The 1926/27 Soviet Polar Census Expeditions

The 1926/27 Soviet Polar Census Expeditions

Edited by

David G. Anderson

berghahn
NEW YORK · OXFORD
www.berghahnbooks.com

First published in 2011 by

Berghahn Books

www.berghahnbooks.com

©2011, 2014 David G. Anderson
First paperback edition published in 2014

Library of Congress Cataloging-in-Publication Data

The 1926/27 Soviet polar census expeditions / edited by David G. Anderson.
    p. cm.
    Includes bibliographical references and index.
    ISBN 978-1-84545-766-2 (hardback) -- ISBN 978-0-85745-044-9 (institutional ebook)
-- ISBN 978-1-78238-097-9 (paperback) -- ISBN 978-1-78238-098-6 (retail ebook)
    1. Indigenous peoples—Russia, Northern—Census. 2 . Indigenous peoples—Russia
(Federation)—Siberia—Census. 3. Ethnological expeditions—Russia, Northern—
History—20th century. 4. Ethnological expeditions—Russia (Federation)—Siberia—
History—20th century. 5. Indigenous peoples—Russia, North—Social life and customs.
6. Indigenous peoples—Russia (Federation)—Siberia—Social life and customs. 7. Siberia
(Russia)—Discovery and exploration. 8. Russia, Northern—Discovery and exploration.
9. Siberia (Russia)—Census. 10. Russia, Northern—Census. I. Anderson, David G.
II. Title: Soviet polar census expeditions.
    GN585.R9A18 2011
    305.800947—dc22

                                                                                    2010051903

British Library Cataloguing in Publication Data

A catalogue record for this book is available from the British Library.

ISBN: 978-1-78238-097-9 paperback
ISBN: 978-1-78238-098-6 retail ebook

Contents

Figures

Tables

Acknowledgements

This book is the result of the collective work of a large team of people. The work on locating, classifying and digitising the primary manuscript records of the Polar Census began in 2000 and continues as this book goes to press. I am especially grateful to Ol′ga Robertovna Sordiia, director of the State Archive of Krasnoiarsk Territory, and her team, for helping us design a protocol for organizing and digitising the large collection of material in Krasnoiarsk. I hope that much that we learned then will be used to preserve and to analyse other collections in that archive for future generations. I am also grateful to the team at the Krasnoiarsk Regional Museum for finding and then also designing a new set of techniques for digitising the photographs and glass plate negatives associated with the Turukhansk Polar Census expedition. From our first work in Krasnoiarsk, this project spread to work in archives in North, Eastward and Westward. I would like to thank the archivists Aitalina Afanas′evna Zakharova (Iakutsk), Sergei Gennad′evich Ovchinnikov (Irktusk), Anatolii Alekseevich Okuneev and Oleg Sarafanov (Ekaterinburg), Tat′iana Ivanovna Lakhtionova (Sykyvkar), Ol′ga Ivanovna Korneeva (Arkhangel′sk), and Natal′ia Ivanovna Galaktionova (Murmansk) for helping us work with their collections. I am also thankful to the archivists in the Russian Far East who helped us for many weeks to locate material, even if there were no specific results.

This project would not have been possible without the help of several Russian scholars who devoted several years of their time to finding and interpreting the Polar Census results. All of them are published here as authors in this book, but their work in signing agreements and in digitising materials for a common catalogue went far beyond the range of their own scientific interests, published here.

A large number of computer programmers and web designers have devoted months of their time to making the archive of the Polar Census expeditions accessible both as digitised photographs and as an online database. The three databases used for collecting the texts and statistics were designed by Nikolai Zhukov and Edoardo Pignotii (both of the University of Aberdeen) and Yngvar Natland (of the University of Tromsø). The web-interfaces were designed by Nikolai Vasil'evich Martynovich (KKKM), Darren Shaw (University of Alberta) and Gordon Neish (University of Aberdeen).

Finally we are all grateful to our sponsors who have supported this work involving a team of forty-seven people in ten cities. The Social Sciences and Humanities Research Council of Canada supported the initial cataloguing of the manuscript archive in Canada through a module of its Major Collaborative Research Initiative (SSHRCC MCRI 412-2000-1000). The main work of photographing and entering the records from Turukhansk, Iakutsk and Irkutsk was done through a small grant from the Economic and Social Research Council of the UK (ESRC 22-0217). The digitization of the photographic archive of the Turukhansk Polar Census expedition was supported through a small grant from the British Academy (SG 35555). The Research Council of Norway (NFR 167040) supported the bulk of our work in finding and digitizing collections in the Russian North, Western Siberia, Iakutiia and the Far East. The NFR also sponsored our field research inspired by the Polar Census collection in the Kanin peninsula and in Bodaibo district, Irkutsk *oblast'* (NFR 179316). A small grant from the European Science Foundation EUROCORES BOREAS programme supported one two-day seminar with the authors to discuss the manuscript.

A group of graduate students from the University of Aberdeen and the University of Alberta were employed in preparing this manuscript – and they did an excellent job. Aline Ehrenfried catalogued the initial manuscript collections from Krasnoiarsk. Maria Nakhshina prepared preliminary translations of four chapters. Olga Pak translated one chapter. I am grateful for the help of Joseph Long for helping to alter the syntax and style of two of the chapters. I am especially grateful to Maria Nakhshina who helped to assemble the manuscript and verify the citations, and to chase down missing references.

The editor gratefully acknowledges a publication subsidy from the Research Council of Norway (NFR 202348) to support the publication of such a large number of tables and illustrations.

Note on Cyrillic Transliteration

Words spelled in languages using the Cyrillic alphabet (Russian, and the indigenous languages of Siberia) are in italics and transliterated using a simplified version of the Library of Congress transliteration system. All iotised vowels, excepting 'e', are transliterated with a Latin 'i' without the ligatures that bind the two vowels together. Therefore Якутия is rendered as Iakutiia and not I͡Akutii͡a.

The spelling of names for the aboriginal peoples of Siberia is based upon the root for a singular person (or a singular male person if there is not generic root). A Latin 's' is added for plurals and 'es' if the transliteration system places an 's' at the end of the root, i.e. Nenetses. In the book we use both Imperial and Soviet-era identity markers since these identities were not standardized at the time of the Polar Census.

The Polar Census manuscripts recorded weights and measures predominately in Russian Imperial units. For accuracy, most chapters and tables present the raw data in the original but at the instance of the first citation the editor has added a co-efficient to translate the measure into the metric system. The table of weights and measures in the appendix presents a full set of co-efficients.

Similarly, administrative units were in a radical state of flux in the 1920s, and it was not uncommon for regional boundaries to shift even during the year that the census was conducted. As a result, we have used the names of the units, italised, in Russian with a shorthand translation in square brackets upon first usage, i.e. *uezd* [district]; *raion* [district]. Quotation marks are placed around the names of Soviet-era collective institutions, as is standard practice in Russian texts: 'Red Khomolkho'.

Data from Russian archives is represented in-text with a simplified, abbreviated system of the archive abbreviation and the classmark system. A full explanation of this system, and the abbreviations, precedes the central bibliography at the end of the book.

1 | The Polar Census and the Architecture of Enumeration

David G. Anderson

In 1925, following several years of civil war, the leaders of the new Soviet state began to look northwards. Up until this time Arctic Siberia and the Russian North were considered marginal spaces. Populated with tribes labelled as 'alien-outsiders' (*inorodtsy*), it was a landscape often defined by what it lacked. Lying beyond the reach of roads and the recent railway, it was a difficult and costly region over which to plan resettlement. Further, its climate made the land unsuitable for traditional Russian styles of cereal agriculture. As it became increasingly apparent that the world revolution was not forthcoming, planners realised that Northerners would also have to become active parts of the Soviet project. As a prelude to the first Five-Year Plan, the Central Statistical Agency of the Soviet Union designed a series of surveys setting the groundwork for a social experiment aimed at transforming relationships among people and between people and their lands. Part of these preparations involved a well-known general population census which, for the first time, would provide a universal standardised picture of the population built-up from the enumeration of individuals and rejecting Imperial-era estate categories such as 'peasant' or 'alien'. A less-known project of this era was the no less ambitious attempt to conduct a total economic and demographic survey of the polar and taiga regions then known as the Northern Frontiers (*severnye okrainy*). Unlike its cousin, the 1926/27 Polar Census was designed to take place over eight months and to fold together a demographic survey with an inventory of household architecture, equipment, livestock and budgets and a general inscription of what for the lack of a better word were called 'settlements' (*poselennye*). Over the course of the year, the enumerators of the Polar Census would survey no less than 33,000 settled, nomadic and semi-nomadic northern households and return hundreds of thousands of pages of tabular data, narratives, diaries and photographs covering a vast region stretching from the Kola to the Chukot Peninsulas. Epic in its scopes and aims, the Polar Census had a deep effect on the Soviet North, training an entire cohort of statistician-ethnographers and coining the lexica by which the Soviet North was addressed, mapped, collectivised and appropriated.

The purpose of this volume is to introduce English-speaking readers to the published and unpublished documents generated by the Polar Census expeditions. The volume is the product of eight years of collaborative research involving a large team of archivists and scholars working in twelve cities of the Russian Federation. The heart of our work was to discover and re-assemble the primary record cards of several of the Polar Census expeditions, which as this book goes to press, consist of an archive of over 6,000 household cards (representing over 30,000 individuals), 800 community diaries and a large archive of photographs, correspondence, diaries and memos.[1] Reading collections of the primary manuscript records, we were able to flip the telescope of statistical interpretation to look back upon the families, and in some cases the individuals, whose lives were represented in the published aggregate figures. We also found it interesting to turn the census instrumentation inside-out to query the central and local administrators who were asking the questions. Many of the authors in this volume are also field ethnographers who were able to contextualise the surviving archival records through the memories of those living in the same Northern communities today. This ethnohistorical approach, we argue, not only breathes life into the documents but also helps us to settle some theoretical questions about how statistical enumerations structure people's lives. The Polar Census occupies an interesting place in this regard. While many scholars have shown an interest in how enumeration supports the structure of power in state socialist societies, this particular collection also speaks to how local understandings of residence and identity percolated through the documentation, somewhat blurring the crisp categories on the forms. The authors in this volume come from a variety of scientific traditions including anthropology, history, demography, geography and archaeology and use these records to address debates in their disciplines. We hope to demonstrate that this comprehensive description of northern peoples and their lands served not just as a prelude to the dislocations and expropriations that were to follow in the 1930s, but that it offers several alternative genealogies that are still evocative as Northern societies revitalise themselves today.

This introductory chapter has three goals. First, I wish to give an overview of the arguments and themes running through the ten substantive chapters in this collection. Second, I wish to contextualise the design of the Polar Census within a history of Imperial-era enumerations of Siberia and the Russian North. Finally, I will address some of the theoretical debates that the Polar Census archive evokes, making special reference to the analysis of colonial enumerations worldwide. The appendix to the volume provides a guide to the finding-aids we constructed to collections in regional archives with the hope of encouraging further comparative work with this valuable resource.

A major theme running through this volume is the entangled nature of the Polar Census inscriptions, which provided not only a record of people, but their relationships to wild and domestic animals, evocative landscapes and the economic and ecological relationships binding them together. The complex nature of this enterprise is hinted at in its official title. While most modern censuses enumerate individuals living within an administrative region, these expeditions surveyed an ecological frontier. The *pripoliarnaia perepis'* speaks to a survey of households clustered 'around' the Arctic Circle – a cartographic metaphor describing places that were just beyond the infrastructure of roads and railways of the Russian steppes (fig. 1.1). At its heart this exercise was an exploratory one – the exercise of a state taking a close look at a poorly understood region. For the sake of convenience, we have translated this inscription (*perepis'*) as a 'census' – although in a strict sense the inventory of humans occupied only a small part of this exercise. Reflecting this quality, the chapters in this volume analyse the primary records according to two themes.

The analysis of *cultural landscapes* predominates in every chapter. As this introduction will demonstrate, the detailed instrumentation for the Polar Census provided a frame within which households were inscribed into named places. As this exercise crossed several cultural boundaries across the Russian North, the manner in which place articulated with identity was not always the same. In many of the chapters we find that identity and 'nationality' often gloss with the landscape. We learn from Elena Volzhanina (chapter 3) that the names by which Nenetses in Western Siberia were known parallels the geographic description of their homelands. Further, we understand from Peter Jordan (chapter 2) that it is impossible to reconstruct any 'community of *iurty*' in Western Siberia without understanding the specific hydrology of the rivers and the resources they offer. True to this particular culture region, landscapes are seen not only as reservoirs of proteins and calories, but as 'sacred' places (Jordan) which 'sustain' life (Klokov, chapter 7). The historical ethnography of sacred or sustaining landscapes blurs the traditional definition of landscape by enlivening it with moral qualities. Anomalies in the way that communities were classified in the manuscript data often show the intersection of geography and cultural practice. This is evident in subtle designations, such as those in use in the Russian North, where an open treeless landscape could be sub-divided into one or more 'tundras' (Semenov, chapter 6; Kiselev, chapter 8; Klokov). As Anderson, Ineshin and Ziker illustrate through their fieldwork in Irkutsk *oblast'*, forest glades which still survive today, are markers of special places or nodes where people kept animals over several hundreds of years (chapter 9). Several of the contributors to this volume have dealt with this complex portrait of cultural landscapes graphically by using their present day knowledge of the tundra and taiga to draft maps of the relation of families to one another, and of the extent of their movements. The maps by Peter Jordan (chapter 2), Igor

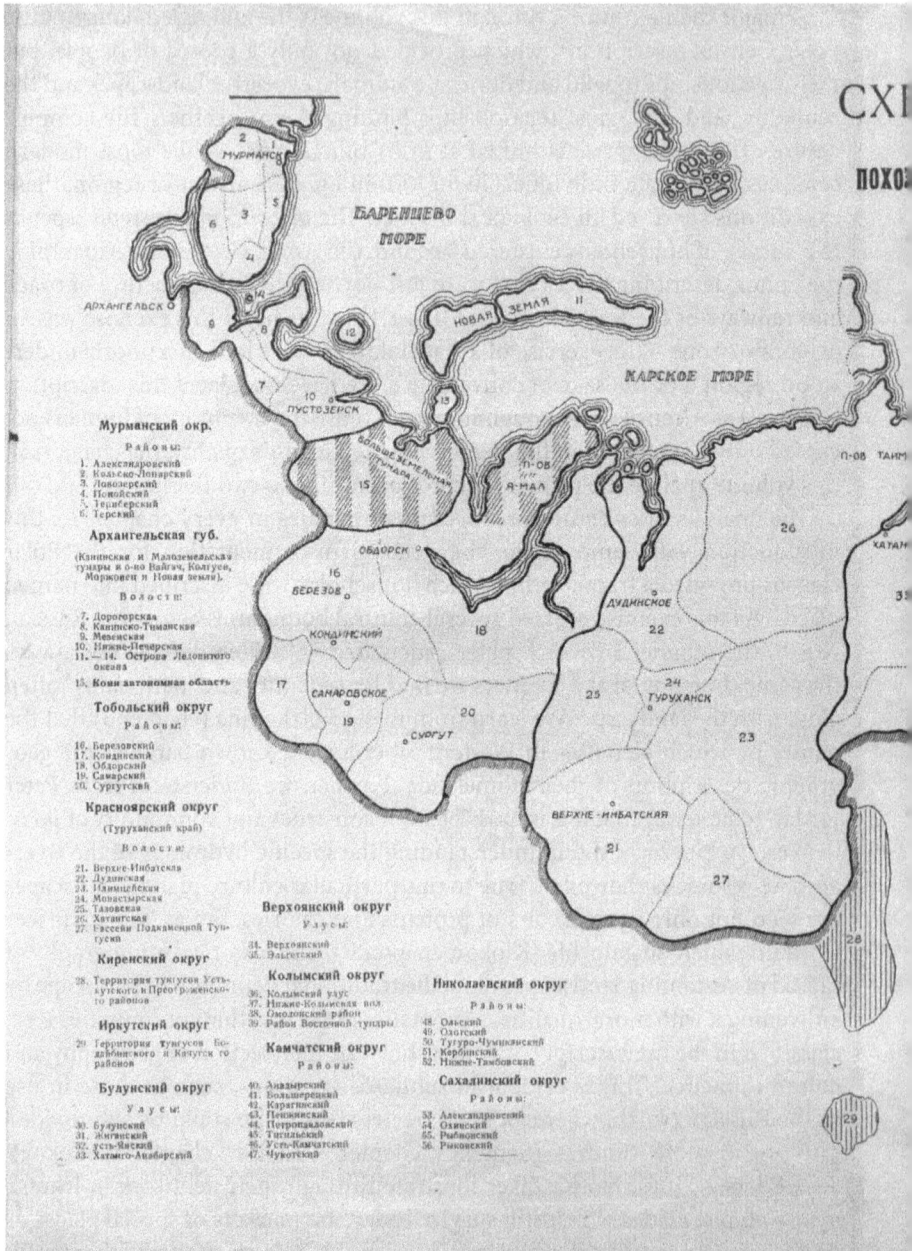

Figure 1.1. The Census Districts of the Polar Census of 1926/27 (TsSU 1929)

ЧЕСКАЯ КАРТА
ИВНОГО ДЕЛЕНИЯ ТЕРРИТОРИИ
ПЕРЕПИСИ ПРИПОЛЯРНОГО СЕВЕРА
1 января 1927 г.

Semenov (chapter 6) and John Ziker (chapter 11) illustrate how historical data can be represented visually to accentuate ecological relationships.

Building on this theme, several chapters tease out aspects of cultural identity based on the *lifestyles* of groups of people (Klokov; Kiselev; Semenov; Ziker; Argounova-Low, chapter 10). These contributors use the primary source material to document the well-remarked fact that cultural identities (or 'ethnicity') are not existential convictions but are linked to what people do. For Argounova-Low the types of fish consumed give an important clue to the identity and the misinterpretation of status among Essei Iakuts. Konstantin Klokov, in a creative reading of the primary documentation, demonstrates how human groups can be differentiated not through their declared identity but through their tools and the efficiency with which they applied themselves to the hunt of the Arctic fox. Kiselev notes that raw numbers of reindeer and hunting equipment similarly give clues to different strategies that people employ to survive chaotic times, be they the Russian civil war or the dislocations of *perestroika*. John Ziker notes certain long-term continuities of hunting practice that can be described through the strategy of designing task-based 'encampments'. The chapters by Igor Semenov and Tatiana Argounova-Low also remind us that at the start of the Soviet period, subsistence practice was closely linked to politics, and the *wrong* type of practice could be dangerous activity. The question of how these census results were used as a form of state surveillance is an all-too-common one in the history of colonial censuses and is one that this introduction will treat in more detail.

The case studies presented here cover the entire range of the surviving manuscript material from the Russian North to Central and Eastern Siberia (the manuscript material of the Polar Census in the Russian Far East has not yet surfaced). In the first part of the book, chapters from Western Siberia (Jordan; Volzhanina; Glavatskaya, chapter 4) discuss the spatial and demographic anomalies that can be read from the primary manuscript data. The Russian North is featured in the central section of the book. Gunnar Thorvaldsen (chapter 5) compares the demography of a range of well-known and less-known identity groups from the manuscript records from the Kola Peninsula. This is followed by three chapters on the history and contemporary subsistence dynamics of Nenets and Komi on the Bolshezemel' tundra (Semenov; Klokov; Kiseleev). The book concludes with three chapters from Eastern Siberia focusing on subtle arguments about identity and the use of landscape in what is today Taimyr, Evenkiia and Irkutsk *oblast'* (Anderson, Ineshin and Ziker; Argounova-Low; Ziker).

An important contribution of this collection is its historiographic technique. The results of the Polar Census were arguably best known by their weakest quality: that of their published aggregate results.[2] Here, in this volume, almost all contributors mix together summaries from the published aggregate data, with results published in regional publications, as well as anomalies scribbled in the margins of the primary record cards. Contrasting the 'census-makers' to the existential puzzlement their questions often elicited has become a bit of hallmark in the critical analysis of colonial censuses in India (Cohn 1987, Peabody 2001) or even the 1897 Imperial Russian census (Cadiot 2004, Darrow 2002). An unexpected finding of our group was an intermediary level of negotiation and interpretation. Scholars working for provincial statistical agencies often elaborated on the centrally-designed questions to the extent that they published their own forms and, most importantly, published alternate and often competing conclusions to those in the central publications. While population data was culled from the record cards to help fill several of the 56 published volumes of the 1926 All-Union census, a series of locally organised research agendas filled an alternative cannon of regional publications and manuscripts, many of which can only be found in provincial archives.[3] In the chapters by Elena Volzhanina and Igor Semenov we have particularly good illustrations of how a careful comparison of the analyses done by individuals sitting at different levels of authority allow researchers to expose the aspects of social and political life that were most open to interpretation. The varied pictures that can be gleaned from central versus regional tabulations does not speak so much to the accuracy of the Polar Census as it does to the competing interpretations of how people were related to space.

Before turning to analyse these records in light of the historiography of post-colonial surveys in general, I would like to describe first some of the terms of reference of the survey itself and how it fits into the history of surveys in the region.

A Survey of Inaccessible Places

The unique quality of this survey lay not so much in its comprehensiveness as in the fact that the organisers sought to personally interview every single household head across a difficult terrain. Spurning the term 'polar', Kirill Shavrov (1929) of the Far-Eastern census expedition described this project as a survey of places that were 'difficult to reach' (*trudnodostupnye*) placing the accent upon the logistical problems of reaching these places, but also the difficulties of describing them (fig. 1.2). In this sense, accessibility provides an interesting interpretive frame within which to analyse this material.

In 1926 (and to some extent today) most of the regions subject to this survey were located far from central transportation corridors. However, distance and terrain at this time often served as a metaphor for resistance (Scott 2009). What was less commented upon in the official publications, but well-known, was the fact that large parts of Siberia and the Far East, as well as in European

Figure 1.2. A census transport caravan at the head of the Moiro river, Evenkiia, 9 January 1927 (AKKKM 7930-1/02-16) Photograph by N. P. Naumov.

Russia, had been inaccessible due to the civil war. The Bolshevik administration had previously attempted and failed to survey many of these regions in 1917, 1920 and 1923.[4] With these recent failures in mind, the Central Statistical Administration agreed to extend the 'critical day' of enumeration from one day (17 December 1926) to nine months (roughly June 1926 to March 1928) allowing census teams the time they needed to reach all outlying households by boat or reindeer sledge, or on foot. These romantically-stylised logistical difficulties served as a convenient pretext for local civic and government agencies to plan their own independent surveys of nomadic peoples – a goal that some archival evidence suggests they had coveted for many years. To some degree, the Polar Census enterprise was a goal in itself – a proof that every regional authority had the capacity to make contracts with local translators and guides and held the necessary geographic knowledge to reach every corner of their domains. 'Accessibility', then, served as a convenient slogan to release resources both for a central administration with its eye on the first Five-Year Plan, and for local scholars interested in detailed descriptions.

The archived discussions leading up to the survey itself carry an unmistakable impression that this census was a unique event – a spirit which flowed over into a wide-ranging debate on instrumentation. The cornerstone document of the general All-Union census was a small 'personal form' (*lichnyi listok*), eliciting basic demographic information on individuals including 'new' data on nationality and more traditional data on mother tongue, occupation and military service.[5] Given the efforts invested into reaching Northern places there was a call to augment the personal form with more comprehensive tools. Provincial statistical bureaux began their campaign with a special request to combine together the general population survey of December 1926 with a survey of rural economy (*sel'skoe khoziaistvo*) originally planned for the previous summer. Rather than sending enumerators twice around remote tundra and taiga locations, many of which were only accessible in the winter, the regional statisticians successfully lobbied for a single survey that gathered the details of the personal form along with very specific information on various economic 'sectors' (such as 'fisheries', 'hunting and fur-trapping', 'reindeer husbandry'), the tools and dwellings held by households, and their main consumption items. In April of 1925 regional statistical administrations were asked to plan and budget for a combined survey 'in one excursion' (*za odin ob"ezd*) initiating a wide discussion on the types of data that were representative of these difficult-to-access places (GAAO 187-1-848: 17). As the appendix to this volume documents, the results of this discussion varied from region to region. However, all agencies administered a double-sided A3-sized form to every household head (on which the questions of the personal form were a small, compressed part) and each community was documented on a sizable 32-page 'community diary'. Some regional agencies also collected additional information on sanitation, kinship relationships and ethnography. By comparison, the general 1926 census project fell into the background. In 1928, the central agency even had to remind each regional agency that they were to extract the 16 data-points on each individual from their complex instruments onto a personal form in order to complete the aggregate picture of the Soviet Union.

Aspects of this 'survey of inaccessible, northern places' were also linked to alterity. Before the Council of People's Commissars stamped a neutral geographical label on this special survey, the preparatory documentation described it as an enumeration of indigenous peoples; literally a 'census of people-in-their-places' (*tuzemnaia perepis'*).[6] This conceptual distinction also influenced the design of the instrumentation, which incorporated extremely detailed questions on reindeer husbandry, elicited descriptions of 'tribal' and 'clan' affiliation and place names (often in native languages), recorded the main encampments in a presumed seasonal round, and left spaces open for enumerators to record artefacts or practices that to them seemed important in classifying everyday life. What is striking when one first glances at the cards is the sheer quantity of questions documenting domestic animals, subsistence practices, collective identities and relationships *between* people. Leaving aside the bulk of the questions of the household card, 75 per cent of which comprise a check-list inventory of tools used and species hunted, an important subset of questions submerge the discrete identity of a household head under a number of overlapping categories describing language fidelity, territorial use, and a mixed matrix of both Tsarist and Soviet administrative categories. In order for the documentation to be submitted, each household in turn had to be nested in a fixed, named community (*poselennyi*). That place was further documented in the community diary with an exhaustive description of its seasonal phrenology, access to transportation corridors, customs and rituals, and incorporation into the regional markets judged by lists of prices. The questions on the community diary pushed the enumerator to go well beyond human demography to explore unfamiliar social and natural environments.

The question arises of whether or not this exercise is best described as a census at all in the modern sense. Most historians of science make a distinction between numeric inventories designed to facilitate a particular task (such as tax collection) and a survey designed to sketch the contours of a biopolitical entity such as a 'population' (Hacking 1990; Curtis 2001; Peabody 2001). Task-specific registers, like lists of baptisms submitted by Orthodox missionaries, have an ever-expanding quality wherein another pagan family or another newborn can always be added to the ecumene. Population enumerations, by contrast, have a hermetic quality circumscribing the universe that they represent. The task-based lists often serve to define relationships. For example, an individual could conceivably ask a clerk to consult the list to confirm his children's baptism, or to prove that he had already extinguished his fur-tax obligations. By contrast, population enumerations are ideally anonymous such that an individual is defined only by relationship to a broader category such as being one of the 24.6 per cent of the population that is male and between the ages of 18 and 59, or one of the 15,083 enumerated nomadic Tunguses.

It perhaps will come as no surprise to learn that the Polar Census does not fit easily into one of these two types. The logistical challenges of surveying these remote regions made the census often look more like an open-ended population registry. Due to the fact that this survey took place over the better part of a year, enumerators used the nominal data to construct a population list in order to guard against repeat registrations. The census was not finished even when the forms were returned since regional statistical offices would exchange forms with each other in order to help each other achieve a complete picture of citizens crossing the boundaries of their newly designed districts. The fact that almost all of the primary nominal forms survived only in provincial archives speaks to the fact that regional administrations coveted them as registers and not just as draft sketches towards some greater, super-organic picture.

On the other hand, the terms of reference for the Polar Census make it clear that the goal was to create a picture of a northern population (*naselenie*). In the words of Konstantin M. Nagaev, the head of the Siberian Statistical Agency, as he was lobbying for funds for a multi-volume set of publications based on the census manuscripts:

One should not forget that although we have controlled the Polar North of Siberia for over three centuries we hardly have a complete and coherent description of either this gigantic territory or its mysterious inhabitants – and this despite sending out all sorts of different expeditions almost every year. We still even don't know with any accuracy the population and a list of populated places. A large group of people, including local and central administrations, many northern [trading] organisations, and just those who are interested in the North have high hopes that the Polar Census will fill this lacuna (*probel*). (GARF 3977-1-355: 32–32v)

The same spirit is echoed in an important speech by Mitrofan P. Krasil'nikov (1926: 2, 9), one of the organisers of the All-Union Census, who spoke of the importance of surmounting the 'colossal distances' and 'unusual difficulties of travel' in the North in order to create a seamless 'public inventory' (*narodnyi balans*).

This same 'need to know' is echoed in the introduction to almost every central and regional publication of the census results. The extraordinary efforts invested into interviewing every single household head in these hard-to-reach regions signalled a new era of relationships. Imperial-era surveyors, be they missionaries or tax-collecting Cossacks, were content to know the 'aliens' at the level of large legal collectivities such as the tribe or administrative clan. The fact that it was thought possible to subdivide these alien groups into households, and to identify household heads who could be interviewed, were important innovations that would change the relationship between Northerners and the state. In Moscow, administrators might look upon northern minorities vaguely as representatives of 'nationalities' which might be 'disappearing' or in need of development or liberation from ruthless speculators. However, for regional administrators, this exercise gave each household a name, and that name was now linked to inventories of animals, equipment and geographic knowledge which could be marshalled to build a civic infrastructure.

Mediating the political importance of this survey is what can only be described as a type of enthusiasm which comes through from archived correspondence and field diaries, and occasionally in turns of phrase on the cards themselves. In his overview of manuscript records of the early Soviet period, the historian Gololobov (2004: 58) distinguishes the Polar Census manuscripts from other records for their living character:

[The manuscript records] combine quantitative data with descriptions and occasional personal statements about how affairs stood in the North. The latter debate the reasons for the positive and negative aspects of certain economic activities, or, of state policies towards Northern Peoples. The [personal quality] of the text comes through emphatic underscoring, corrections, question marks set against quantitative indicators. … They help researchers get behind the dry lines of numbers and official indicators … to see the real life and the real person with all of his problems, difficulties, challenges, and needs.

Borrowing the words of Richard Smith (2000: 7), a historical sociologist of the British surveys of colonial India, the manuscripts show a clear anxiety of 'not knowing and wanting-to-know'. The prosaic quality of these expeditions is amply framed in almost every introduction to the material of each regional expedition, often stressing the hardship and fellowship of the road (fig. 1.3). The chapter by Elena Glavatskaya (chapter 4) captures the 'heroic' quality of the writing especially well. Rather than evoking a panopticon of measurement, the archival material more often than not represents what Justin Stagl (1995) has identified as a sense of 'curiosity' in early European travel writing. Nevertheless, the enthusiasm of travel is always tempered with a drumming concern: Almost every enumerator at some point describes himself or herself as introducing isolated Northerners to new institutions and new hopes.

The Polar Census as a Local Inscription

In describing the manuscript archive of the Polar Census it is easy to get lost in hyperbolic descriptions of the scale of the enterprise. On the one hand, administering a household card with over 1,200 possible answers seems like an impossibly naïve goal. On the other hand, the effort invested at obtaining a 100 per cent sample over rough terrain seems over-ambitious in its own right. This level of detail and this yearning for social inclusion falls into a long legacy of reform amongst scholars and administrators pre-dating the Revolution. David Darrow (2002: 150), in his analysis of the 1897 All-Russian Imperial census, describes the vision of conducting a general empire-wide survey as an extremely late manifestation of the Great Reform era with roots extending back to 1860.[7] He argues that the 1926 population census represents a culmination of attempts to impose a horizontal idea of citizenship over the hierarchical definitions of social estate that preceded it. It is a great irony that this special effort to extend a horizontal, estate-blind enumeration to Siberia and the Russian North provoked the design of exceedingly complicated instruments which created *new* hierarchies. It is almost as if collapsing hierarchical social categories evoked the need to imply social position through the texture of every object that a family held and every person with whom it was linked. This call to statistical involution also has deep roots in *zemstvo* statistics – a set of local Russian statistical traditions which bears a great similarity to the intuition that went behind the design of the Polar Census.

The *zemstva* of late Imperial Russia were agencies of local self-government, primarily in European Russian and Southern Siberia, which had an important duty to extend infrastructure and public services to more or less autonomous rural peasant communes (Darrow 2001; Emmons and Vucinich 1982; Abramov and Zhivozdrova 1996; Svavitski 1961). Detailed statistical house-

Figure 1.3. Konstantin M. Nagaev of the Siberian Statistical Administration posing with three unidentified enumerators – two of whom are dressed in Dolgan winter clothing. The photo is titled 'before departure' (AKKM 7930-1/01-17) Photograph by A. P. Kurilovich.

hold inventories were important instruments for these agencies in setting policies and entitlements. The homology between Polar Census instrumentation and *zemstvo* surveys sits mainly at the level of structure and method, rather than in the details of the questions themselves. A classic late *zemstvo* survey in the period of 1907 to 1913 would include a household card (then called a *podvornaia kartochka*) with 'hundreds of questions' administered to a household head (Koval´chenko et al. 1988). It would also include a collective or community document (often called a *poselennyi* or *obshchinnyi blank*) which captured general information about a single built settlement or a string of settlements. Both instruments immediately recall the household card and the community diary of the Polar Census. As Darrow (2001) argues, the unique quality of the *zemstvo* surveys was their ability to make a single household (*dvor*) legible from the tangled obligations that rural dwellers maintained with their neighbours and to their plots (the boundaries of which were periodically reassigned). As with the *zemstvo* documents, one of the most creative and perhaps arbitrary element of the Polar Census was also the way discrete households were linked to fixed places. The *zemstvo* statisticians were guided by the hope that the precise measurement of property in tools and animals or of access to land would help them to discover the communal peasant ethos. Ironically, their obsession with counting property led them unwillingly to the opposite conclusion that peasant households were straining to become private entrepreneurs independent from the commune (ibid.). A similar process can be observed with the Polar Census instrumentation. The detailed inventories of animals trapped and reindeer harnessed tended to create an image of a landscape populated with autochthonous families, some struggling more than others. If the *zemstvo* statisticians were consciously or unconsciously rehearsing debates on Russian populism when they designed their instruments, the statisticians behind the Polar Census clearly were revisiting concerns about the 'disappearance' of primitive peoples which obsessed late nineteenth century liberals and Siberian regionalists (Kovalashchina 2007). As with the *zemstvo* statistical tradition, there is a strong argument to be made that the instrumentation itself created a frame that over-accentuated certain structural qualities relating to how property in things and animals was attributed to groups of people attached to specific places. Nevertheless local concerns were not silenced. As the contributors to the volume demonstrate, it is possible to understand how classification and inventories reflected social life by using oral testimony and a critical interpretation of the sources.

The dualistic instrumentation of the Polar Census arose out of a long process of debate between the Central Statistical Administration and regional statistical bureaux and was developed through of a wide circulation of draft questionnaires.[8] It is clear from the correspondence that the individuals working in the regional agencies felt themselves to be part of an intellectual community and that they held special skills when it came to the enumeration of remote areas. It is undoubtedly a significant fact that two of the most active correspondents, the head of the Arkhangel´sk Statistical Bureau, Vladimir Plandovskii, and the statistician in charge of the Polar Census instrumentation for the Central Statistical Agency, Mitrofan Krasil´nikov, were *zemstvo* statisticians as well as authors of important late Imperial treatises on census methodologies (Plando-vskii 1898; Krasil´nikov 1913). The intensity of the debate, and the variety of survey instruments proposed, suggest that this event created the opportunity for regional agencies to develop local inscriptions rather than a monolithic statistical instrument.

The regional archives contain a large number of draft survey instruments, circulated in the period between 1924 and 1926, which foreshadow the design of the final household card and the community dairy. The draft that comes closest to the design of the final household card was a large A3-size handwrit-ten 'family card' (*semeinaia kartochka*) designed by the fifth medical research brigade of the Siberian Red Cross Society based in Krasnoiarsk (GARF 3977-1-87: 18–19v; GARF 3977-1-75: 17–17v).[9] That card was likely used in the 1925 Red Cross expedition to Tururkhansk Krai to investigate the social conditions of aboriginal (*tuzemnye*) peoples suffering the aftermath of the civil war (Kyt-manov 1927, 1930; Malysheva and Poznanskii 1998). Some of the material from this complex card seems to have found its way into the prosaically titled 'skin-lodge card' (*chumovaia kartochka*) which was approved by the Statistical Agency of Enisei *guberniia* [province] on 4 September 1925 (GARF 3977-1-75: 12–12v).[10] The Arkhangel´sk Statistical Administration, after tabling cop-ies of their special forms designed to survey the nomadic Samoed reindeer herders 'of the [Northern] dead zone' in 1920 and 1925 (GARF 3977-1-87: 34–39v), also drafted an alternate A3-size 'skin-lodge' card designed to survey the 'heads of skin-lodges' (*glava chuma*) of the 'nomadic tundra population' in the autumn of 1925 (GAAO 187-1-848: 27–30)[11] Their intuition of focussing on the architecture of the household, rather than its membership, was a signifi-cant invitation which I will show below is an important detail in understand-ing the meaning of the Polar Census survey (fig. 1.4).

There are also many surviving lists of regional-level questions which may have gone into the formation of the community diary.[12] In the State Archive of Arkhangel´sk *oblast´* there is a series of drafts of a document alternately called a *gruppovoi blank* for reindeer herders, a *tuzemnyi poselennyi blank* and fi-nally a typescript *poselennyi blank* drafted by the Siberian Territorial Statistical Administration in Novosibirsk (GAAO 187-1-848: 45–77). The drafts show an evolution from a short form aimed purely at northern reindeer herders to a general form with sections on herding, fishing, hunting, etc. (and specific questions about the territorial implications of each). Each draft also shows an increasingly complex list of questions relating to the prices of trade goods. The surviving archival evidence suggests that the Siberian Statistical Admin-istration was the driving force behind the design of the community diary, and what motivated it most was a desire to understand trading relationships and

Figure 1.4. A family of Sym River Tunguses near their skin-lodge (AKKKM 7930-1/12-19) Photograph by L. V. Girshfeld (June–July 1926).

prices.[13] The concern over the monetary value of social practice, again, was a small detail which would have great effects in the further development of Northern societies.

The fact that there survives documentation of a wide-ranging debate over the content of the instrumentation for this survey shows that this event was open for input from regional government agencies.[14] As with the pre-revolutionary *zemstva*, the regional agencies showed a deep concern for accurately measuring draft-animal power – which, in most areas, was assumed to be provided by reindeer.[15] Typically, the worry of administrators was the correct rendering of age and sex categories for reindeer, horses and dogs – data which could be used to deduce herd dynamics. Other correspondence stresses the importance of recording detailed budgets of the consumption items purchased by families. Here the concern was often for specifying the context of debts (to state organisations, private organisations or kin) or to extending shopping lists to include particular commodities or tools which may have been of interest to one or another statistical office. Each discussion rehearsed well-trodden debates concerning the material source of entrepreneurial power which could break apart communal relationships (Darrow 2002; Anderson 2006: 38–41). As it would turn out, the section of the household card recording the numbers and age-classes of domestic animals held, and the one recording consumption goods, were the two sections that were most cautiously completed by all expeditions across the North.

However the manuscript cards also preserve anomalies which can be interpreted as the attempts of local individuals to fit aspects of their own lives in the boxes of the forms. As several chapters in this collection demonstrate, it proved very difficult for the central statisticians to distil the 100 or more hear-say identity categories into the centrally authorised list of census nationalities.[16] Further, household structure did not always match the expectations of European Russian enumerators, as Volzhanina and Thorvaldsen point out in their contributions to this volume. The anomaly most commented on in the marginal notes of both regional and central publications was the difficulty of identifying a single *place* where a nomadic family belonged – since that family would regularly carry out transactions in more than one place and often in more than one administrative district. Finally, the inventories of objects would often be extended to include the names of products, or species or classes of animals, in indigenous languages that spoke to a different way of classifying the world.

The two-part instrumentation of the Polar Census forced enumerators to identify people as living in households, as following a yearly budgetary regime, and as living within named places. As such, it framed social life in a novel way. As intuitive as this relationship might seem today, in 1926 for many rural residents of Siberia and the Russian North the notion that they planned their lives out in autonomously functioning units within a limited spatial and time horizon must have seemed a mystical idea. The designation of fixed households would require the deliberate fracturing of bilateral kin connections and the massaging of complex seasonal rounds into an abbreviated list. To many local hunters, fishermen and reindeer herders, the wealth that they harvested looked to them more as gifts of the land rather than the result of a canny accumulation strategy within a yearly budgetary cycle. Many Northerners would not even share the same calendar as the urban-based statisticians, as in the case of Northern Nenetses who saw every cycle of summer and winter as *two* years. These misunderstandings appear as crossed-out cells, annotations on the primary material, estimations, and in some cases as clarifications published more often than not in regional publications.

The sociologists of colonial enumerations tend to use a number of dramatic metaphors to signal the transformational power of census categories. For Hacking (1982) the pre-modern interest in enumeration produced an 'avalanche' of numbers. Appadurai (1993) navigates an 'ocean' of numbers. Benedict Anderson (1983) diagnoses colonial enumerators as somewhat 'feverish'. These metaphors and descriptions often overstate their case and shout overtop the evidence of local voices and local agency in enumerations (Peabody 2001; Smith 2000). Were the voices of Siberian peoples smothered under the 1,600 tiny cells of the household card?

Having worked with the primary manuscripts, the impression of our team is that this exercise generated not so much that of deluge of numbers as a deluge of questions (many of which informants chose not to answer). While it is true that there is a strong argument to be made that the detailed two-part instrumentation either deliberately or unintentionally triangulated a household within a budgetary cycle and a fixed and named place, this is not the same as concluding that local perspectives were washed out of the material. If one compares centrally published tabulations to regional publications, and then the regional publications to the manuscript material, one can find evidence of a number of adjustments in terminology and in counts that show evidence of instead of a debate over what was important to measure. Rather than smothering local initiatives, at worst the Polar Census provided a very strong model of how complex relationships *might be* described as the fidelity of economically evocative households nested in specific places. This nuance, suggesting that that the published results were somewhat more prescriptive than authoritative, is an important one in understanding both the meaning of this survey and of colonial enumerations in general.

The Enumeration of People in Places

To better understand how households might be framed by the instrumentation, it is important to trace a shift from Imperial to modern Soviet ways of encapsulating people. Up until the 1926 census, people were thought by census takers to live in groups known as *dvory* – an old Russian word evoking a clear metaphor of a rural family dwelling within an architectural ensemble consisting of a house, but also of corrals, storage sheds and animal barns. Only at a very late date in the development of the Polar Census instrumentation – towards the summer of 1926 – the language shifts to favour the documentation of people living in *khoziaistva* – an equally evocative but newer word for a domestic unit invigorated by an economistic idea of improvement and mastery.[17] Both words are commonly translated as 'household' in Western European languages – a fact which obscures this interesting ambiguity.

This shift to a quantifiable, commoditised definition of a household was developed deliberately at the end of the nineteenth century to allow statisticians to put an end to the predominance of estate categories in the enumeration of the population (Kotz and Seneta 1990). The older Imperial language of social estates was also an architectural metaphor writ large wherein distinct social groups (peasants, merchants, non-Russian aliens) all had a defined position vis-à-vis the Tsar irrespective of their populousness or the place where they lived (Freeze 1986; Slocum 1998). By contrast, the economic 'strength' (*sila*) or 'vitality' (*moschchnost'*) of a household could be calculated once a group of individuals was circumscribed locally and temporally defined in terms of a monthly, seasonally or yearly economic cycle. To adapt Patty Gray's (2004: 93) terminology,

Northern households were seen to be 'moveable parts' which floated independently from their settings and which could only be understood by an external measure (such as a yearly income, or an inventory of capital resources).

Despite a seemingly crisp division between these architectural and economistic metaphors, the two often became linked in the practical work of doing the census. Given the history of the development of the polar census instruments, the household card itself stressed a number of architectural elements ranging from a very subtle description of built structures (cells 217–234), to exhaustive counts of all manner of tools and transport infrastructure. To some degree, these different types of data not only vied with each other for space on the form, but also for meaning. For example, the size of reindeer herds then as today swell or contract depending on the season. Smaller herds might be merged together in seasons when herders would prefer to join together to pasture animals co-operatively – as in the case of the Lake Essei reindeer magnates (Anderson 2011). In order to describe a unified regional herd numerically, the enumerator would have to somewhat arbitrarily divide these animals up between different segments of an extended family who happened to be co-resident at the time. Similarly, the ecological realities of hunting migratory wild reindeer or of fishing might drive some hunters to form transitory 'encampments' or 'community *iurty*' to help structure mutual aid (see Ziker, chapter 11; Jordan, chapter 2). In these cases, the inscription of co-residing kin gives a somewhat arbitrary picture of household composition. Even an inventory of consumption trade items did not always prove to be simple task. Elena Glavatskaya notes that stocks of 'pink soap' or 'castorum' in trading posts might be kept to cater to ritual rather than consumption needs (chapter 4). Real-life paradoxes such as these often led enumerators to develop a methodological shorthand in order to help them quickly complete their task and to move on to the next encampment. This shorthand more often than not defaulted to the older, familiar architectural metaphor where people and resources were described on the basis of how they were tangibly placed together.

Even an ad-hoc application of an architectural model of enumeration proved to be a complex task. If we look at how architecture itself was described, a close reading of those parts of the household cards where caribou and moose skin tent panels were counted shows that often a single conical lodge might in fact be constructed out of panels belonging to two or more nuclear families who happened to be co-resident (Anderson 2007). Petr Terletskii (1929: 31), in his published introduction to the centrally published aggregates of the Polar Census, confessed that the data from Chukotka often did not consistently distinguish between two independent families living within one *iaranga* and the *iaranga* itself.

Further the idea of a 'budget' for people working in a non-monetised subsistence economy must have seemed very abstract both to informants and to enumerators. Nikolai Sushilin, one on the enumerators of the Turukhansk Polar Census expeditions captures his frustration in recording budgetary data in a letter to the head of the expedition Adam Kurilovich:

> I am grouping together the Tungus households by the Clan Soviets that unite them and not by one particular settled place. There seems to be no other way. If I was forced to record them by place every single Tungus would have to have his own group. I have also filled out several budget forms. In my opinion, these records under current conditions will not have any value. There is not a single Tungus who can answer them, although I have [questioned their] budgets while sitting in their own lodges. This is the one difficulty I have encountered in the course of this entire census. (GAKK 769-1-308: 24–25)

In 1925, the enumerators of the Red Cross survey to the Turukhansk North were advised to record the value of goods in either 'squirrel' or 'Arctic fox' units since it was recognised that there was no paper money economy in the region at that time (GARF 3977-1-75: 17v).

The ambiguity between economic and architectural metaphors of the household can be teased out of the archived documentation accompanying the census forms. While the enumerators for the 1926 All-Union demographic survey were instructed to register only those people who regularly spent a night in one home or flat on the night of the census (and not their guests)[18], the instructions to enumerators of the Polar Census were asked to imagine a broader idea of a 'budgetary unit' which could include spatially remote forms of solidarity. The instructions to enumerators of the Siberian statistical agency are perhaps some of the clearest on record:

> § 12 A household (*pokhoziaistvennaia*) card is filled out for every household, which is defined as a group of people united by family kinship living together and having a common budget of income and expenses. If a household is divided into two or more parts, even for an extended period (for example, one member of the family had gone off to tend the reindeer while other members were engaged in fur-trapping in a different place) the entire family is nevertheless written onto one card.
> ...
> § 20b [The enumerator shall register] members of the family of the household head who may be absent for more than one month (that is, for example, living outside of the household [sic] on trap-lines and so forth) but who have not broken economic ties (*khoziaistvennye sviazi*) with the family and who maintain to one or another degree a common budget of income and expenses with the family. (Siberian Statistical Administration – GAAO 187-1-852: 75–75v)

While first asking that individuals be registered as part of a common budgetary unit, these instructions then contradict themselves with two bracketed examples where a household is described as a built residential place that someone can 'live outside of' or 'go away from'. The instructions from the Komi Autonomous *oblast'* posed an even more elaborate architecturally-informed definition of a 'budget' by asking enumerators to register together separate families, or parts of families who used a common set of nets and deadfall-traps (NARK 140-2-198: 5), even if those units lived apart from one another or maintained separate dwellings.[19]

Looking deeper into aboriginal cosmologies, it is easy to understand why it was difficult to divide economy from the way that practice was built into a place. In what way could an inventory of the numbers of wild reindeer hunted be reconciled with the point of view of hunters who thought that wild reindeer gave themselves to the hunters? This moral economy of respect, where a 'budgetary unit' is an ecological relationship, still governs most northern societies today. Such relational modes of solidarity with the environment and to kin could only be indicated on the census forms through silence or through paradoxes. In this census, it seems more likely that field enumerators used the word *khoziaistvo* heuristically but factually defaulted to the older idea of recording *dvory* – those involved in managing an architectural-ecological ensemble.

The debate over the accuracy of data from any census is often more of an ideological statement than a technical evaluation. Our group found that the paradoxes produced by the interplay of architectural and budgetary definitions of the household could be reconciled through re-interpreting households spatially. Since the Polar Census had not one but two main instruments – a household card and a community diary – paradoxes generated by an over-enthusiastic splitting of kinship groups into discrete households on the household cards would generally re-emerge in the language used to describe the spatially-defined community in the corresponding community diaries. By reading the community diaries and the cards together, it was often possible to tease out vernacular categories of place.

The community diaries, with their deep roots in the Imperial Russian *zemstvo* tradition, took as axiomatic that there was some agreement on the outer boundaries of a community. In European Russia, the struggles over the creation of these outer boundaries had taken place before the *zemstvo* legislation was drafted in European Russia, allowing the instrumentation to focus on ambiguities and partitions within these boundaries. In most of the Russian North and Siberia this agreement about how social life fit into defined territories did not exist in 1926. Thus the community diaries serve as transcripts of contested boundaries – a fact which becomes more and more pronounced as one moves from west to east.

On the Kola Peninsula, communities of Sami reindeer herders were organised into kinship-defined regional units known as *pogosty* (similar to the Norwegian Sami *siida*). Both the community diaries, and the regional aggregates of the Polar Census for Murmansk *okrug* divided the census material between Sami-controlled *pogosty* and settler-controlled 'colonies' (*kolonii*). However, geographically, both units could overlap since they were defined not by their use of space but by their obligations to the state. The surviving community diaries for the *okrug* and the accompanying sketch maps show that the relative positions of *pogosty* and *kolononisty* depended on the season. Certain frontier groups, like the mysterious Fil´men discussed by Gunnar Thorvaldsen in chapter 5, defined themselves by language, religion and possibly an ecological affinity to the mountainous landscapes that gave them their name.

In the Ural North, Tsarist-era enumerators tended to identify clusters of portable lodges known as *iurty* as discrete population features. In the semi-sedentary economy of Ostiaks (Khanty) these architectural clusters tended to reappear at advantageous fishing sites and thus represented a seasonal gloss on the idea of a built community (fig. 1.5). As Peter Jordan discusses in his chapter to this volume, the architectural metaphor of the *iurt* was easily multiplied into an ensemble of 'communty *iurty*'. Through a careful reading of community diaries, these architectural ensembles can be correlated both spatially and longitudinally with the river systems and longitudinally to records from the 1897 census and to a present day subsistence activity.

A similar phenomenon is reported by Anderson, Ineshin and Ziker (chapter 9) who note that among Eastern-Siberian Zhuia River Tunguses the unit of

Figure 1.5. A community of Samoed *iurty* near Khe. GASO Fond. 'Kollektsiia Surina'. Delo. 145:101 Photograph by L. Surin 1926.

organisation seems to be the geographically defined river-basin (*reka*) which the Polar Census enumerator for that region, Samokhin, clumsily labelled as 'a semi-settled community'.

The Turukhansk enumerators generally identified discretely bounded communities only along the Enisei river. Inland, they produced lists of numerous communities of *chumy* (conical mobile dwellings) which appear in the published regional tables as arbitrary regional 'settlements'. As John Ziker documents in his chapter to this volume, the language of the 'encampment' (*stoibishche*) serves as a reliable way to de-code the manuscript community diaries written by Boris Dolgikh. However when returning to the published data, one has to be conscious of the mysterious workings of 'gravitation' by which the trade-minded statisticians based in Krasnoiarsk naturally drew communities together around one trading post (SKSO 1928; Kurilovich and Naumov 1934; Anderson 2006). When comparing the published and unpublished material it becomes evident that the enumerator and the urban-based statisticians had different definitions of 'budgetary units'. While the enumerator Boris Dolgikh recorded groups of interrelated nuclear families engaged in reciprocity with a specific ecological setting, the census administrators Kurilovich and Naumov saw a group of consumers united by their patronage to a particular trading post. Thus at different levels of resolution the population breaks up into either ecological ensembles or trading ensembles – each engaged in an economic relationship with their environment.

The most radical example of debate over the boundaries of budgetary units comes from the Iakut statistical administration. Here, somewhat like on the Kola Peninsula, nomadic Tungus or Iakut households were organised territorially within a kin-inflected regional unit known as the *nasleg*. The problem with this unit from the point of view of Moscow-based statisticians was that household heads would carry this identity with them as a birth identity and report it even if they happened to be interviewed in a different place. This 'problem' was so pervasive that it prevented the Iakut statistical administration from publishing an authoritative list of population points for the entire republic. A telling paragraph from the introduction to a volume listing only 'winter places' of Iakut cattle pastoralists describes some of the problems involved in inscribing place:

> The named population points in this list, and also our classification of them into types, are unquestionably inaccurate in most cases (and especially for Viliuisk and Olenek *okrugy*). One has to keep in mind that usually one finds a community of *iurty* known by only one name every dozen kilometres after crossing rivers, lakes, islands, mountain valleys and small creek basins (*urochishchy*). [However, these discrete *iurty*] are themselves separated from each other by a number of kilometres (or occasionally up to ten). Moreover, one finds more than one household (*kho-*

ziaistvo) living in one *iurt* in the winter ... On the other hand, one can also find across one large territory, known by one name, over ten households in separate *iurty* perhaps scattered a dozen kilometres from each other ... . The name of these places is taken from the plot of land, place or lake where a built structure stands. (SUIaASSR 1928: xi)

The Moscow-based statisticians, perhaps under the pressure of time, took very extreme measures to standardise these landscape-stratified kinship units. For Iakutiia, the primary results were aggregating into arbitrary administrative *okrugy* that were 'close in population to districts in other provinces of the Russian republic' (TsSU 1928 [vol 7]: v). It would seem that these *okrugy* only existed on paper for the purpose of the federal results – a decision which is still causing our group much grief when trying to reconcile the surviving household cards from that region with those results.

In these four examples, ranging from the Kola to Iakutiia, we see the interaction of many of the same factors generating and mediating paradoxes. The Polar Census instrumentation, focussed as it was on the specification of household solidarity and territorial fidelity, tended to produce dialogues in the field where neither place nor solidarity could be concisely defined. This led to the need for enumerators and respondents together to negotiate the registration of hybrid identities (for example, the 'Mountain' Samoeds), hybrid settlements ('communities of *iurty*'), and hybrid subsistence strategies (such as the Fil'men of the Kola Peninsula). These complex identities which blended together identity and place were either edited or aggregated away in the centrally published results, or remained archived as inconsistencies that appear when manuscripts reflecting different levels of analysis are compared. On the one hand, the aggregate results can be read as a portrait of a polar population. On the other hand, the hybrid categories in the manuscript material point to the complex ways that local people related to a place.

Alternative Genealogies

When writing in English, it is difficult to counterpoise the terms 'census' and 'Soviet' naïvely. Since the works of Benedict Anderson (1991) and Ian Hacking (1982, 1990), scholars are trained to expect that any census schedule is wielded as an instrument of power contributing to the somewhat arbitrary division of living people into competing categories, or biopolitical units. If we note that this particular survey took place on the eve of Stalin's consolidation of power, there is not much interpretive space left for an alternative genealogy. It is true that when reading the Polar Census archive with what we know today, we are immediately suspicious of the exacting inventories of reindeer and capital goods. How could these lists of independently held property not beget the mass nationalisations that were to follow?

There is no direct evidence that census returns were cited in either the construction of collective or state farms or in the violent expropriation of wealthy hunters or herders. Before collectivization reached its giddy heights, there were multiple surveys elaborating upon the methodology first employed federally during the Polar Census methodology that was repeated several times by local agencies. Perhaps the most suspicious survey was a special rural economy census in 1932 that directly enumerated all individuals by their class status as poor, middling or prosperous (Terletskii 1932b). The only evidence that I have discovered of a correlation between these surveys was the perhaps over-enthusiastic attempt of one famous enumerator, Boris Dolgikh, to cross-reference the families that he recorded in 1926/27 to those that he recorded during the 1932 census of the North of Krasnoiarsk *krai* (GAKK 2275-1-13; GAKK 2275-1-227). The strongest evidence that the primary records may have been useful for planners is the fact that in many archives the household cards can be found among the files of the various Territorial Formation expeditions or Departments of Rural Economy which were responsible for collectivization (rather than in the files of the regional statistical bureaus). A stronger argument can be made, of course, that the *logic* of enumeration – of building people into places and of tying them to inventories of property – was implicit in the reorganisations and repressions that were to follow. In this sense the Polar Census served as a rehearsal for regional agencies – giving them information and skills that they drew upon during successive surveys, and when asked much later to implement a policy of collectivisation.

One interesting proof of the open-ended nature of the Polar Census survey comes from a defence that the former co-ordinator of the Far Eastern Census expedition made when answering charges about the accuracy and usefulness of the data. Responding to critics who rejected the results of the Polar Census due to its ambiguities and complexities, Petr Terletskii replied that the material was never intended to produce a map of a general Polar population but instead to produce lists of discrete households:

> With respect to the data of the [Polar] Census it is important to note that they are valid only for individual households. The attempt of the Central Statistical Agency of the Soviet Union to use the data of the census in order to understand the presence of collective or antagonistic roots within Northern households has not been successful, [regardless whether] we analyse collective travel, the catching of fish in collective units (*arteli*), the quality of collective units and other matters such as the presence of conflicts over land resulting from migrations, fishing, hunting (or other types of territoriality). This remains the case if we look at how production was distributed, or how a household was organised. The data that we collected was simply not analysed. (Terletskii 1930: 43)

In the decade when this quote was written this statement could be understood as an apology for the difficulty with which the Polar Census data fed into a class analysis. Perhaps more simply it can be understood as confession that the instruments were never designed to answer these questions of those in power. However today it speaks instead to the nuanced and contingent qualities of these inscriptions.

While it is unquestionable that the census manuscripts provide specific tags – such as surnames, property inventories and geographic locations – that could be used to entrap people by planners who are so inclined, the archive also documents evocative social *practices* which could have been used, and could still be used, to build different projects. While expropriation and repression is unquestionably part of the history of this region, there were other more fortunate projects the value of which is only now being appreciated against the background of a monopolistic market economy. The surveillance on commodity prices undertaken, for example, led to the establishment of a single system of purchase prices which had a great effect on levelling disparities in income between regions. The national autonomous enclaves established in 1930 – which for several generations served as important institutions of identity and self-government for indigenous cadres – were established on the basis of the data of seasonal migration and territorial distribution from this household survey.

This survey of practices is still evocative today suggesting that range of possible imaginaries is not confined to the past. In this volume, Jordan (chapter 2), Ziker (chapter 11) and Anderson, Ineshin and Ziker (chapter 9) demonstrate how the value of careful readings of archived toponymns can help structure archaeological and anthropological research – both by identifying sites for excavation and by helping us build new models of long-term ecological action. The documentation of indigenous land occupancy in heavily industrialised places, like the Lena goldfields, can also potentially be used support future claims to territory should Russian federal laws supporting traditional 'clan communities' and 'territories of prioritised nature use' come into force. Kiselev (chapter 8) shows how the polar census instrumentation drafted in the post-civil war period can help us understand the contingent and fast-moving economic patterns in the post-Soviet period 80 years later. Semenov (chapter 6) demonstrates how a longitudinal analysis of the documents helps us understand the origin of a creolised 'regional society' today which defies the nationality categories so earnestly employed at the start of the Soviet period. Taking ecological analysis more literally, Klokov (chapter 7) combines modern biological studies to show how early records of Arctic fox populations can be used to generate a long-term picture of animal population cycles. In all cases, it is not the register of identity but the description of the architectural-ecological ensemble – of people living in places – which yields an insight into legacies. It is of course impossible to weigh the social value of contemporary historical or ecological studies of this type against the great social costs of the repressions, but the fact remains that this archive remains interesting for those living today who would like to understand aspects of the past in the present.

Where does this leave our evaluation of power and authority which are built into the texture of surveys of this type? Paul Rabinow and Nikolas Rose (2006) reviewed the history of development of the concept of 'biopower', placing their accent on the fact that the concept has been blunted by casual attempts to apply the concept to any form of social inquiry. They note that Michel Foucault himself never provided a 'set of operational tools' by which this evocative concept could be employed. Instead, they remind us, Foucault preferred to evoke biopolitical relationships through the detailed analysis of particular historical circumstances – in Foucault's case the analysis of the development of health and hygiene in seventeenth- and eighteenth-century France. It is clear that parts of the Polar Census survey pushed individuals to describe their fertility, their activity and their health – if not overtly their hygiene – on the specially designed cards for that purpose. However the clumsy inscriptions of households as sometimes *khoziastva* and sometimes *dvory*, not to mention the colourful universe of hyphenated identity markers, create an entangled image of collective actors nested in landscapes. At times, the transcriptions of a household, or of a place, look more like petitions for recognition than labels applied to help individuals 'work on their selves'. While the parts of the census documentation that forced extended families to describe themselves as sets of individuals built into nuclear families fall into line with the a general global tendency for states to interpret their citizens as a work force, other parts mark long-term solidarities between kinship units, complex landscapes, and a type of stewardship towards wild and tame animals evoking status and luck. These local cosmologies also mix the biological and the political, but they do so in a way that is not familiar to sociologists of Western Europe. This study suggests that biopower on the Russian 'Northern Frontiers' is historically and culturally situated and not a generalised, globalised force

If we would like to set this survey within the sociological tradition, we would have to diagnose this survey as representing a biopolitical enterprise where people are placed into a relationship with their lands. If Foucault identified a type of surveillance that monitors the vital signs of an individual torn apart from his or her surroundings – or Rabinow and Rose (ibid.) a type of genetic technology that monitors fractal individuals at the molecular level – here we have seen a type of surveillance that folds individuals into collectivities and into places. This architectural type of biopower is not necessarily liberating, as we know from the story of collectivization, but it also leaves open the possibility for unique forms of resistance.

At the start of the twenty-first century, Northerners in Siberia and the Russian Arctic are confronted with a different set of challenges than their ancestors faced when the Russian Empire collapsed. Their resource-rich landscapes are coveted by transnational corporations whose actions seemingly can only be moderated by local peoples if they make insistent reference to their long-term stewardship over places. Much as during the mid 1920s, the register of officially recognised 'sparse peoples' in Russia is expanding. This constitutional development is fuelling a renewed interest in long-term traditions – an interest that this archive is particularly well designed to serve. The purpose of this collection is to demonstrate the value of these records both to solve theoretical debates in a number of disciplines, but also to continue to write local histories of specific communities facing new social transformations. It also serves as an invitation to imagine the North through the eyes of those experiencing it at the start of the Soviet period, and through those eyes, imagine how it might be different in the future.

Acknowledgements

The research and the work that went into this introduction would not have been possible without the help of all of the archival workers and regional scholars who helped to compile the manuscript material. I am indebted to them. I am especially grateful to Konstantin Klokov, Elena Volzhanina and Maria Nakhshina who kindly agreed to skim over digital copies of memoranda from different regions in order to help me identify relevant quotes to the literature.

Notes

1. Digitised copies of selected information from all household cards, many community diaries, and the photo archive of the Turukhansk Polar Census expedition are available at www.abdn.ac.uk/polarcensus. Selections from the correspondence and diaries have been published in Russian in Anderson (2005) and Glavatskaia (2005b; 2006), and in Klokov and Ziker (2010).
2. The centrally published aggregates can be found in a bilingual French-Russian 56-volume edition (TsSU 1928-1933) where volumes 1, 18 and 35 corresponded to the Northern District (Kola peninsula); volumes 2, 19 and 36 to the Western District including Ural *oblast'*; volumes 6, 23 and 40 corresponded to Siberian Territory; and volumes 7, 24 and 41 to the Russian Far East. There was one centrally published set of results specific to the Polar Census (TsSU 1929).
3. The most important regional publications (from West to East) are from Murmansk (MOSO 1929), Arkhangel'sk (AGSO 1927; AGSO 1929), Syktyvkaar (KOSO 1929), Sverdlovsk (Ekaterinburg) (USU 1928; USU 1930), Novosibirsk and Krasnoiarsk (SKSO 1928; 1929; Tugarinov and Lappo 1927), Iakutsk (SUIaASSR 1928), and Khabarovsk (DVSU 1929a; DVSU 1929b). On the whole the regional publications consist of an authoritative list of population points (following from Imperial practice); often a set of grouped data by nationality and or by community, giving cross-tabulations; and a flurry of articles in local newspapers and in academic journals from regional academic societies. In several archives there are significant unpublished manuscripts that were obviously intended for publication in the early 1930s, but the local agencies were un-

able to win resources to bring them to press (GARF 3977-1-355: 31-41; GASO 2757-1-786; GASO 1812-2-183 [folders 1–5]).

4. The 1916 and 1917 agricultural (*sel'skokhoziaistvennaia*) census took place across the Russian Empire with the exception of parts of the Caucuses, some Eastern Russian provinces, and Iakutiia and Kamchatka – all of which were still under White administrations. That census used both a household (*podvornaia*) card and a community form (*obshchinnyi*) (Gaponenko and Kabuzan 1961). The 1920 general census left out parts of the Russian Far North, the Far East, and many southern regions in Ukraine and the Caucuses (Hirsch 2005: 105; Krasil'nikov 1926)

5. The personal form is reproduced in the appendix to each volume of the central published results (TsSU 1928–1932) and is described in detail, in English, by Francine Hirsch (2005: 114–23). There was a long interest among Russian statisticians in the representation of people in terms of nationality – no doubt inspired by their participation in international statistical congresses. Although the 1897 all-Russian Imperial census did not contain a question on nationality, nationality was attributed to populations often through marginal notes (ibid., 41–42) or through the local analysis of data on mother tongue, social estate and occupation (Alymov 1930). The personal form had a space for recording *narodnost'* ('nationality' building on the Russian root word for 'folk'), the data of which was published as *natsional'nost'* ('nationality' a neologism evoking the Russian word for nation). The Polar Census household card, by contrast, held a little-used space for *natsional'nost'*, the value of which was often attributed by mother tongue and estate/taxation appellations.

6. For an evocative description of the meaning of the word *tuzemets* see Sokolovskii (2001). The term *tuzemets* appears often in the memos surrounding the Polar Census. In GAAO 187-1-848: 69–75 there is a draft plan from Novosibirsk for a *tuzemnyi* community diary dated to approximately February 1926. The research plan by Aizen for the Red Cross survey of Turukhansk (dated to the autumn of 1925) uses the words *tuzemnye khoziaistva* GARF 3977-1-214: 61–63.

7. The 1897 All-Russian census was the first Imperial survey which aimed to interview every household head and relied upon solicited interview data rather than the lists compiled by local authorities. Its results were aggregated and published to produce a picture of the Imperial population (TsSK 1899–1905). The information from household heads was recorded on small personal forms. These were then bound together in a larger form which recorded the general qualities of the built environment within which the household members lived. Despite the lofty methodological aims of this census, special exclusions were made for the 'alien-outsiders' (*inorodtsy*). Some places would be surveyed by counting the number of dwellings and by multiplying that number by a co-efficient, or the enumerators might interview the person appointed by the state to collect taxes (*kniaz'*) (Cadiot 2000: 131–35). It was an interesting but evocative peculiarity of this census that there was no category of declared identity other than social estate and mother tongue. Siberian *inorodtsy* were often represented by their 'administrative clans' through which they paid their obligatory fur-taxes creating to this day some difficulty in linking those populations with modern territorial and nationality categories. This late Imperial peculiarity often seems to be an oversight since many of the organisers of the 1897 census deeply wanted to survey the Empire through a category of declared identity. This led to some energetic but extremely complex attempts to cross-reference social estate, mother tongue, and often marginal notes on the primary census cards to deduce pictures of particular nationalities (for example Patkanov 1906; Hirsch 2005: 41–42).

8. There is scattering of examples of this correspondence in the central archive GARF 3977-1-87, and in many regional archives between April 1925 and May 1926. One of the best surviving collections is in Arkhangel´sk (GAAO 187-1-848). In that compilation, a short memo from the Central Statistical Administration dated 8 April 1925 (received 14 April 1925) asked the Arkhangel´sk Statistical Bureau (and presumably each of the other regional offices) to draft a plan for a combining the 'agricultural (*s.kh.*) and demographic census of the northern frontier … in one excursion' (GAAO 187-1-848: 17). The memo spoke of the instrumentation as similar to the 'personal form of the 1923 census, [and] the household card (*podvornaia karta s. kh.*) similar to the questions of the 1920 census'. Following this memo, there is a series of copied correspondence extending to roughly February 1926 from many statistical bureaux enclosing many different draft sample forms (l.27; 36–77v.). On 7 May 1926 a shipment of 5,000 pre-printed household cards was shipped from Moscow to Arkhangel´sk, signalling an end to the debate (GAAO 187-1-852: 21).

9. This double-sided folio has 192 questions divided into unnumbered sectors. The sectors include: basic information on the identity of the household head [1–8] [identical to the final card], a summary of the nomadic round [9–11], demographic information on the family [12–24] [abbreviated], an inventory of tools and dwellings [29–59], an inventory of dogs and reindeer [60–74], an inventory of furs, berries and other goods sold – broken down by three categories of counts, sold and price [75–117], a relatively open list of squares to document consumer goods broken down by eight categories [2 extra categories than the final variant] [125–152], an exacting list of debts [153–161], a list of trading posts visited from 1922 to 1925 [not on the final card] [162–168], a list of goods that are urgently needed [169–170], a longitudinal list of furs sold from 1922 to 1924 [171–180], a longitudinal list of summer reindeer in pasture from 1914 to 1924 [183–187], and a list of employees [188–197]. The instructions for filling out the form are filed in GARF 3977-1-214: 61–63.

10. The *chumovaia kartochka* can be found in typeset form in a non-curated folder in the Krasnoiarsk Regional Museum (KKKM bez fond 'Perepis'). A photograph of its face page was published in Anderson (2006: 33). A typescript draft form of the same card can be found in GARF 3977-1-75: 5–6. It is important to note that this project for a 'skin-lodge card' was accompanied by several rather detailed forms on reindeer husbandry and hunting, the content of which seems to have been folded into the community diary (GARF 3977-1-75: 7–11). Although the 'lodge card' in a purist manner never mentions the word household, the accompanying cards use the word *dvor* for 'household'.

11. This folio featured 138 questions divided into eleven numbered economic sectors with a heavy emphasis on trade. The sectors include: I) a simple count of the human population, II) a simple count of dwellings, III) a simple count of domestic animals, III) [sic] a longitudinal count of cattle 1924–1926, IV) a detailed table of the sale and purchase of reindeer products, V) a detailed count of dogs by type, VI) an inventory of transport sleds, VII) an inventory of hunting equipment, VIII) an inventory of fishing equipment, IX) an inventory of furs trapped by species, and X) a count of purchased groceries and trade goods.

12. The draft 'skin-lodge' card of the Siberian Territorial Statistical Agency was accompanied by several other instruments focussing on the 'sectors' of reindeer herding and hunting. The questions on these forms are similar to those that appear in the final community diaries (GARF 3977-1-75: 7–9). A long list of questions used for a Red Cross expedition to Turukhansk Territory, which included questions on ritual practices and shamanism, is also filed together with the Polar Census materials in Moscow,

suggesting a link to this document (GARF 3977-1-214: 72–82). On the verso side of a draft household card from GAAO (187-1-848: 27v) there is a list of 23 specific questions designed to elicit information about nomadic movements and trading practices.

13. The head of the Siberian Polar Census expedition, Adam Kurilovich, later became an important administrator in the Soviet trading organisations of Central Siberia (GAKK 827-1-18: 2–5). Aside from surveying prices, the questions on trade often asked informants to specify *from whom* they bought their consumer goods. In the early period following the civil war, Soviet trading organisations still competed with privately owned trading outfits.

14. The main discussion on structuring the final card can be found in a memo of a meeting in Moscow on 4 December 1925 with representatives from all eight regional bureaux (RGAE 1562-336-39: 9–11; GASO 1812-2-1-181.1: 44–48). As a preparation for that meeting it seems that seminars were held in each regional office. For minutes from the Krasnoiarsk meeting of 4 September 1925, see GARF 3977-1-75: 12; and for the meeting of 31 December 1925, see GARF 3977-1-153: 24–25. For Arkhangel'sk, see the minutes of 27 January 1926 GAAO 187-1-848: 26–26v. For the Ural expedition, see the minutes of 5 and 9 November 1925 in GASO 1812-2-1-181.1: 35–39). The state planning commission, after approving the budget, also requested some minor additions to both the household card and community diary (of which the most interesting, and puzzling, was the specification of different types of tea and sugar [cells 384 and 385]) (RGAE 1562 -336-39: 24v).

15. There is a humorous but credible second-hand account of the attempts of the representatives of the Far Eastern Statistical Agency to convince the Muscovite statisticians of the importance of counting male and female dogs separately in order to understand systems of dog transport in the outer corners of the Union (DVSU 1929).

16. The digitised archive of only one-quarter of the original household cards enumerates 97 identifiers, the majority of which are hyphenated geographical identity terms (of the type 'Beregovoi Eneseiets' (lit – 'A person of the Enisei River living along its banks' – now known as a Ket) (see Anderson 2006).

17. The idea of a *podvornaia karta* was the main theme of discussion at the key meeting over the design of the instrumentation in Moscow on 4 December 1925 (although this document gives a rough count of households across Russia as *khoziaistvo*) (RGAE P1562-336-39: 9–11; GASO 1812-2-181.1: 47–48). As late as February 1926, the Central Statistical Administration circulated a typeset, but draft, *podvornaia kartochka* to the regions for discussion (GAAO 187-1-848: 36–36v). The first coupling of the word *khoziaistvo* with the idea of a Northern census occurs in the decree of the Soviet of People's Commissars on 23 February 1926. Following that, the term appears in a letter to the Central Statistical Administration from the State Planning Commission approving a budget (296,000 roubles – a larger budget than that requested) (RGAE 1562 - 336-39: 24). A letter to the Committee of the North of the Central Administrative Committee from the Central Statistical Administration on 7 April 1926 uses the term fluently (RGAE 1562-336-39: 26). There is an impression in the manuscript archives that the census became *khoziaistvennaia* when the Central Statistical Administration had to lobby for funds. There is some parallel evidence that the economically evocative term *khoziaistvo* circulated in somewhat different intellectual circles than the geographic language of *dvor*. The Komi Statistical Administration, which distinguished itself from all other provincial statistical agencies for its obsession with budgets and a monetaristic definition of social life, from a very early date consistently used the word *khoziaistvo* in its correspondence (see GAMO 536-1-74: 9–11v). By contrast, the intellectuals working within the geographical tradition of census taking preferred the

architectural term. Mitrofan Krasil´nikov, one of the co-ordinators of the All-Union census, still spoke of a *podvornaia kartochka* in his speech to the Union of Statisticians on 1–7 December 1926 (Krasil´nikov 1926: 4).

18. The instructions for the general demographic survey are reprinted in the appendix to every volume of the published results. On this point see, for example TsSU (1928 [vol 1]: 287).

19. This elaborate definition of a household is probably more traditionally described as a patrilineal related clan (*rod*).

2 Seasonal Mobility and Sacred Landscape Geography among Northern Hunter-Gatherers

Peter Jordan

Introduction

Three rival themes continue to jostle for the high ground of hunter-gatherer research: adaptation, long-term history and local perception. Interest in the cultural ecology of foragers rose to academic prominence in the late 1960s, and for some, continues to provide a unique inter-disciplinary field with a distinctive identity, methodological rigour and theoretical coherence (Ames 2004). More recently, the degree to which ethnographically-documented foragers represent 'pure' and timeless adaptations to local environments has been extensively debated, to the extent that most hunter-gatherers are now viewed as active participants in more complex historical trajectories. It is now conceded that all interact with states, agro-pastoralists and traders who each exert crucial influences on their social organisation and subsistence strategies. A third theme cross-cuts these ecological and historical approaches: the examination of how hunter-gatherers perceive and symbolically engage with resources and environments, with a focus on cultural landscapes as expressions of social identity and cosmology.

Siberian ethnography is a relative newcomer to these tangled debates, and further analysis of the region's hunter-fisher-gatherers is well-placed to contribute to all three perspectives, which are often presented in academic literature as competing and even contradictory. More importantly, a fresh programme of Siberian research, focusing on the abundance of historical documents, and aided by ongoing opportunities for ethnographic fieldwork, might also signal how these divergent themes might be better integrated, thereby generating fuller understandings of the agency and variability of hunter-gatherer societies both past and present.

As a point of departure into this wider endeavour, this chapter focuses on the community diaries (*poselennye blanki*) of the 1926/27 Soviet Polar Census, which provide a unique historical record of the economy, mobility and living conditions of groups of households in Russia's Arctic and Sub-Arctic prior to the major changes of the Soviet period. In the present case study, I integrate an analysis of these documents with a critical reading of the wider ethno-historical literature, and combine this with insights form my own recent fieldwork (from 1998 to 2005) amongst the direct descendants of communities depicted in these diaries. My aim is to generate a dynamic perspective on how hunter-fisher-gatherers, living in the remote taiga wetlands of Western Siberia, were responding to the challenges of northern ecologies and the colonial encounter, adopting new innovations, and developing social and ritual institutions for 'holding the land'. Here, I focus on one Khant regional society which lived along a single tributary of the river Ob'. However, the insights generated by the pilot study signal productive potential for a larger regional-scale analysis of the Polar Census materials, which would employ the same methodology developed here.

West Siberian Hunter-Fisher-Gatherers in Historical Context (1600–1921 AD)

How do northern hunter-fisher-gatherer societies organise their activities spatially and seasonally?

How do they 'hold' the landscape ideologically, symbolically and practically?

How were northern lifeways transformed through interaction with states, empires and external markets?

What strategies are open to individuals and households within these long-term trajectories?

This chapter considers all these questions through an ethno-historical analysis of transformations affecting Eastern Khant subsistence and mobility during the decades between 1890 and 1930. Additional insights are derived from recent ethnographic fieldwork among contemporary Khant communities still living on the land.

Khants are one of the northern indigenous peoples of Russia who numbered 15,611 in 1897, rising to 22,283 in 1989 (Glavatskaia 2002: 103). Along with Mansis, Nenetses, Sel'kups and other native groups, Khants reside in the vast West Siberian lowlands (fig. 2.1) and are traditionally divided into three groupings – northern Khants, who live around the Lower Ob' and practice a mixture of hunting, fishing and large-scale reindeer husbandry (Perevalova 2004; Martynova 1998: 80–137); southern Khants – now largely assimilated – who lived along the Irtysh river, and practised hunting, fishing and also agriculture and cattle breeding, which they adopted from the South Siberian Tatars and later Russians (E. Fedorova 2000; Martynova 1998: 12–79); and ap-

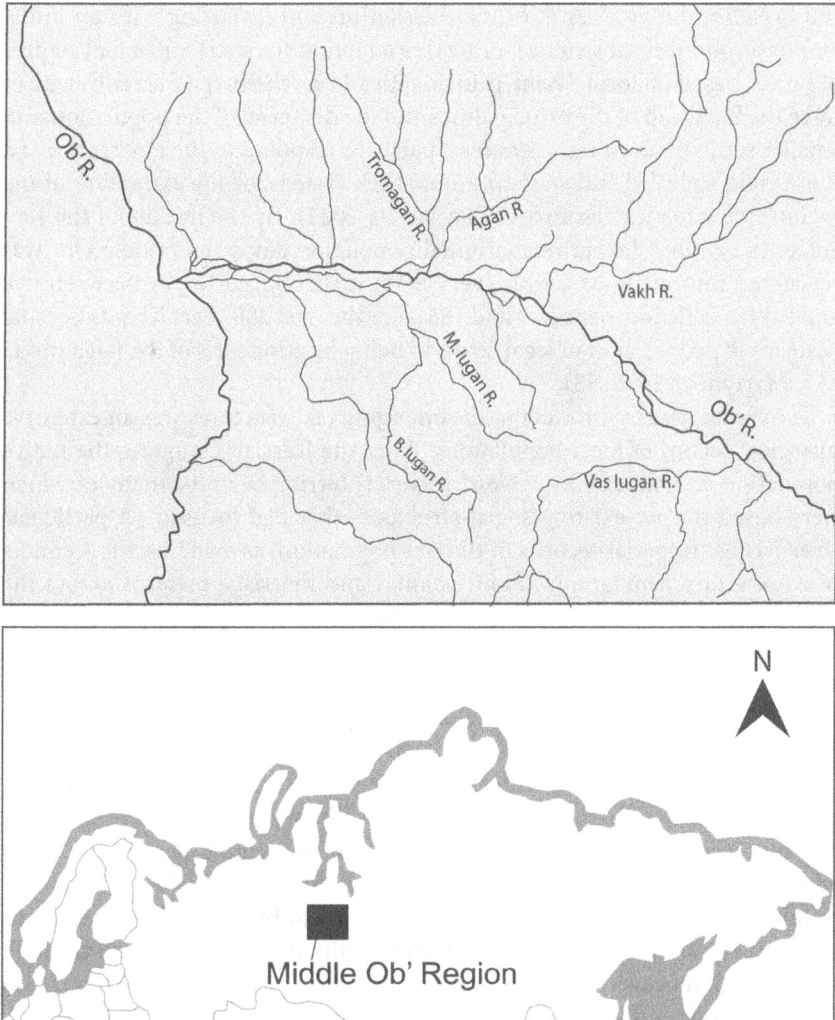

Figure 2.1. Middle Ob´ region (Western Siberia)

proximately 5,000 Eastern Khants, who live in the forests and wetlands of the middle Ob´ and its main tributaries, traditionally practising hunting, fishing and some small-scale reindeer herding (E. Fedorova 2000; Golovnev 1993; Jordan 2003; Martynova 1995, 1998: 138–202; Viget 2002a).

Russians conquered Western Siberia in the late sixteenth century and gradually subjugated native populations into a fur-tax regime (*iasak*). Their initial methods, such as hostage taking, were built on an earlier tribute system that had bound native groups into the medieval Tatar Khanate. It is possible to trace a cumulative historical transformation in indigenous economy and social organisation as a result of the Russian presence, starting with an initial emphasis on local subsistence, limited production for trade and small centres of power based on local Khant 'principalities' (*knaizhestva*). Gradually, we can trace the break-up of the principalities and the dispersal of the population into smaller settlements in remoter areas, partly in response to the emergence of a more rigid state-led and state-monitored tax system for the extraction of the region's valuable fur resources (Glavatskaia 2002). By the middle of the seventeenth century the entire aboriginal population along the middle Ob´ was registered into tax books, with every adult male obliged to pay between five and twelve sable furs per year (ibid.: 83). For the next 300 years Khants became 'state *iasak* people', akin in legal terms to being hunting serfs of the taiga (ibid.: 113; Martynova 1995: 88).

A bureaucratic by-product of the emerging tax structures was an extensive historical record of local populations. After the Russian conquest, the native population was allocated to *volost´* [district] territorial units, many of which were based on pre-existing social structures that had focused on particular river basins. Imperial records of district populations provide useful accounts of community demography, family names and marriage patterns across the wider region (Martynova 1995, 1998). State interests in protecting the fur trade also led to formal legal protection of native economic territories and a ban on the in-migration of Russian settlers from European Russia (Shimkin 1990; Konev 1998: 127–28; Lukina 1985; Martynova 1995; Jordan 2003). Along the middle Ob´, Khant *volost´* populations were characterised by very infrequent interaction and inter-marriage with Russians, which ensured a relative ethnic 'monolithicity' of the Eastern Khants between the seventeenth and nineteenth centuries (Lukina 1985: 16). At the same time, most districts where Khants lived were geographically remote from one another. Khant communities living along different drainages tended to be weakly integrated with others (Martynova 1998: 209). Each community distinguished itself through notable differences in dress, subsistence economy, material culture and also dialect (Shatilov 1931).

It is clear from these accounts that trade, local geography and ecology were crucial factors influencing aboriginal subsistence and mobility practices, and by the end of the Tsarist period several distinctive aboriginal adaptations were emerging along the Middle Ob´ (Dunin-Gorkavich 1996; Martyona 1995; Golovnev 1993; Viget 2002a). A broad historical and ecological distinction can be drawn between the Khant communities living along the main Ob´ river, and those on the *lower* reaches of the main tributaries. The latter practiced what Golovnev (1993: 202) described as a 'river-edge subsistence complex' which by the end of the nineteenth century made these communities dependant on aquatic resources to support their mainly settled strategy. In contrast, communities living on the upper tributary rivers grew to rely on a 'deep-taiga economic complex', combining mobile hunting and fishing (ibid.). It is interesting that these two adaptive strategies can also be identified in the detailed records of the 1926/27 census and to some extent are still visible today (Jordan 2003).

Early state surveillance of native peoples was focused on maintaining a rigid account of valuable pelts extracted by hunters registered to individual *volosty*. However, there was only limited state interest in the details of how households organised their subsistence and land holding practices and these were left largely to local negotiation (Martynova 1995: 110; Jordan 2003: 241–42). Until 1858, the location of specific settlements was not even noted in tax records (Martynova 1998: 141). This situation began to change at the end of the nineteenth century as the state began to take a more systematic interest in the settlements and subsistence activities of its indigenous peoples. A comprehensive geographical survey of Western Siberia was prepared by Dunin-Gorkavich (1996) using results from the 1897 census, and this provides a remarkably detailed account of Khant local communities with which to compare the 1926/27 census results, as we will do below.

Relations between Siberian peoples and the early Soviet State are best characterized as a period of observation and documentation rather than intervention or direct social transformation. In fact, the political shifts in the European part of Russia were slow to affect Siberia's indigenous peoples. The Civil War raged up and down the Ob′ to such a degree that it was only by the mid 1920s that the Soviet state could show an interest in native peoples.

The Soviet Polar Census of 1926/27 was designed to equip state planners with a better understanding of the native peoples living along its long northern periphery, with the ultimate aim of integrating them fully into state economic and political structures (Glavatskaia, this volume). It seems that the enumerators of the 1926/27 census along the middle Ob′ used earlier lists of communities described by Dunin-Gorkavich. The lists of communities in both surveys have a one-to-one correspondence, providing a remarkable opportunity to compare these important sources. Although building on the earlier Imperial-era work, the community diaries take state surveillance of its indigenous peoples to new levels of detail, often discussing *specific* households and their precise movements over the landscape at different times of the year.

This constellation of sources generates unique opportunities to reconstruct the household-scale lifeways of hunter-fisher-gatherer populations prior to the major reorganisations of the Soviet period. Here, I focus on the theme of household mobility in order to introduce a broader discussion of other aspects of indigenous lifeways, including the challenges of task-scheduling, attitudes to new innovations, rising social inequality and the roles of social institutions and ritual practice in land tenure and community interaction.

Iugan Khants: 'People of the River'

This chapter focuses on the community diary archive of the Iugan River Khants and concentrates, in particular, on the activities of households occupying remoter areas of upper-river taiga wetlands. A close reading of these historical records enables us to break open the general economic and ecological type-categories that have characterised some recent scholarship, and glimpse the agency of individuals and households as they reacted to, and participated in, the transformation of the taiga economy between 1890 and 1930.

Understanding these relationships requires attention to both ecological setting and historical context. The Iugan River has two branches – the 'Great' (Bol´shoi) Iugan River, over 1,000 kilometres in length; and the 'Small' (Malyi) Iugan River, which runs for 550 kilometres (fig. 2.1). These rivers converge and flow into the Iugan Ob´ and then the main Ob´ River, close to the city of Surgut, which was founded in 1594 as part of the Russian conquest. To the East of the Iugan drainage are the Balyk and Salym Rivers; to the East is the Kul´egan´, with the Demianka River to the Southwest and the Vasiugan to the Southeast. In the areas between these low-lying drainages are extensive tracts of uninhabited wetland.

The earliest Russian records of *iasak* fur-tax payers living on the Iugan, Iugan Ob´ and Balyk Rivers document the male population as 116 in 1629, rising to 125 in 1645, followed by 133 in 1680, and 148 in 1706. This might indicate either a steady growth in local households, or reflect the improved reach of the tax system into remoter areas (Martynova 1998: 140). Later sources recorded the entire population and indicated that the Iugan Ob´ population hovered around 350 from 1782 and 1897, but that populations on the Malyi Iugan went through a major decline, from 352 down to 141, and populations along the Bol´shoi Iugan showed a steady rise, from 493 in 1792 to 554 in 1897 (Martynova 1998: 140–41).

Interactions with Russians were limited and very infrequent – even at the end of the nineteenth century there were only 140 Russians, living mainly in Surgut and local administrative villages, alongside 5,964 Eastern Khants in the wider middle Ob´ region (Surgutskii *uezd* [province]) (Lukina 1985: 16). Local marriage strategies tended to reinforce links within the Iugan basin with few marriages concluded with neighbouring communities in other river basins (Martynova 1998: 140–42).[1] With most interaction and marriage contacts along – rather then between – the rivers of West Siberia, it is clear that the network of remote waterways provided a scope for local senses of collective identity linked to particular drainages. For example, Khants living along the Iugan waterways described themselves as *Iagun Iakh* ('People of the River'), their regular interactions ensuring that they formed a rather uniform ethnic group (Martynova 1998: 140).

The term *iurt* was used in many sources to describe Eastern Khant settlements. Over the years – and among authors – the term has been used in slightly different ways, appearing in both the singular (*iurt*) and the plural (*iurty*), and leading to some terminological confusion. In one sense, a *iurt* is a general term for a permanently built structure, the design, materials and location of which will often vary from season to season, due to the climate and mobile nature of the hunting, fishing and gathering adaptation. Over the year households occupied a number of structures at seasonal base camps located in different parts of the landscape – hence the terms winter *iurty* or summer *iurty*. For example, Dunin-Gorkavich (1995: 149) described how the Iugan Khants built a log cabin *iurt*. However, the community diaries of the Polar Census listed clusters of Khant households as living at *iurty*. In a second sense the term *iurt* had a more collective social meaning (Martynova 1995: 92), and refers to a group of households who lived together and exploited a shared economic territory. This '*iurt* community' would break up during certain seasons – for example for mobile winter hunting – but during the intervening times would occupy permanent structures at one or several base camps during the course of the year.

In this chapter I will retain the distinction: *iurt* or *iurty* refers to the built structures of a base camp, and '*iurt* community' to the group who lived there and shared a common economic territory. Dunin-Gorkavich provided a base map of late nineteenth century Khant *iurty* along the Iugan drainage. The same framework was used in the 1920s Polar Census, with a community diary taken at each of these settlements, recording the lifeways of the households living there (fig. 2.2). Interestingly, there is also remarkable continuity in these settlement patterns through to the present day, with many contemporary *iurty* existing at the same locations (Bakhlykov 1996: 164; Jordan 2003: 58), enabling recent ethnographic fieldwork to inform historical reconstruction of land use and lifeways.

Despite long-term continuities from the Imperial period to the Soviet era in the structure of *iurt* communities, Soviet power brought some major changes during the twentieth century. The first impacts of Soviet policies began to be felt in the 1920s, with the establishment of the Iuganskii *raisovet* [district soviet], with its centre in Iuganskoe containing five sub-departments over the different branches of the river (table 2.1, below) (Glavatskaia 2002: 108). Bakhlykov (1996: 129–72) provided a useful account of the subsequent Soviet era transformations. The former Ugotskie *iurty* emerged as Ugut, centre of the Iugan Khants, with the formation of the Ugutskii *sel'skii sovet* [village soviet], and with the first boarding school opening in 1929 and a hospital in 1931. Between 1932 and 1935 shops opened in Taurovy and and Tailakovy. Collectivisation was only enforced post-war, with permanent village centres built in Kiniaminy, Kaiukovy, Tailakovy and Taurovy, and further development in Ugut, where most Malyi Iugan Khants were gathered.

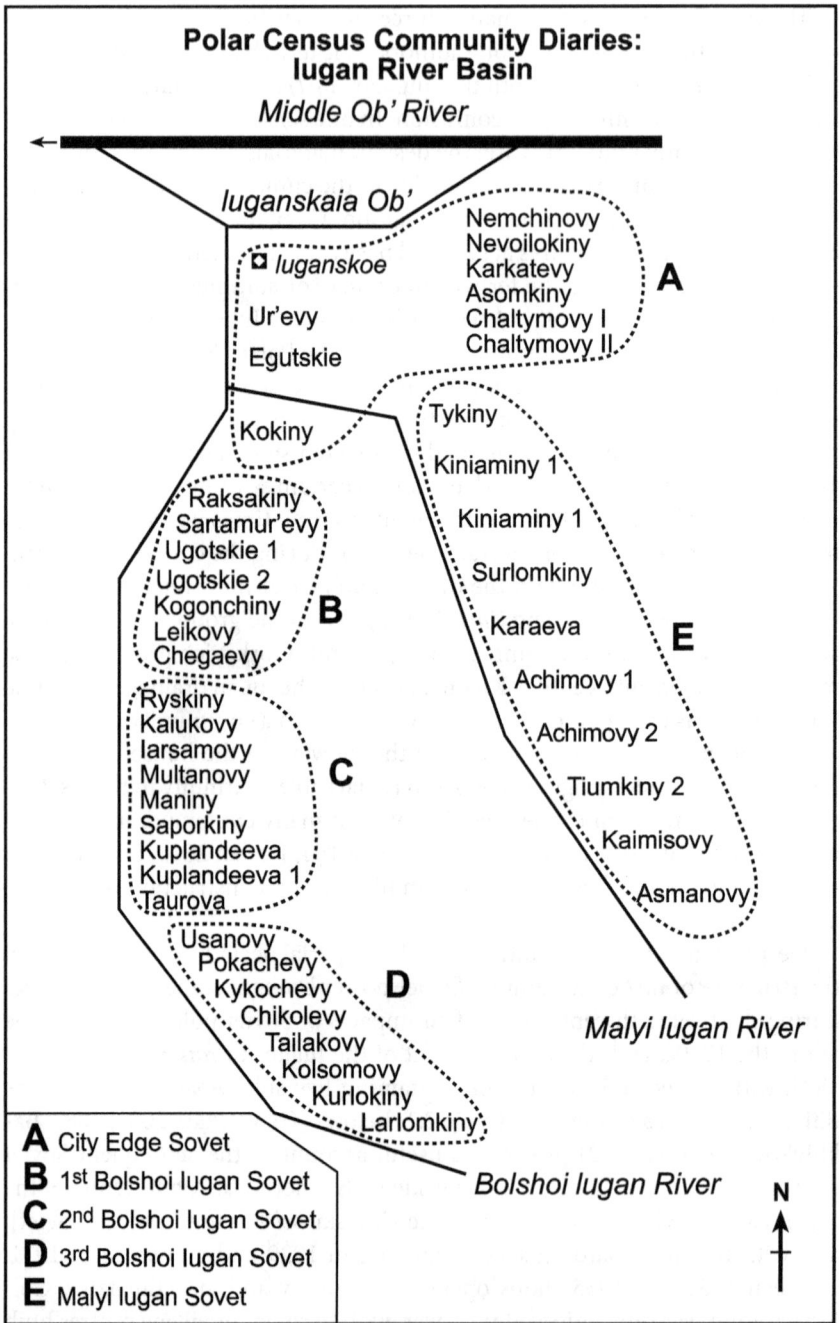

Figure 2.2. Polar Census community diaries: Iugan River basin (see also table 2.1)

Nevertheless, the Soviet development of the traditional economy was built on long-standing subsistence practices. The fulfilment of fur quotas required hunters to return to their ancestral territories, sometimes alone but also with families. In early summer, cutters were dispatched to the top of the rivers to collect the entire native population and tow them in a caravan of boats down to the lower river and Iugan Ob′ for collective fishing. This enforced mobility also precipitated a collapse of reindeer husbandry on the river as there was no one left in the *iurty* to tend herds over the summer months. Hunters reverted to using dog sleds. In the 1960s, five fur farms were established, and by the 1970s all native peoples undertaking traditional economic activities (hunting, fishing and gathering) became state employees of the Ugutskii POKh.[2] However, POKh directors, understanding the need for hunters to live in their clan territories, turned a blind eye to most households drifting back to the historical *iurty* that they had occupied since at least the late nineteenth century (Bakhlykov 1996: 164).

As oil and gas development gathered pace in the middle Ob′ region during the late 1970s, a large section of land between the Malyi and Bol′shoi Iugan Rivers was eventually set aside for the 1982 establishment of the Iugan Nature Preserve, which protected the pristine ecology but truncated earlier native land use patterns. Expeditionary fishing collapsed in the early 1990s but large numbers of Iugan Khant households continued to live out on the land, practising traditional branches of the economy: localised hunting, fishing and gathering, partly for subsistence, but also selling fur, berries and nuts to commercial markets. Although the Iugan Khants have fared better than many other native communities and maintain many traditional aspects of kinship, national clothing, language and ritual practice, their contemporary mobility patterns are much constrained, and a closing ring of oil and gas development is further reducing areas for hunting, compounded by an influx of urban hunters and the development of roads and pipelines, which affect animal migration patterns (Jordan 2003; Jordan and Filtchenko 2005; Viget 2002b).

'Hunters in Transition': Iugan Khant Lifeways (1890s–1920s)

These present changes render insights into the historical land use documented by the community diaries all the more important. We now return to the pre-Soviet era, and examine the main economic opportunities presented by the local Iugan ecology. The Iugan River is located between 59 and 61 degrees north (Dunin-Gorkavich 1995: 138) and has a strongly seasonal climate marked by long, dry summers and bitterly cold winters, with lasting snow cover. The terrain is low-lying, with few areas of higher elevation, and the spring snow melt brings widespread flooding. There are four distinct ecosystems (Viget 2002b: 189): extensive bog-lands occupy the poorly-drained areas between watersheds; pine forests cover sandy hills and ridges; cedar forests run along the better-drained river margins; and a unique ecosystem of willows, taller grasses and wild rose exists along the water edges.

What adaptive strategies emerged in this ecological setting? Recent archaeological surveys of the Bolshoi Iugan basin (Karacharov 1999) have provided indications of a shift in settlement and economic activity, away from an earlier post-glacial focus on localised subsistence. Earlier sites from the Bronze and Iron Ages are concentrated exclusively in areas where several ecological zones converge, providing stable access to subsistence resources, for example, around Kaiukovy *iurty* (figs. 2.2 and 2.3). By the later Medieval period (from the twelfth through the sixteenth centuries), as part of a wider intensification of trade and exchange, the basis of which in the Middle Ob´ was fur, settlement begins to expand outwards from these areas, and into areas not particularly suitable for human existence – e.g. the pine forests along the upper stretches of the Bol´shoi Iugan River, where there are insufficient subsistence resources even for small and mobile populations (Karacharov 1999: 232–33).

Interestingly, the scale and extent of the later Medieval dispersed settlement patterns anticipated the widely scattered and historically-documented *iurty* along both the Malyi and Bol´shoi Iugan, depicted in seventeenth-century maps (Viget 2002b: 189) and surveyed in more detail in the late nineteenth century by Dunin-Gorkavich. However, from Larlomkiny to Iarsomovy *iurty* there were no sites earlier than the later Medieval period; Karacharov therefore concludes that these archaeological surveys demonstrate that the indigenous economy was already undergoing transformation prior to the Russian conquest (1999: 233), with the roots of a new economy extending back to the later medieval period, and with a shift to specialisation in fur hunting and other branches of the economy eventually becoming subsidiary.

The trend towards the intensification of the fur trade continued after the Russian conquest (Lukina 1985: 17), producing a general switch from emphasis on meat to fur hunting in the seventeenth century (Glavatskaia 2002: 115), and forming one aspect of a series of profound regional economic transformations and reorientations affecting native economic complexes in Western Siberia between the sixteenth and nineteenth centuries (Golovnev 1993: 160). It is possible to trace these developments as they play out along the Iugan (Viget 2002b; Dunin-Gorkavich 1995).

The Iugan emerged in the sixteenth century as an area extremely rich in fur resources. As sable was quickly over-hunted, attention switched to squirrel, which were in demand in Chinese markets due its to high quality and unusual colours. Even at the start of the seventeenth century, Iuganskoe held one of the largest trade fairs in the region, enabling merchants to meet with hunters from across the wider Middle Ob´ region (Viget 2002b: 189). If Iuganskoe was located on the lower Iugan meadows, enabling the population to keep cattle and horses, and also to grow crops, then it was surrounded, upstream by traditional *iurty* settlements inhabited by Khant hunters and their nuclear families. These households spent their winters hunting in the remoter forest and migrated downstream in summer, engaging in fishing – the products of which they either sold to local merchants or dried and used as winter supplies to subsidize their diet. Across the region, flour had also come into widespread usage to supplement diet and enabled a fuller focus on fur hunting (Glavatskaia 2002: 116). Khant contacts with Russians and wider trade networks enabled them to gain access to new fishing and hunting technologies, including nets, guns and metal traps, and to use the weirs and self-triggered bows less.

A series of significant ecological changes which affected the basin throughout the nineteenth century had major practical repercussions for this indigenous economic strategy. Devastating forest fires swept through the taiga destroying hundreds of thousands of hectares of mature woodland – forests along the entire western side of the Bol´shoi Iugan were destroyed in the 1840s; a further fire in the 1860s wiped out the forest above and below the confluence of the Malyi and Bol´shoi Iugan Rivers. Regular fires continued in these areas into the 1860s; also, in the 1870s and 1880s the entire forest on either side of the Negus Iakh (a major tributary to the Bol´shoi Iugan) also burned (Viget 2002b: 190; Dunin-Gorkavich 1995: 143). As a result, there was very little mature woodland left by the end of the nineteenth century, and these environmental problems exerted major pressures on the local hunting economy. For example, good hunting areas became in short supply and sable largely disappeared from the Bol´shoi Iugan basin. Hunting activities began to extend outwards into the surrounding forests of the Salym, Balyk and Demianka Rivers. It is estimated that 60 per cent of the population eventually began to hunt outside the Iugan basin. This seems to have been a successful strategy allowing Iugan hunters to procure up to 100,000 squirrels per year (Dunin-Gorkavich 1996: 148–49) and up to 600 sables in a good year (ibid., 156).

Since fish resources were not as plentiful in the upper headwaters, Upper Iugan River groups began to rely on moose and particular wild deer for their fall, winter and spring food supplies. This generated a very diverse set of subsistence strategies across the *iurt* communities. Some households now focused entirely on squirrel, and some hunted squirrel and used guns to hunt wild reindeer; others built fences for hunting moose and wild deer while hunting squirrel as well; others hunted both squirrel and sable while also maintaining fences for wild deer and moose (Viget 2002b: 191). It is into these changing circumstances marked by an expansion of hunting territories and a specialization on certain species that Khants somewhat hesitantly adopted transport reindeer (Viget 2002b: 191). The first records of Khant reindeer holding date to the early nineteenth century (Golovnev 1993: 100). The use of reindeer was only weakly developed by the end of the nineteenth century (Dunin-Gorkavich 1995: 144–45; 1996: 25) – as the community diaries show, even by the 1920s some upper river households did not have reindeer. The development of reindeer husbandry may have been linked to more general responses to the extensive forest fires, which were driving hunters to appropriate and more distant hunting areas. As we will see, adoption of domestic reindeer may also have been closely linked to the local institution of establishing both 'winter' and 'summer' *iurt* communities.

The Iugan River Community Diaries

The communities diaries collected during the 1926/27 Polar Census capture in great detail the way that specific *iurt* communities, and in some cases, individual households, adapted to these changing environmental and economic circumstances. The State Archive in Ekaterinburg has a full collection of community diaries from the Polar Census of 1926/27 for the Iugan watershed, although the accompanying household cards for this region have not been found.[3] As outlined in the appendix to this volume, the community diaries give a semi-structured narrative covering a large number of topics ranging from meteorology and hydrology to customs and traditions. This particular set of diaries gives an especially evocative picture of how groups of households made decisions about their subsistence and of their households' mobility over the course of a year.

The enumerator of this region travelled up two tributaries of the Ob´ River – the Bolshoi Iugan and the Malyi Iugan – documenting *iurt* communities in much the same fashion as during the previous 1897 census. He derived the official settlement name from the location of the summer *iurt* community. In this chapter I focus on families who lived at the headwaters of these two rivers. In general, as one reads the census accounts starting from the main river up to the headwaters one observes that the enumerator documented a greater degree of mobility (table 2.1). This mobility was documented both overtly and subtlety in the detail of the diaries. Each community was first categorised as being settled (*osedloe*) or semi-nomadic (*poluosedloe* i.e. 'half-settled'). However, most – but not all – diaries also documented the movements of semi-nomadic communities between their separate summer and winter *iurty*, summer fishing grounds and winter hunting areas, including their distance, river basin, and compass direction. Table 2.1 summarises this information. Here I record whether the communities were classified as settled or not. If they were classified as semi-nomadic, the table specifies the distance between summer and winter *iurt* (or if the households only used a summer *iurt*). In the table, I also coded their mobility strategies into 'local' and more elaborate strategies which are classified as 'shorter-', 'medium-' and 'longer-range mobility'.[4]

Table 2.1. Overview of Iugan Khant settlement, household mobility and economy (Polar Census Community Diaries (*poselennye blanki*)) (See fig. 2.2)

Folios*	Settlement Name	N Households	Description of the degree of settlement (distance between summer and winter *iurty*)**	Description of Winter Hunting Strategies (Range in km)
Area of Iuganskaia Ob´				
390–406	Nemchinovy	6	Settled	Local
373–389	Nevoilokiny	12	Settled	Local
118–134	Karkatevy	6	Settled	Local
018–033	Asomkiny	3	Settled	Local
661–677	Chaltymovy 1	2	Settled	Local
678–693	Chaltymovy II	5	Settled	Local
Bolshoi Iugan River				
728–745	S. Iuganskoe	41	Settled	Local
627–643	Ur'evy	6	S/W (1)	Local
068–084	Egutskie	2	S	Local
169–185	Kokiny	3	S/W (4)	Local
424–440	Raksakiny	4	S/W (1.5)	Local
475–491	Sartamur'evy	1	S/W (6)	Local
560–575	Ugotskie 1	8	S (on both banks)/W (1.5)	Longer-range (60–c.250)
610–626	Ugotskie 2	4	Share S with Ugotskie 1/W (16.5)	Longer-range (90–c.250)
152–168	Kogonchiny	9	S/W (3)	Longer-range (45–c.230)
322–338	Leikovy	4	S/W (2)	Shorter-range (35–45)
694–710	Chegaevy	2	S/W (3)	Longer-range (70–160)
441–457	Ryskiny	5	S/W (2)	Longer-range (40–140)
135–151	Kaiukovy	11	S/W (3)	Medium-range (50–90)
746–762	Iarsamovy	8	S/W (3)	Longer-range (0–250)
356–372	Multanovy	3	S/W (4)	Shorter-range (0–45)
339–355	Maniny	2	S/W (2)	Local
458–474	Saporkiny	3	S/W (2)	Medium-range (0–60)
220–236	Kuplandeeva	5	S only	Longer-range (190)
203–219	Kuplandeeva 1	2	S only	Longer-range (80–220)
526–542	Taurova	3	S only	Longer-range (40–220)
644–660	Usanovy	8	S only	Longer-range (50–280)
407–423	Pokachevy	4	S/W (10)	Longer-range (90–180)
254–270	Kykochevy	3	S only	Medium-range (70)
711–727	Chikolevy	2	S only	Local
509–525	Tailakovy	7	S only	Longer-range (0–170)
186–202	Kolsomovy	2	S/W (0.5)	Longer-range (0–240)
237–253	Kurlokiny	3	S only	Longer-range (240)
305–321	Larlomkiny	4	S only	Longer-range (60–200)
Malyi Iugan River				
543–559	Tykiny	2	S only	Shorter-range (20)
271–287	Kiniaminy 1	2	S only	Medium range (20–65)
288–304	Kiniaminy 2	7	S/W (2)	Medium-range (70)
492–508	Surlomkiny	4	S/W (2)	Shorter-range (19–35)
101–117	Karaeva	2	S/W (15)	Shorter-range (20)
034–050	Achimovy 1	2	S/W (0.5)	Shorter-range (20)
051–067	Achimovy 2	1	S/W (2)	Shorter-range (30)
576–592	Tiumkiny 2	2	S/W (1)	Medium-range (100)
085–100	Kaimisovy	9	S only	Longer-range (65–220)
001–017	Asmanovy	3	S only	Medium-range (45–85)

*All data taken from GASO 1812-2-206 from the cover sheets sections I.3, I.4 and IV.1. Settlements on the Bolshoi Iugan and Malyi Iugan rivers are listed in order from their mouths to their headwaters.
*S=summer iurty, W=winter iurty (distance apart - km)
**min/max distance in km

As discussed in the appendix to this volume, the diaries also give short narrative descriptions of different economic activities.[5]

The analysis of the data from the community diaries generates several insights. First, the entire basin was settled almost exclusively by 'Ostiak' (an older name for Khants). Of the 64 diaries, only two recorded the presence of Russians. The first site was Iuganskoe – the site of the first Orthodox Church (founded in 1716) and an Imperial-era administrative centre. Aside from this centre, there were six mixed Russian-Ostiak households at Nemchinovy on the Iugan Ob´ near Surgut.

Second, this strong ethnic division was closely reflected in basic subsistence patterns. Agro-pastoral farming was only present at the Russian village of Iuganskoe. Settled Khants on the lower rivers had not taken up agriculture but combined some animal husbandry with intensive fishing, most likely grazing horses and possibly cows on the extensive flood meadows. As noted by Dunin-Gorkavich (1996: 144) the lack of pasture higher upstream made further expansion of cattle rearing impossible, and Khants on these stretches were mostly engaging in hunting and fishing, with varying degrees of reindeer herding.

Third, the diaries recorded a strong, geographically organised range of mobility. Khants living on the lower part of the river were largely settled on a year-round basis, practising sedentary fishing and/or farming. In contrast, almost all Khants along the Malyi Iugan undertook a summer fishing migration to the lower river. If we refer to table 2.1, we can see that on the Bol´shoi Iugan there was a more graded transition. Almost all Khant communities above Kogonchiny made a summer migration downstream. However between Kokiny and Ugotskie 2 a mixture of strategies existed. In winter, the mobility of almost all up-river communities remained very high, with some households travelling out over 200 kilometres to hunt in the Salym, Balyk, Demianka, Vasiugan and Kul´egan´ basins. In a few *iurt* communities, for example Larlomkiny on the top of the Bolshoi Iugan, individual households were undertaking annual round trips of 2,000 kilometres for fishing. In winter, households from this *iurt* were also journeying 400 kilometres out into their hunting and back again – a figure which does not include day-to-day movements during the actual practice of hunting.

Fourth, further details contained throughout the diaries indicated the commercial transportation of fish and fur out of the lower Iugan, which were floated out by boat or hauled by horse-drawn sleds into Surgut. On their return journeys they brought flour and other goods. On the upper rivers, Khants were returning from their summer migrations with dried fish and flour, some also made additional winter reindeer-sled journeys to bring in further supplies from Iuganskoe.

In sum, this broad-brush analysis of the community diaries illustrates the distinction that Golovnev (1993: 202) made between the settled 'taiga river-edge' adaptation and the more mobile 'deep-taiga economic complex' of the upper rivers. Going beyond Golovnev, these data suggest that the households on the upper rivers consisted primarily of commercialised hunters who adjusted their seasonal round and procurement strategies to ensure that they could direct their main economic efforts to winter fur hunting. Summer fishing provided additional income for participation in trade and exchange. Meat hunting and subsistence fishing merely provisioned them through the winter months, while transport reindeer facilitated easier access to markets and distant fur hunting grounds.

Tracking Variability in Household Mobility and Settlement Strategies

A closer reading of the community diaries reveals that although all upriver Khant households participated in Golovnev's 'deep-taiga economic complex', they were doing so in *very different ways*. In particular, the 1920s data illustrated how hunters were fine-tuning their activities and movements, making deliberate choices between several alternative strategies. Can a renewed focus on the *household-scale* aspects of these adaptations generate better insights into the dynamic transformations affecting the pre-Soviet boreal forest economies?

If we focus now on the mobile upper river communities, we can first note that the individual households making up most *iurt* communities practised very different summer and winter mobility strategies. Reading through the diaries it is clear that the census taker often struggled to capture a sense of this diversity in annual household mobility – there are numerous corrections and crossings-out. Usually, one mobility strategy was written out in Section I.3. However, in Section I.5, several other household strategies were also recorded. It is exactly this attention to the details of household-scale mobility that sets the Polar Census diaries apart from the more general descriptions of Dunin-Gorkavich.

One good example of this complexity is the community diary for Kaiukovy *iurt*, summarized in figure 2.3. Here 11 households were registered to summer *iurty* on the left (west) bank of the Middle Bol'shoi Iugan. The community's general mobility was recorded as first moving to winter *iurty* located in a forest 3 kilometres to the east. Next, they journeyed out to the upper Malyi Balyk river, 60 kilometres to the northwest, spending the earlier and later part of the winter here, and in the middle of winter, they were back at the winter *iurty*. In summer they migrated first back to the summer *iurty*, then 250 kilometres down to the fishing grounds on the lower river. In fact, only 6 households followed this 'main' strategy: three households made a 50-kilometre migration to the upper Bol'shoi Balyk; one household went to the Salym River 90 kilometres to the east, and one did not migrate at all, spending the winter only in the (winter) base camp. In summer only five households migrated downstream; six remained in the summer *iurty*.

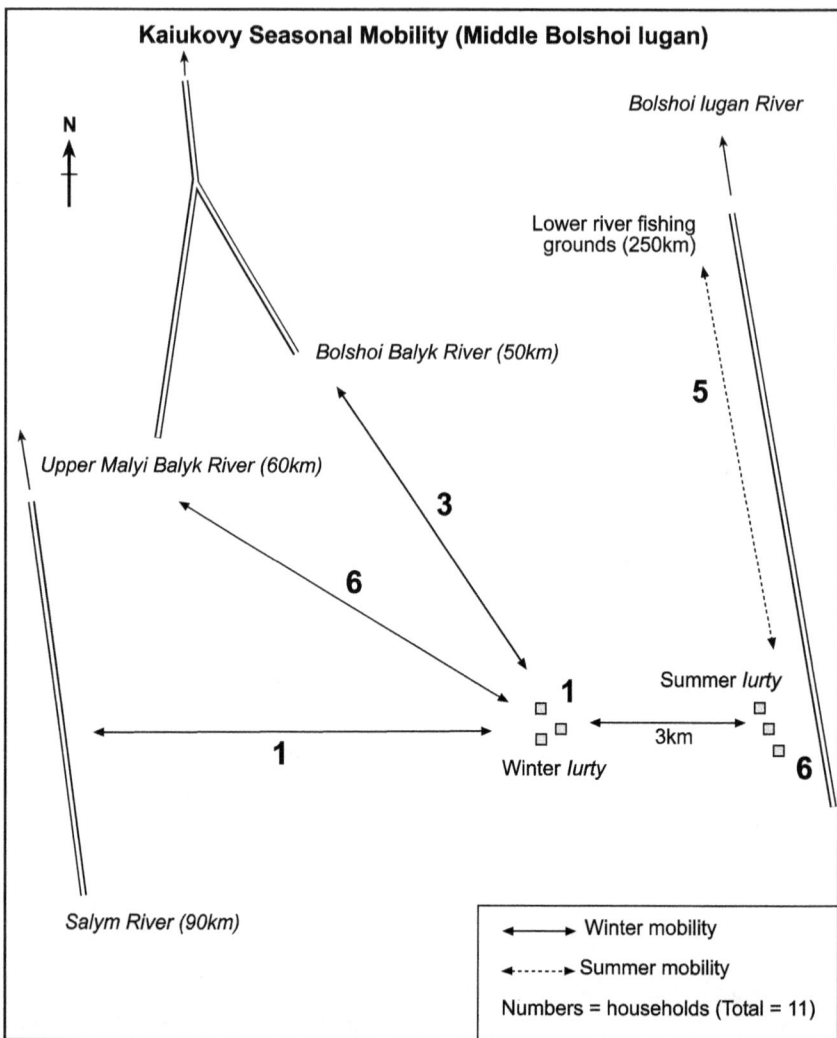

Figure 2.3. Kaiukovy seasonal mobility (middle Bol'shoi Iugan)

If we apply this household-scale analysis across the Iugan region we can generate a general model of mobility and interaction for the upper river *iurty* (fig. 2.4). This exercise enables us to capture some essential features of Khant adaptations to boreal wetlands during the 1920s, but also enables us to establish a base-line strategy that we can use to explore how and why certain households and *iurt* communities might have adopted and/or deviated from this overall strategy. With hunting and fishing the primary economic activities, the most likely solution to seasonal task-scheduling challenges would have been

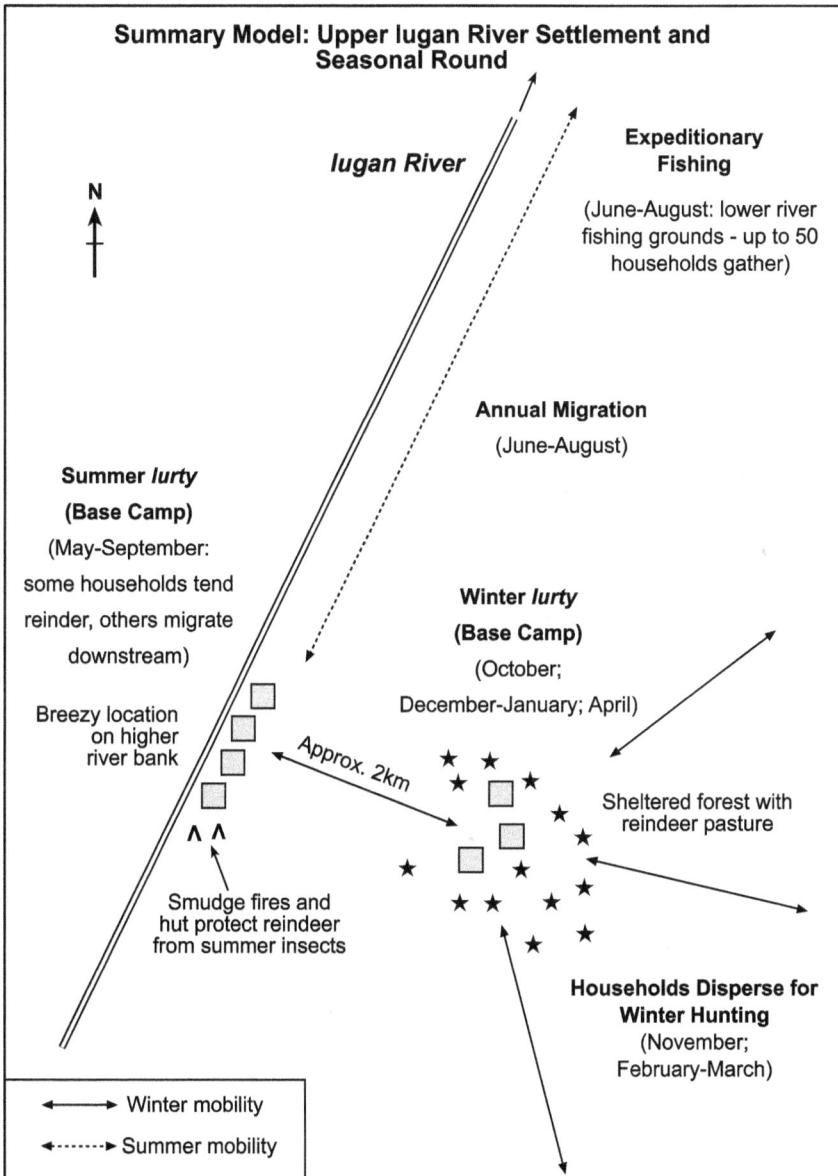

Figure 2.4. Summary model: upper Iugan River settlement and seasonal round

collective residence in a riverside base camp at the turn of the main seasons, group migration downstream in the summers, and dispersal into the remote forests for household based winter fur hunting. The general model captures many basic features of this solution – many communities had only a single summer base camp, and the majority of *iurt* communities did 'break up' in the hunting season as households moved out into the forest, and many migrated downstream in summer.

However, there are several other aspects that need explaining. First, why did some communities have *both* summer and winter *iurty*, sometimes only 500 metres apart (e.g. the settlement Achimovy 1)? Second, why were almost all *iurty* manned by at least one household over the summer; and third, why did some households only migrate between summer and winter *iurty* and not further?

The last question might be explained by the fact that households with very young or very old members may not have been able to undertake winter hunting, and so they stayed behind at the base camp. Households occupying the winter *iurty* of Iarsamovy, Multanovy and Saporkiny may have reflected this, and at Maniny all households stayed at the *iurt* in winter, hunting only locally. The localised hunting strategy documented at Achimovy 2 might also reflect an older or infirm household. The fact that no summer migrations were undertaken from this latter *iurt* also strengthens this generational interpretation of settlement and mobility patterns. However, the presence of older community members does not really explain why many communities had *two* base *iurty*, nor does it provide a full justification for what appears to be the systematic occupying of riverside *iurty* by at least one household over the summer, just as many other households migrate downstream (see table 2.1). For example, even smaller *iurty* composed of only two households like Karaeva and Achimovy 2 appear to have been deliberately deciding to split up, resulting in one household travelling alone to the fishing grounds – and there meeting scores of other families – while the other household remained alone throughout the long summer months. Even at the very remote upper reaches of the Malyi Iugan, one Asmanov household was 'abandoned' for the summer. The most likely explanation of these behavioural patterns is the presence of transport reindeer within the 'deep taiga economic complex'.

New Innovations – The Uneven Adoption of Transport Reindeer

Having the ability to access a wider range of hunting areas would have had an immediate attraction to Iugan households as they sought out new hunting areas. Iugan Khants already kept a large number of hunting dogs, which also assisted in pulling small sleds. However reindeer could pull bigger loads and travel much faster. They could also assist in packing in flour and other supplies from Iuganskoe, and also out to remote hunting camps. In the upper headwaters, other forms of domestic animal traction would have been impossible to develop. Keeping horses, as some households did in the lower river settlements, would have required putting up hay, winter stalling and daily tending.

Upper Iugan families were able to provide neither since there were insufficient meadows and winter was the most important time for fur hunting. In
contrast, reindeer were ideal low-maintenance winter transport animals for
taiga hunters. They could easily be corralled and when not in use they could
be hobbled to prevent them from straying; they could also feed themselves by
digging through the snow cover to the mosses and lichens below (Kulemzin
and Lukina 1992: 67–71).

Keeping reindeer through the summers, however, was far from easy. The
swarms of mosquitoes, black flies and other insects make the taiga hot season
extremely difficult for both humans and animals, and while the large-scale
reindeer pastoralism characteristic of Northwest Siberia involved long trans-
humances out onto the windswept tundra and/or to the higher ground of the
Urals (Perevalova 2004: 274; Golovnev 1993: 75–106), this option was not
available to forest groups, who had to complete their migrations within their
more limited fur hunting territories (Golovnev 1993: 80). Instead, taiga-zone
herders developed their own unique methods, protecting their herds by light-
ing smudge fires and building special shelters (Vizgalov 2000: 127) to protect
animals from the sun (Dunin-Gorkavich 1995: 164–5; Martynova 1998: 150–
152). In the worst weeks of what was known as 'mosquito time', animals would
voluntarily come into the deer huts seeking relief, returning out to feed only at
night (Vizgalov 2000: 126).

The adoption of even small herds of reindeer on the Iugan may have therefore required subtle shifts in the settlement pattern. In summer the optimal
herding locations were higher river banks where there was mixed feed and an
open aspect where the steady breezes reduced the insects; in winter in some
areas the animals needed pasture out in the forests, requiring that a second
base camp be built for these periods (Vizgalov 2000: 125–26). Adoption of
transport reindeer also demanded that *iurty* be manned by at least one household over the summer to tend the smudge fires. In short, both these features
are present in the general settlement model (fig. 2.4).

Historical sources, however, present a more complex portrait of Iugan reindeer herding, which might explain why several households depicted in the
1920s community diaries were deviating from this general model. Between
the fifteenth and nineteenth centuries there was a gradual southerly dispersal
of transport reindeer husbandry (*transportnoe olenevodstvo*) into Khant areas
(Golovnev 1993: 100). The Iugan basin forms the most southerly extension of
this form of reindeer herding (Kulemzin and Lukina 1992: 67) – and at the end
of the nineteenth century formed a unique 'intrusion' of reindeer pastoralism
south of the middle Ob' (Dunin-Gorkavich 1995: 164). Historical data backed
up by folklore suggest that the practice had been adopted from Nenetses via
Kazym Khants (Golovnev 1993: 100; Martynova 1998: 152). Lukina has argued
for an indigenous invention of unique herding methods on the Iugan based

primarily on the fact that Iugan Khant reindeer sleds are enlarged versions of a dog sled, rather than the characteristic Nenets sled used by other Khant groups to the north (Lukina 1985: 336; Dunin-Gorkavich 1996: 141). Whatever the origin it was certainly a new innovation on the Iugan, with evidence for a limited uptake in the 1820s, a possible decline in the 1840s (Golovnev 1993: 100), followed by limited adoption and development among the Iugan Khants at the end of that century, but it was far from a fully developed and adopted practice, with 79 out of 123 households keeping reindeer above Ugotskie (at 23 out of 30 base camp *iurty*) (Dunin-Gorkavich 1996: 144). Average herd sizes can be calculated to around 3 animals per household but that obscures the fact that 36 per cent of households had no deer at all, suggesting either that households were choosing *not* to use reindeer, preferring to haul sleds with people and dogs, or that they were *not able* to marshal the material resources and social relationships that were essential to acquiring and keeping them (Dunin-Gorkavich 1996: appendix 26).

In further discussions Dunin-Gorkavich also explains how reindeer herding is an extremely challenging and expensive transport technology. Most Khants bought individual animals from the northern Samoyeds (Nenetses) via intermediaries for cash (7 to 10 roubles). Some of these imported reindeer survived on the Iugan, though many died, others reverted to the wild; some even escaped and tried to return north. Overall, none were able to reproduce locally, forcing herders to import more reindeer at great cost (ibid., 144–45). According to the community diaries from the Polar Census, it is clear that even in the 1920s reindeer had not fully been adopted in all areas, raising some interesting questions about variations in wealth, long-range mobility and general subsistence strategies between households in the key era of 1890 to 1930.

Comparing the optimal model in figure 2.4 to the details in table 2.1, we can identify a number of *iurt* communities that do appear to have been succeeding in combining long-range hunting with summer-winter base camps and summer fishing migrations – for example, Kogonchiny, Iarsomovy, Kolsomovy and others on the Bol'shoi Iugan. Insights from these iurt communities point to a smooth integration of reindeer herding into the economy. Other variations are easy to explain- Long-range hunters like the Kaimisovy on the Malyi Iugan and many upper Bol'shoi Iugan River *iurt* communities may not have actually required second (winter) base camps if there were sufficient reindeer pastures nearby, but all were clearly manning their summer base camps.

Some *iurt* communities did deviate more significantly from the model. Across all *iurt* communities, full summer abandonment *was* very rare, but was being practised, for example, at Tykiny, Kiniaminy 1 and Tiumkiny 2 on the Malyi Iugan, and at Chikolevy on the higher reaches of the Bol'shoi Iugan. There is definite confirmation in the diaries that Chikolevy had no reindeer,

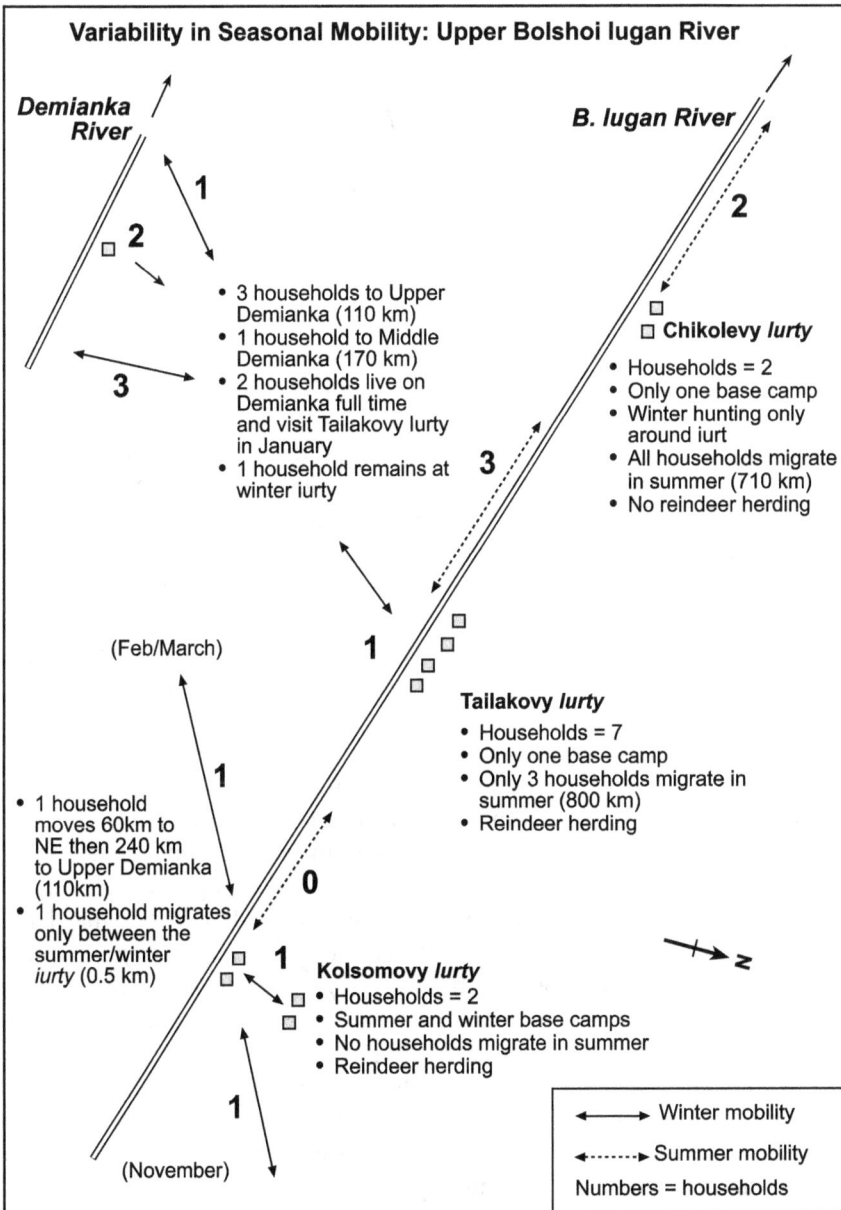

Variability in Seasonal Mobility: Upper Bolshoi Iugan River

Demianka River

B. Iugan River

- 3 households to Upper Demianka (110 km)
- 1 household to Middle Demianka (170 km)
- 2 households live on Demianka full time and visit Tailakovy Iurty in January
- 1 household remains at winter iurty

□ Chikolevy *Iurty*

- Households = 2
- Only one base camp
- Winter hunting only around iurt
- All households migrate in summer (710 km)
- No reindeer herding

(Feb/March)

Tailakovy *Iurty*

- Households = 7
- Only one base camp
- Only 3 households migrate in summer (800 km)
- Reindeer herding

- 1 household moves 60km to NE then 240 km to Upper Demianka (110km)
- 1 household migrates only between the summer/winter iurty (0.5 km)

Kolsomovy *Iurty*

- Households = 2
- Summer and winter base camps
- No households migrate in summer
- Reindeer herding

(November)

→ Winter mobility

·····→ Summer mobility

Numbers = households

Figure 2.5. Variability in seasonal mobility: upper Bol´shoi Iugan River

and that they could only bring in winter flour supplies by boat. All this signals that there are practical challenges inherent in any transition, and perhaps that some Khant households were coping with these changes better than others.

The community diaries suggest how variations in households' strategies might have been linked to dynamics within the household. Figure 2.5 explores some of the variability on the Upper Bol'shoi Iugan. The members of Chikolevy had no reindeer, which perhaps forced them to hunt just around their *iurt,* reducing their income from furs. For them, their well-being would have depended on the success of the summer fishing. Therefore, both households abandoned their winter *iurt* for the three summer months. At the larger *iurt* of Tailakovy just upstream the situation was very different. Here, the members had much higher mobility, probably facilitated by reindeer, with the community dividing into half over the summer, and some remaining while others undertook migratory fishing. They could bring in both fish and flour in summer or winter. Higher upstream, Kolsomovy was also a small *iurt* with only two households. One household was not very mobile while the other travelled long distances, perhaps with reindeer. In summer they did not migrate, as the reindeer needed tending, and so as a smaller *iurt* they were forced – as Chikolevy – to make a strategic choice between undertaking either summer fishing or keeping reindeer to support long-range winter hunting. Faced with this choice Kolsomovy appear to have opted for being hunter-herders, and not fisher-hunters.

Figure 2.6 illustrates a very similar situation on the Upper Malyi Iugan. The people of Tiumkiny 2 also appear to favoured summer fishing, but they had two base *iurty* (summer and winter) which suggests that they do have reindeer. This may have forced them to give care of their animals to other adjacent *iurt* communities over the summer, as documented by Martynova (1998: 151), perhaps at Achimovy 2. This may be evidence of smaller *iurt* communities doubling up tasks and sharing favours with others – in winter both Tiumkiny 2 will probably need reindeer as both households migrated right out to the Kul'egan' River, 100 kilometres to the east, but to do this they may have been reliant on bringing enough dried fish or flour back to the *iurty* at the end of the summer. In stark contrast, the nine households at Kaimisovy appear to have been balancing tasks more effectively within their community – six households undertook summer fishing migrations, leaving three households behind, but the reindeer enabled them to access a vast hunting range, spanning the left bank and Upper Malyi Iugan River, out east to the Kul'egan' (150 kilometres) and also south as far as the Vasiugan river (220 kilometres). The size of the Asmanovy *iurt* community was intermediate – three households – but they do appear to have been effectively balancing hunting, herding and summer fishing.

Detailed exploration of the recurrent variation surrounding a general model of upper river subsistence and settlement takes us beyond crisp categorisations and enables us to glimpse into historical transformations as they spin out over the landscape and through community lives. In particular, the rich house-

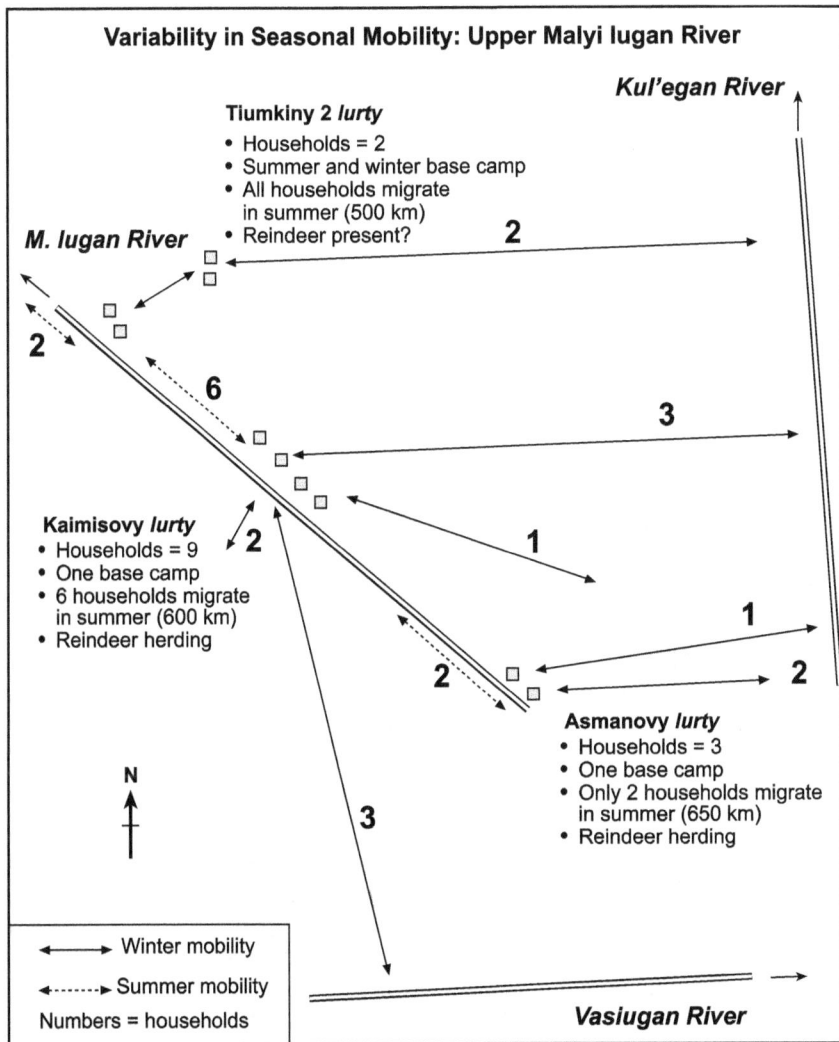

Figure 2.6. Variability in seasonal mobility: upper Malyi Iugan River

hold-scale mobility data in the community diaries illustrates some of the challenges of integrating the sometimes *contradictory* branches of the pre-Soviet economy. They signal enormous task-scheduling tensions *within* and *among* households, the *iurt* communities and wider social collective, for example in deciding who would travel in summer or winter, and who would remain. They also hint at the need for communities to have shared favours and material aid. They perhaps explain emerging social wealth differentiation, as some *iurty* communities became larger, enabling them to become more mobile and access wider hunting areas and perhaps also to become specialist hunter-herders with domestic reindeer as a food reserve. If we add to this picture a sense of different generations passing from infancy into marriage and old age, we sense an enormous need to continually negotiate strategies at different social and spatial scales in order to resolve longer-term scheduling and land use issues.

Mobility, Kinship and Inter-Generational Land Tenure

Can the community diaries help us to understand how these communities negotiated long-term land tenure? Most community diaries record free use of productive territories (*ugod'ia*) in 1926/27. During winter hunting, most households moved out to the remoter forest, setting trap lines and tending hunting fences. Bows and triggered bows were still in wide use at this time, with some dog and gun hunting.

We are able to extrapolate from the community diaries using historical sources and recent interviews (1998–2005) to build a picture of land tenure. What Khants describe today as the traditional hunting system involved the man of the household skiing out on hunting trips, returning each evening. The woman remained at temporary stopping points where open shelters were set up, preparing wood for the fire and processing kills. Households may have camped together, but hunting was individual. When an area had been covered, the household(s) moved further, eventually returning to the base *iurt*. Ownership was based on first use and continuity in practical activities in an area (Martynova 1995: 111), for example through investment in fixed features like fish weirs and hunting fences. Groups also had rights to bounded territories, known as *dacha* or *votchina* (ibid. 1995: 110–112). These subsistence areas were not officially registered but were demarcated by features of the natural topography and drainage, with the boundaries of *ma my* (my land) well-known and respected, and disputes regulated by customary laws (Martynova 1995: 110–11). Use rights were inherited from one generation to the next.

Both contemporary fieldwork and historical accounts tell us that long-term land tenure was largely patrilineal and patrilocal (Jordan 2003: 69). Traditionally, after marriage a woman virtually severed her links with her father's line as she joined a new lineage, and yet within her husband's lineage she remained *chuzherodnaia* ['of a different birth'] and was subjected to a range of prohibitions, both relating to ritual and etiquette, especially until the birth of her first child (Martynova 1995: 102). Long-term continuity in the family names of (male) household heads within the Iugan points to the antiquity of this system (Martynova 1998: 141). Many of these surname lineages correspond to the names that we find in the community diaries (e.g. families Asmanov, Kaimisov and 'Ochimov' (perhaps Achimov) on the Malyi Iugan and Kurlo(m)kin (perhaps Kurlakin), Kogonchin, Kaikov, Kupladeev, Ryskin and Usanov. In social terms this means that base camp *iurty* were inhabited by several male generations within a lineage. In larger settlements with many households, several lineages may be present, e.g. at Kaiukovy (Martynova 1998: 154), but this appears to have been an exception. At a larger scale each lineage (*patronimiia*) fell into a number of exogamous non-localised clans (Khant: *sir*). For example, on the Malyi Iugan lineages fell into bear, elk and beaver clans (*Pupi Sir, Nekh Sir* and *Makh Sir*) (Jordan 2003: 69–71).

These accounts help us to understand the emergence of a traditional settlement, land-holding and kinship system, but as normative descriptions, they do not help us explore what happens when these systems are subjected to external stress, or how individuals and households operating within these historical contexts would have responded to new opportunities and lingering challenges. The community diaries add some human dynamism to the analysis. Shortage of game and hunting territory was certainly a major problem in the nineteenth (Martynova 1998: 150) and well into the early twentieth century on the Iugan (Vizgalov 2000: 80). In addition, the population on the Bolshoi Iugan had risen from 493 (1798) to 554 (1887), further exacerbating the problem (Martynova 1998: 140–41). In the diaries, the inhabitants of Ugotskie 1, for example complained that the Raksakiny are hunting in 'their' area – their protest was based on the fact that their grandfather hunted there (GASO 1812-2-206: 560-575: Section IV.9). This suggests that, far from there being a concrete system of tenure, the edges of land use areas may be open to dispute and renegotiation.[6]

There are other hints at wider pressures and solutions. The diaries recorded the households Ugotskie 1 and Ugotskie 2 as hunting on the Negus Iakh (between the Bol'shoi and Malyi Iugan) and also on the lower Malyi Iugan, with some households starting to venture out over 200 kilometres to the Demianka, forcing them to cross through other territories to get there.

The diaries also documented substantial variability in the size of *iurt* communities and this may have affected their solutions to the land-shortage problems; for example, there was only one household at Achimovy 2 but nine at Kaimisovy on the upper Malyi Iugan. Shifts in the appropriation of the landscape may therefore have been linked to the decline, growth and splintering of particular lineages, all of which would have required renegotiation of immediate territoriality and also long-term tenure. In a time of general land shortages requiring new solutions, larger lineage populations may also have been able to combine different economic strategies more effectively, for example by assigning one household to summer reindeer herding while the rest undertook summer fishing to build up stores and earn money to buy flour. In turn, keeping a reindeer herd would also have provided household and *iurt* community with improved access to winter hunting areas, the ability to travel further if game in one area were few, and also generated opportunities to bring in more flour supplies over winter – both to the base camp from Iuganskoe village, and from the base camp out to remote hunting camps. If more reindeer could be kept, they could eventually start to serve as a source of meat rather than transport alone, generating a form of hunter-herder adaptation that transcends the more general hunter-fisher subsistence strategies that can be partially combined with transport reindeer. Interestingly, Dunin-Gorkavich reports that reindeer Khants (*olennye ostiaki*) were already present at the Ugotskie, Kogonchiny and Kaikovy *iurty* in the late nineteenth century (1995: 144–45), and in 1926/27 each of these *iurty* was still very large, with twelve, nine and eleven households respectively (if Ugotskie 1 and 2 are combined).

In contrast, smaller lineages of perhaps one or two households may not have been able to herd reindeer over the summer due to a commitment to older systems of migratory fishing. This decision, which would have reduced capacity for winter mobility, may have prevented them from seeking out and holding new areas. They would become even more reliant on the diminishing returns of a smaller territory, perhaps resulting in poorer general nourishment, especially if game levels remained low within the vicinity (as historical accounts suggest). And with control of land based on continuity of occupation and active exploitation, failure to maintain a productive physical presence out in the wider forest (e.g. maintaining traps and hunting fences) may have enabled others to encroach on the outer margins of their land without challenge. These smaller lineages would also have been far more vulnerable to the accidental deaths of adults – drowning is common even to the present day – especially male hunters, whilst larger lineages could probably have absorbed these changes more easily. Through time these dynamics could have eventually amplified, so that smaller lineages became more vulnerable as they became locked into a declining cycle of reduced mobility, declining territory, poverty, poorer nourishment and declining health. At the same time, larger lineages could maintain benefits of a fully-diversified economy with access to many more resources.

Interestingly, recent fieldwork confirms that the entire Achimovy 2 lineage eventually died out, possibly not long after the 1920s census, and was replaced by Kel'mins migrating in from the Bol'shoi Iugan. Tiumkiny 2 also died out and is now occupied by incomers from other adjacent *iurty*. These changes along the middle Malyi Iugan appear to have triggered a wider renegotiation of land use around this stretch of the river – households from the adjacent Achimovy 1 settlement reported that they hunted on *both* sides of the river in the 1960s and 1970s. However, their 1926/27 community diary lists them only as hunting to the *west* side – where they faced encroachment from Karevy households – while the single household from Achimovy 2 hunted to the east. Growing lineages may also splinter. The Kaimisov *iurt* community remains large and prosperous to the present day, with several households splitting off some decades ago to form new settlements along adjacent stretches of the river. On the Bol'shoi Iugan, the Usanovy lineage of eight households recorded in 1926/27 eventually broke up and became three separate settlements. Land pressures appeared to have continued after the 1926/27 census. Several Kaikovy and some Kogonchiny households, each from already large *iurt* communities, eventually colonised the the Salym basin permanently in the 1930s, primarily as a response to enduring land shortages (Vizgalov 2000: 79–80), with records indicating that there was a catastrophic decline in sable, deer, moose hares, and even 'mass' fur-bearers like squirrels (ibid., 80).

In summary, historical records and more recent ethnographic accounts tend to single out the more enduring normative aspects of kinship, territoriality and land use. The general region *does* appear to have been characterised by long-term continuity in many of these key social institutions. However, in recording life at a micro-scale the community diaries force us to grapple with the issue of variability and explore some of the more flexible aspects of these institutions that households are manipulating and transforming as they react to the profound environmental changes affecting their commercialised fur-hunting adaptation. These insights take us beyond a shallow understanding of the typical and force us to appreciate the repeated need for renegotiation of year-to-year territoriality and inter-generational tenure (Jordan 2003: 231–74) *within* the wider landscape, despite close links overall among this tenure system, settlement and the patrilineal kinship system.

Community Mobility and Sacred Landscapes Geography

With an informed reading some 'hidden' aspects of the community diaries hint at other aspects of land tenure and social interaction, in particular, how communities *perceived* and interacted symbolically with the cultural landscape. While the place names of many *iurty* are descriptive, recording characteristics of place (*pugol*= village) (e.g. Nevoilokiny – *Liarkut-pugol* = 'between the flood meadows village'; Ur'evy = *Uri-pugol* = 'old river bed village'; Chikolevy – *Savytov-pugol* = 'boggy clay lake village'). Other native place names, however, have close links with indigenous sacred landscape geography, for example, both Kaiukovy and Achimovy 1 are named as: Lun-pugol or *'spirit - village'*, referring to the fact that both *iurt* communities are guardians of major sacred sites which have regional significance for the Eastern Khants.

As with many other northern peoples the Iugan Khants continue to understand the landscape to be inhabited and owned by non-human 'presences' including spirits, deities and ancestors. Engagements with these entities ensure health, welfare and general hunting success, and found their clearest expression in gifting rituals at sacred sites (Jordan 2003). These were usually marked by a stilted sacred structure (Khant *labas*) inhabited by wooden idols which protected the local *iurt* community, performed specialist roles to the wider community or even served as guardians of entire river basins. There were two sacred structures close to Achimovy 1 and several around Kaiukovy, where a carved image of the deity Iugan Iki 'migrated' seasonally between the different locations. One site at Achimovy 1 continues to house images of Ai Ningken, daughters of Pugus Anki, the motherhood goddess. Until the collapse of collectivized fishing in the early 1990's, these deities were carried by communities during their summer expeditions to the lower river. In fact, almost all *iurt* communities traditionally had a local protector spirit, housed close to the base camps, often a short way inland from the river bank.

In turn, these local deities were linked by a network of divine kinship to a wider pantheon of animal spirit masters, gods of the underworld and the supreme god, *Torum*, who ruled over the upper world. For human persons the conduct of daily life involved a complex process of negotiation with these beings to ensure health, general welfare, and continued luck in the conduct of subsistence activity. The location of sacred sites, the rituals conducted there (*pory*), and the corresponding built structures and material residues are now well-documented and discussed (Jordan 2003). However, interpretation of the content and significance of these rituals has tended to view the sacred sites against the partially truncated territoriality and interaction patterns of a post-Socialist Russia, in which migratory fishing has collapsed, reindeer are no longer kept and large tracts of land within the Iugan basin have been lost to a nature reserve (*zapovednik*) (Jordan 2003).

In addition, widespread use of motor boats, snowmobiles, winter roads, helicopters and radios means that the rhythms of social interaction along the river has been transformed, and is at present best categorized as being increasingly frequent and more casual – many individuals make frequent trips in and out of the administration centre in Ugut. In these interpretations the primary importance of sacred sites is their role as primary places of communication and reciprocal engagement between a mobile human collective and the wider spirit world (ibid., 280–81). Analysis of the community diaries provokes reconsideration of some other key aspects of sacred site ritual practice and also enables a more detailed examination of how the location of holy places relates to the details of historical mobility and interaction across the wider Iugan basin. Several new insights emerge.

First, the immense geographic extent and apparent flexibility of 1920s winter mobility is impressive and underlines the fact that many households in the pre-Soviet period were entirely alone for extended periods of the year, perhaps migrating periodically with another household, but almost always living and working in very remote tracts of forest with no means of external communication or contact. This would have included winter hunting but also those families left behind in the summer to tend reindeer. Periods of profound isolation would have been offset by the gathering of the *iurt* community in its base camp at the change of the seasons, the traditional time for sacred site visits and *pory*. The collective rituals at the site would, of course, have re-established links with the spirit world, but would also have performed a second social role by re-establishing inter-household relationships and obligations at fundamental junctures in the year, either when returning from, or about to depart into, months of separation.

Second, there was an explicit emphasis on *sharing*, both in the consumption of food and drink at the sacred sites, but also in sharing out left-over supplies that were taken back to individual households. This deliberate emphasis on equal exchange also extended to clothes and the skins of sacrificed animals that were shared out across the extended community, emphasising and reinforcing a multi-faceted and cross-cutting reciprocity that spanned the world of humans, animals and spirits. Sacred site guardians were also drawn from male members of the local *iurt* community. Duties included tending the site and providing much of the food and drink for events. The role was eventually passed on between generations, but in larger *iurt* communities was also circulated between households within the same generation, so that guardians served for a set time.

Third, social obligations to sacred places often extended *outwards* across several lineages. For example, the carved wooden dolls inside the shrines were made by men from outside the local lineage. When that man died it was thought that some of the idols' power also followed the soul of the carver into the next world, and so a new set of images had to be carved by an male elder from a different lineage, and when housed and clothed, a major *pory* was performed. Some sites, for example on the upper Malyi Iugan were traditionally visited sequentially, bringing together two lineages. Guardians of very sacred deities – for example, the Ai Ningken, goddesses described above – also took their local idols to places of major community aggregation, for example, to the summer fishing grounds. In this way, the idols could be venerated by the wider river basin collective. Finally, women along the river were invited to provide clothing and footwear for the idols, and women from across the region traveled to do *pory* at the site.

Fourth, visits to sacred places appear to have been built into the seasonal round, reinforcing a sense of collective identity along rivers. On making the long upstream return from the summer fishing grounds, elderly informants described how every sacred place was visited during the journey home (fig. 2.7). In Khant cosmology the downstream direction of the river – and a journey in that direction – was thought to be fraught with images of danger and death (cemeteries are always located downstream or inland from the *iurty*), and movement upstream was thought auspicious. In doing *pory* not only local spirit guardians were invited but also the main deities, animal spirit masters and other protector spirits from other sacred places. In this way, we might

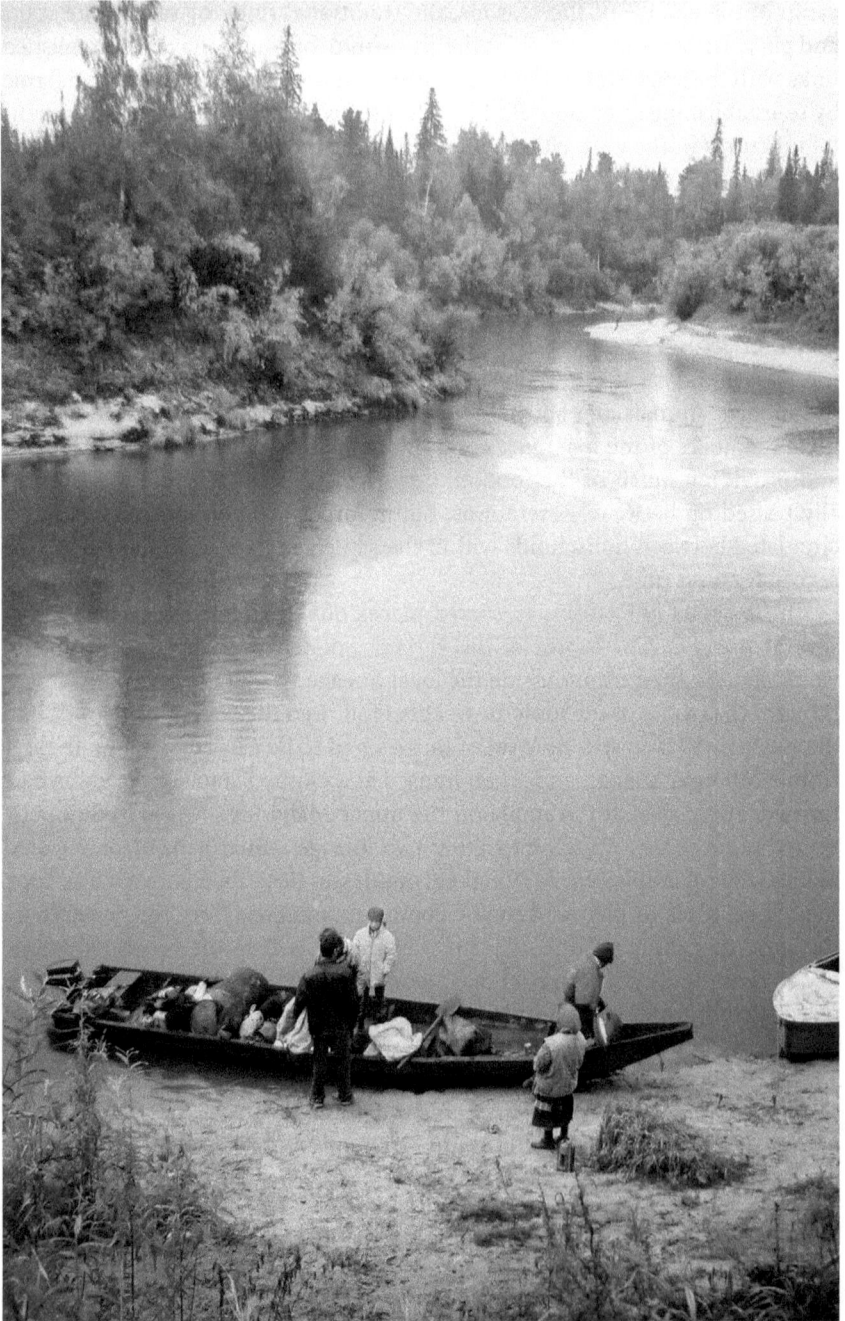

Figure 2.7. Boat travel along the Malyi Iugan River. Photograph by Peter Jordan.

see these earlier summer fishing migrations as a form of collective pilgrimage as well as the simple dispatch of task groups to build up winter supplies. Again, the river becomes central as a focus of both practical and ritual activity, and the collective nature of rituals and the shared web of spiritual obligations, highlights the importance of the larger drainage basin as a focus of goup identity above and beyond the household and patrilineage.

Finally, what is also striking from analysis of the immense scale of 1920s household mobility is that almost all the *labas* sacred places, which formed a focus of collective ritual, were actually situated inside a narrow central cordon of communication that ran along the main riverways and adjacent sledge routes, and included also the summer and winter *iurty* and cemeteries. In other words, almost all significant places were located within a few hundred metres – and no more than a couple of kilometres – of the main river edge. There were other kinds of sacred places – the *kot mykh* ('earth house') – which had close associations with *Wuhnt Lung* (the forest spirit). While these are slightly further outside the river edge zone they are certainly not scores of kilometres away.

What these distributions suggest is that the key places in local sacred geography tended to be closer to settlements and rivers and that they were relatively fixed places. In contrast, procurement out in the wider tracts of the landscape still had a ritualized dimension in that animals were owned by spirit masters, and the entire forest was 'animated' by divine forces, but in this remoter domain human engagements with this relational world were more pragmatic, immediate and flexible, determined more by day-to-day travels and events than the more formal obligations to *labas* sacred sites. This more open and flexible relationship to the forest and game spirits – and therefore spiritual tenure of the remoter land – also appears to have extended to practical usage of the land which may have been much more open to annual and inter-generational renegotiation. Through time, the extent of a household's or lineage's most distant annual hunting areas could therefore be collapsed or expanded to suit local needs and abilities without reordering the fundamental logic and location of the river's primary sacred places.

In summary, integration of insights from the community diaries and recent fieldwork enable us to explore from new perspectives some of the social and ritual ties that bound remote and highly mobile communities together. They also enable us to understand better the local *perceptions* of movement through a landscape cross-cut with reciprocal relations to spirits and other social groups. In a time of clearly emerging distinctions between the economic strategies of different households and lineages, some apparently prospering, others struggling to find new ways of coping with a degraded environment and new innovations, these community gifting rituals may also have served to dampen some of the potential strains of growing social inequality, task-scheduling and emerging tensions within and among patrilineages. Rather than serving as arenas for 'competitive' feasting and political advancement the explicit emphasis on community sharing and material redistribution hints that gifting rituals may have served as a counter-weight to a wide range of more divisive social and economic forces impacting local communities in the early Soviet period, including the collapse of hunting yields, new transport technologies, and opportunities to exploit further areas and to buy in further goods and services through successful trade, all of which would have placed a major strain on some households but led to material gains for others.

Conclusion: Eastern Khant Identity, Social Institutions and Sacred Landscapes

It was noted in the introduction that the competing themes of adaptation, history and perception continue to carve up hunter-gatherer studies into rival research domains. This Western Siberian pilot study anticipates a more integrated future for hunter-gatherer research, and has aimed to illustrate new ways of understanding the dynamic interplay between different aspects of hunter-gatherer behaviour and social action.

A fine-grained analysis of the fine-grained Polar Census community diaries, combined with critical readings of the wider ethno-historic record and inputs from recent fieldwork with descendant communities, together provide glimpses of the *agency* of forager households as their long-term adaptation to the commercialised fur trade is faced with sudden ecological change, new innovations and fresh challenges of task-scheduling and land tenure within a remote boreal environment.

In seeking out the *variability* of household strategies, rather than presenting the more common typological overview of boreal forest adaptations, this fine-grained analysis highlights the social and practical tensions that appear to have been central to the 'hybrid' upper river hunting-fishing-herding adaptations in the Middle Ob' region as they struggled to deal with local environmental degradation, decreased game and a shortage of hunting areas.

In turn, these insights generate new questions about the role – and flexibility – of core Khant social and ritual institutions, including the kinship system of localised patrilineages, and the locations and community gifting rituals conducted at sacred sites. In understanding better the links between subsistence, mobility and ritual, we are also better equipped to understand the cosmological significance of journeying and procurement activity in a relational landscape where humans must maintain reciprocal relations with both people and spirits.

The study also hints at the many spatial dimensions to identity that arise from, and are embedded in, wider land-use practices in the Iugan basin. These include gender, ancestry and ethnicity and may also extend to task-based identities, especially where the decision to pursue long-range hunter-herding, summer migratory fishing or localised agro-pastoral farming would generate very different patterns of mobility and social interaction over the annual round, and the effects would be even more pronounced if amplified over several generations. Running through these cross-cutting identities are the main branches of the Iugan River, which serve as central arteries of seasonal movement, social contacts and ritualised journeys. The importance of waterways as a main axis and focus of indigenous social life has also been reflected in outsider categorisations and surveillance of local populations – from the very start of the Russian conquest, river basin communities formed a basic administrative framework for monitoring, taxation and control, an approach that was developed and refined into the Soviet period.

The productive conclusions generated by this study also signal how the approach outlined here could be rolled out across the wider region to examine mobility patterns *within* and *between* other Eastern Khant river basins, which are characterised by a fascinating array of intermeshing economic regimes and local environments. And in balancing an analytical focus among regional ecology, long-term history and household-scale trends in interaction, subsistence and ritual, the expansion of this research across Western Siberia would make a refreshing contribution to some of the entrenched debates that retain a stranglehold on hunter-gatherer studies.

Acknowledgements

The author would like to express his grateful thanks to the Iugan Khant communities visited between 1998 and 2005. Thanks also to Andre Filtchenko for assisting in the translation of some of the more difficult place names, and to Elena Glavatskaya and Konstantin Karacharov. Fieldwork funding was provided by: the Finno-Ugrian Society, British Academy and Leverhulme Trust. I am very grateful to David G. Anderson for his encouragement to pursue this case study as part of a wider programme of research into the Polar Census archive across the former Soviet Union. I am particularly grateful again to Elena Glavatskaya and her colleagues who so quickly digitized the community diaries for the Iugan as part of the Polar Census research project at the University of Tromsø financed by the Research Council of Norway. This chapter forms one of a series of comparative ethnographic studies of northern hunter-gatherers being conducted by the author and is an output of the international research project 'Early Networking in Northern Fennoscandia' which was hosted by the

Centre for Advanced Study at the Norwegian Academy of Science and Letters during the 2008–09 academic year.

Notes

1. For example, 19 per cent of all mid-nineteenth-century marriages were conducted within the Malyi Iugan, 28 per cent with the Bol´shoi Iugan, 40 per cent from the Iugan Ob´ and Balyk, and the rest from elsewhere, e.g. 6 per cent with the Tromagan Khants. On the Bol´shoi Iugan 30 percent of marriages were internal, 23 per cent with the Malyi Iugan Khants, 25% with the Iugan Ob´/Balyk rivers, and the rest involving more distant communities. However, most of these marriages involved other Khant communities, with inter-ethnic marriages (e.g. 5 with Sel´kup, 5 with Nenets) totaling only 0.6 per cent of all Eastern Khant marriages recorded from the seventeenth to the nineteenth centuries (Martynova 1998: 140–42).
2. POKh *Promyslovo-okotnich´e otdelenie ot Surgutskogo koopzveropromkhoza.*
3. Editor's Note: The Iugan River community diaries form a complete set of 46 documents held at classmark GASO 1812-2-206. With the help of the archivists at GASO, over 700 pages of documentation have been both photographed and entered into an XML database which can be consulted online.
4. 'Local' winter hunting strategies were often described in the diaries as 'hunting around the *iurt*' – an activity which probably did not involve an overnight stay. 'Shorter-range' journeys refer to mobility of up to 50km. 'Medium-range' referred to travel of 50–100km. 'Longer-range' referred to movement over 100km. This column also records the most and least mobile household, for example '(0–160)' records that one household doesn't leave the base *iurt*, and one travels up to 160 km.
5. Sections VI.1–IV.10 record pastoralism; sections V.1–V.13 record cereal agriculture; and sections VII.1–VII.14 record reindeer husbandry. Occasional disputes over land rights are formally recorded under Question IV.9.
6. Occasional disputes over land rights are formally recorded in the community diaries under Question IV.9. In the set of 64 there were nine recorded conflicts. The majority of the conflicts were over access to fishing sites, but there are three cases of dispute over hunting territories. It is interesting to note that the diaries only list the claims of the aggrieved parties while the families using the areas appear to feel that their tenure is legitimate. In general, however, the diaries appear to record relatively few territorial conflicts along the river, suggesting that resource areas were allocated via negotiated consensus, probably drawing on a wide range of social mechanisms.

3 | The Interpretation of Nenets Demography in the First Third of the Twentieth Century

Elena A. Volzhanina

With the establishment of Soviet power in the north at the beginning of the 1920s, the new administration set out on an ambitious programme of territorial, cultural and economic reform, and demanded reliable and complete information about both indigenous people and Russian settlers (TsSU 1929: v; Kopylov 1994: 127, 147). Up until then, from the seventeenth to the beginning of the twentieth centuries, scholars relied primarily on the archives of the *inorodnye upravy* [public administration boards] for information about the indigenous peoples of the Russian North. These data represented only male hunters who were responsible for paying *iasak* fur taxes. In 1897 the Imperial government organised a general census experimenting for the first time with the then new enumeration practices of conducting a comprehensive survey and allowing people to self-declare their identity. Nevertheless, this census did not collect data on nationality but instead only on social status (*sosloviia*) and mother tongue.

The Polar Census, and the territorial formation expeditions (*zemleustroitel'-nye ekspeditsii*) of the 1920s and 1930s, provided a new type of information detailing the identities, economy and demography of northern peoples. The new statistical practice was also unique for both its comprehensiveness and its use of modern categories for identity. Based on these sources, this chapter reviews demographic debates on Siberian Nenetses living within the administrative borders of the contemporary Iamalo-Nenets Autonomous Okrug of Tiumen' *oblast'*. The boundaries of the Okrug were set in 1930. Between 1924 and 1930 this territory belonged to the Obdor *raion* and partially to the Surgut *raion* (the Piaku-Pur River basin) of Tobol'sk *okrug* of Ural *oblast'* (fig. 3.1).

The first demographic studies of northern peoples, based on this new registration system, were published immediately following their collation. Following pre-revolutionary traditions, early Soviet researchers focused on the issue of population growth among the indigenous peoples. If at the end of the nineteenth and beginning of the twentieth centuries this population was

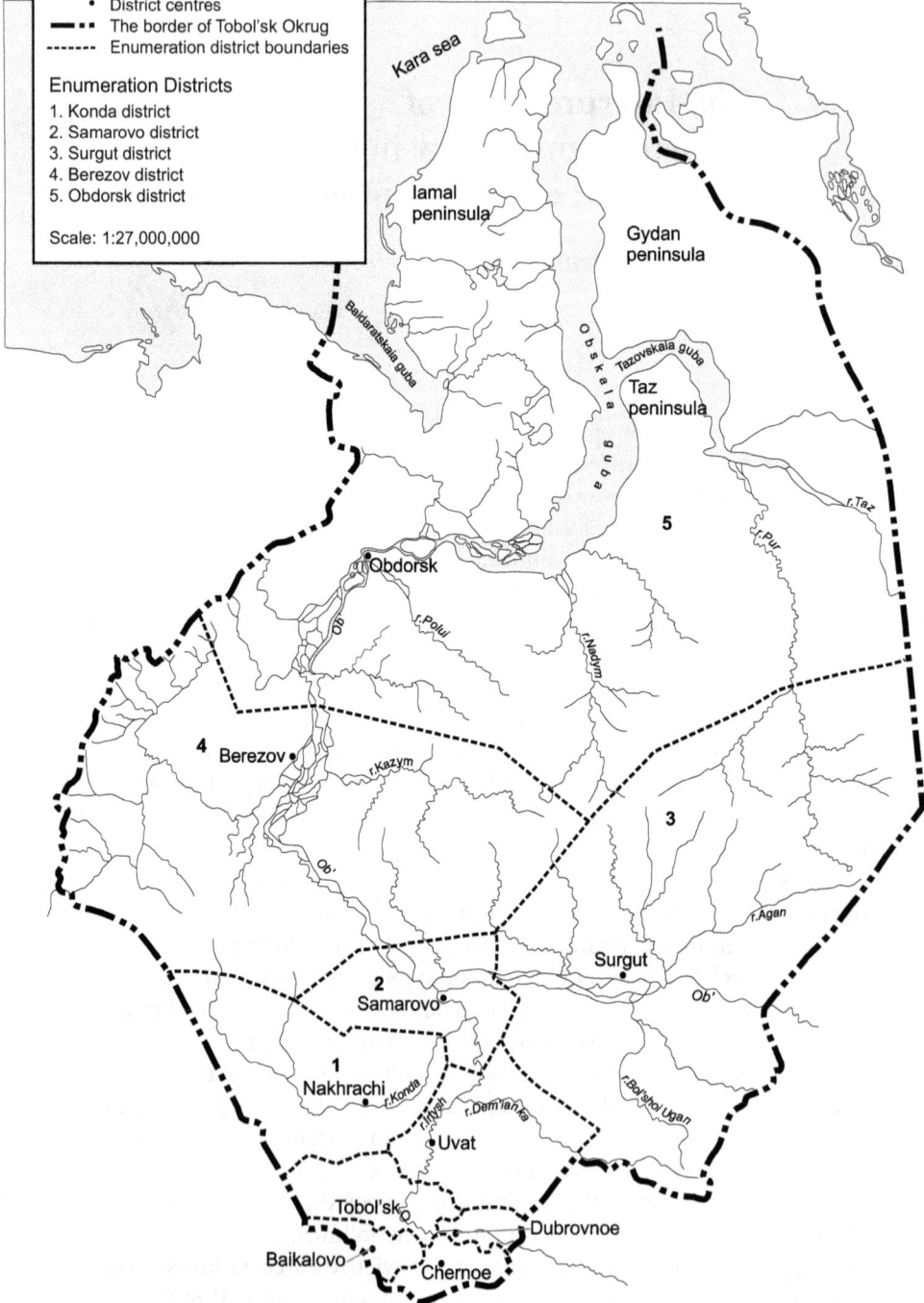

Figure 3.1. Map of the Polar Census Enumeration Districts in Tobol´sk Okrug

characterized as lacking vitality and moving toward extinction (Iakobii 1893; Patkanov 1911a, 1911b; Dunin-Gorkavich 1995; Iadrintsev 2000), in the early Soviet period the researchers now noticed that the population was growing. A discussion surrounding these findings appeared in 1925 in the journal *Severnaia Aziia* where Plotnikov, Bogoraz-Tan and Shternberg noted that northern peoples had a 'mechanism' of self-preservation.

Plotnikov initiated this debate with an analysis of statistics on various peoples collected between 1897 and 1924. He argued that the idea of the extinction of northern peoples had been devised by Siberian regionalists (*oblastniki*) 'in order to attract the attention of the government to indigenous peoples' whereas 'despite unfavourable economic, domestic, and hygienic conditions, the native tribes of Siberia are not becoming extinct and, despite all these conditions, demonstrate considerable vitality'. He concluded that 'the law of the inevitable extinction of the natives cannot be proven' (Plotnikov 1925: 25). Both Bogoraz-Tan and Shternberg criticized this interpretation and suggested other explanations for the phenomenon. In particular, Bogoraz-Tan was among one of the first scholars to suggest that northern peoples had a demographic homeostasis in which demographic growth and decrease were balanced (Bogoraz-Tan and Shternberg 1925: 28).

Until the 1980s, most studies on the social and demographic development of northern peoples had explained population growth as an outcome of state policies such as the transition of nomadic peoples to a settled way of life (Gurvich 1987). P. E. Terletskii's (1932a) analysis of the Polar Census is one of the earliest examples of this framework. Despite criticism from his contemporaries (Bogoraz-Tan 1932; Sergeev 1933), this work became a significant contribution to scholarship insofar as it was among few studies that modelled the demographic characteristics of the native peoples of Siberia in the late 1920s. Terletskii modelled three categories of northern peoples – Russians, settled natives and nomadic natives – on the basis of their respective decreases in birth rate, increases in mortality rate and the possible relationship between these figures to living conditions. In his opinion, this relationship created 'a certain pattern of population growth: the Russians, being a more cultivated population and leading a settled way of life, show a rather positive growth; the settled natives, being at a lower cultural level, demonstrate a lower increase; finally, the nomadic population, living in utterly unfavourable conditions with respect to fertility and mortality, reveal a moderate birth rate, high mortality and extremely low fertility slipping to an average of just 10 people for 1000 for all nomadic peoples in general' (1932a: 48). It is striking that Siberian Nenetses – a nomadic people – are well-known for contradicting Terletskii's model. If we examine the aggregate data from the 1926/27 census and that of the 1939 census, the Nenetses of the Iamal-Nenets *okrug* show not a moderate rate of growth but a high rate of more than 150 per cent in only 13 years (fig. 3.2).[1]

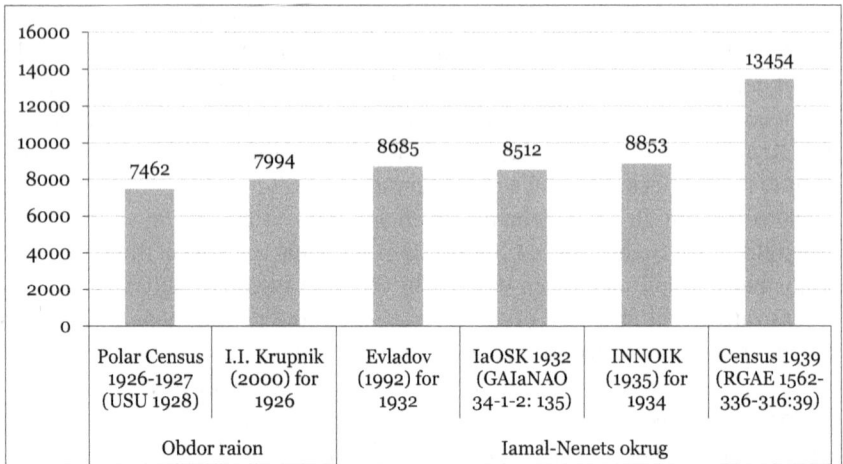

Figure 3.2. The population of Nenetses in the area of the contemporary Iamal-Nenets Okrug in the first third of the twentieth century

Such a sharp rate of growth is impossible to explain by natural factors. By applying contemporary techniques to analyse newly discovered archival sources, as well as centrally and regionally published data, I can try to explain this apparent contradiction.

Here, I will critically analyse historical data for Nenetses living within the boundaries of today's Iamal-Nenets Okrug on sex and age distribution, marital status, household composition, number of children, and natural population size dynamics from the All-Union Censuses of 1926 and 1939, the Polar Census of 1926/27, as well as from reports of the ethnographic and territorial formation expeditions. Although the nominal household level data is far from complete, it nevertheless gives us an interesting point of comparison from which to judge the statistical picture presented in the published sources, shedding new light on the question of the vibrancy of the Nenets population. I will evaluate the accuracy of the primary sources but will also apply some insight from my own ethnographic work to suggest where certain European categories of time, naming traditions, and household composition may have contributed to a misinterpretation of some of these sources.

From the Polar Census I have consulted the published census material, which provides overall population numbers, and distributions by age and sex (TsSU 1928–1933: vol 4: 94–305; TsSU 1929; Kopylov 1994: 278–79). I have also taken detailed demographic information from a small number of surviving digitised household cards. In total, the enumerators of the Obdor district submitted 3,545 household cards of which only 75 are preserved, representing only 2 per cent of the total (GASO 1812-2-181.04: 15) (fig. 3.3). These cards

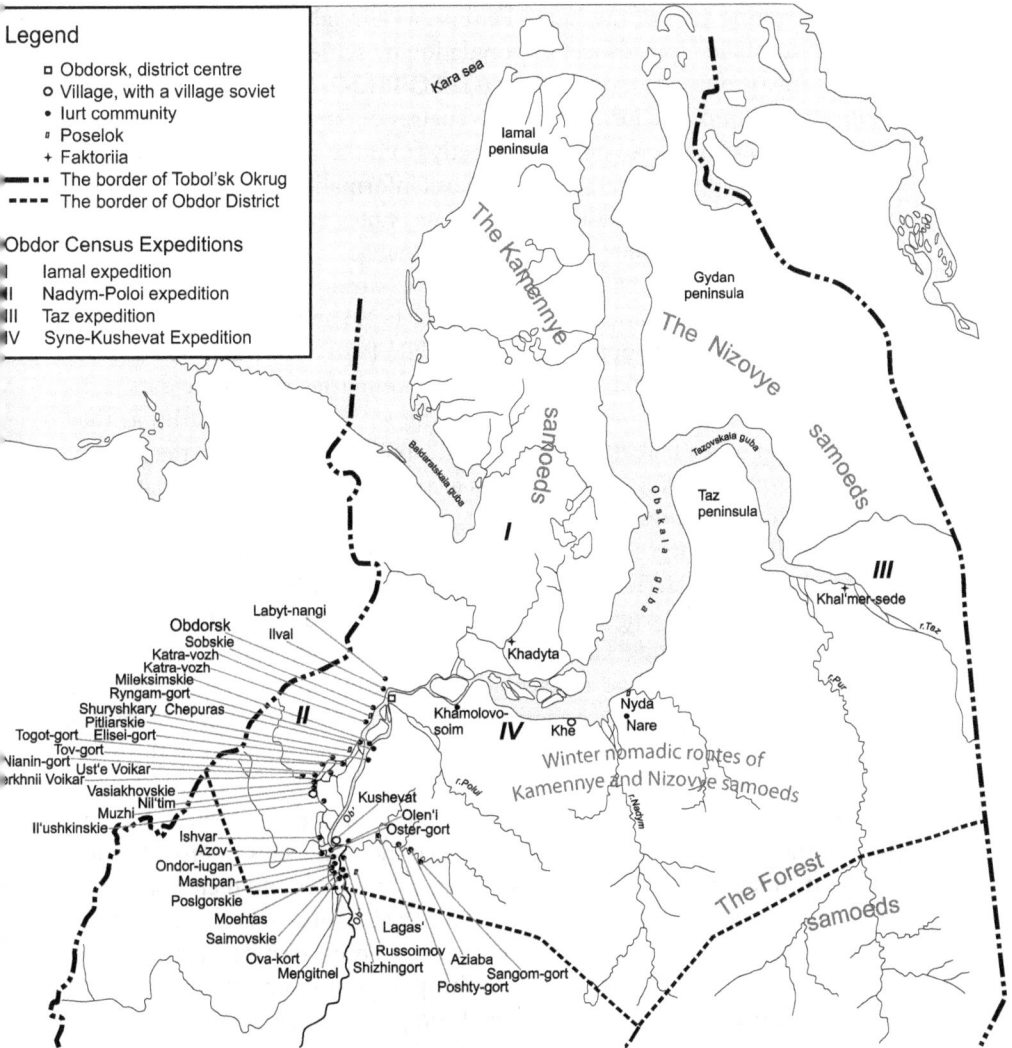

Legend

- □ Obdorsk, district centre
- o Village, with a village soviet
- • Iurt community
- ▫ Poselok
- + Faktoriia
- ▬▬•• The border of Tobol'sk Okrug
- ▬▬▬ The border of Obdor District

Obdor Census Expeditions

- I   Iamal expedition
- II   Nadym-Poloi expedition
- III   Taz expedition
- IV   Syne-Kushevat Expedition

Kara sea

Iamal peninsula

The Kamennye

samoeds

Gydan peninsula

The Nizovye

samoeds

Baidaratskaia guba

Tazovskaia guba

Obskaia guba

Taz peninsula

III

Khal'mer-sede

r. Taz

Labyt-nangi

Obdorsk   Ilval
Sobskie
Katra-vozh
Katra-vozh
Mileksimskie
Ryngam-gort
Shuryshkary   Chepuras
Pitliarskie
Togot-gort   Elisei-gort
Tov-gort
Nianin-gort   Ust'e Voikar
Verkhnii Voikar
Vasiakhovskie
Muzhi   Nil'tim
Il'ushkinskie
Ishvar
Azov
Ondor-iugan
Mashpan
Poslgorskie
Moehtas
Saimovskie
Ova-kort
Mengitnel   Shizhingort

Khadyta

Khamolovo-soim   IV   Khe

Nyda
Nare

II

Kushevat
Olen'i
Oster-gort

r. Poloi

Lagas'

Russoimov   Azlaba
Sangom-gort
Poshty-gort

Winter nomadic routes of Kamennye and Nizovye samoeds

r. Nadym

The Forest

samoeds

Figure 3.3. Map of Obdor district (1929) showing regional groups of Nenetses

account for that section of the Iamal Peninsula where nomadic summer camps were spread out around the Seiakha and Mordhyiakha River basins (GUTO-GAT 690-1-49, 54). Despite the lack of materials for a complete analysis of the demographic situation among Siberian Nenets, analysis of the primary sources for this one case study does reveal some important insight into demographic processes in the first third of the twentieth century.

As a proxy for the missing household cards, I have used a set of archived community summaries for the Taz Village Soviet (GAIaNAO 12-1 *dela* 4–

5) then covering part of the Iamal Peninsula (GU IaNOMVK : "Poselennye Itogi"), a summary spreadsheet of population by settlement for nomadic and settled native groups of Obdor district (GASO 1812-2-184: 85–89), and a set of community summaries for the Forest Nenetses of Surgut district (GAIaNAO 12-1-6). All of these were compiled directly from the now missing household cards. These sources contain settlement level information (names and populations), population distribution by sex and age, notes on levels of literacy, residents' occupations, income, and population change.

Using the community summaries, the Central Statistical Administration published its territorial summary (TsSU 1929) and regional offices published their registers of population points (USU 1928). The published data for Tobol'sk *okrug* differs from the community summaries in that the data is divided into nomadic and settled groups living within the boundaries as they existed at that time (TsSU 1929: 226–27). The published register of the population points of Ural *oblast'* also provides a column with some information on Nenets migratory routes (USU 1928).

In this chapter, I have also tried to compensate for the lack of the primary data by also using materials from territorial formation expeditions which travelled through Iamal *okrug* in the 1930s, mapping land and water use. These sources typically include family-household registration forms (*posemeino-khoziaistvennye blanki*) and household registration cards (*pokhoziaistvennye kartochki*) filled out on every household by the expedition members, as well as secondary data from various reports on the economic conditions of the *okrug* (INNOIK 1935; GASPITO 23-1-258; GAIaNAO 12-1-189).[2]

Finally, I used the published accounts from a number of scientific expeditions to the territories of Nenetses held since the mid 1920s to provide additional information on the number of Nenets households and their population size within the areas of research. Gorodkov (1924), Mitusova (1926, 1929a–e), and Verbov (1939) conducted fieldwork among Forest Nenetses aimed at collecting ethnographic, statistical, and anthropological information along with artefacts for museum collections. Several comprehensive expeditions to Iamal were subsequently organised (Evladov 1930, 1992; Verbov 1936). Kol's (1930), Kostikov (1930), Skalon (1931a, 1931b) and Kurilovich (1934) all studied lowland (*nizovye*) Nenetses. Startsev (1930) also completed an historic and ethnographic study of Samoeds that summarised materials existing at that time.

Ambiguities over Nenets Identity and Territorial Affiliation

Nenetses are a hunting and reindeer-herding people living in the far north of the Russian Federation. Their language forms part of the wider Samoed Uralic language family. An official Russian government register recognises them to-

day as one of the 'less-numerous' minorities of the Russian North. The ethnographic literature distinguishes four ethno-territorial groups. European
Nenetses,[3] Siberian Tundra Nenetses and Siberian Forest Nenetses, are all described in the literature since the seventeenth century (Vasil´ev 1979: 6; 1994:
29). Enisei Nenetses are generally described as a group formed in the first half
of the twentieth century (Vasil´ev 1970: 108; 1975: 144). The ethnonym 'Nenets' became fixed in the titles of administrative districts from 1929 to 1930
(Nenets, Iamal-Nenets and Dolgano-Nenets) and came to be used generally
only in the 1930s. Until that time Nenets were known either as Samoeds and
Iuraks.[4] The old category 'Samoeds' was still used in many documents well into
the 1930s. The Forest Nenets were often referred to as 'Pian-Khasovo' or 'Piaki',
a name given to them by Tundra Nenetses.[5]

Associating specific Nenets communities to one of these standard ethno-
territorial groups has proven to be a difficult task. For example, in the Polar Census household cards on the region, the section recording the 'tribe' of a household
head could contain labels such as 'Samoed', 'Iamal Samoed', 'Kamennyi Samoed',
'Nizovoi Samoed', 'Forest Samoed' or 'Iurak'. Dunin-Gorkavich (1995: 106) provided a key to these identifiers at the beginning of the twentieth century:

> The migration routes of the Kamennye Samoeds stretch from the head of the Sob´
> river along the Ural Mountain ridge down to the Kara Sea. Here they join the Pus-
> tozerskie Samoeds of Arkhangel´sk *guberniia*. To the east, they reach the Ob´ Bay.
> The migration routes of the Nizovye Samoeds spread between the bays of Ob´ and
> Taz and, in the east, they adjoin the Iurakskie Samoeds of Enisei *guberniia*.[6]

The designations of 'Kamennye' [Mountain], 'Nizovye' [Lower] or 'Iamal'skie'
[Iamal] Samoeds referred to the landscapes within which groups were migrating at the time of registration or from which they had arrived. As noted in
other chapters in this volume (Jordan, Semenov), these landscape-derived
designations can be traced back to the eighteenth century. The term 'Kamennye Samoeds' is derived from an Old Russian word *kamen´* referring to the
Ural Mountains, and 'Nizovye Samoeds' take their name from the 'Nizovaia
Storona' region or the 'lower side' tundra areas lying to the east of Ob´ River
mouth (Dunin-Gorkavich 1909: 11). It is also argued that Kamennye Samoeds
to the west are mostly Iamal Nenetses whose summer migrations occupied
the Iamal Peninsula, whereas Nizovye Samoeds to the east consisted mostly of
Taz Nenetses, who migrated in summer within the territories of the Taz and
Gydan Peninsulas (Dolgikh 1970: 89; Khomich 1995: 28).[7] 'Mountain', 'Lower'
and 'Forest' differ from each other according to linguistic attributes, and in ac-
cord with the instructions to the 1926 census they were considered as separate
tribes (GASO 1812-2-181.01: 105v.).

When interpreting longitudinal data, like those in figure 3.2, it is also important to take into account the shifts in the jurisdictional boundaries within

which the data was collected. An act passed by the All-Russia General Executive Committee (*VSIK*) on 10 December 1930 divided the territory on which the Siberian Nenets lived between the Iamal (Nenets) and Ostiako-Vogul' National Okrugs.[8] Before the Revolution the indigenous population of this territory lived under the administrative regulations of the *Obdorskaia Inorodnaia Uprava* (Native Administration Board) of Berezov *uezd* in Tobol'sk *guberniia*. From 1919 to 1923 the territory was a part of Obdor *volost'* of Berezov *uezd* of Tobol'sk *okrug* of Tiumen' *guberniia*. From 1924 to 1930, it lay within Obdor *raion* of Tobol'sk *okrug* of Ural *oblast'*.[9] The shift from Obdor *raion* to the national *okrug* greatly increased the number of Neneteses falling within the boundary of specific territories and can partly explain the large jump in the population portrayed in figure 3.2 in 1939.

In addition to problems over the official organisation of identities, enumerators faced difficulties with the way that identity might be declared. During the Polar Census, enumerators were instructed to ascribe *natsional'nost'* 'according to self-identification and ethnic characteristics' of an individual' (GASO 1812-2-181.01: 105).[10] For mixed families, in which neither father nor mother felt able to ascribe a nationality to their children, the nationality of the mother was to be ascribed to children (Kozlov 1969: 80). This official regulation contradicted the customs of northern peoples in this region, according to which the father's identity was usually ascribed to offspring.

Enumerators also faced a challenge with certain identifies which might overlap with groups outside of Nenets territories. The participants of the Nadym expedition of 1933–1934 noted the following ambiguities of self-identification:

> It is difficult sometimes to strictly separate Khants and Nenetses because some families of one and the same clan call themselves Nenetses while others identify themselves as Khants. It is worth mentioning that natives belonging to the clans of Anagurichi, Porunguy, Solinder, and Nerkagy are in fact Khants penetrated to the territory of Nadym *raion* from Priural' and Shuryshkar districts. Living among Nenetses, descendants of Khants have, in most cases, lost their mother tongue and call themselves Nenets. It is often possible to see mixed marriages between members of these Khants clans and Nenetses ... (GAIaNAO 186-1-1: 39)

A concrete example of this overlap can be found in the case of the Ostiako-Samoeds. This territorial group was listed separately in both the censuses of 1897 and 1926. Kastren used the category of Ostiako-Samoeds to refer to Sel'kups in order to emphasize their linguistic affinity with Samoeds and other cultural practices in common with Ostiaks, today known as the Khants (Sokolova and Tugolukov 1983: 80). In the areas of the Greater and Lesser Iamal, the lower reaches of the Ob' and Taz Rivers, within the Nadym basin and the Gydan tundra the term 'Ostiako-Samoed' usually referred to the Samoedified Ostiaks who may have lost their mother tongue but retained Khant self-consciousness and some elements of their spiritual and material culture (Verbov 1939: 62–63). These were members of Salinder, Nerkygy, Tibichi, Niadyngi, Pando, Porongui and Lar clans who referred to themselves collectively as 'Khabi', the Nenets term for Khants. The entire group was classified by scholars as a group of Nenets of Khant origin (ibid., 60–61; Dolgikh 1970: 74–75).

In order to untangle these ambiguities of identity it is useful to keep in mind the structure by which primary household records were transformed into aggregate results. After the data were collected, they were compiled and analysed in a number of intermediary forms (see also Semenov, this volume). This first stage of aggregation creates a dimension around which there can be a difference in population numbers. In order to simplify accounting, some mixed groups were included in larger groups. As a result, data presented in different published sources varies. In the regional published results Samoedo-Zyrians, Ostiako-Samoeds and Iuraks are all classified as Samoeds (USU 1928: iv, xxxiv; GASO 1812-2-184: 85). However, in the official federal published census results Ostiako-Samoeds and Iuraks are categorized separately (TsSU 1928–1934: vol 4:104). In addition, some mixed groups were classified as having identities other than Nenets. For example, in the regional publication for the nomad Ural district, 335 mixed 'Samoedo-Zyrians' were recorded as being part of the Zyrian [Komi] language group (USU 1928: 164–65).

In general, as one moves from the beginning to the middle of the twentieth century there is a tendency for the official publications to simplify the territorial distribution of Nenets groups. For example, the published *Register of Population Points of Ural Oblast'* (USU 1928) gives a detailed account of the ethnic composition of nomadic Samoed language groups (7,376 individuals) within Obdor *raion* with Samoeds representing 81.1 per cent of this population, Forest Samoeds, 0.2 per cent; Iuraks, 2.6 per cent; and Ostiako-Samoeds, 16.1 per cent (calculated from USU 1928: 164–65). In contrast, the instructions for coding the 1939 Federal Census asked enumerators to classify all of following regional groups simply as Nenetses: 'Nenetsiia', 'Nenetses', 'Khasovo', 'Samoeds', 'Samodi', 'Samoeds-Iuraks', 'Iuraks', 'Iarans', 'Pian-Khasovo', and 'Forest Nenetses' (RGAE 1562-336-205: 30). If we consider the fact that by 1939 the boundaries of what was once Obdor *raion* had been expanded into the larger territory of the Iamal (Nenets) national Okrug, the sharp population increase in that census also reflects the inclusion of approximately 1,065 Forest Nenetses previously classified as part of Surgut district.

The Structure of Enumeration during the Polar Census

If the aggregation of results geographically and within territorial groups created some ambiguity in the history of Nenets identity, the structure of enumeration also creates certain challenges. The Polar Census was unique in that its enumerators worked in direct contact with local people in specially organised many-month-long expeditions, breaking previous practice of taking hearsay information from community elders. To maximize coverage, expeditions to remote areas were organised and registration took place at trading stations located along seasonal migration routes (GASO 1812-2-181.1: 3v.). In 1926 and 1927 the members of the Iamal, Taz, Nadym-Polui and Synia-Kunovat parties were registered as nomads in Obdor district (GASO 1812-2-181.4: 3). The Gydan Peninsula Nenetses were surveyed in the fourth census tract of the neighbouring Turukhansk district (Anderson 2005: 343–48; Kodolov 2005: 129). Due to the difficulty of accessing certain places, however, and limited funding, census officers sometimes had to revert to previous practice by filling in cards based on hearsay evidence (USU 1928: 210–1; GASO 1812-2-181-4: 5v.).

The comprehensiveness of the Polar Census was impressive for its time. According to a report of the Taz expedition, they missed 'no more than twenty or thirty households' among the Lower Samoeds (GASO 1812-2-181-4: 6). It was thought that as few as 15 to 30 Forest Nenets households were left uncounted (ibid., 6v). It is thought that about 80 households were missed among Iamal Nenets (ibid., 7). In total 115 to 140 households, or approximately 575 to 700 individuals if the average size of a household is assumed to have five persons, were not enumerated.[11] This amounts to 7.7 to 9.4 per cent of the counted population.

When the census was taken, a number of supplementary surveys were applied to correct census undercounting (GASO 1812-2-181-4: 12). In particular, three units of the Obdor Veterinary and Bacteriological Institution, sent in the summer of 1927 to Iamal, Northern Ural, and to the Taz basin, were supplied with registration forms and the appropriate certificates in order to enumerate members of the nomadic population that, for some reason, had not been counted earlier. The secretary of the Taz Village Soviet was also supposed to undertake additional census-taking of nomads within the Taz District. Census forms were also sent to V. Gorodkov and L. Kostikov, the heads of an expeditions to the Gydan´ Tundra arranged by the Soviet Academy of Sciences. Expeditions conducted in the 1920s and 1930s by Evladov, Skalon, Verbov and Kurilovich also helped to correct the data of the Polar Census.

Census-taking in the areas populated by the Nenetses of Obdor region took seven months instead of the planned four. Work planned for 1926 to be held 'from the beginning of December until the end of March' in fact started in November to register Zyrians and Zyrian-Samoeds 'descending toward the Ob' river from the Urals before establishing a river crossing' nearby the village Labytnangi. Enumeration continued until the beginning of April and 'partially (for the Iamal section) until the beginning of May' 1927 (GASO 1812-2-181.1: 2; 4: 4, 8v). Northern expeditions in the 1930s needed a year to collect the required information. Families with migration routes close to trading stations that called in for goods and supplies were the first to be registered. It is possible that the families migrating in areas of tundra that were far away from these stations were not accounted for at all.

There were various reasons for differences in the way that Nenetses were portrayed statistically. Perhaps the most important were differences in the way that data was exacted. Most analyses that worked from the household cards would extract identities from the heads of households and then extrapolate them to all individuals in the family. The federal results, however, were compiled from intermediary *lichnye listy* which took data from the individual-level identity cells where certain family members could express differing identities. The fact that the population in question was nomadic also played an important role. Different categories of the population might be absent at the moment of registration, or instead might be permanent residents. The problems of counting nomadic Samoeds are best understood with specific examples. Here I will discuss the enumeration of Iamal Peninsula Nenetses and Forest Nenetses before returning to conduct a critical analysis of the combined figures for the region.

Iamal Peninsula Nenetses

Iamal Peninsula Nenetses had a strong seasonal cycle. They occupied the territory of the Iamal Peninsula mostly in summer. In the autumn they migrated to the forest-tundra areas. The distribution of the population within these territories therefore varied according to seasons. Zhitkov (1913: 208) notes:

> From November till March, Iamal becomes deserted. Sometimes just few *chumy* remain near to the Strait of Malygin and on the Kara Sea shore in order to hunt bears in early spring. One cannot neglect, however, the fact that here and there along the Ob´ Bay, or by big lakes, Samoeds sit with so few reindeer that they cannot afford to start on a long journey and, for years, they do not leave the tundra. Nevertheless, these often join stronger *chumy* to sustain migration…

Figure 3.4 shows the different absolute population figures for Iamal Nenetses taken between 1926 and 1939 and as compiled by seven different agents. The census of 1926/1927 was taken in winter, between the end of November and the end of March, when a considerable proportion of nomads would have already left the peninsula. The territory reaching from the Iamal Peninsula down to the river Shchuch´ia was assigned as a separate region for follow-up expeditions. A further region set aside for subsequent expeditions included the ʻareas of winter migrations of most Kamennye Samoeds that spread between the rivers Polui and Nadym, on the one side, and the shores of the Ob´ Bay and the upper riches of those rivers, on the other' (GASO 1812-2-181.01: 132). Census-taking stations in Iamal were situated at the trading stations of

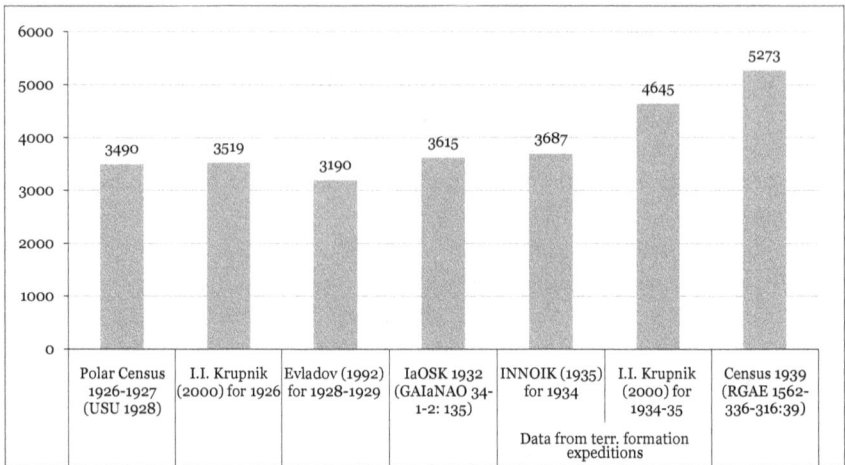

Figure 3.4. The total population of 'Iamal Nenetses' (showing differing amalgamations of Obdor *raion* and the later Iamal-Nenets *okrug*)

Shchuch′ia, Khadatta, Mar-Sale, Nyda, Nore and Khe (ibid.). Iamal Nenetses were registered by the Iamal and Nadym-Polui expedition units. The Iamal unit covered the territory of southern and middle Iamal. Consequently, households that stayed at Iamal through the winter were not accounted for.

Despite this handicap, it should be noted that the numbers provided by the enumerators for the Polar Census seem to match those of other observers. In 1926/27 the published results show that 3,190 Nenetses were registered on the territories of the Iamal Peninsula and islands of the Ob′ delta of the Puikov fishing region (or 3,490 if Ostiako-Samoeds are included)[12] (USU 1928: 164–165, 182–185). The overall number of Samoed and Ostiako-Samoed households amounted to 662. This corresponds to data collected by the zoology technician Korolev, who travelled through the peninsula with Evladov's expedition during 1928–1929. He counted 638 households in Iamal two years later, a difference of only 24 households.[13]

Korolev reported that in summer about a third of households (21.7 per cent) were located within the northern part of the peninsula (186 or 183 households according to expedition and census data respectively), about half (52.6 per cent) occupied the middle area (335 and 426 households in the respective documents), and 18.4 per cent resided in the south (117 households) (Evladov 1992: 253). According to Evladov, in winter there was a redistribution of households. Twenty-four (3.8 per cent) households stayed in northern Iamal, 330 (52 per cent) households migrated to the western part, and 284 (44.2 per cent) households moved to the opposite bank of the Ob′ river to Khenskaia Storona (ibid., 256). If we count that 354 households stayed on Iamal, this means that the winter population was 55.5 per cent of the summer population. Multiplying these numbers of households with the coefficient 5, the approximate size of the Iamal population in summer and in winter would have been 3,190 and 1,770 individuals respectively.

Three years later, the Iamal Okrug Statistics Board records that, as of 1 January 1932, there were 3,615 Nenets registered in Iamal District, constituting 54.8 per cent of the overall district population of 6,600 (GAIaNAO 34-1-2: 135). In 1934 there were 3,687 Nenets in the district, 42.4 per cent of the overall population (GASPITO 23-1-258: 8; INNOIK 1935: 7). According to the household survey conducted that same year by the Iamal territorial formation expedition of 1932–1933, the Nenets population in Iamal amounted to 2,936 individuals (calculated from GAIaNAO 12-1-51~56). Based on data collected in by territorial formation expeditions in Iamal *raion* from 1934 to 1935, Krupnik has suggested the Nenets population at that time consisted of 4,645 individuals (Krupnik 2000: 145). According to official information from the next All-Union census of 1939, Nenetses numbered 5,273 individuals.

The reasons for the jumps in the local population of Iamal Peninsula Nenetses according to these different sources seem to be mostly connected with the structure of enumeration and the way that numbers were later aggregated into published results. The numbers produced by territorial formation expeditions were generally higher than those produced by the regional publications of the Polar Census. The estimates by Igor Krupnik (2000) for 1926/27 and for the 1934–1935 census seem to be the highest due to the effect of the special coefficient he used to compensate for what he saw as an undercounting of the population. A crude comparison of the numbers of 1926/27 and 1939 show an increase in the regional Nenets population of the Iamal Peninsula of 150 per cent.

Forest Nenetses

The reported growth of Forest Nenetses is no less interesting (fig. 3.5). Dolgikh, citing *iasak* books of the seventeenth century, suggests that Kazym Samoeds numbered as many as 770 individuals (Dolgikh 1960: 72).[14] For the end of the eighteenth century, Vasil'ev provides a figure of 476 individuals, based on the materials of the fifth pre-Soviet taxation audits (*reviziia*) of 1795 (Vasil'ev 1994: 52, 56). According to the first census of 1897, there were 467 individuals in the region (Patkanov 1911b: 29). It has, however, been suggested that because Forest Nenetses lived in a remote marshy area without direct contact with the tundra Nenets population, researchers believed that the vast space between the Ob' and Taz Rivers was not populated at all (Gorodkov 1924: 21).

The Polar Census enumerators, however, registered 1,065 Forest Nenetses within Surgut district; 47 within Samarov; and 17 within Obdor (USU 1928: 164). Verbov, who worked with the Forest Nenetses in the early 1930s, thought that the general total of these three districts – 1,129 – was too low (Verbov

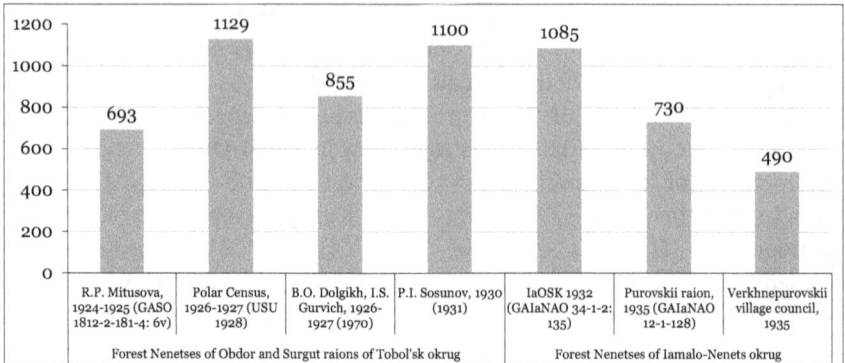

Figure 3.5. Various population figures for Forest Nenetses from 1924 to 1935

1936: 62). According to the map of population distribution for neighbouring native territorial groups of the north in 1926 and 1927 produced by Dolgikh and Gurvich, the Nazym-Liamin, Vat′egan, Verkhne-Pur, Piaku-Pur and Numto groups of Forest Nenetses amounted to 171 households and approximately 855 individuals (Gurvich and Dolgikh 1970: 438) (see fig. 3.5).

The Forest Nenetses of Obdor district were not completely accounted for in the Polar Census due to the illness of Mitusova who was supposed to register them. Attempts to substitute her with census officers from the upper reaches of the Kazym River as well as from Berezov and Taz districts were unsuccessful due to shortages of both transportation and officers (GASO 1812-2-181-4: 6v). As a controlling measure, the Surgut district census manager was advised to expand the area of coverage for the district to the north. This was undertaken only in part with interviews limited to community elders in Nore and Surgut. Consequentially, the households of that area were officially considered as being unaccounted for (USU 1928: 210). During the provisional expedition of 1924 to 1925 to the Pur and Agan River basins, Mitusova recorded 693 Samoeds and Ostiako-Samoeds as dwelling in the area, living in 97 *chumy* and including 380 children under 15 (GASO 1812-2-181.1: 30–30v).

As Sosunov (1931: 42) noted:

> Accounting of this *narodnost′* is presumably complicated by administrative issues, as a significant majority of 'Pian-Khazovo' are administratively ascribed to Surgut *raion*, some of them inhabit the middle lands of the Pur river, probably intermingling here with the Iuraks, and those within the Pur band are included in Taz *raion* [Pur *raion* was separated from the Taz *raion* in 1932, E.V.]; the rest of them migrate along the rivers Chasal′ka and Tol′ka [tributaries of the Taz] and, due to this characteristic, are apparently ascribed, being seen as Ostiaks, to the administrative divisions of Turukhansk *krai*.

By his calculations, the Pian-Khasovo amounted to 1,000–1,100 individuals, of which 750 lived in Surgut district, according to information from members of the Aivasedo clan. One hundred and fifty individuals made up the Pur 'band', and 150 individuals migrated along tributaries of the Taz River (ibid.). Generally, these numbers differ only slightly from those of the Polar Census. In composite data for the districts of Iamal Okrug, as of 1 January 1932, there were approximately 1,005 Forest Nenets in Pur district (GAIaNAO 34-1-2: 139). According to reports by the land-use expeditions of 1935, the 146 households of Pian-Khasovo registered in Pur district added up to 730 individuals (GAIaNAO 12-1-189: 24). The enumerators of the Tazovsko-Pur expedition counted a further 95 households in Verkhnepur Village Soviet, amounting to 490 people (GAIaNAO 12-1-128).

In contrast to the chart of the population of Iamal Peninsula Nenetses, the various figures for Forest Nenetses do not show any sign of an increase in their population. Neither do they show any stable population size. This group had a population of no less than 1,129 people in 1926/27. As we move forward to the 1930s we can state that the absolute population numbers are more a reflection of the strong effect that changing boundaries, dates, and the length of time invested in enumeration can have upon population figures.

Regional Overview of the Nenetses of the Iamal-Nenets Okrug

Having explored the various sources of discrepancies in the regional population for Forest Nenetses and Iamal Peninsula Nenetses, it is useful to return to figure 3.2 in order to better understand the reasons for the jump in the population at the beginning of the twentieth century in this region. In figure 3.2 we can see the results of several different aggregation strategies. In 1926/27, if one chooses the regional household-level aggregation (USU 1928) over an individual level aggregation (TsSU 1929) one already sees an increase in the population in that year of 532 individuals. According to the Central Statistical Board, their numbers included residents of their administrative regions present in the then-boundaries of Obdor *raion* at the moment of census-taking (USU 1928: IV) which would have included Samoeds from Komi *oblast'* and Turukhansk *krai* as well as Forest Samoeds (509 individuals) from Surgut *raion*.

If we move forward to 1932 and 1934, we can see that the data from the land use expeditions show that the overall Nenets population of Iamalo-Nenets Okrug in the first half of the 1930s did not exceed 9,000 individuals. However, the All-Union Census of 1939 records a population of 13,454. Following the observations above it can be suggested that this number is an outcome of both a more accurate enumeration and a simplification of the way that identities were grouped. In this region, the main increase is likely due to the fact that

Ostiako-Samoeds, Samoed-Zyrians and Iuraks, formerly considered separately, became registered, in most cases as Nenetses.

In the next section I will examine the cultural concepts of the person which may have contributed to differences in the way that demographic data are represented.

Nenets Ideas of the Person in Conflict with Enumeration Practices

Comparative analysis of the primary sources shows that the enumeration of Nenetses was further complicated by traditional Nenets beliefs associated with a person's name and age as well as birth, death and marriage. Detailed descriptions of these views can be found in the ethnographic studies of Tereshchenko (1966, 1967), Khomich (1976, 1995) and Susoi (1994). Enumerators who lacked an understanding of Nenets cultural practices could sometimes produce missing, incomplete or unreliable demographic information. According to Nenets customs, a person could have up to three names, for example: the ancestor's name (of limited use), a nickname given due to circumstances of birth, and a Russian name might all be used (Khomich 1976: 117). Furthermore, the increased usage of Russian names occurred along with the Christianization and baptism of some Nenetses. Often those names existed only on paper and were forgotten by their bearers and people around them (Minenko 1975: 20).[15] The traditional Nenets anthroponymy can be glimpsed in the header section of the household card for the Polar Census. The household card recorded both Russian and native surnames and forenames, middle name and a nickname. A Nenets native surname was considered to be the name of the clan to which the head of household belonged. Either one or two forenames could be recorded. In the case of one name being recorded this could be a Russian or Nenets name or a nickname. Where two names are recorded this may be a Russian and Nenets name, a Nenets name and a nickname, or a Russian name and a nickname. Most commonly a Nenets name alone was recorded; second most common was a recording of a Russian name along with a Nenets one; and third most common was the recording of a nickname.

The possibility of a person having three names caused concern about the possibility of overestimating the Nenets population where individuals may have been entered several times (GASO 1812-2-181-4: 7). To avoid such a mistake, all registered nomads were given certificates to show that they had been counted.

In the 1920s and 1930s, Nenets names and nicknames outnumbered Russian names. For women, in their position as wives or daughters-in-law to the head of household, the names of their natal clan were sometimes recorded instead of their first names. Nenets anthroponymy did not give patronymics due to traditional prohibitions and so the corresponding columns were left blank. In family-household registration forms of the 1930s, it was often only the name of a head of household that was recorded. His wife was sometimes referred to by a name relating to the name of the oldest child: for example, *Aiu nebia* or *Ene nebia,* meaning 'mother of Aiu' or 'mother of Ene'. Sometimes a woman was named according to her natal clan such as Vanuito, Susoi or Lapsui. Taboos existed on pronouncing a person's name aloud after a certain age or a significant event, and the usage of substitutions could also result in misunderstandings if an enumerator did not know the Nenets language and culture. There are also examples where, instead of names, terms of kinship such as *meia, niapa* or *niaba* ('daughter-in-law'), *niabako* ('elder sister'), or *ne* ('woman', 'wife') were recorded. In some cases, names of a wife, children and other family members were not recorded together.

Recording a person's age might also have been difficult for enumerators. In the worldview of demographers, 'age' refers to the number of calendar years lived. If a respondent does not know their date of birth they may be asked how old they were on their latest birthday (Medkov 2002: 418). Nenets could not give a precise answer to such questions, however, because in Nenets culture, a person's age is not measured in years. The date of birth, for example, was taken from the moment an infant's umbilical cord fell away and their age was only counted for the first four or five years of their life (Susoi 1994: 36, 50). In general, the number of years lived was less significant for Nenets than the ability of a person to perform certain social functions – for women, the ability to bear children for example (Khariuchi 2001: 156).

Moreover, differences in length of the Russian and the Nenets years added confusion to calculation of individuals' ages in years when this was attempted. The traditional Nenets calendar is divided into two periods: summer and winter (Susoi 1994: 49; Golovnev 1995: 302; Khomich 1995: 199). Each of these periods was seen as a separate year and a self-contained life cycle. During an *oblast'* Healthcare Department expedition to Circumpolar North of Tobol′sk *okrug* in 1926–1927, doctor Shapiro-Aronshtam reported that Nenets 'cannot count well. [They] cannot tell the age of a child. Aged people, being of 50 years old, give a number from 75 to 100 years...' (GUTOGAT 695-1-78: 30). She continues, 'Samoeds do not understand measurements of time, that is why they do not know their age. A child's age is known only until they are three. A Samoed person cannot tell if he or she is 25 or 40, so their age has to be guessed' (ibid., 87v.). One example given by Shapiro-Aronshtam suggests that Samoeds in close contact with Russians and Zyrians were similarly imprecise in their reckoning of age. On questioning, one simply answered: 'Do you know Sanka Shakhov? My son was born the same year or a year later...' (ibid., 89).

Instructions on filling the household registration card for the 1926/27 Polar Census contained the following recommendations regarding age: 'The age of infants under one year old shall be recorded in months and be asked, whereas the age of adults who cannot give a definite answer shall be determined from the respondent's appearance; for those under 10, the age is to be identified within one-year, for those of 10–29, it shall be reckoned within 5-year age brackets, and for those above 30 in 10 year age brackets' (GASO 1812-2-181.1: 105v.). The task of enumerators for the land use expeditions was somewhat simpler due to the requirement to record only the numbers of those capable of working, teenagers of 12 to 16 years old, children under 12, and those incapable of working. The latter category usually included aged people (GAIaNAO 186-1-1: 40v.). The categorization of adults as capable and incapable of working was determined by registrars' observations as well as respondents' accounts. In a report of the Nadym expedition, it is stated that 'usually Nenets do not know their age... old men who are 60–70 actively participate in household activities and are considered capable of working, whereas old women of the same age are seen as incapable of working, although they can perform some minor household tasks...' (ibid., 40).

The presence of age rounding can lead to considerable distortion of the age data in our sources from the 1920s and 1930s. This shows that enumerators often had to estimate a respondent's age from his or her appearance, recording an approximate number of years instead of an accurate one. Transformed into graphs, the data show the tendency to cluster toward ages ending with '0' or '5'. For example, in the data collected from household forms from the territorial formation expeditions in 1932 and 1933 the age of people above 40 is usually indicated by the numbers 40, 45, 50, 55, 60, 65, 70 and 75 (fig. 3.6). The coefficient of age accumulation, calculated in relation to ages ending with '0' and '5' in 1926 is equal to 4,916.6 per cent; in 1932–1933 it is equal to 3,069 per cent; and for the Forest Nenets of the Verkhnepur Village Soviet in 1934 it is 1,435.2 per cent. The appearance in the data of Nenets of 100 years old and above is the result of age estimation by sight in the first half of the twentieth century. The actual data contains information on men and women of 98, 103, 110 and 115 years old.

The existence of a small number of primary records for households allows us some perspective on the overall accuracy of the regional published results. In figure 3.7, I compare age-sex pyramids constructed from the published Federal results for the Obdor region (where data was compiled from individual records) to the raw data for the Mordy River valley of that region recompiled from a set of digitised household cards. The rough patterns, unsurprisingly, are the same in both diagrams. The benefit of using the recompiled data however comes in the fact that we can separate data for the age cohorts 30 and over, which in the published data were compressed into 10-year age groups. When these data are disaggregated into 5-year age groups the progressive population pattern for this small regional group of Nenetses is much more easily seen. The picture of the Mordy regional population, as small as it is, does show a very sharp decline in the numbers of children after age nine, suggesting a high level of child mortality – a feature that the aggregate statistics also show (as I will discuss below).

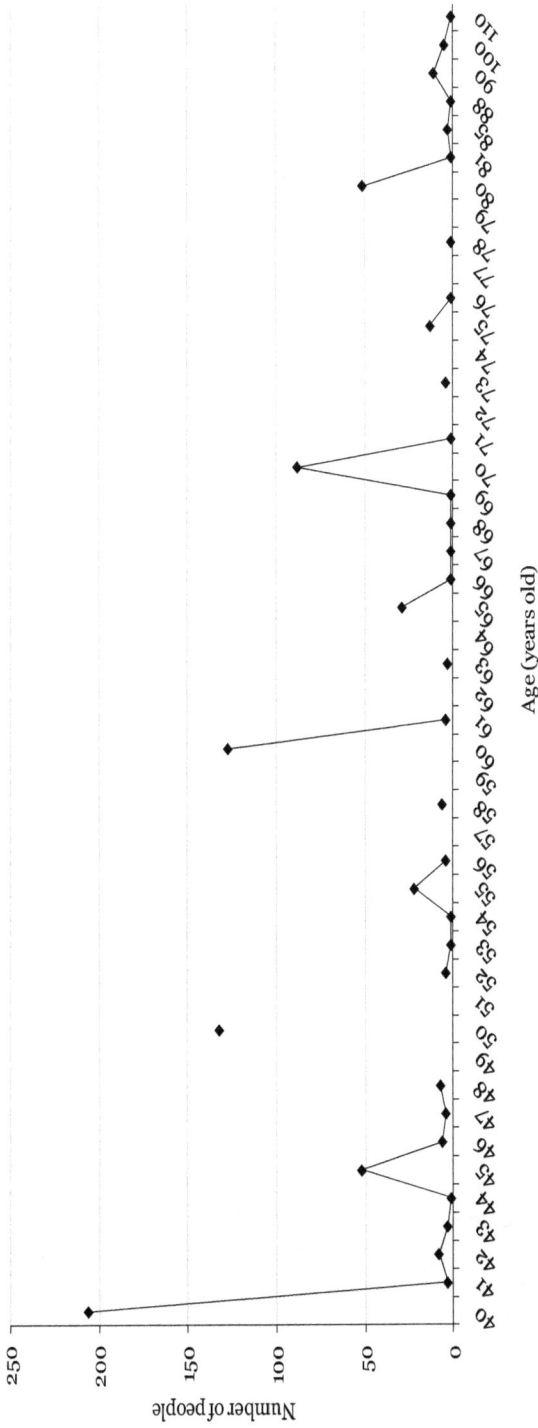

Figure 3.6. Age rounding of Iamal Nenetses more than 40 years old, calculated from the household forms of the territorial formation expedition of 1932–1933

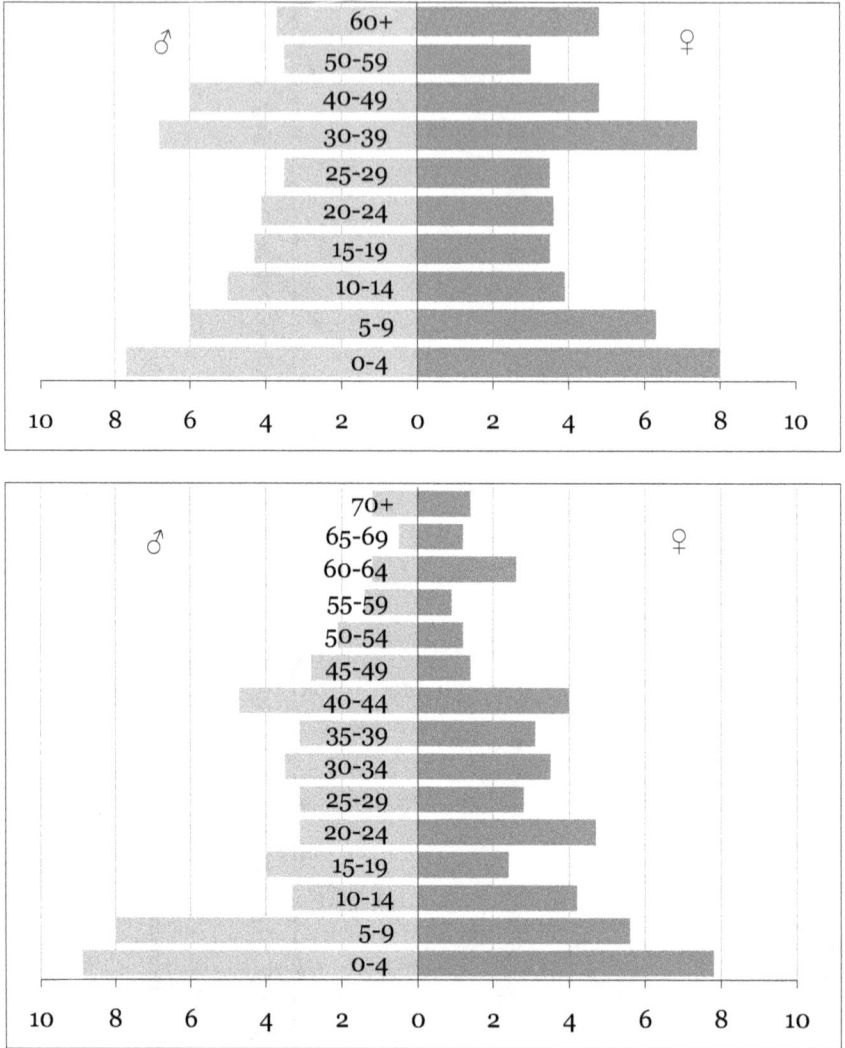

Figure 3.7. Comparative age-sex pyramids for Samoeds of the Obdor *raion* (top) [from TsSU (1928)] and for the Mordy River valley (bottom) [from digitised household cards]

The comparison of nominal records from the archives to published records also allows us a new perspective from which to judge the accuracy of historical demographic data. For example, Igor Krupnik (2000) developed a method for determining the accuracy of statistical data by looking at the ratio of men to women. Krupnik argues that, for the given period, one would expect to find a ratio of 90–96 women to 100 men. Variations from this ratio would stand as evidence of undercounting. In his analysis of the primary sources for the nineteenth and twentieth centuries, he comes up with an average sex ratio of 93:100. Therefore, by applying Krupnik's method to the data from 1932, it is possible to estimate the undercount for Forest Nenetses at 15.2 per cent and for the Nizhnepur Nenetses at 7.2 per cent. In addition, Krupnik's method suggests incomplete registration of men among Iamal Nenetses according to the materials of the Iamal land use expedition of 1932–1933. This undercount amounted to 110 individuals or 3.7 per cent. According to the statistics of both All-Union censuses of the first half of the twentieth century, namely those of 1926 and 1939, men represented 51 per cent and 50.6 per cent of the Nenets population respectively. My analysis of the household registration cards and family-household forms of the 1930s provide similar proportions (table 3.1, top rows), confirming Krupnik's conclusions.

The Definition of 'Households' and the Nenets Kinship System

Information about Nenets family composition was also not always accurately recorded. In the Nenets language, there is no term designating 'family' (Dunin-Gorkavich 1932; Verbov 1937); the concept is borrowed from Russian (Teresh-chenko 1965: 156). The words *miad'ter* or *miadnder* meaning 'inhabitant of a chum' may be seen as equivalent (ibid., 186). The enumerators of the 1920s and even of the 1950s sometimes recorded the name and sex of household members without comments about their relation to the head of household, considering them as 'family members'. Difficulties describing Nenets family composition are also caused by the differences between the Nenets and the Russian family structures that are described in the studies of Startsev (1930), Verbov (1936), Kupriianova (1954), Khomich (1995) and Simchenko (1974).

Nenets kinship terminology may also have created problems for Russian census-takers. With the exception of the mother or the father of the person being interviewed, all consanguinal and affinal kin older than the speaker are referred to by the same descriptive term (Khomich 1995). The same term may be used for individuals of two different generations (ibid., 174). This system sometimes affected data collection, notably on family-household forms and household books which could contain erroneous records regarding lines of descent. Someone recorded as 'grandmother' may in fact have been the aunt of the head of household (according to the Russian classification system). The same can be said about a 'grandfather' who later turned out to be an uncle. Similarly, Nenets terms used for children and grandchildren are identical, namely *niu* for son or grandson or *ne niu* for daughter or granddaughter. Coupled with the fact that enumerators often approximated age, this could have resulted in a household card where aged or old parents were recorded as having fewer children than may have been the case. Moreover, the same term was

Table 3.1. Demographic data on Nenetses derived from household cards and family-household sheets of territorial formation expeditions

Demographic indicators	Taz *raion*	Pur *raion* (Forest Nenetses) of Verkhnepur village council	Nadymi *raion*	Iamal *raion*
Total Population	1402	490	1174	2935 (3045)*
- % men	51.0	53.5	51.6	49.9
- % women	49.0	46.5	48.4	50.1
Ratio of men to 100 women	104	115	106	99.5
% of children below 12 years old	25.6	27.3	36.8	33.3
- % boys	13.2	15.9	18.7	16
- % girls	12.4	11.4	18.1	17.3
Ratio of boys to 100 girls	106	139	103.7	91.9
% of teenagers of 12–16 years old	10.2	10.8	6.3	7.5
- % boys	5.5	6.5	3.4	4.0
- % girls	4.7	4.3	2.9	3.5
% of able to work (from older than 16 years old to ≈50 years old)	60.0	50.2	52.5	46.6**
- % men	31.0	25.9	28.5	24.1
- % women	29.0	24.3	24.0	22.5
Ratio of men to 100 women able to work	106.8	106.7	118.8	107.1
% of unable to work (sick, disabled, elderly)	4.2	11.6	4.3	12.4
- % men	1.4	5.1	0.9	5.8
- % women	2.8	6.5	3.4	6.6
Average age		men 24.9; women 27.2; both sexes 25.9		men 26.6; female 26.4; both sexes 26.5
Median		men 20; women 22; both sexes 20		men 22; women 22; both sexes 22
Total households	242	85	221	580
- households with children and teenagers	78.9	77.6	78.2	75.5
Average number of children and teenagers in a household	2.6	2.8	2.9	2.7

Table is based on: GAIaNAO 12-1-51-56; 90-91; 128; 135
Notes
* () Number received as a result of recalculation according to a method by I. I. Krupnik.
** Women – 17–50 years old; men – 17–59 years old.

used for cousins, nephews and nieces, and younger siblings. I have taken this agglomerating quality of Nenets kinship into account when compiling table 3.2, which gives a summary of the major family types among Iamal Peninsula and Forest Nenetses. Instead of limiting the representation to nuclear and extended families I specify extended families where cousins, uncles and aunts are declared, as well as more than one spouse.

Table 3.2. Family composition of Iamal and forest Nenetses according to data from territorial formation expeditions

Family type	Iamal Nenetses Total families	Iamal Nenetses Number of people	Forest Nenetses Total families	Forest Nenetses Number of people
Total families	557	2912	84	489
Complete families: simple	296	1448	40	197
1. Couple with children	258	1370	34	182
- more than one wife	17	121	4	33
2. Couple without children	38	78	6	15
- more than one wife	2	6	2	7
Complete families: composite	193	1224	33	255
3. Couple with children and in-laws	25	134	8	51
- more than one wife	1	6	—	—
4. Couple with children and grandchildren	2	15	—	—
5. Couple with children, grandchildren and the parents of one spouse	—	—	—	—
6. Couple with children, grandchildren and in-laws	2	15	—	—
7. Couple with children and the parents of one spouse	38	213	3	20
- more than one wife	2	14	—	—
8. Couple with children, the parents of one spouse and in-laws	21	150	4	28
- more than one wife	1	8	1	7
9. Couple without children and other relatives	36	136	3	16
- more than one wife	3	15	—	—
10. Two and more couples without children and other relatives:	69	561	15	140
- married brothers	17	133	3	26
- parents and married sons	51	418	12	114
- uncle and nephew	1	10	—	—
with more than one wife	6	54	3	36
Incomplete families: simple	46	163	7	23
11. Mother with children	34	119	5	17
12. Father with children	12	44	2	6
Incomplete families of various types	22	77	4	14
13. Mother (father) with children and grandchildren	2	10	1	6
14. Mother with children and one of her parents	1	7	—	—
15. Father with children and one of his parents	4	22	—	—
16. Mother (father) with children and relatives (grandchildren and one of spouses' parents altogether)	3	10	—	—

Due to the paucity of household cards from the Polar Census, my characterization of the Nenets family structure as it existed in the beginning of the
twentieth century is based on the materials of the land use expeditions of the
1930s. Most families (up to 53 per cent) in the first third of the twentieth century were two-generational and consisted of parents with children. Along with
complete nuclear families, there was quite a large portion of complex families
including various relatives (up to 39 per cent). Within the second group were
large families encompassing three generations: a married couple with their
children and one of their parents; a married couple with their children, one
of their parents, and collateral relatives (mother or father and sisters and/or
brothers of the head of household); or two or more married couples. According to the family-household cards, up to three married couples could reside together: parents (a head of household with his one or two wives) and their two
married sons. Sometimes two married brothers could have a joint household
and occupy different parts of the same *chum* or live in separate *chumy*. Such
large-family collectives had similar family structures to the patrilocal groups
that had existed among Nenetses in the past as described in sources of the seventeenth to nineteenth centuries (Gurvich and Dolgikh 1970: 197).

Incomplete families constituted a small fraction of the total number of
families, constituting approximately 12 per cent of Iamal and Forest Nenetses.
Families consisting of a mother with children dominated this group. A single
father with children or a mother with children and relatives or brothers and
sisters were less frequently observed. Due to the patriarchal nature of traditional Nenets society, it was the man who always headed incomplete family
households, usually a woman's older son or brother. In some cases, a head of
family could be as young as 10 years old.

Marriages were both monogamous and polygamous. Old age, illness of a
wife, her sterility or the lack of a workforce for a large household could be
the reasons for a man acquiring a second or sometimes a third wife. Only
prosperous Nenetses could afford this, however (Tarasov 1915; Khomich 1995:
172), and polygamy was considered the privilege of energetic and rich men
(Golovnev 2004: 44). A widow could occasionally become the second wife of
a married younger brother of her deceased husband (Mitusova 1929a–e: 15)
and often two sisters could be wives of the same man (GUTOGAT 695-1-78:
88v; Khomich 1995: 175). All marriages were patrilocal. After marriage the
wife moved to her husband's or his parents' *chum*. Nevertheless, the number of
polygamous marriages was gradually decreasing in the early twentieth century.
During the first half of the 1930s, 7 per cent of men among the Forest Nenetses
of the Verkhnepur Village Soviet (11 in total) and 3.6 per cent of Iamal Nenets
men of marriageable age (32 in total) had two or three wives. According to the
materials of the Iamal *kul'tbaza* in 1937, 40 out of 800 Nenets men of the Iamal

Peninsula had two or three wives (Brodnev n.d.: 61). No man was identified as having more than three wives.

Ethnographers observed that Nenetses preferred not to have big families (Zhitkov 1913: 219; Khomich 1995: 186). A head of family tended to separate his sons after their marriage into self-sufficient households (Khomich 1995: 186). Usually the youngest son would stay in the *chum* of his parents (Startsev 1930: 100).

The published data from the Polar Census can also shed light on differences in the average household size of families pursuing reindeer herding, hunting, and fishing. Reindeer-herding households were considerably larger than the other types (Terletskii 1932a: 13). According to archived the Community Indices (*poselennye spiski*), the average household size of settled Samoeds was 3.13 individuals, semi-settled households averaged 4.4 inhabitants, and nomadic reindeer-herding households averaged 5.4 (calculated from GASO 1812-2-184: 85). Forest Nenets households were larger than those of the Iamal and Taz tundra Nenets populations. The former had on average 7.2 individuals (GAIaNAO 12-1-6) while the Taz populations had 6.1 individuals (GAIaNAO 12-2-4~5) and the Iamal had 5.3 (GUIaNOMVK "Poselennye").

Furthermore, the households of Nenetses migrating within the interior tundra were larger than households located in coastal areas and in the basins of large rivers and lakes. Using the published regional data from the Polar Census the average size of households residing in the Peski area was only 4.8 individuals, for example, whereas Nenetses of Gydan-Taz sub-region, those of Gydan tundra, the Iavai and Bezimiannyi Peninsulas, and of the Taz River area averaged 5.9 individuals per household (calculated from USU 1928:164). At the same time, the average household size for Nizhnepurovskie and Nadymskie Nenetses was 5.7 and 5.3 persons respectively (ibid.). Of the Iamal Nenetses, smaller households were characteristic for Nenetses migrating within the area from the Iuribei River to the River Erkut, Lake Iarroto, and Novyi Port – an area of mostly reindeer-poor Samoeds who had to switch to fishing for subsistence (ibid.). These examples lead me to assume that decreases in household size among Nenetses related to changes in the activity type and transition to a more settled way of due to the loss of reindeer and consequent impoverishment. At the same time Ostiako-Samoeds, along with Samoeds inhabiting the shore areas, tended to have larger households (ibid.). The size of the reindeer-herding households, sometimes uniting several related families, was determined by whether subsistence activities required the collaboration of more than two families (Golovnev and Konev 1989: 80–81). In such cases, related families, forming a compound family, had an advantage.

According to the Iamal land-use expedition of 1932–33, of 68 households with 7 to 9 members, two thirds included two married couples or one couple and an incomplete family that included the mother or father of one of the couple as well as further siblings. Of 23 families with more than 10 persons, 17 consisted of two married couples (GAIaNAO 12-1-51-56). A similar situation is observable from the Family Lists (*posemeinye spiski*) for the Forest Nenets of Verkhnepur Village Soviet in 1935 (GAIaNAO 12-1-128). There the average size of a compound family was almost 1.5 times larger than the size of a simple one. For Iamal Nenetses these family types averaged 6.3 and 5.3 persons respectively, for the Forest Nenets, 7.7 and 5.3 respectively (calculated from table 3.2). The average size of families consisting of two or more couples was 8.1 for Iamal Nenetses, and 9.3 for Forest Nenetses (calculated from table 3.2). Up to 16 persons could live in a household simultaneously, up to 19 persons for Taz Nenetses (table 3.3).

Due to high child mortality rates, most families had only a few children (Khomich 1995: 188; GUTOGAT 695-1-78: 30). In the data from the 1930s, a higher number of children could be found in larger households with a complex composition such as polygamous marriages or the second marriage of widowed man. The average number of children in simple families as well as compound families with one married couple was lower than that in the families with two or more couples. Iamal Nenetses had an average of 2.8 children per nuclear family, and Forest Nenetses had 2.5, while complex families with two or more couples had 3.2 and 3.7 children respectively (calculated from GAIaNAO 12-1-51-56, 128). These numbers demonstrate insignificant growth in the rate of reproduction by the Nenets population, in contradiction to the aggregate results.[16]

The new census household data from the 1920s and 1930s is also important for the fact that it began to register births and deaths. Nenets seem to have been strongly opposed to the registration of births and deaths (Kopylov 1994: 128,

Table 3.3. Distribution of Nenets households according to number of people derived from household cards and family-household sheets of territorial formation expeditions

Expeditions	*raion*	Number of households by the number of individuals in each											
		1	2	3	4	5	6	7	8	9	10 and more	Max N of people	Ave. N of people
Tazovsko-Pur expedition, 1934–1935	Taz *raion*	5	7	36	40	48	28	17	26	16	19	19	5.8
	Pur *raion**	1	7	13	11	15	7	11	7	3	10	16	5.7
Nadym expedition, 1933–1934	Nadym *raion*	10	17	34	31	28	37	21	22	7	14	14	5.3
Iamal north expedition, 1932–1933	Iamal *raion*	23	59	84	103	90	62	77	25	34	23	16	5.06

*Data for Verkhnepur village council

144, 153). The refusal to register the dead was explained on religious grounds. According to my own research in Nadym district in 2006, according to the traditional Nenets beliefs, the name of a deceased person was not allowed to be said out loud as it may disturb the dead person, who would then lift his or her head. It was also held that speaking the name of a dead person aloud would hurt him or her (Khomich 2005: 464). The deceased were usually referred to as 'the missing one' or 'our one who has gone' (Tokhole 1996: 26; Lar 2003: 68). It was considered offensive to pronounce the name of a dead person in the presence of their relatives (Khariuchi 2001: 154). In relation to this taboo, while it was customary for Forest Nenets to give a new name to every child, if one of two persons with the same name died, the second had to change their name (Khomich 1976: 117).

The Polar Census also provided the very first data on the birth and mortality rates for the Obdor Samoeds taken from a 98.8 per cent sample (GASO 1812-2-184: 85). These valuable materials are practically the only source of data showing Nenets birth and death rates in the first half of the twentieth century (Terletskii 1932a: 47). My own study of modern municipal registration archives (ZAGS) confirms their uniqueness since even this institution did not collect data on Nenets at that time (GAIaNAO 34-1: 2, 66, 77, and others). Needless to say, the number of registered births and deaths was still underestimated (Lebedev and Kolupaeva 1929: 32; Terletskii 1932a: 46). Recalculating the raw data using P. E. Terletskii's method of taking data over a two year period (in this case from 1 October 1924 to 30 September 1926) confirms his hypothesis that settled peoples had a high natural growth rate. The only exception to this were the Zyrians whose natural growth coefficient was lower than that of the neighbouring groups, even though only 25.7 per cent of their population was classified as nomadic (GASO 1812-2-184: 85). The Obdor Samoeds, with 96.4 per cent of their people being nomadic, had a characteristically low birth rate of 41.9 per cent and a death rate of 14.5. Their rate of natural increase (27.5) took third place after the Russians and the Ostiaks. They were the only group to have a negative growth among the settled and semi-settled population and a positive growth rate among the nomads (table 3.4).

Lebedev pointed out the incompleteness of mortality data on the nomadic population of Obdor and Berezov districts. Compiling the tables of mortality for Ural *oblast* in 1924–1927, he found that, because of this data, mortality in Tobol'sk okrug was underestimated (Lebedev and Kolupaeva 1929: 32). Thus, the relatively high natural growth rate is likely to be a result of undercounted deaths. The presence of a high birth rate and low life expectancy among working-age population and high level of child mortality can be inferred from the percentage cohort distributions reported for four regional populations (table 3.1, middle rows). All four regional groups show a very low proportion of elderly ('not employable') people of between 4 and 12 per cent, suggesting a low

Table 3.4. Indicators of birth and death rates and natural increase of the Obdor *raion* population according to the Polar Census data of 1926/27

Population		Birth rate	Death rate	Infant death rate	Natural increase
Samoeds		41.9	14.5	4.8	27.5
Zyrians		53.5	29.2	10.4	24.3
Ostiaks		44.2	14.8	4.3	29.3
Russians		52.5	20.7	8.8	31.8
Settled and semi-settled	Samoeds	22.2	25.9	7.4	−7.4
	Zyrians	57.9	34.4	12.3	23.5
	Ostiaks	44.6	14.8	4.0	29.8
	Russians	53.4	21.1	8.9	32.3
Nomadic	Samoeds	42.3	14.26	4.8	28.1
	Zyrians	40.8	14.1	4.9	26.7
	Ostiaks	41.4	14.6	6.0	26.7
	Russians				

Calculated from average data from 1 October 1924 to 30 September 1926.
GASO 1812-2-184: 85-86.

life expectancy (if a level of 20 per cent is standard for urban populations). The proportion of the population between 0 and 16 years in all regions is close to 40 per cent, suggesting a high birth rate. If we turn to the aggregate the data of the All-Union Census of 1926, 36.9 per cent of their population consisted of children up to 14 years of age, 54 per cent of the population were of an employable age (from 15 to 54 years), and 8.6 per cent were elderly. This progressive structure is also suggested by the data in figure 3.7. All of this data suggests that the age structure of the Nenetses in this region of Siberia was progressive.

Conclusion

The introduction of new principles of population accounting in the first quarter of the twentieth century allowed the collection of statistical information about Nenetses that was qualitatively different from that in the previous period. However, the new censuses and administrative registers did not immediately solve the problem of getting reliable and complete demographic data. Due to traditional Nenets beliefs and language differences, the information obtained from respondents was distorted, particularly where an enumerator's language fluency was limited. The situation was further complicated by the Nenets unwillingness and lack of understanding of the necessity to provide information about themselves and their families to an outsider. The nomadic way of life and seasonal migration further complicated population accounting. Once the data was analysed in the regional centres, the complex way that it was aggregated often led to an oversimplification of territorial patterns among Nenetses. This analysis of various statistical and ethnographic data for the given time period reveals that the high absolute growth of the Nenets population presented in the aggregate data is an artefact of a better enumeration strategy and certain simplifications in the way that identity groups were grouped together. When we re-calculate the census results using household-level nominal records, primarily from the 1930s but also from the Polar Census, the basic demographic parameters of family size, fertility and mortality suggest that Nenetses had a simple reproduction rate which would have led to a constant population size, and not a burgeoning one. This finding agrees with the classic models of nomadic populations.

Translated by Olga Pak

Notes

1. If we compare data for all Nenets populations in Western Siberia from 1897 to 1939 we find an astonishing level of growth of 300 per cent over 42 years.
2. The family-household forms were collected under name of the head of household and have the following information: address (*raion, sel'sovet* and settlement), type of household (nomadic, semi-nomadic or settled), family composition, household economic activities and migration routes followed. For each family member there are records on position within the family, sex, age, nationality, literacy, disability and incapability of work, and primary occupation. I analysed 580 such forms collected in expeditions in 1932 and 1933 among the population of the Southern-Iamal', Iarsalin, Neitin, Tambei, and Teutei Village Soviets, settlements of Kutop'iugan, Nangi, Vanuito, Vorkuta, Khe, Khadytta, Puiko, and Iada in Iamal Okrug (GAIaNAO 12-1-51 & 56). The household registration cards were effectively shorter versions of the family-household forms. They were filled out in the name of the head of household. They contain information on the migration routes and economic activities of a household. The demographic profile includes the number of people in a household, specifying teenagers of 12 to 16 years old and children under 12, those able to work and the disabled, all divided according to gender. In the GAIaNO, I identified 221 household registration cards collected during the Nadymskaia Expedition of 1933–1934 (12-1-90 & 91) and 327 cards of the Tazovsko-Purovskaia Expedition of 1934–1935 (12-1-128 & 135).
3. From the seventeenth to nineteenth centuries, the European Nenetses were known as the Arkhangelogorodsk Samoeds.
4. Nenetses from Taz *volost'* who communicated with Enets became officially called Iuraks in the nineteenth century (Vasil'ev 1979: 162). The term 'Iurak' translates as 'Nenets' in the Enets language (*diurak kasa*) and the Nganasan language (*diuriake*).
5. Among the European Nenetses the term *nenets* translates as 'person'. Among the eastern groups (Iamal, part of the Gydan, and Enisei groups) the term *nenei nenets* means 'real, original person'. The term *khasava* (person, man) is also used (Kostikov 1930: 115; Prokof'eva 1956: 608; Tereshchenko 1965: 94, 214). The term *neshchang* among forest Nenetses is phonetically different from the other names.
6. Dunin-Gorkavich (1909: 106–16) further subdivides Nizovye Samoeds into the Samoeds of the Nyda River; those of the Taz Bay (Nial-Pay, Iam-Khazovo); those of the

Taz River (Tazu-Iam-Khazovo); those of the lower riches of the Pur River (Puraiam-Khazovo) and the Stepnye Samoeds (Enisei Samoeds).

7. In folklore texts, Nenets inhabiting the Taz Tundra and the Gydan Peninsula were called Tasinii (Tasinyangy) in opposition to the so-called 'Pe Ter', a name referring to Iamal Nenetses, Ural Nenetses and those living to the west of the Urals. Both terms corresponded to Nizovye and Kamennye Samoeds (Khomich 1976: 65; 1995: 28).

8. In 1940, Ostiako-Vogul' National Okrug was renamed Khanty-Mansiiskii. In 1977, according to the new constitution of the USSR, national okrugs were given the status of autonomous okrugs.

9. Obdor raion was formed from the northern part of Berezov *uezd* with the addition of the lower reaches of the Taz River and some territory of the Gydan Peninsula (from Enisei Guberniia). In 1930, with the formation of Iamal (Nenets) National *okrug* within the borders of Ural *oblast'* and with its centre in Obdorsk its territory included Obdor *raion* (except the territory of Shuryshkar raion), the upper reaches of the Pur River (from Surgut raion) and peninsulas of the Arctic Ocean. In the west, Iamal *okrug* bordered upon the Nenets National *okrug* of Northern *krai* and Komi Autonomous *oblast'*. In the east it adjoined Turukhansk raion of Eastern Siberian *krai*. The southern border ran 'along the line of the beginning of the mass habitat of the Ostiak population south from Obdorsk and toward the Synia river, along the watershed of the Polui river and the Kunovat-Iugan area including the whole of the Nadym and Nyda river systems as well as the lower courses of the rivers Pur and Taz' (Kopylov 1994: 180). In January 1934 Iamal (Nenets) *okrug* was incorporated into Ob'-Irtysh *oblast'*; in December 1934, it became a part of Omsk *oblast'* and in August 1944 it joined Tiumen' *oblast'*.

10. Later censuses also emphasized self-identification (GASO 1812-2-191: 2; Pod"iachikh 1957: 31; Kozlov 1969: 79–80).

11. To reconstruct the population size on the basis of the number of households in the first half of the twentieth century, I used the index of the average family size provided by Krupnik as a result of his analysis of the 1926/1927 Polar Census and of materials of the use-of-land expeditions in Iamal raion from 1934 to 1935 (Krupnik 2000: 148). This indicator also appears in reports referring to the first half of the twentieth century (GAIaNAO 12-1-189: 24v).

12. Twenty-nine less than the 3,519 put forward by Krupnik (2000: 145).

13. According to information provided by Dolgikh, in reference to Evladov's oral report, the Iamal expedition of 1928–1929 counted 1,243 families (Dolgikh 1970: 67; Evladov 1992: 253, 256).

14. From the seventeenth to the nineteenth centuries, the Forest Nenetses belonged to the *iasak* paying population of Kazym *volost'* of Berezov *uezd* and therefore the name Kazym Samoed became associated with them.

15. I noted such instances in my own fieldwork in Pur raion in 2005 and Nadym raion in 2005–2006.

16. The specification of the rate of reproduction relative to the level of child mortality was analysed according to the scale of V. A. Borisov (1987: 203). According to him, a simple population structure is guaranteed if families with average and large numbers of children constitute no more than 51 per cent of the population. In other words, the average family size should be 2.6 children. The final line of table 3.1 shows values close to or a little above that figure.

4 | Undaunted Courage: The Polar Census in the Obdor Region

Elena M. Glavatskaya

Introduction

The Obdor region of northwestern Siberia is unique for its remoteness, severe climate conditions, low population density and relatively slow history of Russian settlement. It was also famous for its role in the Russian fur trade starting in the eleventh century and becoming prominent from the sixteenth to early twentieth centuries. The region's status as a compact, semi-autonomous and relatively isolated territory makes it special among other Russian territories and lends a peculiar flavour to its ethnic history. By the late nineteenth and early twentieth centuries, several outstanding scholars had conducted field research among the indigenous people. Zuev (1947), Castrén (1853–1858), Beliavskii (1833), V. Shavrov (1871), and others left valuable ethnographic descriptions. Pápay (1988–1995) collected materials on Khant and Nenets folklore and mythology. Dunin-Gorkavich (1904) and Patkanov (1911a, 1911b) published extensive materials on the statistics and ethnography of the region. However, the Ural expedition of the Polar Census, in 1926 and 1927, in contrast to earlier forays, gave the first complete and universal survey of every Obdor household based on face-to-face interviews. Its field-based method yielded rich data not only on demography but on economy, religion, medicine and geography. The enumerators recorded extensive data on the everyday life of Obdor indigenous peoples on the eve of the dramatic social changes imposed by Soviet power in the late 1920s.

Here I will make use of the recently discovered primary records of several Census parties working in the Obdor region which our team discovered and digitised in two regional archives in the cities of Ekaterinburg and Tobol'sk. I will pay particular attention to the descriptions of trading-posts (*blanki faktorii*) and to the schedules of individual family budgets (*biudzhetnye blanki*) which represent a unique set of documents seemingly not present in other regions of Russia. One of my preliminary conclusions is that while the standard census forms were printed in Moscow, the enumerators of the Ural expedition showed much initiative, creativity and flexibility, which resulted in a larger variety of documents and the documentation of a wider range of topics than their Moscow supervisors had anticipated. Their efforts made this archive an interesting source for ethnohistorical work.

This chapter contains three related sections. First, I present a brief introduction into the Obdor region and its ethnic history. Next I summarise the Russian tradition of identifying and enumerating indigenous peoples in this region with a focus on the Polar Census: its organization and uniqueness, and its enumerators. Finally, I analyse some of the primary sources for this region in order to reconstruct indigenous life as it was seen and recorded by the enumerators.

The Obdor Region from a Bird's-Eye View

As outlined by Elena Volzhanina in chapter 3, the territory of the Obdor region represents the tundra part of western Siberia and is formed by the eastern slope of the Polar Urals, the Iamal Peninsula, part of the Gydan Peninsula, the gulfs of the Ob´ and Taz Rivers together with the Nadym, Pur and Taz River basins. It received its name from the settlement of Obdorsk (today's Salekhard), a fortress founded by the Russians in 1595 or 1596 on the site of an Ostiak (Khant) fortress-town at the mouth of the Ob´ River known as Polnovat-Vosh. In Tsarist Russia, the region was part of Berezov *uezd* [district] and subordinate to a governor located in Tobol´sk. In the early Soviet period, the Obdor region was made into Tobol´sk *okrug* within Ural *oblast´*. Today, the region's territory roughly corresponds to that of the Iamalo-Nenets Autonomous *okrug* with its capital in Salekhard (Minenko 1975: 217–23; Kopylov 1994; Poberezhnikov 2005: 19–34) (see fig 3.1 in the previous chapter).

According to the Khants and Nenetses (formerly known as Ostiaks and Samoeds, respectively) a people known as Sikhirtia lived on the territory before Russians arrived. One of the latest hypotheses on the origin of Sikhirtia suggests that they were Ugro-Samoedish settlers of Western Siberia who moved to the northern tundra in the sixth century, bringing reindeer herding and metallurgy to the region (N. Fedorova 2000: 45–66). Sikhirtia lived in coastal areas where they took advantage of the driftwood necessary to build their buildings. Their metal-fashioning skills and produced artifacts made them distinct from other peoples who dwelled in the Obdor region and are used to distinguish their sites archaeologically today. The arrival in the region of different metal items produced by Russians made the skills of Sikhirtia unnecessary and they, as Khant folklore puts it, 'disappeared under ground' (ibid., 66). This trade-related disappearance of a people perhaps explains why there is no record whatsoever on the Sikhirtia in Russian sources. It is interesting that even from the earliest times, the Obdor region's ethnic history was affected by trade to the point that it defined its ethnic composition.

Russian traders who penetrated beyond the Ural mountains in the eleventh century brought back myths about a 'Midnight country', rich with furs, where 'squirrels and reindeers fall from heaven' (Machinskii 1986). Russian fur traders from the Novgorod republic arranged sporadic trade expeditions and exchanged metal goods for furs with local hunters. Subsequently, the Obdor region, due to its geographical location became one of the earlier gateways for the Russian colonization of Siberia.

With the founding of the Obdor fortress, which followed several trade expeditions and successful military raids by the Moscow state into the area, the whole territory became known as the Obdor *kniazhestvo* [principality]. Its people were proclaimed tax subjects of the Russian tsar and forced to pay *iasak* – a fur-tax collected most often in sable pelts. However, the Obdor principality kept a semi-independent political and economic status. The Ostiak princes of Obdor were officially incorporated into the structure of Russian society as noblemen and were recognized as rulers over their people and territories until the eve of the nineteenth century (Bakhrushin 1955; Minenko 1975; Kopylov 1994; Perevalova 2004). In return they had to collect *iasak* from their own people and the neighboring groups of Samoeds. Their intensive fur-based tax and trade with the Russians forced the indigenous hunters to travel longer and longer distances in order to obtain furs of the required quality and quantity. Given that sledges pulled by reindeer were the main transport, the evolving fur market encouraged the intensification of reindeer herding among Obdor indigenous peoples. The warlike Obdor princes managed to spread their power over the tundra Samoeds living as far east as the Taz River gulf (Bakhrushin 1955: 134). The remote location and severe northern climate of the Obdor region slowed down Russian settlement in the area. It did not, however, prevent the arrival of Zyrians (contemporary Komi), who started migrating into the area in the seventeenth century and adopting local reindeer herding traditions.

The Russian government's attempt to modernize this region, and others across Siberia, is associated with Count Speranskii's 1822 *Ustav ob upravlenii inorodtsev* [Regulations Concerning the Management of Indigenous Peoples] (Ustav 1999). The new administrative system subdivided the indigenous peoples of Siberia into three separate categories: settled, nomadic, and 'wandering' (*brodiachie*). Those referred to as 'settled' were to be incorporated into Russian peasant communities, while the others were to be allowed to keep their indigenous institutions. The Ustav classified the Obdor Samoeds and Ostiaks as 'wandering' and thus eligible to preserve their traditional institutions. The Ustav, for example, legitimized traditional religious practices for the nomadic Obdor Ostiaks and Samoeds with the statement that 'wandering non-

Figure 4.1. A family of Samoeds in the far northern area of Ural *oblast'* 1926 by L. Surin
GASO 'Kollektsiia Surina' – 785:048

Christians may freely observe their beliefs and worship their gods' (ibid., 89). While some of the Obdor princes were introduced to Christianity already early in the seventeenth century, the process of Christianization started much later and never resulted in mass baptism. The resistance of the Obdor Ostiaks and Samoeds to baptism slowed down the expansion of Christianity in the north. The Russian Orthodox Church did its best to adapt Christian rites to make it more relevant to northern peoples. It approved certain variations to ritual practice, ritual time and ritual space, which were distinct from the Russian Orthodox Church canons (Glavatskaia 2005a). This flexibility further enhanced the autonomy of the Obdor region and explains the prevalence of non-Christian rituals in the documents of the Polar Census.

A History of the Enumeration of the Indigenous Peoples of the Obdor Region

The enumeration of the Obdor region started with the Russian colonization of the area and was driven by taxation. People whom we would today describe as indigenous peoples were given a special social status (*soslovie*) as the 'Tsar's *iasak* people' [*gosudarevy iasachnye liudi*]. This was a common status shared by other Siberian peoples who hunted and thus were able to pay the fur-tax. The tribute collectors obtained their information on the local population from local elites and kept their records in *iasak* books. The earliest *iasak* book of Berezov *uezd*, which included Obdor principality, was dated 1629. The Russian administration also distinguished groups of people by their language. The peoples of the Obdor region were recorded as the Tsar's *iasak* Ostiaks and Samoeds. The books also recorded a person's name and age, the quantity and type of fur-pelts submitted, and information about former and current debts. However, the problem is that the *iasak* books recorded only adult male taxpayers and not women or children. Today, most surviving *iasak* books can be found in Moscow at the RGADA (Rossiiskii Gosudarstvennyi Arkhiv Drevnikh Aktov). Dolgikh (1960) has provided the most authoritative analysis of these books.

Peter I reformed the system of taxation in the beginning of the eighteenth century and introduced a unified state enumeration system called 'State revisions' [*gosudarstvennye revizii*]. During a revision, the community leaders provided information to the state agents, who then recorded them in 'Revision Notes' [*revizskie skazki*]. The new system was much more detailed in that it listed all household members and how they were related to the head of the household. The notes recorded the *iasak*-payer's name, patronymic, surname, age and language. Language was the main marker to distinguish one people from other. It also provided the same information on the *iasak*-payer's wife but also included her place of birth and the name of her closest male relative. For the children in the household the notes recorded only their names and either their age or birth dates. The names of dead relatives and their dates of death were also recorded. The data collected in the Revision Notes gave a reliable basis for detailed demographical studies of the population dynamics of the Obdor region in the eighteenth and nineteenth centuries (Dolgikh 1960; Sokolova 1983; Vasil'ev 1979; Krupnik 2000). Most Revision Notes for the Obdor region are kept in Tobol'sk in the GUTOGAT Archive.

In 1897, the first general Russian census took place. This marked a new stage in the process of enumeration. Enumerators used a standard form that contained the following information: surname, name and patronymic, relation to the head of the household, age, gender, marital status, social status, places of birth and permanent residence, religion, native language, literacy and occupation. This census still lacked a question on national identity. Following established traditions, language still served as the main quality to distinguish people despite the fact that spoken language and ethnicity did not necessarily go together in the Russian Empire (Patkanov 1911a, 1911b; Dunin-Gorkavich 1904; Cadiot 2005). In the next part of this chapter I will show that some indigenous people of the Obdor region, while speaking Samoed (Nenets), nevertheless considered themselves Ostiaks (Khants) or Zyrians (Komi).

The next Russian general census was postponed several times first due to the Russo-Japanese War, then the Revolution of 1905, and then because of World War I and the two revolutions in 1917. In 1920, however, the new Soviet government tried to conduct a federal census. The 1920 census form had 18 questions, and included a question on nationality for the first time. The census took place during the unstable conditions of the civil war and therefore was not completed in all territories. The coverage of the Obdor region was incomplete. It was only by 1926 that the Soviet state was ready to collect complete data on the population to assist the planning of economic development.

As if to make up for the partial qualities of the earlier census, the Polar Census of 1926/27 was designed to thoroughly describe every indigenous household including its composition, economy and everyday life. The Polar Census in the Ural region was made up of several large and complex expedition parties. No other country had attempted an undertaking as ambitious as this before. The records of this census are especially valuable since they were gathered at a time when socialist reforms had not yet influenced the traditional life styles of northern peoples.

The census in the Ural *oblast'*, which included the Obdor region, was conducted by the Ural expedition under supervision of Statistical Administration of Ural *oblast'*. I have analysed its unique history and organising principles elsewhere (Glavatskaia 2005b: 16–19). Here I focus upon the primary materials for the Obdor region. These consist of a very partial sample of household cards and community diaries, and a unique set of budgetary questionnaires and descriptions of trading posts. The surviving primary materials for the Obdor region are described in table 4.1.

The material recorded in the household cards and the community diaries was common throughout the north. In addition to these main instruments the members of the Ural expedition were asked to collect data on the household budgets of selected reindeer-herding families. The enumerators had to pick up and register a certain amount of 'typical' households (judged in terms of prosperity) which were to be stratified on the basis of their herd size. Those with

Table 4.1. Inventory of documents filed and discovered from the four Obdor Polar Census parties of the Ural Polar Census expedition

	Document class	Number of items submitted (GASO 1812-2-181(4): 215-217v)	Found in archives
1	Region forms	1	—
2	Community Summaries (PI)	12	5
3	Community diaries (PB)	138	50
4	Household lists (SKh)	178	4
5	Household cards (PK)	3,545	75
6	Budget cards (BB)	9	9
7	Economy cards	6	—
8	Trade cards (TK)	20	20
9	Descriptions of trading posts (FB)	29	29
10	Sketch maps	70	4
11	Photographs	257	Approx. 10

more than 1,500 reindeer were to be classified as rich; those with more than 500 reindeer as wealthy; those with 100–500 as small herd owners; and if they had less than 100, as poor (GASO 1812-2-181.01: 38). The information they collected included household property, reindeers, dogs, constructions and tents, sledges and skis, implements and tools, kitchen utensils and male/female clothing (specifying if they were sewn at home or purchased). The enumerators filled this information into a specially designed Budget Questionnaire. These documents also contain comprehensive information on the annual family catch of fish and other animals, what would be consumed (whether raw or cooked) and what would be sold. In addition there was information about how much work time they would spend, and the male/female labour time distribution (GASO 1812-2-191). I will return to these documents in the next section.

Four separate parties conducted the census among the nomadic people in the Obdor region. Two students, Lebedev and Voznesenskii, an interpreter Zotov, and the leader Vladimirtsev made up the Iamal Party. Their team was attacked by wolves on the very first day of their work on 28 November 1926. The expedition lost most of its transport reindeer and had to follow its route towards the Shchuch´ia River trade posts with only one light sledge and no tent (GASO 1812-2-181.04: 6v; Glavatskaia 2006).

The Taz expedition consisted of an agronomist with some experience in statistics, P. Iordanskii, and two enumerators – an exiled lawyer, P. Brzhezinskii, and local resident Vitiazev (GASO 1812-2-181.01: 210–210v; Glavatskaia 2006). Their work was also delayed by problems in hiring guides with transport reindeer due to a recent epidemic that affected local herds. To add to their misfortune, one of the enumerators, P. Brzhezinskii, was severely wounded by a magnesium explosion while he was taking pictures (GASO 1812-2-181.04: 4v, 6; Glavatskaia 2006).

Raisa Pavlovna Mitusova, a professional ethnographer from the Russian Museum of Ethnography in Leningrad, headed the Nadym-Polui expedition.[1] The expedition consisted of two enumerators – the student ethnographer Natal´ia Kotovshchikova from Leningrad[2] and the journalist Iurkevich from Sverdlovsk. The two interpreters also provided the expedition with transport and tents. This group had to deal with several obstacles as well: an unusually snowy winter, the underestimation of distances between settlements, and wolf attacks. Additionally, the leader Raisa Mitusova got pneumonia just after her late arrival in Obdorsk and could not undertake overland journeys. As a result she did most of her surveys at the trading posts at Nore and Khe (GASO 1812-2-181.04: 3v, 5v; Glavatskaia 2006).

The Syne-Kunevat expedition was the smallest. It consisted of single enumerator Grigorii Arteev, who was a school teacher from Obdor. He had no need of an interpreter and, being familiar with local Zyrians and Samoeds, enjoyed their hospitality and often received help with transportation.

The enumerators surveying the Obdor also took on a nomadic lifestyle. In an area with almost no infrastructure, they had to carry everything they would need during their long journeys on the tundra. Each expedition member was provisioned with enough food to last for at least a month. Their rations included frozen bread, meat, smoked food, cereal rolls, butter, tea, sugar, caramel, dried fruit, mustard, pepper, salt, bay leaves, vinegar, tobacco, soap, citric acid and cranberry extract (to prevent scurvy) (GASO 1812-2-181.04: 8). Enumerators often exchanged their purchased food with the local people for fresh meat and fish (GASO 1812-2-181.04: 13). They also bought local fur clothes. Each enumerator and interpreter was also issued with one bottle per month of vodka 'bread wine', and a first-aid kit (GASO 1812-2-181.04: 8, 8v). The head of the census Leonid Shul'ts wrote in his report that it would have been better if they had more medical supplies so that they could help not only themselves but also the local people. He recognised that such assistance often created goodwill towards their work (GASO 1812-2-181.04: 13v).

There were very few instances recorded of residents refusing to speak with enumerators. In most cases all residents provided basic information on family composition, the nomadic cycle, the equipment held by the household, and their diet. On the whole, people with fewer reindeer were more willing to provide information on the size of their herds whereas those with many reindeer usually tried to conceal the actual amount which enumerators had to discover by other means. The census in Ural *oblast'* was planned to run from 26 November 1926 to April 1927 (GASO 677-1-49: 171).

The Obdor Region as Represented in the Polar Census Forms

The primary data contained in the surviving household cards and the collection of community diaries, descriptions of trading posts, and household-budget cards yields rich data on the lives of indigenous people. For my interpretations on the social dimensions, I will use data primarily from household budget cards for the Obdor region (GASO 1812-2-191: 22–75), supplemented by the aggregated data published by the Central statistical body (TsSU 1928 and 1929). To interpret the ethnic dimension, I will use data from the 75 household cards in GUTOGAT (690-1-49; 690-1-54) which were compiled mostly by the Iamal expedition (and partially by the Nadymo-Polui expedition) representing approximately a 2 per cent sample of the population,[3] supplemented by aggregated data. My summary of the economic dimension is based on a collection describing trading posts, some of which were completed by the renowned ethnographer Mitusova (GASO 1812-2-187; GASO 1812-2-188). Finally, for the analysis of the religious dimension I have used information contained in a nearly complete collection of community diaries for the region, which contained a section on local religious practice, and materials from the descriptions of trading posts.

Social Dimension

The population of the Obdor region belonged to six village councils or *sel´sovety*. As table 4.2 clarifies, 55 per cent of the population was classified as nomadic.

The published aggregate statistics show that literacy level among the population was not high. Only 1,133 men and 585 women in the region were able to read and write. Russians made up 66 per cent of the literate residents while only 10 per cent of the indigenous peoples were literate. If the focus is changed to gender, 66 per cent of the men were literate but only 4 per cent of the women (TsSU 1929: 110–111). Nearly half the population, 9,474 people, were employed outside their own household. The main activities were the same for men and women: agriculture, reindeer herding, fishing, sea hunting, hunting, transportation, trade and craft. Reindeer herding, fishing and hunting prevailed.

The family budgets recorded by the enumerators provide a rich insight into the property of indigenous people, their access to European trade goods, and to everyday life. The form was designed to be applied selectively to a small proportion of households from each region with five households representing each economic group. Each form consisted of five folios and in structure is very similar to that of the household card. Information on family composition, dwellings and other buildings, and employment of wage labour (sections 1–3) is almost exactly the same as the standard card. Information on household equipment and the consumption of trade goods (sections 4–10) are not only unique for the amount of detail collected on how an item was purchased (and if it was later gifted, broken or sold) but also on the number of hours spent in different sectors of the household economy. This broad concept of a budget would today be described as a combination of a time budget summary and a credit-debit accounting of every item in a household. It is not surprising that few of these forms were filled out.

The Obdor enumerators produced nine budget descriptions. Among these nine registered households, four households were considered poor, three 'middle' income, and two prosperous (*zazhitochnye*) (GASO 1812-2-191). Poor households had between 2 and 32 reindeer. Those with a middle income

Table 4.2. The number of *sel´sovety*, settlement, households and people by their nomadic or settled status (TsSU 1928 (vol 4): 97)

Type of economy	Village Soviets	Settlements	Households	%	Population	%
Settled	6	161	1,886	52	8,058	45
Nomadic	0	201	1,751	48	9,645	55
Total	6	362	3,637	100	17,703	100

had from 26 to 157 reindeer. Prosperous households had between 148 and 701 reindeer. It is evident that this local classification was different from the instructions sent out centrally, as mentioned above. This speaks to the fact that local enumerators did not blindly follow central patterns but instead corrected and improved the procedures when they felt the need. The budget forms show an interesting direct correlation between a household's size and its wealth. Those referred to as prosperous had between 7 and 17 members. Presumably the larger numbers of people were necessary to help to take care of their large herds. All families, whether poor or wealthy, lived in conical lodges labelled as *chumy* by the Russians. Their inventory of tools usually consisted of 1 to 2 axes, a saw, hammer, *peshnia* [ice axe] and scraper. Middle and prosperous households had up to 20 sledges. The hunting equipment included guns and traps of different types. While well-to-do herders had 3 to 4 guns, the poor did not have more than one and usually hunted with traps (for example GASO 1812-2-191: 64–69). Fishing was done using seines and nets. Reindeer meat (raw or boiled) and fish formed the main part of people's diet irrespective of whether they were rich or poor. Meat from wild animals was usually given to dogs. Cooking equipment consisted mainly of cups and saucers, a couple of cast-iron pots and copper kettles and sometimes birch-bark containers. The clothes were usually home-made of reindeer skins. The richer families purchased clothes more often than others.

Ethnic Dimension

According to the published data, ten different nationalities lived together on the territory of the Obdor region. There were Slavic peoples such as Belorussians, Ukrainians, Poles and Russians; Altaic people represented by Tatars; Ural (indigenous) peoples such as Zyrians, Votiaks (Udmurts), Ostiaks (Khants), Samoeds (Nenetses) and Iuraks. Samoeds made up nearly half the population; Ostiaks and Zyrians made up one-fourth; Russians were not more than 8 per cent; and the Iuraks made up 1 per cent. Other peoples made up less than 1 per cent. An analysis of the 75 household cards provides an extra dimension of detail to this question.

In addition to a person's nationality, the household card registered the person's 'tribal' identity (*plemia*), which sometimes specified a hyphenated mixed identity: 'zyriano-samoed', 'ostiako-samoed' or a regional identity such as 'mountain' or 'plain' Samoed. The enumerators were forewarned that nationality and language might not coincide. In this respect it is interesting to look at the case of an Ostiak household head who reported his native language as Samoed. The enumerator recorded him as a 'Samoedified Ostiak' in the 'tribal' cell in order to emphasise his strong relationships with the majority Samoed population around him (GUTOGAT 690-1-36: 74–77).

Table 4.3. Population of the Obdor region according to nationality and language (TsSU 1928: 254–255)

Nationality	Male	Female	Total	%	Native language	Male	Female	Total	%
Samoeds	4,072	3,922	7,994	45	Samoed	4,237	3,988	8,225	103
Ostiaks	2,249	2,019	4,268	24	Ostiak	2,244	1,891	4,135	96
Zyrians	1,780	1,931	3,711	21	Zyrian	1,965	2,093	4,058	122
Russians	708	662	1,370	8	Russian	729	674	1,403	102
Iuraks	130	95	225	1	Iurak	—	—	—	—
Tatars	22	6	28	—	Tatar	19	5	24	85
Poles	7	5	12	—	Polish	6	5	11	92
Byelorussians	2	1	3	—	Byelorussian	0	0	0	0
Ukrainians	1	2	3	—	Ukrainian	1	3	4	133
Votiaks	1	0	1	—	Votiak	1	0	1	100
Total			17,615						

Zyrian, Nenets and Russian languages dominated in the region. Many people with other identities considered those languages their native ones (table 4.3).

According to the official instructions, enumerators were instructed to record nationality as it was stated directly by an informant. If a person could not answer the question, the mother's nationality would be recorded (GUTO-GAT 695-1-191: 5v). However, as it was already shown above, the enumerators did not always follow these instructions. They often recorded children as having the same identities as their fathers. In some families, sons were recorded as having their father's identity and daughters as having the identity of their mother (GUTOGAT 690-1-36: 8–11, 60–64, 70–73; GUTOGAT 690-1-49: 15–19, 76–80).

Polygamous marriages were a distinguishing feature of Obdor region families. Although the Orthodox Church prohibited them, not all of the population was baptised and some people held onto their traditions. The surviving materials show the existence of three such families registered either as Samoeds or Samoedified Ostiaks (GUTOGAT 690-1-36: 35–38; 690-1-49: 10–14, 15–19). In all three cases men were married to two women. The significant age difference between the husband and older wife can be explained by the fact that either the men themselves, or their parents, preferred that they marry experienced women who were able to run the household. Also, a man was often responsible to care for a widow in the event of the death of his elder brother.

It is often stated in the literature that Samoeds were a privileged ethnic group in the territory of the Obdor region. This can be seen from the data on the composition of mixed families. Samoed women rarely married Ostiak men (Golovnev 1995; Perevalova 2004). Meanwhile, the surviving household cards show the existence of at least three such families (GUTOGAT 690-1-49: 81–84, 85–88). The first names of both the household heads and their wives and children suggest that they had been baptised. Perhaps in these three cases, religious identity was a more important criterion in the choice of a spouse than traditional identities.

Economic Dimension

Most of the population of the Obdor region was engaged in reindeer herding, hunting and fishing, which met most of their needs. Other goods were bought at one of the 32 *faktorii* or trading posts in the region. These posts replaced the famous Obdor trading fair, whose activity was undermined by the civil war and subsequent policy of 'Military Communism' which was designed to ensure that the state monopolised trade. The trading posts took primary products from the people in exchange for industrial trade goods. The trading posts were often deliberately placed near habitual places where herders might stop for several days. The nomads were most likely to visit the posts twice a year, during the periods from 1 November to 1 January and from 1 March to 1 May. One trading post, for example Shchuch´ia river *faktoriia* of the joint-stock company 'Syr´e', could serve up to 500 households (GASO 1812-2-188.10: 5).

The enumerators observed that the economic situation in the Obdor region in 1926 was worse compared to the pre-war time. For example, the enumerator in Nyda reported that a decline in reindeer herding was linked to a decline in fur hunting (GASO 1812-2-188.7: 7v). Herders who sold furs at the larger posts near the regional centre were often paid in cash, due to the lack of trading goods at the posts. People from smaller remote settlements preferred to be paid in kind since, according to the enumerators, they were not interested in money (GASO 1812-2-188.7: 7v). In the case of barter, squirrel pelts and Arctic fox furs served as money equivalent, much like the muskrat skins used as currency in the nineteenth-century American Indian trade (Dopp 1919: 496) or the 'made Beaver' in the early trade with the Hudson's Bay Company (Ray 1978). Table 4.4 shows the price equivalents of standard trade goods in squirrel currency, and the 45 per cent inflation in terms of trade since the start of the century (GASO 1812-2-188.12: 7).

The standard trade goods in the Obdor region included bread, butter, tea, sugar, leather, cloth, tobacco, ironware (axes, knives), rifles, powder, shot and caps (GASO 1812-2-187.20: 7v). However, what is remarkable about the collection of documents on trade is the list of goods that were in great demand but rarely available at the trading posts. These were: enamel ware, cracknels, haberdashery, leather goods, soap, copper and cast iron, salt, fishing tackle, threads, resin and tar. Rather than counting consumption goods that were present, the forms often record shortfalls of goods that were in demand. These chronic shortfalls often led people buy things from well-to-do Ostiaks middlemen, paying them three times as much (GASO 1812-2-190.20: 8). Enu-

Table 4.4. Prices of the goods most in demand at the trading post Syr´e in Nyda from before World War I and in 1926 (GASO 1812-2-188.12: 6v-7)

Name of product	Measures and weight	Price Pre-war In roubles	Pre-war In squirrels	Current (1926) In roubles	Current (1926) In squirrels
Butter	1 *pud*	0.40–0.50	1.3–1.6	0.80	0.75
Powder	1 *pud*	0.70	3	0.90	0.8
Shot	1 *pud*	0.20	0.7	0.45	0.4
Tobacco	1 *pud*	0.20	0.7	0.60–0.70	0.55
Kerosene	1 *pud*	—	0.17	0.10	0.1
Salt	1 *pud*	0.01	0.03	0.25	0.02
Flour	1 *pud*	1.00	3.3	3.08	2.8
Chintz	1 *arshin*	0.15–0.20	0.5–0.65	0.40	0.3
Matches	1 box	0.10	0.3	0.15	0.15

merators also noted a lack of beads, bells, snuff boxes, chains, colour cloth and beaver skins. The lack of fatty foods at the trading post in Khal´mer Sede settlement led to an enormously high level of reindeer slaughtering which affected the state of reindeer herding in this area (GASO 1812-2-188.4: 7; GASO 1812-2-188.6: 7v). Hunters often used poisoned bait and especially strychnine in Obdor region. A shortfall in the supply of this poison led to a reduction of hunter earnings from fur hunting (GASO 1812-2-188.7: 8v–9). This was specifically blamed on the increase of the wolf population in the Shchuch´ia River valley (GASO 1812-2-188.10: 8v).

Temporary shortfalls in consumer goods could also exacerbate difficulties in provision. Those who came to the trading post first could get everything that was in stock there. People arriving later had to take what was left. The number of things a hunter could take depended on the amount of fur he brought. Therefore the poor, who could not pay for a large amount of goods, would be tempted to take credit in order to take advantage of goods that were in stock. At the same time, the rich had to waste their time searching for things they needed at other trading posts, covering long distances and often in vain. As scarce products could only be exchanged for fur, the traders refused flatly to exchange these prestige items for money. An enumerator concluded that problems of shortfalls discredited the work of trading posts in the eyes of the people (GASO 1812-2-188.12: 8).

Reindeer herders would often seek to trade fur to foreigners who sailed near their migratory areas. Thus, workers at the trading post Syr´e in Muzhi settlement talked about contraband trade at the coast of the Arctic Ocean in 1925 (GASO 1812-2-188.9: 9). The enumerator Iordanskii wrote that fur was traded to English and other foreign sailors in Novyi Port and in the north of Gydan Peninsula (GASO 1812-2-188.4: 8). Besides that, some fur was sold to private buyers. Voznesenskii reported that people from Tobol´sk came to the trading post Pripoliarnyi Krai during summer navigation and exchanged vodka, onion and honey-cakes for fur and ready-made fur clothes with the local people (GASO 1812-2-190.18: 9).

Often commodities sold at trading posts were not of good quality. Sometimes people preferred old guns to new ones. The new guns could not stand the severe climatic conditions of the Obdor region. They were said to rust-up and that their springs were subject to freezing (GASO 1812-2-190.20: 14v). Traps sold at the posts were said to be too small and to break quickly. R. P. Mitusova considered it necessary to sell traps produced in Norway that were reliable and popular among the local people (GASO 1812-2-190.20: 14v). According to her notes, the lack of good foreign traps and rifles indirectly allowed the wolf population to increase, which in turn caused a decrease in the size of reindeer herds.

Aside from food and tools there was a great demand for goods that were special in the everyday life of the Ostiaks and Samoeds. Among these were chests for keeping tea services and a special set of copper castings, rings and bands for making the false plaits that were a distinguished feature of the traditional clothing of local women (GASO 1812-2-188.07: 8v). Mitusova, who was an expert in northern traditional culture, advised the trading posts to sell castoreum which was in big demand among the reindeer herders. She wrote that castoreum was used for perfuming women and for purification processes in general (GASO 1812-2-188.09: 7v).[4] Samoed men who held big herds bought binoculars at the trading posts. Blue glass that protected the eyes from snow-blindness was especially in demand (GASO 1812-2-187.19: 10v). Many posts experienced a lack of 'pink soap': According to the census materials, pink-coloured soap, or wild strawberry soap with a strong smell, was a widely used traditional medicine for eye disease.

The process of exchanging fur with hunters at the trading post could take a very long time. Mitusova described the situation at trading post of the 'Ob´trest' in Nore on 18 February 1927:

Sometimes the process of trading fur, especially from rich Samoeds is very tiresome for a trading post officer. He does not want to lose a good client and therefore tries to be careful and polite towards a Samoed. The latter would take out one Arctic fox pelt and exchange it for goods or money. Then he would take out another one. [The Samoed customer] never displayed all the fur he had brought immediately. He did this for two reasons. First, the man was afraid to make a mistake in his calculations if he exchanged a lot of fur at once. Second, if he did not like something, he could leave for another trading post with the rest of the fur. As a result, the trading post officer sometimes had to stay up late into the night or did not go to bed at all. Once a Samoed hunter brought 60 Arctic fox pelts and sold all of them one by one. The trade went on for the whole night. (GASO 1812-2-188.08: 10v)

Obviously, the trading posts influenced the economy of the people of the Obdor region. For example, one enumerator reported that a reduction in the price of an Arctic fox pelt without tails caused a sharp increase of delivery of fur with tails. Hunters began to skin animals more carefully using special tools, which increased the quality of the traded fur (GASO 1812-2-187.15: 15).

The founding of trading posts had a positive impact on the economic situation in the region. People with few reindeer could now trade for necessary products at the post instead of buying them from rich reindeer herders (GASO 1812-2-187.19: 12v). However, enumerators also noted that poor herders developed a high dependence on the new trading organisations. Lebedev wrote that 'Ob'trest' took advantage of there being no other competitors in the region by issuing large credits to encourage people to take unmarketable and useless goods (GASO 1812-2-188.05: 14–14v).

Some trading posts offered small favours in order to attract new customers. Thus, a post in Kushevat provided reindeer herders with free oil to make ointments for scabs (GASO 1812-2-188.07: 16). Enumerator Iordanskii observed that people often asked for medicine at the trading post in Khal'mer Sede. Due to their contacts with trading post officers some Samoeds learned to bake bread (GASO 1812-2-188.04: 13v). Lebedev noted that people also came to trading posts to solve their legal problems. He wrote: 'A Samoed lodged a complaint that his wife was stolen. The chief of the post was in the role of a judge and six Samoeds came as witnesses (GASO 1812-2-188.10: 6). After interrogation the verdict was made that the wife could stay with the abductor because the whole thing happened by mutual consent. The former husband, although not pleased promised to lay no claims to the defendant (GASO 1812-2-188.10: 15v).

According to Mitusova, local people were very interested in news from the region's center. Samoeds were especially interested in technical achievements such as electricity, airplanes and trains which they heard of by hearsay (GASO 1812-2-187.19: 13). Being illiterate, they did not ask for papers or books but looked curiously at pictures, especially those of cities and houses (GASO 1812-2-188.09: 14v).

Trading posts influenced the life of the Obdor region's population by the very fact of their existence. Mitusova wrote that first of all, people began to look at their environment differently. They started to spit less while being inside trading posts and their homes as well. They also received some information about culture and public life in other places (GASO 1812-2-187.19: 13).

The life of trading post officers was not easy. Sometimes people worked and slept in the same room, and when the nomads came it became very crowded and dirty (GASO 1812-2-188.10: 17v). It was especially hard for those who worked in small remote trading posts, where there was no post office or telegraph. Enumerator Iordanskii described the life on a trading post in Khal'mer Sede: 'Needless to say there was no comfort. Taking into account the lack of any reasonable entertainments and newspapers together with unusual climatic conditions, it is no wonder that everybody considered his stay there tempo-rary and therefore turnover of labour was inevitable' (GASO 1812-2-188.04: 16–16v).

Describing a trading post in Khe, Mitusova noted that spring was the hard-est time for people because there was no sugar left and it was difficult to ob-tain either fish or meat. The only entertainment available was reindeer sledge driving, hunting, playing cards and drinking beer (on which the sugar was depleted) (GASO 1812-2-187.19: 14–14v). She added that almost all trading post officers complained about the unfriendliness of Zyrians. She thought it was due to Zyrians being culturally more backward compared to incomers. Also, they preserved many traditional features of their everyday life and were sensitive to mockery. At the same time, Zyrians showed keen interest in many things and attended performances and talks willingly. She concluded that it was possible and even necessary to involve them in social activities and to possibly have an impact on Samoeds and Ostiaks via them (GASO 1812-2-187.19: 15).

Religious Dimensions

Indigenous religion has always played an important role in the molding and maintenance of Northern peoples' identity, composing one of its most pro-nounced and manifested dimensions (Rydving 1993; Glavatskaya 2004). Regretfully, the Polar Census household card did not contain a question on religion. That fact makes it almost impossible to get a clear picture on the re-ligious landscape of the Obdor region. However, data found in community diaries, supplemented by information occasionally registered by enumerators in trading post inventories, allows some reconstruction of the manifestations of indigenous religious traditions. Here I will examine records on Ostiak and Samoed religious practices.

According to the data gathered by enumerators in the territory of Obdor, Muzhi and Kushevat sel'sovety, the local population often sought out shamans for help. They did so especially in cases of disease or hunting failure. Although people from the Obdor sel'sovet flatly denied the existence of shamans among them, the enumerator who filled in the community diary for Ostiak village of Chepuras was doubtful. He added a comment that 'because shamans are prosecuted, their existence is thoroughly concealed'. On some forms direct ob-servations of shamanic practice were recorded. Thus, Ostiaks from Ryngam-gort and Mileksim iurty asked shamans from nearby settlements to heal them (GASO 1812-2-214: 273–384).

According to the data gathered by enumerators, people from three set-tlements in Muzhi sel'sovet, namely Il'iushinskie, Tov-gort and Nianin-gort *iurty,* stated they had shamans and resorted to their help frequently. Many people from Kushevat *sel´sovet* used local shamans as well. Ostiaks from Vyengort *iurty* in Muzhi *sel´sovet* said they did not have their own shamans but they often used those from other settlements. The same applied to Ostiaks from Muzhi settlement and people from Nil´tim-gort and Vasiakhov-gort *iurty.* People from Ust´e-Voikar *iurty* indicated there were shamans in Verkhnii Voikar *iurty.* Ostiaks from Togot-gort, Ust´e-Voikar and Nil´tim-gort *iurty* said they resorted to shamans from the Ostiak settlement Elisei-gort. As for Ostiaks from Elisei-gort themselves, they told enumerators they did not have any shamans and that people applied to the nearest settlement with an aid post in case somebody was sick. This contradiction can be explained by the fact that people wanted to conceal the existence of shamans from the authorities.

Ostiaks from Lagas´-gort admitted they resorted to help from shamans but justified it by the lack of doctors. Ostiaks from Aziaba-gort, Vyli-gort (Olen´i), Poshty-gort, Sangom-gort, Khalasoim-gort and Ondor-iugan *iurty* did the same. Besides that, people from Lagas´-gort, Pitta-gort, Poshty-gort, Sangom-gort and Khalasoim-gort could perform shamanic practices themselves. Those who lived in Vyli-gort, Lagas´-gort, Poshty-gort, Sangom-gort and Khalasoim-gort also made offerings in case of diseases (GASO 1812-2-216: 209–224).

There were some areas with a sacred status, where hunting was prohibited due to purely religious reasons. Ostiaks from Elisei-gort referred to Saimov and Shizhin-kort as having such a place where people did not hunt for religious reasons apart from when they had to make an offering. It is possible that Ostiaks from Elisei-gort made offerings in that area themselves. Enumerators also gathered interesting data on animal veneration. For instance, the commentary on the form on Lagas´-gort says that 'bears and wolves venerated here have no economic significance; they are not hunted and are killed only when they "ask for it"' (GASO 1812-2-216: 65–80).

Enumerators working in Kushevat village where there were only Russian dwellers, collected detailed information on religious traditions of the indigenous population. It seems that Russians were well acquainted with the ritual practices of Samoeds and Ostiaks and shared that information easily as they were not afraid of consequences. The community diary said that 'when hunting starts, several settlements arrange together to buy a reindeer, cow or horse. The animal must be many-coloured. Then they make an offering. If the hunting is successful they make offerings again. If they hunt a bear, they dance for seven evenings. If the hunting fails, people question the shaman about the cause and obstacles encountered. The shaman performs a certain ritual and tells hunters about possible obstacles such as irrelevant offerings or weapons not having been fumigated with castoreum (GASO 1812-2-216: 145–160).

There is some information about sacrificial practices in Muzhi settlement registered in the descriptions of trading post inventories. An enumerator wrote that Ostiaks needed reindeer in order to perform sacrifices. They exchanged them from reindeer herders for fur and were always in debt, sacrificing their best animals in a hope to receive more in the future (GASO 1812-2-187.16: 15v).

Regretfully, the Polar census enumerators were not interested much in religious issues. Given the atheistic essence of the Soviet power it is not surprising that the inquiry on religion was not included in the main card. As a result there is no complete picture on the religious composition of the Obdor region's population. The supplementary forms tell us that some Obdor Ostiaks and Samoeds had shamans, performed ritual purification on a regular basis, venerated wolves and bears, and maintained a range of sacred places. We also know that many of the Obdor indigenous people embraced Christianity from the late nineteenth to the early twentieth century.

Conclusion

The Polar Census was an outstanding event in terms of statistical and ethnographical study of the Obdor region. The data collected by enumerators presents a wide basis for understanding the cultural landscape along ethnic, demographic, social, economic and religious dimensions. For the first and only time in Russian history the lives of indigenous peoples were documented in a comprehensive manner. The primary Polar Census data contains unique information on the Obdor region's population, which requires further analysis. Even a brief survey undertaken in this chapter proves the advantages of using primary data in comparison with the statistical summaries. The aggregate statistics published by the Central Statistical Administration simplified the complex ethnic situation in the region. It rather reflected the mainstream state policy towards general unification (assimilation) of the indigenous people in the Soviet Union, just as did the Imperial Russian state.

Following Habeck's (2005: 22) idea that 'people choose to highlight their common identity in order to achieve certain purposes', one might assume that identities can be formed strategically. The aggregate statistics portray a simplistic picture where the Russian, Zyrian and Samoed languages predominate over the Ostiak language. On the other hand, the primary sources instead point to a more complex reality through the existence of hyphenated identities in ethnically mixed families and among different (regional) groups of the same people.

Most of the Obdor indigenous population preserved a traditional way of life with respect to hunting, fishing, reindeer herding, household management, dress, etc. At the same time they creatively adopted every new element diffused through a net of trading posts, whether it concerned new ways of skin processing, tools, or skills and knowledge.

In general, the economic situation in the area and the level of exploitation of the poor by the rich after ten years of Soviet power was referred to as much worse than it used to be during imperial rule. Starvation, lack of medical care, and poor management in trade were widely reported. However, the very existence of trading posts created the basis for improvement. Founded on the main routes of the nomads, they attracted hundreds of households and were important means in exchanging goods and information. They worked as centripetal forces for the Khant, Nenets and Komi people, who lived on hunting, fishing and reindeer herding, and also manifested their relations with the state. No wonder the trading posts were the sites where most of the information was collected. While trade played a crucial role in molding of the Obdor region's ethnic history, trading posts (*faktorii*) were one of the primary traits of the early twentieth-century Obdor cultural landscape.

The heroic work of the Polar Census enumerators, their interpreters and the Obdor region's people resulted in a firsthand description of the Obdor region's indigenous life.

Acknowledgements

This research was sponsored through the project 'Archival and Living Transcripts' by the Arts and Humanities Research Council (UK) Grant APN16283 based at the Department of Anthropology, University of Aberdeen. The author would like to thank Maria Nakhshina for the translation of an earlier draft of this chapter. The primary archive research for this chapter, also sponsored by the AHRC, could not have been possible without the help of Oleg Sarafanov who helped us first locate and then process a large store of unclassified primary documents. I would also like to thank the State Archive of Sverdlovsk *oblast'* for permission to work with the collection and to share this unique data with other scholars.

Notes

1. Raisa Pavlovna Mitusova was a Russian ethnographer who collected invaluable materials on Siberian peoples, some of which was published. She was arrested in 1937, due to a forged report about her alleged membership in a counter-revolutionary monarchical organization, and shot on 7 December 1937 in Novosibirsk (Karapetova 1999; Glavatskaia 2006). For a bibliography of her work, see Perevalova and Karacharov (2006); and for a summary of her work, see Elena Volzhanina (chapter 3, this volume).
2. Natal´ia Aleksandrovna Kotovshchikova took part in an expedition to Iamal in Winter 1928, where she tragically died from scurvy under uncertain circumstances, being left

along by both colleagues and guides. Her body was found in snow a few meters away from a tent with diaries and a farewell letter (Chernetsov 1930; Glavatskaia 2006).

3. Editor's Note: There is an additional set of seventeen cards for this region, scattered among 4 folders in NARK, on Izhemetses (Komis). They can be located on the online database with the classmark 18-03.D01.

4. The fact that enumerator Iordanskii registered an acute shortage of castoreum in Kushevat trading post, serves as another indirect confirmation that people were actively engaged in purification rituals (GASO 1812-2-188.04: 6v; GASO 1812-2-188.11: 8v).

5 | Household Structure in the Multiethnic Barents Region: A Local Case Study

Gunnar Thorvaldsen

There is a lively debate over the degree to which people in traditional societies lived in nuclear or extended families. This can be illustrated by the great number of times that one finds references in the literature to Peter Laslett (1983), one of the most influential historians of the family. Using British census material, he argued that the nuclear family predominated in Europe both before and during the industrial revolution. Some researchers have questioned this conclusion. Steve Ruggles (1987) combined census data from different settings with simulation techniques to show that people may have preferred to live in extended families, even if high mortality rates made this possible only for short periods of time during the family life cycle. In his model, parents would die either before or shortly after their children married and gave them grandchildren. Others have found that while the nuclear family dominated Western Europe, households with extended families were more common in the eastern parts of the continent (Engelen and Wolf 2005). Many households of the latter type have been found also in local communities quite far west – for instance in Rendalen in southeastern Norway and on the Åland Islands between Sweden and Finland (Sogner 1990, Moring 1994).

To contribute to this debate, it is most fortunate that we now have access to nominative census material from that meeting place between the East and the West which is the Barents region. While most of the original manuscripts from the national census conducted in the Soviet Union in 1926 have been discarded, many household cards fortunately exist from the special Polar Census conducted in the northern parts of the Soviet Union. These contain detailed information about individuals' names, ethnicity [*natsional'nost'*], language, occupations, as well and other economic assets belonging to households such as livestock, as well as records of fishing and hunting. For the purpose of this chapter, what is most important is that the Polar Census gives information about family relationships within the household so that it is possible to understand which persons lived together. This study will use data on 1,523 persons (313 households) who lived in Aleksandrovsk *volost'* [district] in Murmansk *okrug* [province] on the Kola Peninsula. These household records represent a near complete collection of the original material for the rural population of this district but do not include households in the city of Aleksandrovsk.[1] Aside from another household study on Ter Samis of the Kola Peninsula based on tax records from 1858 (Kuropiatnik 2000), these data are unique.[2]

The present-day Arctic border between Russia and Norway is of relatively recent origin. It was negotiated in 1826 by the Russian tsar and the Swedish-Norwegian king. However, expansionist movements in Finland during the period when Finland was still a Grand-Duchy of Russia began lobbying for a Finnish corridor northwards to the Arctic Sea. Blocked by the Russians, this demand could not be realized until 1920 when the Petsamo area was ceded by the new Bolshevik government (Nyyssönen 2005). Finland lost the Petsamo corridor during World War II, so that Arctic Finland became again landlocked to the North. At that time, the 1826 border between Russia and Norway was re-established. During the 1926/27 Polar Census, the Petsamo region was still part of Finland – a fact which explains the strong influence of Finnish identity markers in the census records on the Russian side towards the east.

Aleksandrovsk district, which ran along the coast North of Murmansk, was still dominated by a traditional, primary economy in 1926. Until the mid nineteenth century there was little permanent settlement on the northern coast of the Kola Peninsula. The coast was used during the summer sailing and fishing season by fishermen trekking across the peninsula from the White Sea and by nomadic Samis (Nielsen 2005: 14). The coast was settled from the 1860s onwards by people from Russia, Finland, Kareliia and Norway. These settlements were recognized by the Russian authorities according to various decrees from 1860 and 1868. The building of the Murman railway during World War I finally broke the isolation of the northern coastal area (Nielsen 2005). The urban settlement Aleksandrovsk, which was founded in 1896 on the western side of the inlet to the Murmansk fjord, was first called Ekaterinina Harbour and had eight Russian households in 1899. It is better known today by the name Poliarnyi, as it was renamed in the 1930s. The district encompassed the fjord and extended south to Murmansk, but did not include the city itself.[3] It had been settled by people chiefly from Finland in the early 1890s as part of a Tsarist colonisation policy (Iurchenko 2005: 97). Three-quarters of the men were fishermen, often combining fishing with agriculture. Other rural minorities hunted or worked as reindeer herders. Traditionally, this district belonged to the Eastern Sami *pogost* called Kil'din (Sergeeva 2000). According to the Polar Census documents, most women were housekeepers, which usually meant caring for the livestock in addition to home and children. A few persons were employed in traditional handicrafts (boat-building, boot-making, baking, repairmen) while the newspaper-editor and the telegraph worker signalled the arrival of modern times also in this remote district.

Ethnic Diversity

In terms of ethnicity, the area displayed a most interesting mixture. Although it was dominated by Finns, it can be called the meeting place of at least five nationalities: Finns, Russians, Karelian, Sami and Scandinavians (Norwegians and Swedes). In this region, we can find data on ethnic identity in the field titled *natsional´nost´*. This category was an innovation in this census, replacing the previous Imperial concern with *soslovie* [estate] and language, presumably in an attempt to link to the German concept of *Nationalität* or the French *nationalité*. Since the English concept of 'nationality' often carries connotations of citizenship, in this chapter I prefer to translate *natsional´nost´* as 'ethnicity'.

Data on *natsional´nost´* was collected in two places on the household card. The ethnicity of the head of household was used to generate most of the published results. However here I will be using data from columns 6 and 26 within the table, which list information on individuals within the household, the instructions for which, according to the census, were to report a person's own response about his or her ethnicity (table 5.1). The table shows the dominance of Finno-Ugric groups in this region with the main ethnicities being Finnish, Karelian, Sami and a couple of Estonian families. The situation for the original Sami population in Aleksandrovsk district may not have been so different from in Petsamo further west where 'the Finns soon outnumbered the Skolt Sami and pushed them to the margins' (Nyyssönen 2005: 209). The Russian minority was about as big as that of Karelians and Samis, and in addition there were a few persons of Germanic origin: Latvians, Norwegians and a single Swede. Ethnicity went unreported in the original source for 245, or one out of every six persons, most of them children [180 were under fifteen years of age].

Table 5.1. Self-reporting of identity in Aleksandrovsk district according to the 1926/27 Polar Census

Identity (*natsional´nost´* – language)	Sum	Female	Male
Latvian	9	6	3
Russian	6	54	72
Estonian	2		2
Norwegian	3	3	
Karelian	150	60	90
Sami	105	56	49
Fil´man	65	24	41
Finnish	982	452	530
Swedish	1		1
Karelian-Finnish	8	3	5
Russian-Karelian	2	1	1
Missing	70	39	31
Sum	1,523	698	825

We shall return to how the ethnic groups intermarried and whether there were differences between them with respect to family structure.

While the other four ethnic groups are well-known from the literature about the Barents region today, more needs to be said about the group of Fil´man who have disappeared from more recent ethnographic classifications. According to the 1926/27 Polar Census, seventeen households supporting people with the somewhat mysterious Fil´man identity spoke a mixture of Lapp, Karelian, Finnish, Fil´man, Finnish/Lapp and Lapp/Fil´man. This mixture lent support to the view that they were Finnish Sami, the smallest of the colonizing groups on the northern coast of Kola (Iurchenko 2005). The Russian-German etymological dictionary defines Fil´mans as nomadic reindeer herding Sami in the Petsamo area who had kept their Protestant religion; 'Fil´man' should allegedly be Swedish for 'man from Finland' (Vasmer 1953, 3: 209). Their Lutheran religion is confirmed in the Kola-Sami dictionary by the Finnish language expert Itkonen who had travelled most extensively in the area, but who defined their geographic origin as Varanger *'lutherischer lappe (aus Varanger)'* (Itkonen 1958, 2: 818).

However, the etymology of this ethnonym is more complex since it also forms part of a local pidgin language known as Russenorsk (Russian-Norwegian) where *Fielmain* or *filmann* is simply translated as synonymous with 'Sami' (Broch and Jahr 1981: 64). Since this language was used by Pomor traders bringing goods between the Arkhangel´sk area and Northern Norway, it is not surprising to find such pidgin ethnonyms along the coast of the Kola Peninsula. Aleksandrovsk was a well protected harbour only a short distance from the main sea route. Analogous words in pidgin Russenorsk are *russmann* for a Russian person and *burmann* for a Norwegian fisherman/farmer. It is tempting to compare the word Fil´man with the concept of *Fjellap* or mountain Sami which can be found in Norwegian census manuscripts. Connotations about nomadic people living parts of the year in the mountains with their reindeer easily arise. This may find support in some sources where Fil´man is contrasted with *Burmann*, the latter word being used about farmers or more literally the resident or non-nomadic. All of these ethnonyms were juxtaposed in a pidgin song cited in the book about the Russian-Norwegian language (Broch and Jahr 1981: 134 [translated by DGA]).

Paa Burmain jes maaja njet vil ha,	I would not want to be a Norwegian fisherman,
Fiska skirom, Firska skirom,	Processing fish, processing fish,
Kak tvoia Rusmain, saa mera bra,	If you are a Russian, then that is better,
Jes paa Skip kom, Jes paa Skip kom.	Come onto the ship, come onto the ship.
Kak ju vil skaffom ja drinke The,	If you would like to eat and drink tea,
Davai paa Skip tvoia ligge ne,	Please, come onto the ship,
Grot paa slipom, Grot paa slipom	First let us sleep, first let us sleep.

Da grot sinfærdi, tak njet schevaa	Very true, it's not important.
Baat pap tvoia	We are brothers
Kak Burmain, fielmain jes karaashchaa	As Burmans, Fielmans, it's very good
Dein paa moia	That's how I see it
Dein gammal Vrei mera bra kladi	The old Evil is best set aside
Paa mi ailsama og Veen, gribi	For me all are good friends, take a glass
Skaal paa tvoja	Here's a toast to you

However, the occupations columns [columns 11 and 31] in the household cards contradict the simple association of Fil′mans with reindeer herding. The 23 Fil′man adults for whom an occupation was recorded were primarily fishermen, with four combining fishing with hunting or farming. Also, Russian-Norwegian has a special term for mountain Sami: *olenamann* which literally can be translated 'reindeer-man' (Broch and Jahr 1981). Thus, by 1926, Fil′mans were more closely associated with the coast and fishing than with mountains and reindeer. There is a suggestion, however, that they were reindeer herders in the past before the destruction of the reindeer herds during World War I (Leinonen 2008).

The prefix of the term 'Fil′man' might alternatively be a gloss on *fin* rather than *fjell*. *Fin* is a problematic and ambiguous ethnonym historically because it could be used to denote both people from Finland and ethnic Sami more generally, regardless of the country of origin. In 1845, 1855, 1865 and 1885 the census instructions for Norway used 'Lapp' and 'Finn' as synonyms for *Sami*. In 1875, 1891, 1900, and 1910; however, the census authorities rather used *Finsk* and *Kvensk* as vernacular synonyms for Finnish in the census instructions and questionnaires, an inconsistency also brought into the published aggregate data (Hansen and Evjen 2008; Thorvaldsen 2008; RHD 2008). The place-name 'Finnmark' for Norway's northernmost province is derived from the former meaning, while the nation-name 'Finland' is derived from the latter. Thus the present-day Russian place name Koloniia Finmanskaia on the coast close to the border with Norway could have a Sami origin but more likely originated from the time when the Petsamo area belonged to Finland. Allegedly, in the nineteenth century this place was called *Fil′manskoe stanovishche* (encampment) (Schrader 2005: 68; Matsak 2005).[4] The Fil′men's Finnish language skills may indicate some background from this Finnish corridor, but could also have been learnt from the majority of their Finnish neighbours in Russia. If they can be distinguished from the local Skolt Sami by ancestry further west, this would be in line with the Finnish philologist Elias Lönnrot who visited Kola in 1842 and contrasted the 'Filmann' with the 'Murmann'. He placed their origin on the coast of Norway eastwards to Hammerfest and meant they spoke pidgin Russian-Norwegian (Broch and Jahr 1981: 151). The Fil′men's names according to the 1926 census may give some clue as to their origin. Their family names do not overlap with those used by other ethnic group in the Kola area, but are similar to names used by Sami families along the southern side of the Varanger fjord in eastern Finnmark such as Oksehode, Inger, Birget, Valle, Halt and Snaula.[5] Also, the Scandinavian origin may be seen in the selection of first names for their children (cf. table 5.2 below).

We should be open to the possibility that the different interpretations of 'Fil´man' need not be mutually exclusive. The nomadic Sami traditionally moved between their winter pastures in the interior of Finland, Sweden and Norway, and their summer camps along the coast, where they interacted with the resident coastal Sami. Many people of Finnish ancestry moved annually to participate in the seasonal coastal fisheries, and many of them settled permanently in Norway, especially during the nineteenth century as so-called Kvens (Niemi 1994). It was not unusual for Samis and the Kvens to intermarry. The settlement of 'Fil´man' on the coast of Kola can thus be seen as the extension of migration patterns that were traditional further west. Their predominant ethnic identity can be argued to be Sami, and their ancestry was probably a mixture of coastal and nomadic Sami as well as some with Finnish background. When migrating eastwards to the Murman area, the easiest would obviously be to travel along the coast. This interpretation that the Fil´men were really an eastward extension of Fennoscandinavian Sami who had become Russian after the nineteenth century border regulations is supported by Russian researchers and source material (Kharuzin 1890: 52). In an 1822 complaint from Russian Sami that soldiers from Vardøhus were taking their wood, sheep and reindeer it was also reported that Fil´men fished and let their reindeer eat lichen on territory used by the Russian Sami. In subsequent meetings where the Norwegian Sami claimed it was Norwegian territory, 'Fil´man' is an ethnonym used by the Russian Sami for their Scandinavian counterpart. This source, with the oldest use of the Fil´man concept describes the incident triggering the 1826 border regulations mentioned above. In other sources, the Fil´men were contrasted with other groups of Sami along the Kola coast as being bigger and darker with different clothes and marriage traditions. They mastered Finn-

Table 5.2. The household of Ivar Skere in Bol´shaia Ura surveyed 10 December 1926

Name	Gender	Age	Relationship	*Natsional´nost´*
Ivar Olafovich Skore	M	40	Head	fil'man
Maria	F	23	Spouse	finn
Khristina	F	13	Daughter	fil'm.
Anton	M	11	Son	fil'man
Svante	M	2	Son	fil'man
Verner	M	5	Son	fil'man
Shelbi	F	1	Daughter	finn
Ivar	M	80	Father	fil'man

ish or Norwegian and would participate in the annual markets at Lake Enari in northern Finland. Maybe their Protestantism was reinforced at Laestadian religious meetings there? Sami people from Fennoscandinavia who from the 1860s onwards moved eastwards together with other colonists would naturally be classified with the original Fil′men who had for centuries lived east of the new border for parts of the year. In order to study the in-migration of the Fil′men to the northern coast of the Kola Peninsula we really need information about the mobility of individual Sami families, and such source material may be hard to find.

A summary of these paragraphs would be in accordance with Alymov (1928b) in his article based on the 1926 Polar Census where he described the Fil′men as a group of Sami (he wrote 'Lapp') origin whose special language was disappearing and about to be assimilated by the Finnish majority population. While Fil′men in the mid nineteenth century may have been important reindeer owners, by the 1920s they had adopted an economy based on fishing in combination with sheep and cattle farming. The men were responsible for the former market-oriented economic activity while the women for the latter subsistence-oriented activity. Each household would keep up to three reindeer which they primarily used for transportation purposes. It is likely they were forced to give up their original economic year cycle of coastal fisheries in the summer and inland reindeer herding in the winter due to nineteenth-century border regulations. Alymov found them to be relatively advanced, living in wooden houses and educated to read and write the Finnish language. Leinonen (2008) provides a detailed account of the Fil′men compiled primarily from nineteenth-century travel literature.

For a concrete example of a Fil′man household from 1926 see table 5.2. The wife and the youngest daughter in this family were Finnish, while the rest are of Sami/Fil′man origin. Since Maria cannot be the mother of the oldest children, we can be certain that Ivar has remarried, probably after the first wife died in childbirth, maybe when Svante was born, which would explain his unmixed paternal ethnicity. The household was extended upwards with the inclusion of 80-year-old Ivar, who is called 'father', but might alternatively be the younger Ivar's father-in-law from his first marriage if we interpret the patronymic Olafovich literally.

The Definition of the Household in the Polar Census

In this census, it may not be straightforward to decide which persons lived together, even if the persons were listed by family and household in the census and the forms are called household cards. Often, households are defined mechanically by some formal criterion such as, for example, declaring that an unmarried person represents an independent household once he or she is an adult, or reaches a certain age. This is fortunately not the case in the Polar Census results for this region: It is not uncommon for adults to be listed together within the families to which they were related. As a point of departure it is tempting to label all persons listed on one household form as a household, since there is no notation for distinguishing the members of different households listed together. For instance, Norwegian census-takers were instructed to identify individuals as belonging to separate households, even if they were listed on the same form, if they ate separately (Thorvaldsen 2007). The official instructions sent to the enumerators of the 1926 Russian Federal Population census defined a household as all people related by blood who were co-resident in the same dwelling, and who shared the same budget. Lodgers and other unrelated persons were to be represented as having separate households (TsSU 1926). With such a sparsely populated region, it is unlikely that there was any need to single out more than one household on the same form.

A more relevant problem may be that households could potentially be divided over two or more questionnaires for lack of space or because census takers were paid by the number of forms they completed. Such problems seem not to be relevant in this case since most enumerators in the Polar census were paid by the day. Further, none of the questionnaires from Aleksandrovsk district show evidence that the enumerators ran out of space.

Still, there is some evidence that competing definitions of household relationships were in use, which should alert us to the possibility that household relations might extend across census forms. Most household heads (256) were recorded as *khoz* – an abbreviation for *khoziain* – in columns 2/22 on family relationships. This can be translated as 'household head' but in some contexts also as 'owner' or 'master'. However in columns 11/31 data was also collected on the status that they held in their occupation. It is interesting that here only 109 were redundantly classed as *khoz* (masters) of their subsistence farms. Others were classed (50) as *sam* (literally meaning 'by himself' or 'independent') which can be interpreted as leading an independent subsistence existence (and not as a paid worker for another individual). One wonders, then, if individuals who were 'masters' might be masters of more than one household. The ambiguity between being the legal head of a family and holding an economic role here might help us to understand the role of family relationships in this subsistence economy.

We can find further ambiguities in six cards where the term 'father' is listed first. This is for instance the case with the Latvian family of Eduard Petrovich Ul'pe (GAMO 536-1-98: 8) which is listed on a separate card from the family of his son Bernard Eduardovich Ul'pe (GAMO 536-1-98: 9) although they were enumerated at the same place (Sredniaia Guba) and were both fishermen. According to the instructions, the title 'father' should only be written if

that person lived in a household formally lead by the son. Therefore these two
cards might represent an extended household with two families spread over
two cards. This is far from certain, however. For example, there are no clues
that the Finnish family of 'father' Juhan Ivanovich Siekkinen (GAMO 536-
1-99: 4) are living together with people listed on other cards. Thus, it seems
quite safe to indeed define as a household the persons listed together on the
household cards for the purpose of our analysis. Of course there were family
relations between neighbouring households due to intermarriage or because
relatives such as brothers had migrated to settle in the area, but that phenomenon is another matter entirely and can be found in any census. In a traditional
economy it would also be common for household members to work together,
basically forming an economic unit.

Household Structure

Here, I have classified the households living in Aleksandrovsk district in 1926
according to a modified version of the Laslett system. The system allows us to
identify the proportion of households with extended kin systems. One simplification should be mentioned immediately: I have linked the 35 adopted
children in the sample as belonging to the household specified on the form
unless another type of family relation is specifically mentioned (for example,
one adopted son is listed as a grandchild).

Even if just over half the households in the Aleksandrovsk district were
standard nuclear family households consisting of parents and children, table
5.3 shows an interesting variation with respect to household structure. Just
over one-fourth of the households must be classified as extended since other
kin resided with the nuclear family. About every tenth household contained
only one person. In addition, every twentieth household consisted of just one
married couple. One out of twenty were single heads of household with children. Also, twelve extended households were headed by an unmarried person.

A closer look at the background material shows that nearly one-third of the
households were extended downwards
with grandchildren, while more – about
one-half – were extended upwards by
including the parents of the household
head and/or his wife. Many of the latter, and a few other households, were
also extended sideways with siblings
as household members. So far we can
conclude that the extended household

Table 5.3. Household types in
Aleksandrovsk district 1926

Household type	N	%	Average age of head
One person	29	9	
Couple	15	5	48
Single head	13	4	
Nuclear	163	52	43
Extended down/up	86	27	63 / 35
Other/unspecified	7	2	
Total	313	100	

was a structure that many families employed in this part of the Barents region in order to take care of their parents and grandchildren when the need arose. With the high mortality in the region, it can be assumed that the need arose quite often (Nyyssönen 2005).

A single census can only give a snapshot picture of the household structure at a specific point in time. It cannot show the full extent of a household's life cycle over the years. Obviously households have to be reclassified when parents die, siblings marry, children are born, etc. An indirect method to grasp this dynamic process is to calculate the average age of the household heads for each of the household types in table 5.3. In the households extended downwards the head had an average age of 63. In those households consisting of only couples, the head had an average age of 48. In the nuclear households the average age of the head was 43, and in those households extended upwards the age on average was 35. Even if we have not really followed families and households over time, we might on this basis hypothesize that the following household cycle was typical. After marriage the couple was often joined by one or more of their parents. After a few years the parents died and left a nuclear family with children behind. When the children left, the married couple would be on their own for a while, until they either took care of grandchildren or moved in with their children after these had established their own families. Naturally, some families would go through their household life cycle remaining consistently nuclear. We would have needed longitudinal data from other sources to follow people over time in order to figure out how many households remained nuclear, and for how long others formed extended households of different kinds. The Demographic Database provides longitudinal sources for multiethnic areas in Sweden (www.ddb.umu.se), and there are plans to combine information from several Norwegian and Russian sources in order to construct a inter-regional longitudinal population register (Thorvaldsen 2008).

Which Ethnic Groups Lived Together?

Even if household structures in a region shift over a life-cycle, a census can still show which groups of people live with non-nuclear kin for parts of their lives. Such differentials can also provide clues with respect to the reasons why some households become extended. Several types of background factors might be in play. Among economic factors, people might choose to live together because their home was organised around their work, as in the example of a family producing traditional handicrafts or a group of fishermen sharing the catch of a common fishing boat. Only some families might be able to afford to look out after parents living independently in their own homes. Economic necessity might force some individuals to abandon their homes to move in with others due to old age or the death of a breadwinner.

Another background factor is cultural. In this context it seems especially relevant to see if there are any significant differences in household structure between the different ethnic groups. One should also be certain that the effect of the economic or cultural factors is not confounded by large differences in the average age between household heads belonging to separate ethnic or occupational groups. Fortunately, the average age of the Finnish, Russian and Karelian heads of household lies between 42 and 44 years, while we should keep in mind that Samis are somewhat older, with an average head-of-household age of 47.

Before venturing into an analysis of the ethnic differences in household structure, we ought to understand the extent to which people from different ethnic groups lived together, and most importantly, to what extent did they intermarry? The extent of intermarriage will of course influence any ethnic or cultural differences in marriage structure. The ethnicity of the 230 married couples is reported in table 5.4.

The main impression from table 5.4 is one of ethnically homogeneous marriages. Out of the 230 married couples, 197 or 86 per cent were noted to have a partner from the same ethnic group. The large group of Finns had the best chances of finding an eligible partner within their own group, and this was also the case with Samis who likewise had access to partners from Sami groups across the border to the west. Otherwise the smaller groups married out more frequently in relative terms, Karelians being popular both among the Finns and the Russians. The Karelian language was close to Finnish, and many Karelians shared the Orthodox faith with the Russians. Given that Karelians were in the position to act as a catalyst, the lack of marriages between Finns and Russians is remarkable. The most likely obstacle would have been that that Finns living in Russia would have to convert from the Protestant to the Orthodox religion in order to be wed to a Russian partner. This explanation also applies

Table 5.4. The ethnicity (*natsional'nost'*) of married partners, Aleksandrovsk district, 1926
*Two Latvian couples were not included in the table.

	Nationality of the Bride	Unknown	Russian	Norwegian	Karelian	Sami	Fil'man	Finnish	Total
Ethnicity (*natsional'nost'*) of the Groom	Russian		14	1	4				19
	Karelian		5		14		1	4	24
	Lopar'					19			19
	Fil'man						4	4	8
	Finn	2		2	6	1	2	144	157
	Swede							1	1
	Sum	2	19	3	24	20	7	153	228

to Fil'mens, who were also Lutherans and married either Finnish partners or among themselves, but not Orthodox partners even if they were Sami. Due to the Finnish connections listed in the Polar Census, however, we must conclude that endogamy among Fil'mens was less strong in 1926 than it was said to be in the nineteenth century (Leinonen 2008). One must remember that in the nineteenth century, Russian 'Lopari' and Fil'men were prevented from marrying each other due to religious intolerance or antagonism. After visiting a Scandinavian, a Russian Sami would go to the priest to report his sin and it was also considered a sin to eat from the same plate as a Fil'man. This intolerance was most likely developed due to Russian Orthodox influence in areas of multiple religious confessions. Thus, the strongest attitudes against out-marrying were found among the Russian Sami, even if they would usually select brides among Sami outside their own locality. Other ethnic groups considered themselves more high-standing and also lacked the skills needed for the Sami way of life (Kharuzin 1890: 261f). Less weight placed on religiosity in the Soviet state combined with collective economic cooperation are likely explanations why the Fil'men disappeared as a distinct ethnic group in the second half of the twentieth century. Already in the early 1930s increased intermarriage and assimilation is reported among for instance the Norwegians on the Kola coast, but the latter were moved out of the territory as a measure by the Soviet state to get rid of any potential fifth column before the start of hostilities during World War II (Iurchenko 2005; Jentoft 2001).

Household Types by Ethnic Group

Because of the largely ethnically homogeneous marriages and the predominant tradition of hypergamy in the region, it was decided to use the ethnicity of the head of household when tabulating household types by ethnic affiliation. In addition to the married couples cross-tabulated above, a number of single household heads such as widows are included in the following analysis (figure 5.1). The cross-tabulation shows, as expected, that the majority of Finnish and Russian households lived in nuclear families, although a considerable minority (a fourth or a fifth) were extended. However, nearly half of Sami (10 out of 24) and Karelian (13 out of 31) households were extended. This tendency is so clear that it can hardly be explained by the somewhat higher average age among Sami heads of household. It is also supported by other research on the eastern Sami (Utvik 1985: 69ff).

Since fishing (with agriculture), followed by reindeer herding, dominated as occupations among the household heads, we can only analyse how household type is related to these two occupations. There is a slight tendency for fishermen to have nuclear households in comparison to the general population,

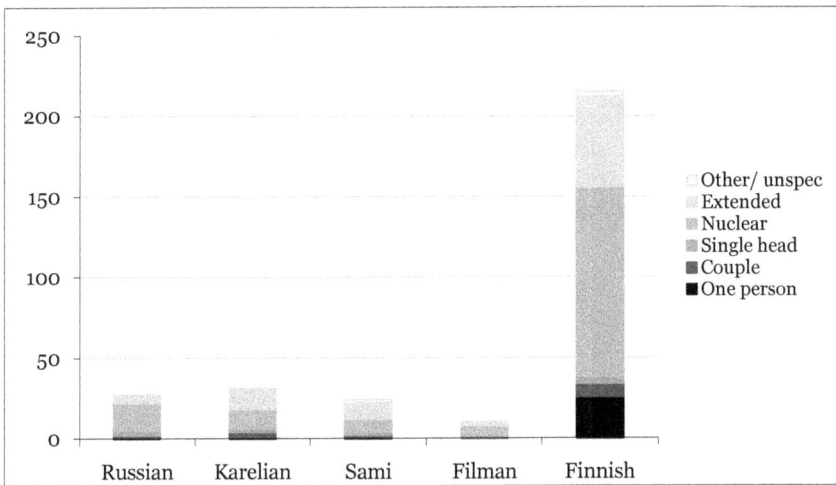

Figure 5.1. Household structure by ethnicity (*natsional'nost'*) in Aleksandrovsk district

but this could be due to fishing being more popular among relatively young and fit men. Reindeer herders, by contrast, organised themselves into four nuclear families and six extended households. Household structure here shows a strong correlation with ethnicity. Since we believe that these preserved household cards are representative, we can therefore conclude that in Aleksandrovsk district household structure depended most on what stage people were in their life cycle and their ethnicity. The occupation of the household head mattered little or not at all. Another striking result is the lack of servants and other employees in the households. Thus, the common criticism against household structure studies that they only take blood-related kin into consideration does not apply here. A Finnish and Karelian widower were both assisted by young servant girls, and two Sami nuclear families each employed 'workers' who were 13 and 15 years old respectively. Forming extended households by taking in extra kin must have been a welcome way to get the help of some extra hands in the labour-intensive life within the primary sector economy.

Reliance on subsistence farming, fishing and other primary sector activities was intensified by World War I and the Soviet takeover which brought an end to the lucrative Pomor trade by Russian ships along the coast of Norway's two northernmost provinces. Until the end of the 1920s the region was economically isolated, and people on the Murman coast had to produce most of the household articles themselves (Portsel' 2005: 148). This may also explain why they were too poor to afford keeping servants. It was not easy to pay salaries that could compete with a share from the rich fisheries in the Barents Sea or marriage with one of the fishermen. An alternative interpretation is that it was politically undesirable and potentially dangerous to exploit workers by hiring them as servants, but this presupposes that communist ideology had already become influential among the minorities in this region. This was probably the case only after 1926 (Carrère d'Encausse 1992: 213). The region was still not socially or culturally isolated which can be seen by the registration of Richard Bodin in Aleksandrovsk district during the 1926 census. This prominent Norwegian communist leader had probably gone with one of the fishing boats from Vardø where he lived in order to visit his parents who emigrated east in 1920).[6]

Age at Marriage

The population pyramid in figure 5.2 distinguishes the population of Aleksandrovsk *volost´* by five-year age cohorts, gender and marital status. The larger numbers of men in their thirties must be a result of in-migration. This excess of men resulted in marriage being nearly universal among women in their thirties, a majority of the women marrying before they were 25 and some even before they were twenty. The male surplus made it less likely for men to be married or widowed in all adult age groups. The smaller groups of children at progressively higher ages could be the result of differential fertility over time, but more likely it was primarily caused by generally high child mortality. Until the children married they stayed at home helping the parents with domestic work, the fisheries, reindeer herding and agriculture. There was always the need for extra hands in a non-mechanized primary sector economy.

Even if we lack marriage protocols stating the age of marriage of each of the partners, it is still possible to compute the average age when men and women married. This can be done with a technique called singulate mean age at marriage (SMAM) which computes this from the age group information in the censuses (Schürer 1989). SMAM is not directly or completely comparable with the average age computed from marriage registers such as church records, since the latter will include information about those couples who outmigrated after marrying. The use of SMAM here will reflect people residing in the Aleksandrovsk district, but also those who had married elsewhere. Also, SMAM will be somewhat affected by any differential mortality between those who married and those who did not, and it is usual to find higher mortality among unmarried than married men. It is also typical for married women to experience more deaths due to puerperal fever and other complications at birth. The basic data for the calculation of SMAM, which was also used for the population pyramid in figure 5.2, gives an average age at marriage of 21 for the women and 26 years for the men. This is considerably lower than the average for Norway at the time, where men on average married when they were 29 and women at 26 (SØS 13, table 13: 47). Even in Finnmark the average age at

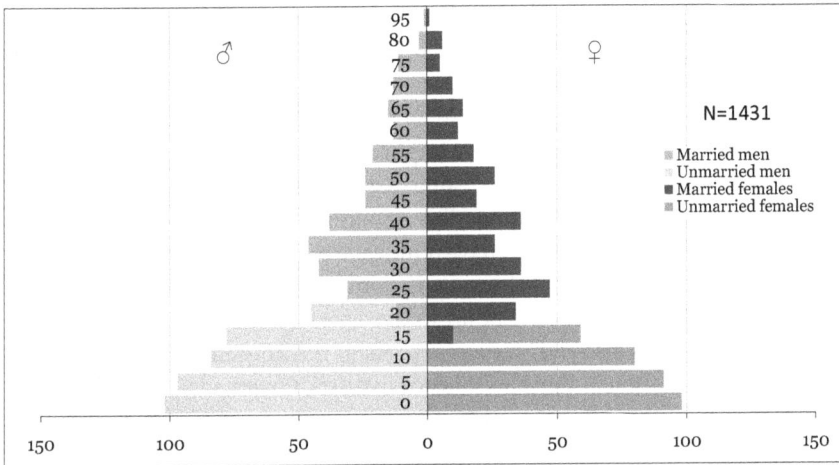

Figure 5.2. Population pyramid for Aleksandrovsk district in five-year age cohorts, gender and marital status
*39 persons with unknown ages were omitted.

marriage for men was nearly 29 years as late as 1910. With such clearly differ-ent results, the reservations about the SMAM measurements listed above do not apply. Supposedly, the rich fisheries in the Barents Sea made it relatively easy to establish new households and may explain why it had been popular to migrate eastwards from Finland and Norway. Also, the demography implies that the years of crisis elsewhere in the Soviet Union in the early 1920 were less serious in the Aleksandrovsk district where people could always fall back on the rich fisheries for their subsistence. These results are supported by a study of the demography among contemporary Norwegian families on the coast of the Kola Peninsula, and the Finnish settlers in the Petsamo area, giving a picture of young in-migrants with high fertility and high death rates (Portsel' 2005; Nyyssönen 2005: 216). It seems that the main factor preventing early marriage was a lack of eligible female partners, which was especially the case in the Pet-samo area after the establishment of the nickel factory in the 1930s.

Conclusion

This chapter analyses the ethnic composition, household structure and mar-riage patterns of the population in Aleksandrovsk *volost'* north of Murmansk according to the Polar Census taken in 1926. The census gives a comprehen-sive picture of the population and its resources, but still only a snapshot of the situation at a specific point in time. We should be aware that with the shutting down of the Pomor trade towards the west and the establishment of the Petsamo corridor, changes may have been even more dramatic on the northern coast of Kola than generally in the Soviet Union. Especially, people may have reverted to relying more heavily on the primary economic sector and self-subsistence than before World War I. The majority of the population in the Aleksandrovsk district was ethnically Finnish with important minorities of Sami, Karelians, Russians and a few Scandinavians. Some Samis were called 'Fil´man', probably in-migrants from the coast and possibly also inland further west who had kept their Protestant religion but given up reindeer herding as their main economic basis and become Sea-Sami fishermen in combination with husbandry. Samis generally had the highest likelihood to live in extended households, but the other ethnic groups also did so during parts of the household life cycle. Men, and especially women in the Aleksandrovsk district married young, an indication that moving here from areas further west made it more easy to establish new households due to the rich fisheries in the Barents Sea.

This research ought to be extended by comparing it with results from other multiethnic settings, such as Kuropiatnik (2000), Thuen (1987), Gjessing (1960) and Thorvaldsen (2009). The work which is currently carried out to computerize and encode the 1910 census for Norway will facilitate household analyses among Samis and Finnish groups along the coast and in the country's interior. Similarly, work on the late-nineteenth-century censuses and cathechismal records for Sami parishes in the interior of northern Sweden will further strengthen the possibilities for comparison. Even if these sources are from a few decades earlier than the Polar Census, such comparative analysis may throw light especially on the background of ethnic groups who had migrated from Fennoscandia to northern Russia.

Notes

1. Editor's Note: The sample from Aleksandrovsk *volost´* is made up of households from 46 rural communities and excludes the district capital at Aleksandrovsk. In comparison to the published records for the region (MOI 1926), the sample is 76 per cent complete, with large numbers of records missing for Tsip-Navalok, Zubovka and Belokamenka. Nevertheless the sample represents a very good sample of both inland and coastal communities.
2. See Rantala (1996) for a bibliography on Samis in Russia.
3. Editor's Note: The administrative divisions within Murmansk *okrug* changed while the Polar Census was in progress. At the beginning of the survey, the *volost´* was centered around Aleksandrovsk. By the autumn of 1927 Aleksandrovsk *volost´* was extended until it reached the border with Finland as in figure 1.1 in chapter 1 of this volume.
4. The assertion by Schrader (2005) that Fil´manskoe was further southwest, also close to the Norwegian border, a few hundred metres from the Orthodox church consecrated to St. Boris and St. Gleb must be a misunderstanding.
5. Personal Communication from Prof. Ivar Bjørklund, November 2007
6. Personal Communication from Prof. Ivar Bjørklund, November 2007

6 | Statistical Surveys of the Kanin Peninsula and the Samoed Question

Igor Semenov

Introduction

Identity is a complex expression of a person's feeling of belonging and many other political and ecological factors. In this chapter I present an account of a region in the far north of European Russia – the Kanin Peninsula. Classically, this peninsula, located in the middle of the Arctic Ocean, is known to be the westernmost 'homeland' of reindeer-herding Nenetses (Khomich 1970: 100) and to have been recently settled by Pomor Russians on the coast of the White Sea in the eighteenth century and then by Komi Izhemetses in the interior in the nineteenth and twentieth centuries. Today the region is best described as a complex regional society where all locals rely upon one another for help and may be interrelated with each other. The Kanin Peninsula, which in the Russian Empire formed part of Arkhangel'sk *guberniia,* for various reasons outlined here was intensively studied by scholars who we would recognise today as statistical investigators or local historians. Despite its remote location there is a wealth of information and even layer after layer of household (or 'skin-lodge') censuses aimed at describing and specifying what came to be known as the 'Samoed Question'. The 'Samoed Question', in brief, was the question of what public policy was necessary to either support, develop or change a group of people defined by their primitiveness in the nineteenth and early twentieth centuries. This issue was linked to the broader liberal issue of the 'Aboriginal Question' [*inorodcheskii vopros*] which circulated in Russia at this time (Iadrintsev 1892; Kovalashchina 2007). The urgency of the question was created by what seemed to be the in-migration of a group of large, wealthy reindeer herders (called in the documents the Zyrians or Izhemetses) who were thought to be disrupting the lifestyle of what came to be known as an aboriginal population much later in the twentieth century. The Polar Census of 1926/27 was one of the instruments used to gather data on this question and played an important role in forming early Soviet policies on access to land and redistribution of capital resources under collectivization. These public policies were developed from the summary results of the Polar Census, which in turn were extracted from the primary documents collected from enumerators. To state representatives, these general population counts showed an alarming growth of Izhemets families over Nenets families and led to a direct public concern over the representation of Samoeds in new collective farms. Through analysing these summary results in detail, and by comparing the summary results to other ethnohistorical sources, I show here that the 'threat' of a burgeoning Izhemets population was a statistical fiction created by taking what we know of the primary documents out of context. It provides a good lesson about the dangers of statistical analysis. Through re-analysing the history of surveys in the region I demonstrate that the 'regional society' [*lokal'noe soobshchestvo*] of the Kanin Peninsula existed also in the early twentieth century but that the statistical instruments used to measure this society were not subtle enough to describe it. To use the terms of the historian of science Ian Hacking (1990), this chapter will distinguish the picture of the *population* of the Kanin Peninsula from the history of the *people* of the region.

The chapter is based around intensive fieldwork between 2005 and 2008 both in the regional archives in Arkhangel'sk and Mezen' as well as with Nenets and Komi reindeer herders in both the Arkhangel'sk and Komi regions. Most of my fieldwork on the Kanin Peninsula was done as the co-ordinator of a two-month ethnographic expedition to the Kanin Peninsula in the summer of 2007 celebrating the 80th anniversary of the Polar Census (figure 6.1). As part of a group of scholars interested in the nominal archival data records of indigenous people in Siberia and the Russian North, I spent many months searching for the Polar Census household cards for the Arkhangel'sk region. Unfortunately, it seems these records did not survive or at least have not yet been discovered in the major regional archives. Instead, this chapter relies upon a near complete set of community diaries for the region (GAAO 187-1-892). In order to bring the information of the community diaries to the level of the household, I used a handwritten index sheet of the missing household cards which recorded the names of the heads of the household, the day they were surveyed, and even the index number of the missing household card (GAAO 187-1-857: 52–53, 60–63v, 74). I was able to expand this information by using a second form, one usually used in the general Federal Census, the 'Homeowner List' (*poselennyi spisok domokhoziaev*). This was a second index of household cards on a settlement-by-settlement basis (GAAO 187-1-888: 240–274v). The homeowner lists gave me lists of names, nationalities and locations which I was then able to use to organise earlier household records from 1920, 1905 and 1897. These three documents allowed me to trace the identity of specific families longitudinally in time. In this chapter, the nominal results of the 1920 special survey of the nomadic reindeer-herding families of Arkhangel'sk *guberniia* will play an important role (GAAO 187-1-891: 268–283v). In order to trace the ethnohistory

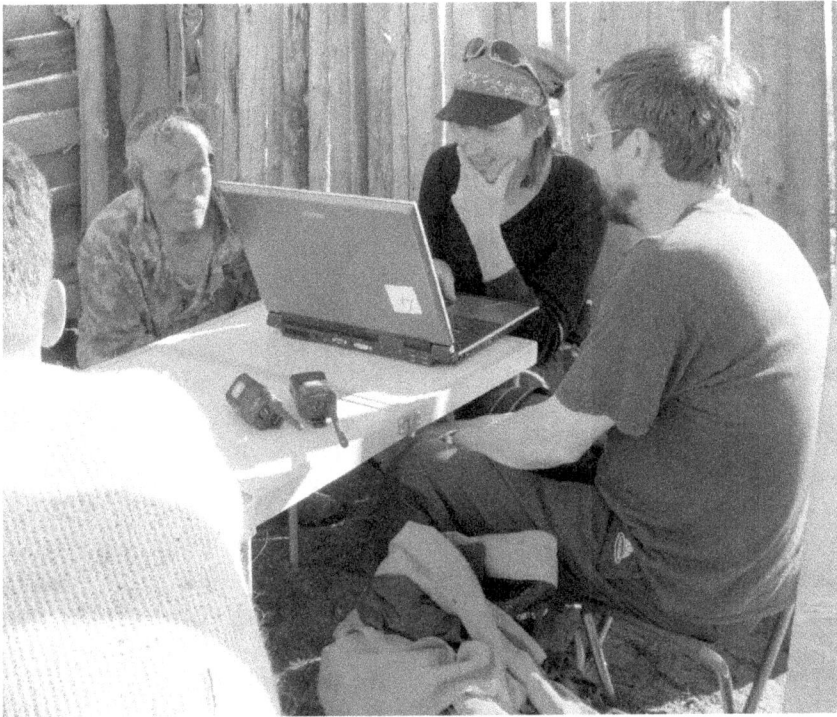

Figure 6.1. Members of the Northern Expedition of St. Petersburg University interviewing Vasilii Ivanovich Kaniukov, Brigadier, Brigade 10
From left to right: V. I. Kaniukov, the author Igor Semenov, and K. B. Klokov

of the late 1920s and early 1930s I also make extensive use of an oral history archive held in the village library of Nes', copies of which are in the archives of the Northern Expedition of St. Petersburg University (ANE). In the terms of this volume, this chapter demonstrates a method for the critical analysis of summary records at the community level, which in turn played their own role in generating the published results.

The Samoed Question on the Kanin Peninsula

Until the start of the twentieth century, the Kanin Peninsula was one of the least studied regions in the Russian European North. Located far from large administrative centers, and entirely beyond the Arctic Circle, it separates the White Sea from the Barents Sea. The area of the Kanin Peninsula is about 11 thousand square kilometres and stretches from north to south for more than 300 kilometres. Today the Kanin Peninsula is part of Nenets Autonomous *okrug.* It borders with Mezen´ *raion* of Arkhangel´sk *oblast´* in the west. The Kanin tundra covers almost the entire territory of the peninsula. The Timan tundra begins in the southeast and the forest-tundra zone in the southwest in the basin of the rivers Mezen´ and Peza. The nomadic population of the Kanin tundra belongs to municipal unit Kanin *sel´sovet* with its administrative centre located in the village of Nes´ (Nenets Autonomous *okrug*).

It is difficult to reconstruct the ethnic map of the Kanin Peninsula in the 1920s due to frequent changes of administrative units within which the nomadic population of Arkhangel´sk *guberniia* was registered. The borders of the tundras themselves were poorly defined. For example, it is rather difficult to draw a distinct boundary between Kanin and Timan tundras. In the 1920s there was a convention of setting a border along the rivers Grabezhnaia and the river Oma. The Kanin tundra was located to the northwest of these rivers, bordering Chesha Bay, and then including the Kanin Peninsula. The Timan tundra extended northeastwards up to the river Indiga (Saprygin and Sinel´nikov 1926: 62–63) (see fig. 6.2).

In the second half of the nineteenth century the people living on these tundras became actively integrated into the economic networks of the Russian Empire. Moving northwards, Russian people colonized new territories and made contacts with Samoeds, a reindeer-herding population of the tundra. These processes caused changes in the state policy of managing tundra ter-

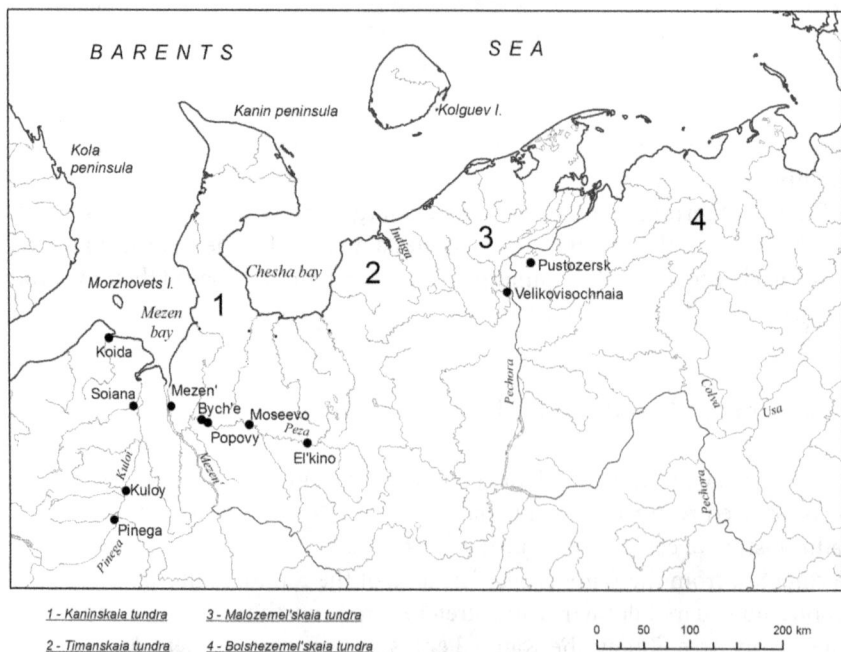

Figure 6.2. Map of the Timan, Kanin and Bol´shezemel´ tundras circa 1840

ritories. During the second half of the nineteenth century and first quarter of the twentieth century both state officials and liberal critics of the state began to discuss the 'Samoed Question'. The discussion started on how best to establish relations with the peoples of the tundra, and moved on to broader questions of whether to integrate them into the social and economic life of the country, carry out reforms, or to preserve their traditional culture.

In 1892 the government issued a law titled 'On the non-Russian (*inorodtsy*) people of Arkhangel'sk *guberniia* called the Samoeds' (GAAO 6-8-153). The law regulated the system of relations both within Samoed society and between Samoeds and Russians. It allowed Samoeds to travel freely on the Timan, Kanin and Bol'shezemel' tundras, except in those areas that had already been assigned to Russian settlers in 1840 (GAAO 6-8-153: 1).

However, this law did not settle the 'Samoed Question'. At some point in the 1890s, Komi Izhemets reindeer herders began to move into the tundras of Arkhangel'sk *guberniia* including the Kanin Peninsula, putting pressure on the nomadic Samoed population. At the same time, groups of Samoed reindeer herders also started to settle down in villages, which complicated relations with Russian hunters. The conflict of interests between these different groups in the region coincided with the government crisis of the 1920s that was caused by the transition of the state to new political and economic principles of management. In the early Soviet years the 'Samoed Question' gained a new currency and played a crucial role in establishing the basis of national policy during the sovietisation of the tundra. Incoming Izhemetses were now portrayed as rich and exploitative. Government workers made the argument that their rapid population growth was overrunning the local population, which still preserved positive primitive communal features. As this chapter will describe, the policy then reversed in the 1930s when the experience of large scale Izhemets reindeer herders was recruited to help form collective farms. At this time, any argument that associated moral traits to nationalities was suddenly discouraged.

The particular geographical conditions on the Kanin Peninsula, like in many places in the circumpolar North, were not those for creating seamless, bounded discrete populations. Although the peninsula is noted for its population of Nenetses, Russians and Komis today, at the end of the nineteenth century the boundaries among these groups were not as clear. Nevertheless there has been a rich literature retrospectively describing the ethnographic qualities of each component group.

Nenetses (Samoeds)

According to L. V. Khomich (1970), Nenetses of the Kanin Peninsula have preserved many elements of their national traditions, in spite of long-lasting contacts with the Russian population. Their culture is very different from the cultures of all other Nenets groups that live eastwards up to the right bank of the Enisei River. Kanin Nenetses differ from other groups of tundra Nenetses in language, as well as in the material and spiritual aspects of their culture. The dialect of Kanin Nenetses is different from the dialects that were used to create the literary Nenets language, such as Bol'shezemel' and Iamal' dialects (Khomich 1970: 101–02).

Lev Geidenreikh (1930: 6) noted that the language of Kanin Samoeds in the 1920s had a distinct phonology and simplified lexica. He noted that they borrowed many many ideas and names for objects from their neighbours, mainly Russians, since they lacked terms in Samoed. At the same time, Geidenreikh noted that the language of Kanin Samoeds was much different from that of Timan Samoeds and even more so from Bol'shezemel' Samoeds.

Liudmila Khomich (1970: 102) notes that the Kanin Nenetses are noted for their *kulemy* deadfall traps used for trapping Arctic fox and other fur-bearers, as described by Klokov in this volume. They were unique for worshiping the skulls of dead shamans and had special types of clothing. Khomich linked the differences in Kanin clothing to the persistence of archaic traditions, which may indicate that they were direct descendants of one of the first groups of Nenetses to inhabit the tundra. The closest groups to them in language and style are those Nenetses living directly south (ibid., 191–21).

Vladimir Vasil'ev (1979: 134–56) places the Kanin Nenetses into an ethnic history of all European Nenetses in the nineteenth century. Working from censuses and local church and population registers, he showed that Nenetses in the nineteenth century and at the beginning of the twentieth century increased considerably in numbers and expanded the borders of their habitation. This was matched with changes in their social structure. By the beginning of the twentieth century, clans lost their territorial unity, which led to increased intermixture of Nenets families from different geographical regions and to the development of a common ethnic identity.

Komis (Zyrians, Izhemetses)

The Komi people, who immigrated to the Kanin Peninsula, have never been the focus of research in either Soviet or Russian anthropology, despite the fact that today they represent up to 30 per cent of the reindeer-herding population. However, there is a well-documented tradition of studying the interethnic relations between Komis and Nenetses. Within this tradition the focus has been upon a sub-group of the Komi population known as the Komi-Izhemetses. Zherebtsov (1982a, 1985), Konakov (1985, 1991), Konakov and Kotov (1991) and Lashuk (1972) theorised about the ethnogenesis of the Komi-Izhemetses along with that of other groups. Their publications document how they adopted a form of northern reindeer herding in the eighteenth century and started to occupy the tundra zone. These researchers stress the way that Komis adopt the customs of neighbouring peoples. The Russian ethnic element is present in all Komi groups and is often said to be the strongest external trait in their culture (Zherebtsov 1982b: 116). Zherebtsov (1982b: 117–156) notes that borrowings mainly went in one direction from Russian to Komi culture.

The question of the relations between Komis and Nenetses in this literature is more complex. Komis borrowed reindeer herding and related elements of material culture from Nenetses, improved them and then gave the new version back to Nenetses. The latter in turn borrowed some elements of Komi material and spiritual culture. According to Zherebtsov (1985: 116–17), it was partly under the influence of Komis that Nenetses started to settle. Relying on the local statistics of the nineteenth century, Vasil´ev (1979: 125) observes that it was common for Nenets men to marry Komi-Izhemets women. At the same time, Izhemets men rarely married Nenets women. On the whole, most contemporary researchers admit a high complexity of Komi-Nenets relations throughout history. Until now, there is no single opinion on this process among scientists. There are exaggerations in favour of both positive and negative results of these contacts.

Russians

Descriptions of economy and way of life of Russians living on the Mezen´ Coast appeared already in the first half of the twentieth century. They demonstrated the role of economic relations between Russians and reindeer-herding populations (Rostislavin 1926).

Contemporary works on the European north-west of Russia are concerned with the question of formation of the Pomor ethnographic group whose ethnic history has been directly related to nomadic groups of the tundras (Bernshtam 1978).

Russian villagers traditionally interacted with reindeer-herding groups in the Kanin Peninsula and its border territories. This interaction was significant both culturally and economically. The two groups supported a vibrant trade in meat, skins, winter clothes, footwear and the mutual marketing of food and goods. However, the degree of interaction varied considerably. Some Russian and reindeer-herding families have known each other for more than a century paying regular visits and maintaining friendly relations. Russian people from such families usually have a nuanced and positive perception of reindeer-herding cultures.

However, the majority of Russian population has little idea of the tundra and its inhabitants perceiving the latter as strange incomers who appear for a short period of time when their migratory routes pass near their villages. The decline of Russian economy in the Kanin Peninsula also led to a decrease in contact with reindeer-herding populations.

Our fieldwork materials from 2006–07 revealed a complicated picture of identity. On the whole, informants confirmed the widespread view among researchers that Komi cultural traits are prevailing over Nenets traits. Many informants spoke about the fast spread of Komi language, cultural traditions and consequently Komi identity in mixed families. However one has to be careful how one defines these traits. Within the area of material culture there is evidence of mutual borrowing. It is true that a certain type of light Komi sledge, called an Izhemets sled, became widespread among Nenetses as well. Komis also borrowed many aspects of tundra reindeer breeding from Nenetses such that their herding practices are indistinguishable from each other. When asking of mixed marriages we also encountered complex relationships. In 2006 in the Kanin tundra, I interviewed Grigorii Mikhailovich Latyshev who is Nenets and his wife Elena Gennad'evna who has both Nenetses and Komis among her relatives. Grigorii and Elena Latyshev both identify themselves as Nenetses. According to Elena, nationality and cultural tradition in mixed families follows the husband's line (ASE 'Semenov 2006': 48-50). Conversations such as these have directed our attention toward understanding which elements are defined as culturally significant traits. On this topic, statistical investigations have played an important role.

Statistics and the Creation of the Kanin Peninsula Population(s)

Despite the interdependence of Nenetses, Russians and Komis on each other, there is a long tradition of using statistical research to separate each population. The story that these statistical accounts often tell is of the steady growth of the Komi Izhemets population on the Peninsula. However, as this section will show, a close look at these records show a more complicated picture. Table 6.1 provides a summary of the most relevant population indicators.

The first descriptions of the Kanin Peninsula were made by travellers, geographers, officials and missionaries in the eighteenth and nineteenth centuries. The Samoeds were considered to be the main population group on the tundra at that time. Lepekhin (1795), who travelled over vast distances in Russia in the eighteenth century, provides some general information about the Samoeds of the Arkhangel'sk tundras. During the first half of the nineteenth century Islavin (1847), Kastren (1999) and Shrenk (1855) travelled through the European North creating what are known today as the classic descriptions of Samoed cultural tradition, history and language.

The detailed study of the Kanin Peninsula population started only in the second half of the nineteenth century. In 1849, Aleksandr Savel'ev published an essay titled 'The Kanin Peninsula' in the *Journal of the Internal Affairs Ministry* distinguishing the Kanin Samoeds as separate 'native' (*korennaia*) group

Table 6.1. A summary of the available statistics for Kanin Samoed and Izhemets populations by year showing households and populations (1856–2006)

Year	Samoed (Nenets after 1926)	Izhemets (Komi after 1926)	Total population	Source
1849	431 men		[860 Samoeds]	Savel'ev 1849: 385–86
1856	470 men; 477 women		[947 Samoeds]	IRGO 1858: 26
1861 Timan-Kanin	202 *chumy* 850 men; 911 women		1761 Kanin and Timan Samoeds	MVD 1861
1895	299 men; 301 women		600 Samoeds	GAAO 6-8-168: 18v–19
1897	78 nomadic households 218 men; 217 women		435 Samoeds	GAAO 6-19-87: 6–9v
1905	100 households 502 people		502 Samoeds	Golubtsov 1907
1920	145 households 701 people	10 households (6.5%) 72 people (9.3%)	155 households 773 people	GAAO 187-1-891
1926	149 households 801 people	20 households (11%) 124 people` (13%)	169 households 925 people	GAAO 187-1-852: 269–70
1976	65 households 365 people	21 households (24%) 138 people (27%)	86 households 503 people	AKPS* Pokhoziaistvennye Knigi 1976
2006 Kanin Commune	38 households 298 people	17 households (31%) 67 people (18%)	55 households 365 people	AKPS* Pokhoziaistvennye Knigi 2006

living a nomadic way of life among three main 'tribes' of Samoeds. Savel'ev made the important decision to map each group onto the territory over which they travelled – a description that would anticipate later arguments about aboriginality. The Kanin group, who travelled the most western of all tundras, consisted of 431 men (Savel'ev 1849: 385–86). This labelling convention was confirmed by the anonymous author of a yearbook published by the Imperial Russian Geographic Society for the year 1856 (IRGO 1858) where the practice of associating Samoeds with 'their' tundras was said to be a general practice in Mezen' *uezd*. Accordingly, Kanin Samoeds took their name from their landscape (IRGO 1858: 45). This source gives the first general population figure for the Kanin Samoeds of 470 men and 477 women (IRGO 1858: 26).[1]

A next important step in studying the questions of population size and ethnic composition of the Kanin tundra was the first general census of the Russian Empire in 1897. In this region, it was prepared and carried out by Arkhangel'sk Statistical Committee with the help of numerous officials and local initiators. Since the Samoed way-of-life differed so much from that of the neighbouring Russians and Zyrians, they were singled-out for special attention:

With respect to the Zyrians, Karelians, and even the Lapps there is no need to depart from the general rules [for the 1897 census]. They are a registered [*pripisnoe*] population and do not differ very much or hardly at all from the neighbouring

Russian peasants of Arkhangel'sk *guberniia*. From the latter, they have borrowed so much, including the Russian language, that they have merged [*slilis'*] with them. This has reached such a level that it is difficult to identify them as a separate ethnographic group. However the Samoeds are a different question. (AGPK 1896: 4)

These special measures led to some unique practices in the 1897 census. In preparation for the census a handwritten preliminary list of Samoeds was compiled for 1895 (GAAO 6-8-168). According to this list, the population of Kanin Samoeds consisted of 299 men (26 of them were temporarily absent) and 301 women (GAAO 6-8-168: 18v–19).[2] When the census was organized, the Samoed population of Mezen' *uezd* was registered in a separate census district with special enumeration rules. The most important addition was the fact enumerators were asked to record national identity in the heading designed for 'estate, social condition or status'. This gives perhaps an overly clear boundary between Samoed families and Russian families and allows us to identify mixed families (GAAO 6-19-87: 1–429). According to the census results, there were less Samoeds in the Kanin tundra compared to the preliminary list made in 1895. The enumerators registered 218 men and 217 women (435 people in total) in 78 households. All of them were nomads except for the family of Nikolai Ivanovich Ardeev which had settled down in the village of Nes' (GAAO 6-19-87: 9v; 128–129v). Although oral history records suggest that some Komi-Izhemetses were in the Kanin Peninsula by this date there is no record of them in the primary records of the 1897 census; however, as will be explained below, their lack of large herds of reindeer may have made them 'look like' Samoeds at the time.[3]

A further study in 1905 counted 100 tents on the Kanin tundra with 502 Samoeds (249 men and 253 women) living in them (Golubtsov 1907).

Overall, from the end of the nineteenth century to the beginning of the twentieth century, the scientific interest in the fate of the Arkhangel'sk Samoeds grew. This was reflected in a series of publications (A. Borisov 1906; Zhitkov 1904; Iakobii 1891; Kertseli 1910; Zhuravskii 1909) and the above-mentioned series of statistical studies. The political and socio-economic transformation of the country with the coming of Soviet power gave new impetus to the 'Samoed Question' and with it the need to commission even further studies of the tundra. As part of the incomplete federal census of 1920, the new administration designed a special survey for the 'nomadic reindeer herders living in what is known as the "dead-zone" on the Islands of the Arctic Ocean and in their own territories on the tundras of Arkhangel'sk *guberniia*' (fig. 6.3). This exotically named survey instrument greatly anticipated the household card of the 1926/27 Polar Census.[4]

The primary records of the survey of the reindeer herders of the 'dead-zone' are held in GAAO. The forms contained information about family com-

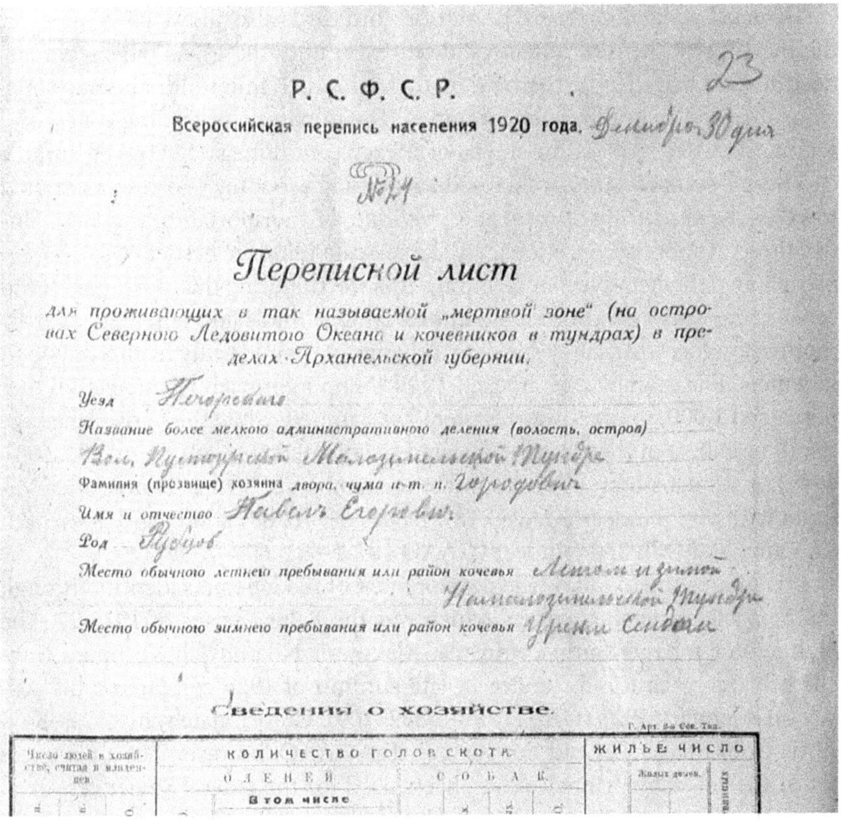
Р. С. Ф. С. Р.

Всероссийская перепись населения 1920 года.

Переписной лист

для проживающих в так называемой „мертвой зоне" (на островах Северного Ледовитого Океана и кочевников в тундрах) в пределах Архангельской губернии.

Уезд

Название более мелкого административного деления (волость, остров)

Фамилия (прозвище) хозяина двора, чума и т. п.

Имя и отчество

Род

Место обычного летнего пребывания или район кочевья

Место обычного зимнего пребывания или район кочевья

Сведения о хозяйстве.

Figure 6.3. Fragment of a card from the Survey of the Reindeer Herding Families of the 'Dead-Zone' (GAAO 187-1-891: 1)

position and economic condition of households (number of reindeer, dogs, sledges, equipment etc.) and their summer and winter migratory territories. For the first time these primary records give a clear record of the incoming Izhemets population. There are 155 surviving sheets with information on the nomadic households of the Kanin tundra, which registered 773 people in the Kanin tundra (379 men and 394 women) (GAAO 187-1-891). The heads of 145 households registered their 'clan' identity as Samoed and ten heads of households registered themselves as Izhemets. The total number of reindeer in all the households made up 18,790 animals. Ten Izhemets households had 72 people (34 men and 38 women) and possessed 2,496 reindeer (representing 13.3 per cent of the total stock of reindeer). The number of Izhemets households represented 6.5 per cent of the total households or 9.3 per cent of the total population.

The level of detail on these primary record cards also allows us to interpret the meaning of the new Izhemets identity. Up until the 1920s Izhemets reindeer herders travelled further and further into the Kanin tundra because they were attracted by trading opportunities. The proximity of trading routes and regional centres such as the towns of Mezen´ and Pinega created favourable conditions for their large-scale reindeer-herding economy which was oriented towards the marketing of meat and providing of transportation (fig. 6.4). Under these economic conditions, any large-scale reindeer herder began to approach an 'Izhemets-type' of economy. It is worth noting that during the 1920 census, members of some rich Samoed families indicated Izhemets as their mother tongue, which may speak to a change in their identity from Samoed to Izhemets. For example, the household of Filipp Egorovich Khatanzeiskii that possessed 1,000 reindeer was registered as Samoed, while the native language for all members of the family was stated as Izhemets (GAAO 187-1-891: 693–694v). A similar situation was found in the families of Semen Timofeevich Vaniuta with 900 reindeer (GAAO 187-1-891: 677–678v) and Gavril Egorovich Khatanzeiskii with 350 reindeer (GAAO 187-1-891: 699–700v).

It is interesting to follow the development of the Izhemets identity through the next major detailed survey which was the Polar Census of 1926/27. The enumerator for the Kanin Peninsula, Aleksandr Nikonovich Kuroptev, travelled through the Kanin tundra in late autumn of 1926 completing his survey on 9 January 1927 (GAAO 187-1-852: 209). Unfortunately, his household cards from this survey did not survive. The GAAO, however, has a complete set of the centrally printed index sheets used for the federal Soviet census of 1926: the 'Community-level list of Homeowners' (*Poselennyi spisok domokhoziaev*) (GAAO 187-1-888: 240–274v).[5] These lists provided the full name and nationality (*narodnost´*) of each household head by community and how many men and women were in his or her family (distinguished by whether or not they were absent on the date of enumeration). As was usual for the Polar Census, the community names were very rural such as 'the headwaters of the Silnitsa river'. According to these lists, 169 households were registered in the Kanin tundra. Out of them, 19 householders were indicated as Zyrianins, 1 as Russian and 149 as Samoeds.

In total, 926 men (466 men and 460 women) were registered in the Kanin tundra during the Polar Census, and 119 people (65 men and 54 women) lived in 19 Zyrian households. The number of Zyrian households made up 11 per cent and its population makes up 13 per cent from the total data for the Kanin tundra. The comparison of statistical data of the 1926/27 Polar Census and the census of 1920 seems to indicate a considerable growth of Izhemets (Zyrian) households in the Kanin tundra (see table 6.1).

In comparing the lists of names generated by the surveys in 1895, 1987, 1920 and 1926/27 it is possible to trace the identities declared by certain individuals

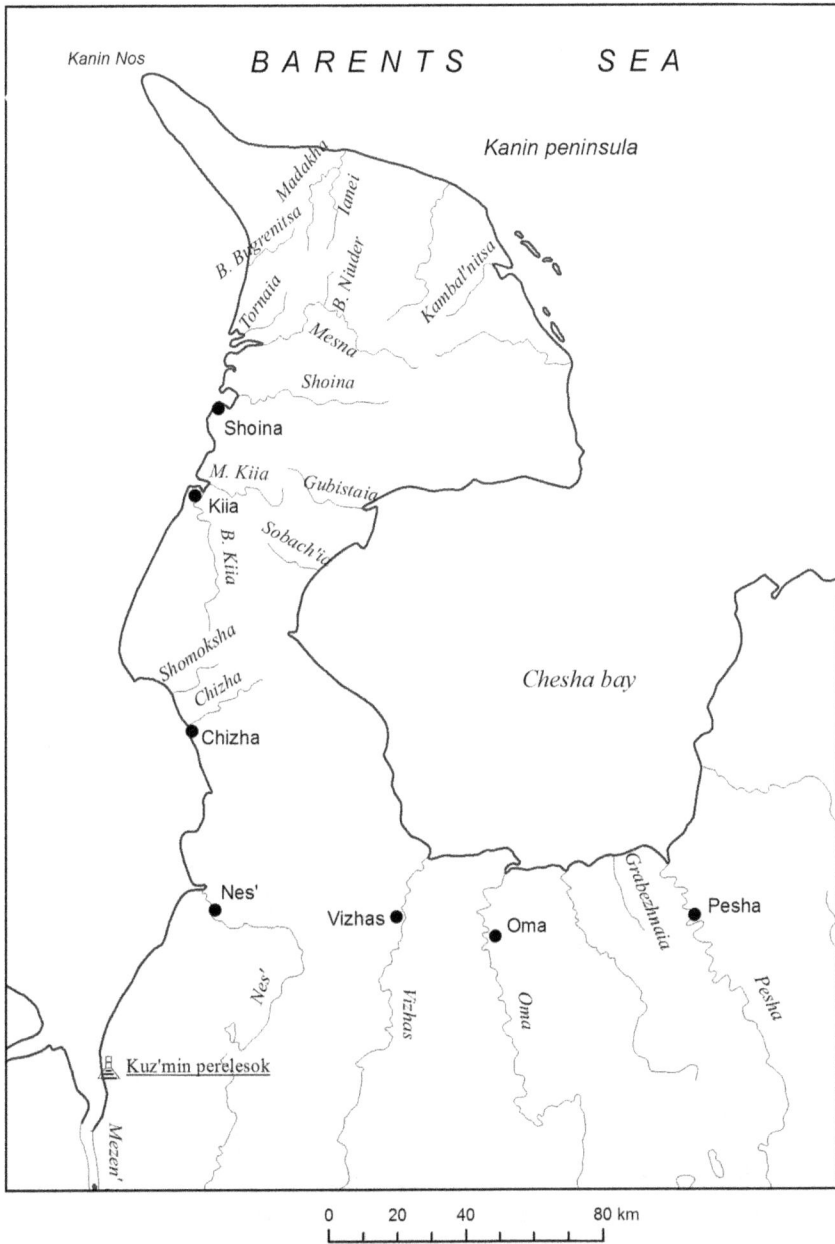

Figure 6.4. Map of the Kanin Peninsula 1926–27

and their descendants over time. A fascinating part of this process is the way that certain individuals change their identity from Samoed to Izhemets, or back again. In the next section, we will use historical and ethnographic sources to illustrate the reasons for these processes.

The Kanin Regional Society: The 'Closed' Tundra

The relations between Samoeds and Izhemetses and their transformation from one into the other can be understood through three different processes. The first process is the formal declaration by former Samoed families of their affinity for Izhemets identity – the process of so-called 'subscribing' to identity [*zapisyvanie*]. The second process is related to a complex process of small-scale Samoed households 'rejecting' the presence of large-scale reindeer-herding households labelled as Izhemets – the process of 'expulsion' [*vytesnenie*]. The third process, which we might call the 'mapping' of identity, led to people being counted as Izhemetses if they simply lived in and around areas with large herds of reindeer. These three processes together can explain the expanding and contracting of different segments of the tundra populations as seen through the differing population figures for 1897, 1920 and 1926/27. In all three cases, economy and the geography were seen as closed objects of study and the identity of the people passively reflected their location and activity.

We can see the process of subscribing to identity clearly illustrated in the accounts left by the geologist M. B. Edemskii during his research in the Klioisk-Mezen´ basin in the second half of the 1920s. Edemskii describes the culture of reindeer herders that he met, noting that from a desire to lead a more cultural way of life, the '*saamodi* would describe themselves as Izhemetses. The reason for this, according to him, is that Izhemetses enjoyed certain civic rights, such as participating in elections and serving in the army, which Samoeds did not enjoy. It seems that enterprising Izhemetses were good in organizing and managing reindeer herding and marketing produce from it, which made a big impression on Samoeds and served as an ideal for them (Edemskii 1830: 34). Those Samoeds who had a lot of reindeer often hired herders among poorer Samoed families and in this respect did not behave any differently from Izhemetses. 'A Samodin called Lambiia [Vaniuta]' who spent winters in Kuloi village registered himself as 'Izhemets' in order to enjoy the same rights and privileges as his Izhemets neighbours; known in town by his baptized name, Semen Timofeevich Vaniuta, slaughtered up to 100 reindeer for sale every year (ibid., 35).

In contrast to the process of subscribing, the archival documents of this period also demonstrate the process of the expulsion of Izhemetses from the Kanin tundra. In the 1920s, according to Zhilinskii (1923), the Kanin tundra was the site of severe conflicts between large-scale reindeer herders. The peninsula was attractive for herders since it had almost no pastures which were infected with epidemic viruses. In the 1920s, a rapid influx of reindeer on the tundra led to a serious depletion of lichen. By 1923, according to Zhilinskii, the regional reindeer population had reached 80,000 head. This severe ecological pressure was a source of constant misunderstanding and even conflicts between Samoeds and large Zyrian reindeer herders. Since there were very few Zyrian households, and their migratory routes were not established according to clan principles (but are instead were described as 'occasional intrusions') there was a growing opinion that the Kanin Zyrians should be expelled. This view was supported by the local Russian hunting population as well (Zhilinskii 1923: 46–47). The policy of expulsion referred to setting a rough boundary at the Chizhi River beyond which Zyrian households were not allowed to migrate with their reindeer in the summer. This forced some Zyrian families to temporarily shift their winter migration route to a far western region near the White Sea in the Koida River basin.

The population of Koida village, in turn, made an official complaint to the Arkhangel'sk *guberniia* executive committee about Izhemets reindeer herders, who having been expelled from the Kanin tundra, led their large, 10,000-strong herds to trample the meadows belonging to people in Koida (V Koidenskoi 1925). In order to avoid a similar situation in the future, the villages asked the executive committee to 'expel once and for all' Izhemets reindeer herders to one of larger tundras such as Timan or Malozemel'.

The data that we collected during fieldwork in 2006–07 confirms the fact that Izhemetses were moved out of the Kanin tundra. People in the Kanin Peninsula recalled stories of confrontations between Komis and Nenetses in the 1920s: 'It was mainly Nenetses who lived in the Kanin Peninsula... Komis started to appear here in the 80–90s of the nineteenth century. Komis were not allowed [to the Kanin Peninsula]; there were only Nenetses in the tundra. When kolkhozes appeared, everything changed...' (ASE Bil'diug fieldnotes 54v–55).

The comparison of data from the homeowner lists and the community diaries also allows us to follow how Izhemetses were expelled from the Kanin tundra, but this task is more like a detective story. The GAAO holds a full collection of seventeen community diaries for Kanin except for diary number 5 for the village of Kuloi where a large number of Zyrian families were registered. Kuloi is located on a river 50 kilometres west of Mezen'. The reason why this particular diary is missing is, of course, an interesting question given the politics of the region at that time. By consulting the homeowner lists, and by using a process of elimination, it is possible to reconstruct the population of Kuloi (GAAO 187-1-888: 250–250v) (table 6.2). From that list it is possible to identify all Zyrian families that were previously registered at Kanin tundra in 1920. There are only two exceptions: the families of E. A. Vokuev and P. A. Terent'ev. These families, with great difficulty, managed to keep their herds on Kanin tundra at the Chizha River, according to the life history of E. A. Vokuev which is documented below (GAAO 187-1-888: 247).

The paradoxical effect of 'subscribing' and 'expulsion' can be seen in the fate of the Vaniuta brothers with whom we are already acquainted from the report of Edemskii (1930). Semen Timofeevich Vaniuta (GAAO 187-1-891: 677–678v) and Iakov Timofeevich Vaniuta (GAAO 187-1-891: 701–702v) were both registered at the northwestern bank of the Kanin Peninsula as Samoeds in the 1920 special census, but it seems that shortly afterwards they made a strategic decision to describe themselves as Zyrians. By 1926/27 they were duly recorded as Zyrians already living in a different place (GAAO 187-1-888: 250–250v). It would seem that their choice placed them in the unfavourable position of being 'Zyrian kulaks' and subject to being expelled under the harsh rules of that time.

The differences in population figures over the 1920s demonstrate some of the fundamental principles of how surveys work with nomadic indigenous people. During the 1920 census, when enumerators privileged the recording of language and of identity, the numbers returned a larger number of Samoed households. During the 1926/27 census, when economic indicators were more important, those households displaying wealth in reindeer were sometimes

Table 6.2. Zyrian households registered at Kuloi in 1926

No.	Surname, name, patronymic of household head	Men	Women	Total
1	Vokuev Egor Andreevich	5	3	8
2	Khoziainov Aleksei Iakovlevich	1	3	4
3	Khoziainov Fedor Grigor'evich	4	5	9
4	Khoziainova Aleksandra Vasil'evna	4	3	7
5	Khoziainov Konstantin Vasil'evich	5	3	8
6	Vokuev Iakov Nikolaevich	2	2	4
7	Khatanzeiskii Artemii Gavrilovich	6	4	10
8	Vaniuta Arkadii Iakovlevich	3	4	7
9	Kaniukov Fedor Iakovlevich	5	4	9
10	Filippov Konstantin Alekseevich	5	4	9
11	Filippov Timofei Ivanovich	4	2	6
12	Filippov Gavril Izosimovich	1	2	3
13	Taleev Stepan Mikhailovich	3	2	5
14	Vyucheiskii Ivan Ivanovich	2	1	3
15	Vaniuta Evgeniia Egorovna	3	1	4
16	Vyucheiskii Aleksei Ivanovich	3	2	5
17	Vokuev Stepan Fedorovich	3	3	6
18	Vokuev Ivan Fedorovich	3	2	5
19	Terent'ev Petr Alekseevich	3	4	7

too hastily classified as Izhemets. Their eye for economic indicators also drove the enumerators to those parts of the landscape where large-scale (wealthy) reindeer herders might expect to be found, hence further exaggerating the figures. The difference between the surveys might be summarised as the difference between privileging a land peopled with residents, and one that privileges a territory with a population maximizing herd sizes. In this manner, through mapping one population onto the grazing reindeer, we can partially explain the sudden rise in the Izhemets population.

The Kanin Regional Society: The 'Open Tundra'

In the previous section, I presented an account of the relations between Komi Izhemetses and Nenets Samoeds from 1850 to 1926 where I argued that the ethnic borderline between them was more an artefact of the peculiar economic conditions of this time enclosed within an economic stereotype of their landscape. With the start of collectivization in 1931 some of the economic impetus that fed into the distinction between identities was removed, and one finds informants saying that the tundra was 'open' for people to express their identity. By the time that the first work-units [*tovarishchestva*] were established in 1934, most of the Izhemetses who had left the Kanin had returned and even occupied prestigious positions in the new Soviet institutions. With the gradual rise in status of the idiom of aboriginality in the 1980s and 1990s one can even say that the processes outlined above had reversed leading some Komis to once again declare themselves to be Nenetses. In this section I argue that making arbitrary divisions between Komis and Nenetses is not the best way to view the Kanin Peninsula. Instead I will portray the region as a 'regional society'.

The oral history archive in the library of the village of Nes´ sheds some light on these reversals (fig. 6.5). The manuscript titled 'Pages from the life of Komi-Izhemets Terent´ev Egor Ivanovich' documents the history of the emigration of the Terent´ev family to the Kanin tundra:

> A small herd belonging to the Terent´evs grazed in the upper reaches of the river Pechora close to the village Niasha that is above Izhma. Suddenly an awful disease came like the wind and many dead reindeer covered the tundra. Ivan took his small family, harnessed six reindeer that miraculously survived and went to the North looking for happiness. Tundra roads brought him to the Kanin Peninsula and the sea. There was no way to travel beyond this point. The Terent´evs settled there. Ivan worked for rich reindeer herders. His son Egor who was young at that time helped him with pasturing. (ASE 'Terent´ev 2006')

In order to verify the chronology of the events, we looked first at the primary records of the special census of reindeer herders conducted in 1920.

Figure 6.5. The Oral History Archive in the village of Nes´. Photograph by Igor Semerov.

Those records contain only one family called Terent´ev. Census sheet number 9 documents a household headed by Ivan Rodionovich Terent´ev (GAAO 187-1-891: 683–684v). At the time of the census, he was forty-five years old, married and had two children. Ivan Terent´ev indicated Izhemets as his native language and said that he was born on the territory of Pechora *uezd*. He moved to the Kanin Peninsula together with his family ten years prior to the census, in 1910. Ivan Terent´ev's son Egor was thirteen in 1920 and he also considered Izhemets as his native language. During ten years of living in the Kanin tundra, Terent´ev's family managed to build an independent household with one hundred reindeer, two herding dogs, two transport sledges and three cargo sledges. In the process, Ivan Terent´ev changed from being a hired-hand to being an independent 'master' (*khoziain*).

The history of the family was closely connected with the change in policies in the 1920s with respect to the roles of Komis and Nenetses. The following excerpt from the manuscript describes the family's life after the resettlement:

> Many years passed before it became possible to accumulate a small reindeer herd that could more or less satisfy needs of the family. Still life was not easy. Kanin Nenetses did not like Izhemetses. They oppressed them, gave them the worst pastures and sometimes simply did not let them into the Kanin Peninsula. It was the conse-

quence of autocratic policy of setting one people against the other. The organization of *kolkhozes* put an end to conflicts between Izhemetses and Nenetses. (ASE Terent´ev 2006)

Terent´ev's family temporarily disappears from statistical data. Neither Ivan nor his son Egor were on the lists of householders of the Kanin tundra in the records of the 1926/27 census (GAAO 187-1-888: 240–274v). This implies that between 1920 and 1926 the Komi-Izhemets family of Terent´ev were forced to leave the Kanin tundra. What made them leave?

The histories of other Izhemets reindeer-herding families shed some light on the events of the mid 1920s. The history of the Vokuev family in Nes´ village library also starts with the history of their resettlement to the Kanin Peninsula: 'The Vokuev Komi-Izhemets family came to Kanin in the beginning of the twentieth century looking for better pastures. They were Egor Andreevich and Iuliia Konstantinovna' (ASE 'Vokuevy 2006'). Sheet number 31 of the 1920 census describes the household of Egor Andreevich Vokuev and allows us to determine the time when his family moved to the Kanin tundra. Egor Vokuev moved to the Kanin Peninsula around 1890 and his wife Iuliia came there five years later. By 1920 they had a big family that consisted of ten people. Their household was quite strong and included two hundred reindeer, four watchdogs, twenty-two sledges, two rifles, five hundred nets, two boats and two pairs of skis (GAAO 187-1-891: 687–688v). Having analyzed primary materials of the 1920 census, we came to the conclusion that Egor Vokuev was one of the first Izhemets resettlers to the Kanin tundra.

An interesting fact is that the family of Egor Vokuev was the only Izhemets family to be registered during the Polar Census in the Kanin Peninsula on a homeowners list (GAAO 187-1-888: 247). They were registered on the left bank of the river Chizha and upstream from the mouth living with a group of five households. The other four households were Samoed. The community diary corresponding to that group stated that the group followed the same routes every year and led a 'classic' [*pravil´no*] nomadic lifestyle. In summer they travelled to the Shomokhov hills of the Kanin Peninsula. In winter they moved southwards to the town of Pinega. The community diary has a question about disputes over pastures [Question VII.12 page 9]. The enumerators documented the fact that the 'Samoeds are pressuring (*vyzhymaiut*) one household to move from Kanin´ which we can assume was that of Egor Vokuev [who it seems did not leave]. There is a note that this group 'keeps its household in an Izhemets way (*po-Izhemski*) and is independent from anybody else.... It also does not come to *suglany*, households meetings or trade posts' (GAAO 187-1-892: 268–283v).

The life histories of Ivan Terent´ev and Egor Vokuev speak to the idea that Izhemets families were expelled from the Kanin tundra in the 1920s. At the same time, they discredit the myth that it was exceptionally rich Izhemets reindeer herders that resettled to the Kanin Peninsula. It seems that Izhemetses from tundras that suffered from the aftermath of reindeer epidemics further south resettled to the Kanin tundra at the end of the nineteenth and beginning of the twentieth centuries initially without attracting any controversy. Indeed since their capital resources were poor, it is entirely possible that the enumerators of the 1897 census simply marked them as Samoeds. Over the same period of time, large Samoed reindeer herders also became attracted to the growing market economy in meat and transport services, which drew them closer to the Izhemets reindeer herders who were successfully establishing themselves. Men from large Samoed reindeer-herding households started marrying Izhemets women, using Izhemets language, and registering themselves as Izhemetses. This promoted the idea of Izhemetses being an exceptionally rich group of people, perhaps threatening development of poorer Samoed families. In this situation some Izhemetses were forced to leave the Kanin tundra, a fact which was caught in the lists created in the materials of the Polar Census. Ironically this fate also affected some large Samoed families who registered themselves as Izhemetses. After collectivization, these special economic conditions changed, removing the reason for competition between these two groups. The Kanin tundra again became open, and the Izhemets herders returned.

It has proven difficult to find statistics to document the way that the Kanin Peninsula changed in the 1930s and 1940s. However, in the manuscript archive of the village library of Nes´ a document titled 'Collectivization on the Kanin´, which was compiled from the administrative documents of the former tundra Soviet Kanin, states that all of the directors of the three new work-units on the Kanin were Izhemetses.[6] The same manuscript states that on 1 January 1935, 27 of 260 households on the peninsula were Komis. The full participation of Komis in the regional society continues up to this day.

The administration of the organization 'Kaninskii *sel´sovet*' has in its archive the materials of local community census of the Kanin tundra population which allow estimating its dynamics and ethnic composition in the second half of the twentieth and beginning of the twenty-first centuries. This data takes into account the population of the Kanin tundra that belongs to the 'Kanin' reindeer-herding community and does not include a group of households that belong to the 'Voskhod' community assigned to Oma village who migrate in the east of the Kanin Peninsula and Timan tundra.

By 1975 there were 86 households registered in the Kanin tundra: 60 Nenets ones,

Table 6.3. The structure of nomadic households on the Kanin tundra by ethnicity in 1975 (Archive of the Kanin village administration).

Type of household	Number	%	Population	%
Komi	17	19.77	106	21.07
Nenets	60	69.77	346	68.79
Mixed Komi-Nenets	9	10.47	51	10.14
Total	86	100	503	100

17 Komi and 9 mixed Komi-Nenets households (tables 6.3 and 6.4). Total population size registered in the tundra made up 503 people (ASE Kanin *sel´sovet* 1972–1975).

Table 6.4. The nomadic population of the Kanin tundra by ethnicity in 1975

Ethnic group	Population	%
Komi	138	27.5
Nenets	365	72.5
Total	503	100

Local statistical data clearly demonstrates an increase of number of Izhemetses in the structure of nomadic populations of the Kanin tundra as compared to 1926–27. On the one hand, it was the result of 'opening of borders' in the European northern tundras after collectivization. Under these conditions Izhemets families were now able to come back to the Kanin tundra. Also, some new households could move there now. On the other hand, lack of any obvious social, economic or political privileges for representatives of any particular nationality (except perhaps Russians) led to the stabilization of identity among nomadic populations. In this regard, identity of children in ethnically mixed families was defined according to cultural factors such as language, economy and spiritual tradition.

Reforms of the 1980s and 1990s caused new changes in the ethnopolitical situation for Kanin residents. According to the Constitution of 1993, the Nenets Autonomous District became a 'subject' within the Russian Federation. In the 1990s and 2000s the government started a policy of economic support towards the 'less numerous peoples' of the Far North which brought economic benefits to Nenetses, but not to Komis. This has led to the situation when it once again became advantageous for some families to signal once again their Nenets heritage on the Kanin tundra. As the main criterion for defining one's national identity was self-determination, there was a tendency to register children from mixed families as Nenets. Statistical data from household books in the Kanin tundra for 2002–2006 (ASE Kaninskii *sel´sovet* 2002–2006) reflect these processes.

Table 6.5. The nomadic households of the Kanin tundra by ethnicity in 2007 (Archive of the Kanin village administration)

Type of household	Number	%	Population	%
Komi	9	13.64	35	9.64
Nenets	44	66.67	248	68.32
Mixed Komi-Nenets	13	19.70	80	22.04
Total	66	100	363	100

In 2007 there were 66 households of the community 'Kanin' migrating in the Kanin tundra in summer 2007: 44 Nenets, 9 Komi and 13 mixed Komi-Nenets ones (table 6.5). The total number of population in the tundra was 363 people (ASE: Semenov Fieldnotes 2006).

Therefore, in spite of a hearsay conviction that Komi traditions are spreading on the tundra, current statistical data show an increase in the Nenets population (table 6.6). This

Table 6.6. The nomadic population of the Kanin tundra by ethnicity in 2007

Ethnic group	Population	%
Komi	69	19.01
Nenetses	294	80.99
Total	363	100

underscores the argument that the Kanin tundra supports a regional population where certain aspects of skill and identity can combine to form one or another nationality under specific political conditions.

Notes

1. According to the data from the 'List of settlements in Arkhangel´sk *guberniia* in 1861', there were 850 male and 911 female Samoeds that migrated in the Kanin Peninsula and tundra living in 202 tents (MVD 1861). However, it is obvious that these data bring together nomadic populations not only of the Kanin but Timan tundra as well.
2. The total figure includes 79 small children (up to 12 years old), which makes 194 men excluding children, and 273 men including children (GAAO 6-8-168: 18v–19).
3. An essay with the analysis of the total Russian Empire Census results of 1897 for the Kanin and Timan tundras was published in 'Memorandum of Arkhangel´sk *guberniia* for 1908'. Apart from the analysis of demographic, social and economic figures, it contained information about the Samoed clan structure. It described the population of each tundra dividing itself into clans which are made up of individual families. There were 12 clans in Timan tundra and 14 clans in the Kanin tundra. Eight of these 26 clans were defined as large clans with ten or more families. On the Kanin tundra the larger clans included 13 families of Arteevy, 21 families of Bobrikovy and 6 families of Kaniukovy (Samoedy 1908: 57).
4. Editor's note: A blank copy of this form can be found in Moscow in the *fond* of the Central Statistical Administration along with other early twentieth century survey instruments as examples of the material that went in the design of the household card (GARF 3977-1-214: 61–91).
5. Editor's note: It is unclear if these centrally printed forms from the general Federal Census were simply used as proxies for the Polar Census variant called a Household List (*spisok khoziaistv*) or if the data from the Polar Census forms was rewritten onto these forms. It is clear that the people recorded here were not homeowners, but nomadic reindeer herders.
6. In 1934 there were three work units (*tovarishchestva po sovmestnomu vypasu olenei*) formed on the Kanin Peninsula. The director of 'Vyl´ Tui' was Ivan Federovich Vokuev; the director of 'Tato' was Artemii Fedorovich Khanzerov; and in 'Vil´ Olem' the directorship was shared by Aleksei Vasil´evich Chuprov and Vasilii Egorovich Vokuev. All four directors were Izhemetses.

7 | The Sustaining Landscape and the Arctic Fox Trade in the European North of Russia, 1926–1927

Konstantin B. Klokov

The manuscript archive of the Polar Census of 1926/27, together with other regional publications of the same period, provide a valuable picture of the lives of the indigenous peoples of the Russian North before they were transformed by the Soviet regime. These sources document particularly well how indigenous peoples interacted with their environment. The use of documents to reconstruct adaptation of different ethnic groups to their environments is a relatively new approach in Russia. However, it corresponds to the work of numerous scholars who seek to relate society and nature (Scoones 1999; Balée 2006). For these scholars, landscape is a fundamental unit of analysis and can be considered to be the material manifestation of the relation between humans and the environment (Vaccaro and Norman 2008).

Through the interpretation of the manuscripts it is possible to understand how people adapted to their environment, but also to understand how they perceived the resources around them and accordingly organized them. This combination of subjective and objective factors can be described as a 'sustaining landscape'. The sustaining landscape, as I define it here, is not nature functioning autonomously from people but rather an ecological relationship in which the social and economic behaviour of people regulate nature. The notion of a sustaining landscape is close to the *kormiashchii landshaft* [literally: the feeding landscape] of Russian ethnologist Lev Gumilev (1993), who used it interchangeably with *mestorazvitie* [literally: place of evolution, native land].

In this chapter, I will use the manuscript archive of the Polar Census to demonstrate the diverse ways in which Russian settlers, settled and nomadic Komis, and settled and nomadic Nenetses created sustaining landscapes in the northeast section of the European part of Russia. The analysis here will focus upon the hunting of the Arctic fox – the most important trade item in the region at this time.[1] The regions examined are the north of Arkhangel´sk *guberniia* (now Arkhangel´sk *oblast´*) and the Komi Autonomous *oblast´* (now the Komi Republic). Today this territory corresponds primarily to the Nenets Autonomous *okrug* of Arkhangel'sk *oblast'* and the districts bordering it.

The chapter will use a variety of manuscript records and local publications. The heart of the analysis comes from digitized versions of the Community Summaries (*tablitsy poselennogo podscheta*) for Dorogory and Mezen' *volosty* of Arkhangel'sk *guberniia* (GAAO 760-1-28: 1–48; GAAO 187-1-857: 56–59) and for the islands of the Arctic Sea (GAAO 760-1-6: 125–138). These large manuscript tables provided community-level summaries of subsistence activity and were used as intermediary charts to collect data before selecting them for publication. The resulting published tables for each *okrug* and *volost'* published centrally and regionally are also an important source here (TsSU 1929; AGSO 1929). For an analysis of what I distinguish as six territorial groups of households living in the Komi Autonomous *oblast'*, I used the digitized versions of the household cards from this region (NARK 140-2-201~212). The interpretation of these cards is a difficult question, discussed elsewhere (Klokov and Semenov 2007). In this chapter, 588 'first-copy' cards were used. This first-copy manuscript set holds data on some 500 extra households which were not included in the published results. The data on Arctic fox are contained primarily in cells 264 and 265, but the numerous local labels applied to Arctic fox at different stages of the animals' life cycle were often also recorded in the user-defined cells. Physical descriptions of particular regions were taken from the complete archive of Community Diaries for Arkhangel'sk *guberniia* (GAAO 187-1-892) and the Komi Autonomous *oblast'* (NARK 140-2-200; NARK 140-2-203: 85–100 [duplicates in NARK 140-2-286]). The narrative descriptions of local territorial groups came from the unpublished manuscript diaries and letters held in GAAO and NARK, as well as many anonymous articles published in the rare regional journals *Komi-Mu* and *Severnoe Khoziaistvo* and one monograph based on the results of the Polar Census in this region (Babushkin 1930).

Fur-Hunting among Indigenous Peoples of the Russian North

According to the published data from the Polar Census, in the 1920s hunting and trapping was the second and sometimes the third most important economic sector for the peoples of the European northeast. There were very few families who hunted exclusively for their livelihood. In the north of Arkhangel'sk *guberniia,* the people who hunted most were nomadic indigenous households where roughly one third of the families (36.2 per cent) reported that the majority of their income came from hunting. Among both settled indigenous households and settled Russian households, the proportions of their incomes earned from hunting were only 21.2 per cent and 8.7 per cent respectively. In the Komi Autonomous *oblast'*, where official results were published only for nomadic households, the figure is as low as 16.8 per cent (TsSU 1929 [table 5]: 152–69). Nevertheless, hunting was still a very important activity since men in nearly every household were involved in hunting, even if it was a supplementary activity. There were also isolated cases of women being registered as taking part in hunting (TsSU 1929 [table 3]: 109).

Hunting was important both for subsistence and for trade. Fur pelts and ptarmigan were the most important commercial resources. Water fowl, such as geese and ducks, as well as ptarmigan were significant sources of food. In this region, unlike others, people rarely hunted ungulates due to their small numbers. Elk was a very rare animal in the European North at that time, and what wild reindeer hunting took place was confined to Novaia Zemlia Island. People also hunted large predators such as brown bears and wolves across the region, although this was also rare.

Fur hunting in the European northeast began earlier than in Siberia and tended to be associated with the Arctic fox. As early as the sixteenth and seventeenth centuries Nenetses from Ust'-Tsilem and Pustozersk *volosty* are recorded as paying tribute at a rate of two white Arctic fox per hunter (defined as any male person owning a bow) (Kirikov 1966: 7–8). By the beginning of the twentieth century no less than 20,000 fur-bearing animals per year were hunted on the tundra of the European northeast. Half of this number were hunted on the Bol'shezemel' tundra and the other half on the Kanin, Timan and Malozemel' tundra regions located to the west of Pechora River. Most people could hunt from 30 to 60 animals in a good year while Samoed hunters sometimes procured 100 animals or more. Their main quarry was the Arctic fox while the European fox, ermine, wolverine and otter were also hunted on the tundra and forest-tundra, and squirrel and marten in the northern taiga. Hunting these other animals was always a minor activity compared to hunting Arctic fox (AGSK 1924: 22–23).

Russian, Komi and Samoed Involvement in Arctic Fox Hunting

In the 1920s nearly all of the population of the European northeast was engaged in Arctic fox hunting in some way. However, what I will define as different territorial and sometimes ethnic groups hunted the fox differently using a wide variety of strategies. The key differences in strategy are associated with what one might call a spatial quality: whether or not a territorial group was nomadic or settled. However, as I will show, the efficiency of the hunt, defined both in terms of the quantity of furs harvested and their quality, in turn tended to be associated with certain identity markers that today are understood as ethnicity.

I have divided the Russian population of this time into three groups, each of which had a different relation to Arctic fox hunting. The number of fox captured is presented in table 7.1. One group, living and working permanently on the islands of the Arctic Ocean as hunters and civil servants (*sluzhashchie*), devoted their time to fishing, sea hunting and hunting wild reindeer. Only 14 families here hunted a small number of Arctic fox.[2] A second group consisted of peasants who lived in the lower Pechora area (Pustozersk and Ermit *volosty*) who did not keep cattle but fished along the Pechora and Indiga rivers and trapped ptarmigan in winter. According to the published records, these hunters took only 1 or 2 Arctic fox per year.[3]

The third, and for our purposes, significant group consisted of Russian peasants who lived in the villages along the coast of Chesha Bay (Oma and Pesha village councils) and the western coast of Kanin Peninsula (Nes' village council). Their households were rich and must have looked like oases in the deserted tundra (AGSK 1924: 16). Their rich grass meadows allowed the peasants to keep considerable numbers of cattle. Each household could have up to 10 cows, 2 to 3 horses and 20 to 30 sheep, and the produce such as milk, cottage cheese, butter and meat were enough to satisfy the needs of a household. The surplus was usually exchanged for fur with nomadic Samoeds. Some peasants planted potatoes, beetroot, radish, horseradish and other crops such as barley (although it did not ripen every year). Cattle-breeding formed the mainstay of their economy. Another important subsistence resource was fishing navaga at the mouths of rivers, and whitefish, peled, grayling, burbot, pike, perch and ruff in tundra lakes. Seals and white whale were hunted at sea. These households hunted fur animals in any free time that they had remaining when they were not fishing. It is interesting to note that the average number of Arctic fox caught by each household was no less than that among the nomadic Samoeds (table 7.1, lower rows).

While the settled Russian population consisted of clearly localized groups, the nomadic peoples are harder to divide and categorise. A distinction has been made between Samoeds and Komi-Izhemetses. Many authors have written about the controversial nature of this distinction at the end of the nineteenth and beginning of the twentieth century (Babushkin 1930: 21–33; Semenov, this volume). Most commentators distinguish the two groups by their economic strategy. Samoed households are characterised as being self-sufficient and concerned with their own subsistence while Komi-Izhemetses were interested in participating in the monetised economy and in accumulating capital in order to sponsor further investments. The Polar Census enumerator K. Korelin also describes this distinction in his manuscript report:

A Komi-Izhemets looks after his herd better. He provides animals with vaccinations, does not harness female reindeer and keeps reindeer in better conditions

Table 7.1. The number of households hunting Arctic fox in the north of Arkhangel'sk *guberniia*

Volosty	Village and Tundra councils	Type of household	Number of households			Hunted Arctic foxes per household			Total hunted Arctic foxes			
			Komi	Russians	Samoeds	Komi	Russians	Samoeds	Komi	Russians	Samoeds	Total
Dorogory	El'kin	settled	—	41	11	—	0.03	0.00	0	1	0	1
	Moseev	settled	—	55	—	—	0.05	—	0	2	0	2
Kaninsko–Timan	Kanin	nomadic	9	—	139	2.3	—	9.4	7	0	1170	1177
	Timan*	nomadic	97	—	46	2.7	—	5.4	16	0	238	254
Mezen	Ness' (partly)	settled	1	9	1	1.0	15.4	4.0	1	139	4	144
	Oma	settled	—	84	1	—	8.3	6.0	0	559	6	565
	Pesha	settled	26	58	7	0.0	0.1	0.0	0	3	0	3

* Data on Arctic fox hunting in Timan tundra and Pesha village council are not comparable with those for the rest of the table because they relate to the season 1925–26 when the Arctic fox population was low.

during winter than a Samoed. A Samoed does not usually count his reindeer. He does not know how many animals per year die naturally, are killed by predators, or slaughtered by him. He justifies this by his illiteracy and says that they just eat reindeer meat as long as they have some. Samoed herds are small, which means they have little offspring per year, and some herders do not have any at all, as all calves are consumed. Therefore the herds increase very slowly. On the contrary, Izhemtses have a lot of offspring, look after it and rear the youngsters. (GANAO 5-1-3: 42–49)

In table 7.1 I have therefore listed Komi and Samoed households in separate columns.

Analysis of the census data, as well as manuscript data from enumerator P. Barskii, suggest that nomadic households in Timan tundra (table 7.1, row 4) hunted less Arctic fox (and more red fox) than the households in the neighbouring Kanin and Malozemel′ tundras (GAAO 760-1-28: 1–48, 187–257). All other published sources state that the hunters of the European northwest tundra, as a rule, hunted many more Arctic fox than red fox. This contradiction can be explained by the fact that Barskii did his survey on the Timan tundra and in Pesha village in the summer of 1926, which would mean that he received information on the winter of 1925 when the population of Arctic fox would still have been low. The numbers from the Timan tundra, therefore, do not correlate with those of other regions.[4]

An analysis of the data in Table 7.1 shows that nomadic Samoeds captured the bulk of the Arctic fox in the region, but if one looks at the number of fox caught per household, certain Russian and Komi households seem to specialize in hunting this animal. In all areas Samoeds harvested much more Arctic fox per household than Komis (see table 7.1).

The bulk of the Arctic fox hunting was conducted by nomadic households. If it is difficult to distinguish between Komi and Samoed households, there is a wealth of classification systems for the nomadic households in the region. Indeed, the distinction between 'nomadic' and 'settled' was one of the primary categories by which the Polar Census data was compiled. For a nomadic household, the significance of fur hunting was closely connected with the number of reindeer they held. Among these, there could be two types of households: the first type had large reindeer herds and made its living by selling produce from reindeer herding. The second type was mainly involved in hunting and fishing and used reindeer for transportation purposes. Polar Census enumerators were very concerned about such differentiations because they were considered to be related to 'class-stratification'.

In his classification system, N.D. Teren′t′ev (1926) observed that there were two types of households on the Bol′shezemel′ tundra – those engaged in reindeer herding, and those engaged in hunting and fishing. Both types had reindeer, but for the latter reindeer played the same role as horses might on a peasant farm (although a peasant household might depend heavily on horses, it is not classified as a horse-breeding household). Ninety per cent of hunting and fishing households in the tundra were Samoed. They were former reindeer herders who abandoned herding for various reasons. No economic or social stratification was observed within such groups. It was, however, possible to distinguish between poor and rich reindeer-herding households.

Anton Vitiugov (1923: 3–10) distinguished three groups of households. The first group consisted of the poor who concentrated on hunting and fishing. They only used reindeer for transport and kept usually from 30 to 100 animals. The size of their herds was not large enough for them to travel out to the taiga, although several of such households could join together in order to move from one site to another. Therefore, these households were not strictly sedentary but had a semi-nomadic quality. The second group was made up of households of average means, for whom reindeer herding was the main activity, and hunting, fishing and sea hunting were secondary. Each family kept from 500 to 700 head of reindeer. Under favorable circumstances, such a household could progress into Vitiugov's third category. That third group consisted of large reindeer-herding households and had two sub-categories. The first consisted of families who kept their own reindeer with numbers of up to two or three thousand head. The second subgroup was a ranching type of household that possessed from three to five thousand reindeer and which hired other people to work for them. The owners of the herd were not involved in reindeer herding themselves and did not live by the herd permanently but visited it occasionally. Most reindeer herding produce was used for sale or processing.

Barskii (GANAO 5-1-3: 18–41) also distinguished four types of reindeer-herding and hunting households in the region: large, middle, small and extremely poor (edomskie). Barskii's scheme was similar to that of Vitiugov differing only in the definition of poor households, which, according to Barskii were far poorer with an average of 13 reindeer per family or 2.6 reindeer per person. Such households could not migrate independently and stayed near lakes (edomy) from spring until late autumn, feeding themselves from fishing.

The several ways that indigenous households were classified at this time reveals two strategies which speak to the question of how people structured the sustaining landscape (see table 7.2). First, the fewer the reindeer held by a household, the more important attention that household devoted to hunting animals for fur. Second, fur hunting was more important for Samoeds than for Izhemetses, as the former, on average, held fewer reindeer. This difference is even more striking if we correlate the quantity of hunted animals to the number of working-age men in a household. For example, on the Bol'shezemel' tundra, a Samoed hunter would catch three times more Arctic fox on average than an Izhemets. In Arkhangel'sk guberniia, the correlation could be even 13 to 1 in favour of a Samoed hunter. If we turn to commercial income, hunting brought twice as much money to nomadic Samoed households as did reindeer herding.

Given the documented differences in hunting strategies between Samoeds and Komi-Izhemetses, it is surprising that the two groups did not differ significantly in the average number of reindeer they owned. On the Bol'shezemel' tundra Komi-Izhemetses owned only 1.3 times more reindeer than Samoeds. This factor rises to 1.7 times in Arkhangel'sk *guberniia*. It would seem that if rich Izhemets reindeer herders almost never hunted, then Samoeds holding a similar number of reindeer were greatly interested in hunting. It is possible that the documented lack of interest of Izhemets households in fur hunting can be explained by something other than their involvement in reindeer herding, such as cultural difference in the way that they thought about economic maximization.

Samoed households in the Bol'shezemel' tundra had, on average, almost 3 times more reindeer than the Samoeds of Arkhangel'sk *guberniia*. It is interesting that these large reindeer-herding households also hunted 1.4 times more Arctic fox than their cousins in Arkhangel'sk *guberniia*. This fact contradicts the first tendency we noted – that hunting is usually inversely related

Table 7.2. A comparison of Arctic fox hunting practices between nomadic Samoeds and Komi-Izhemetses in the European North (TsSU 1929: 30–51)

Indicator	Unit of measure	Komi autonomous oblast' Bol'shezemel'		Arkhangel'sk guberniia	
		Komi	Samoeds	Komi	Samoeds
Total households	number	145	141	45	399
Average size of a household	persons	8.2	6.3	7.0	5.9
Average number of men in a household	persons	3.2	2.2	2.5	1.8
Men in a household involved in reindeer herding	%	89%	89%	70%	84%
Men in a household involved in hunting	%	46%	55%	30%	65%
Average number of reindeer in a household	number	866	642	374	225
Average number of traps in a household	number	7	13	3	6
Average number of wooden traps (*kulemy*) in a household	number	—	—	—	8
Reindeer herding produce sold by one household at an average	roubles	917	415	639	250
Hunting produce* sold by one household at an average	roubles	424	707	173	480
Number of Arctic foxes hunted by one household at an average	number	6.9	13.6	2.9	9.8
Correlation between reindeer herding and hunting produce	times	2.2	0.6	3.7	0.5
Number of hunted Arctic foxes per one man in a household at an average	number	1.8	5.8	0.4	4.7

* Produce from hunting ungulates and predators is also included.

to reindeer ownership – and suggests that some other cultural factor attracted Samoeds to hunting.

If we turn to the unpublished household cards for the Komi Autonomous *oblast'* (table 7.3) it is possible to confirm that Komis and Samoeds had different strategies. If the 588 households are divided into six territorial groups by river basin, it is possible to see that Samoeds chose to hunt far more Arctic fox than Komi-Izhemetses. Of those households that came to the Bol'shezemel' tundra from beyond the Urals for the summer (from Obdor and Berezov *raiony*) only Samoed groups chose to hunt Arctic fox. They also hunted most among all of the groups under discussion.

This region also supported a number of interesting regional groups who followed a mixture of strategies. The so-called 'settled Samoeds' recorded in the Polar Census manuscripts often represented destitute or groups of mixed identities. One poor group of 17 Samoed *edomskie* lake-dwellers lost their reindeer due to an epidemic in 1924 (GANAO 5-1-3: 40–41). The *kolvinetses* of the Usa River tributary of that name were a settled group of hunters reflecting the identities of the contact zone of both Nenetses and Komis. They came about in part from by settled Nenetses who took aspects of the material culture of Komi-Izhemetses (Konakov and Kotov 1991: 98). In table 7.1, we can assume that most of the *kolvinetses* were recorded as 'settled' Samoeds. They are significant for this study in that they lived in a region with the highest concentration of Arctic fox dens and thus contributed to the high rates of hunting for the

Table 7.3. A comparison of Arctic fox hunting households in the North of Komi Autonomous *oblast'*

Groups of households	Number of households hunting Arctic fox		Average number of Arctic foxes hunted by one household		Maximum number of Arctic foxes hunted by one household		Total number of hunted Arctic foxes	
	Komi	Samoeds	Komi	Samoeds	Komi	Samoeds	Komi	Samoeds
Households of Komi oblast'								
Kolva basin (settled and nomadic)	90	65	4.8	11.5	42	80	433	746
Usa basin (settled and nomadic)	203	33	2.5	3.5	20	15	510	116
Lower Pechora (mainly nomadic)	2	30	7.5	10.7	10	40	15	321
Middle course of river Pechora (settled and nomadic)	60	85	3.5	8.3	22	50	208	704
Nomadic households spending winter beyond Urals								
In Obdor raion	1	8	0.0	15.3	0	30	0	122
In Berezov raion	11	—	0.5	0.0	2	0	6	0

Source: Household cards from NARK.

Kolva basin (table 7.3, row 1 ['Samoeds']). I will focus upon their strategies for rearing captured Arctic fox in detail below.

This overview of the six territorial groups of the region establishes a wide difference in the way that different groups relate to the environment and in particular to the hunting of Arctic fox. Groups with high mobility ('nomadic') but who were not distracted by the onerous task of caring for too many reindeer ('Samoeds') tended to have the time and the desire to hunt more Arctic fox. However some settled groups, such as the *kolvinetses*, had developed certain strategies to allow them to hunt Arctic fox at high levels despite their lower level of mobility. In order to explain the differences, we must now turn to understanding the methods of hunting Arctic fox. This discussion will show how the combination of mobility and time could result in more or less successful strategies for different groups hunting in the same geographical environment.

The Arctic Fox: Its Environment, and Local Hunting Practices

The Arctic fox's main breeding places in 1926–27 were located in the Bol'shezemel' and Malozemel' tundra regions in areas overlapping with the traditional territories of Samoeds and Komi-Izhemetses. Small quantities of Arctic fox are also found along the southern coast of Mezen' Bay. The animals did not breed in the northern regions of the Komi Autonomous *oblast'* but were found there in large numbers during migration. According to Sergei Kirikov (1966: 8–11) the Arctic fox's average population in the European northeast remained approximately the same during two first-thirds of the twentieth century. Therefore we can use detailed calculations of its population dynamics made by zoologists from the 1950s to the 1970s in order to estimate an approximate level of the Arctic fox population in the 1920s (Skrobov 1960; Shiliaeva 1982).

The Arctic fox lives in special warrens which are built through the collective activity of many generations of animals in their struggle against permafrost. They can be inhabited for hundreds of years. The warrens occur in complexes of 10-15 placements per 10 square kilometres. The old warrens occupy a territory of 100 to 500 square metres. There are seven such complexes on the contemporary territory of the Nenets Autonomous *okrug* and about 30 thousand Arctic fox warrens today (Skrobov 1960). Rich grassy vegetation grows on top of the warrens making it possible to find them from a distance of up to one kilometre away on level ground. As female Arctic fox often come back to old warrens, hunters valued these warrens highly and often considered them to be their own property. Animals do not usually come back to warrens that have been dug open by hunters.

While the so-called built environment of the warren implies a strong sense of territoriality for the people interested in finding Arctic fox, the demography of the species has the reverse effect. The Arctic fox population is characterized by sharp changes in size due to the instability of their food, namely lemmings. This results in considerable shifts in hunting luck from year to year. The Arctic fox's population size reaches its maximum and minimum at different times in different regions. For example, in Murmansk *oblast´* it reaches its peak every two to six years, and every four years on average. The Arctic fox population in the Nenets Autonomous *okrug* has a clear three-year cycle (Shiliaeva 1967: 91–98).

Due to their cyclic population dynamics, data on the number of Arctic fox hunted in one year cannot be truly representative and may relate to a low phase or to a peak phase. As the Polar Census has data for only one year, it is important to specify the phase of the Arctic fox's population cycle at that time. According to statistics on fur procurement, trade organizations in Komi Autonomous *oblast´* bought more than 19,000 Arctic fox furs in 1927 (fig. 7.1). In the previous year, which witnessed an average size of the Arctic fox population, they bought 5,500 furs, whereas in 1925, which was a minimum phase year, they bought less than 1,000 (Babushkin 1930: 104). Before that, a successful hunting season took place in 1922–23 when about 10,000 animals that had not yet shed their fur (the so-called *krestovatiki)* were hunted even before the start of a hunting season (Pushnoi promysel 1923: 111; Promysly pestsa 1923: 103).

There is also historical data on Arctic fox hunting on the Bol´shezemel´ tundra. Hunters procured 5,000 animals on average per year there from 1903 to 1912. They procured 1,500 Arctic fox furs in the years 1922–23, 1515 in 1923–24 and 987 in 1924 (Bulyzhnikov 1926: 6–7).

It was common in the 1920s to hunt the Arctic fox before the start of a hunting season and before it had finished changing its coat, even though the fur was of less value. The Arctic fox is least afraid of people in the summer, which allowed it to be hunted in numbers large enough to compensate for the lower fur price. Cubs that were still living in their warren were called *norniki* ['from the warren']. Those that had already left their warren but had not achieved the classic white coat were called *krestovatiki* ['cross-like coat'], *siniaki* ['bluish coat'] and *nedopeski* ['not yet an Arctic fox ready for sale'] according to the different stages by which they changed their coat. The Arkhangel´sk *guberniia* executive committee banned hunting of all these types of sub-adult fox in 1922 (AGSK 1924: 22). Nevertheless the hunt of these types continued and the data on these sub-types was often officially recorded during the Polar Census in the free-form cells of the household card.

The pronounced population cycles of the Arctic fox make it very difficult to make judgments about what a responsible or efficient hunting regime should be, as we shall see below. Without any human predation or sharp changes in forage, the natural mortality of the Arctic fox's population could be very high. In an ecosystem with hunters, biologists expect that on average only 15 per cent of the cubs live until the next breeding season while 69 per cent still die

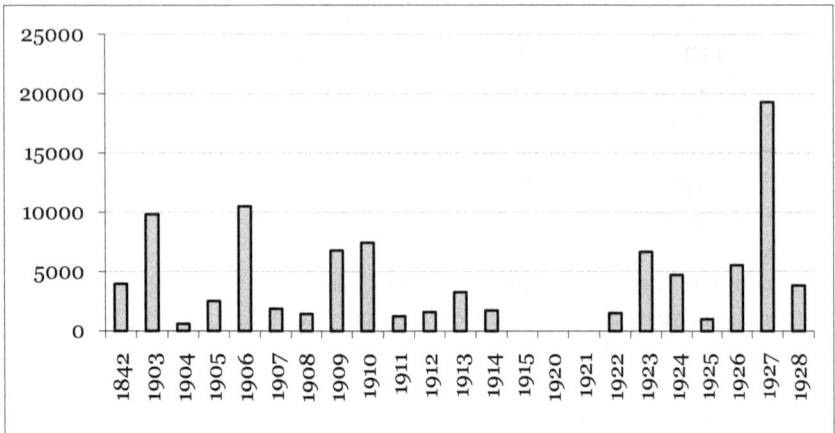

Figure 7.1. Arctic fox hunting in Komi Autonomous *oblast'* (Babushkin 1930)

from natural reasons and 16 per cent are killed by hunters. Intensive human predation of young animals during a peak year of the population cycle could therefore have no measurable impact on the population (Shiliaeva 1982: 1–16). For example, during the period of the 1950s and 1960s when the average level of Arctic fox hunting in the Nenets Autonomous *okrug* approached 6,000 furs per year (similar to the average level of the 1920s), the level of natural mortality was several times higher. The calculation of a natural population is complicated by the fact that the characteristic population cycles of the animal are different in different regions which leads to epic migrations of the animal in one region or another in certain year which might involve up to two-thirds of the population moving (Skrobov 1960; Chirkova 1967). In the Nenets Autonomous *okrug* most of the Arctic fox migrates from the Iamal Peninsula towards the White Sea via the Kanin Peninsula in autumn, attempting to return in spring. These long-distance migrations have been called a 'death march' since ice conditions and a lack of forage mean that most of the migrating animals perish (Chirkova 1967). This demographic background creates specific challenges in how I evaluate the ecological sustainability and efficiency of the aboriginal hunting strategies discussed below.

In the autumn of 1926 there was a large migration of Arctic fox from beyond the Urals, across the Bol'shezemel' tundra to the Malozemel' tundra and further to the west. As a result the Polar Census data suggests an unusual abundance of Arctic fox in the tundra of the European northeast in the winter of 1926–27, which is also indicated in other sources (NARK 1341-1-11: 62–74; GANAO 5-1-3: 42–49).

The largest number of migrating animals moved along the coast. Russian hunters who hunted Arctic fox from shelters called *karaulki* on the coast to the west of Pechora River said that in November and December animals moved along the coast in groups of five to six, and that there could be up to ten such groups each night. Samoeds who hunted Arctic fox by overtaking them with harnessed reindeer sometimes killed up to one hundred animals during one raid. Migrating Arctic fox travelled as far south as the taiga zone. A lot of them were hunted near the town of Mezen´ and in the marshes along the river Kuloi. Some were hunted on the river Pinega and even the river Dvina near Arkhangel´sk (Migratsiia pestsa 1927: 69).

Methods of Hunting the Arctic Fox

There were six main ways of hunting the Arctic fox in Northeastern Europe:

- with metal leg-hold traps (*kapkany*)
- with wooden deadfall traps (*kulemy)*
- through the organization of a collective hunt or 'round-up' (*tolara)*
- stealing-up on individual animals (*skradyvaniia*)
- shooting from a blind called a *karaulka*
- catching young animals before the start of the hunting season, and then feeding them in captivity until their fur thickened (*perederzhka; kormiazhki*)

Leg-hold traps were employed by all hunters and their use was particularly widespread on the Bol´shezemel´ tundra and on the islands of Novaia Zemlia and Vaigach. Traps were rather expensive and hunters treated them carefully. Trap lines were checked regularly in order to ensure the preservation of fur. The number of traps among the settled population varied from an average of 2.5 per household in Dorogory *volost´* to 14 per household on the islands of the Arctic Ocean. The nomadic households on the tundra and islands of Arkhangel´sk *guberniia* owned 4 to 5 traps per household, whereas on the Bol´shezemel´ tundra each household owned 10. Samoed households had 2 or 3 times more traps than those of Komi-Izhemetses (GAAO 760-1-28: 1–48; TsSU 1929: 36–37). According to the community diaries, the settled population involved in fishing and sea mammal hunting preferred to set traps near warrens with bait (GAAO 187-1-892: 607–654). Trapping could be best in autumn when the Arctic fox was still changing its coat but could sometimes result in pelts of a sub-standard, uneven thickness.

The nomadic Samoed population of the Kanin tundra preferred using wooden deadfall traps (*kulemy*)[5] (fig. 7.2). They would build *kulemy* along river valleys and along the sea coast for hundreds of kilometres. There were, on average, 15 to 20 deadfalls per nomadic household in Kanin tundra. However, many Samoed households owned 100 to 200 traps. The total number

Figure 7.2. Roman Sen´ko of the Ethnographic Museum of the Peoples of Russia standing over an old kulema dead-fall trap at the mouth of the Burgenitsa River. Photograph by Konstantin Klokov.

of *kulemy* in Kanin tundra at this time reached 3,000. They were set up in the western part of the Kanin Peninsula along the rivers Bugrenitsa, Mestna, Shoina, Kiia, Chizha and Gornaia; in the Shomokhovsk hills; and in the eastern part of the peninsula from the Kambal´nitsa Bay up to the Sobach´i, Gubistaia and Erennaia Rivers (GAAO 187-1-892: 266–426). Enumerators did not record the use of any deadfall traps either on the Bol´shezemel´ or Malozemel´ tundra as hunters there preferred leg-hold traps (TsSU 1929: 36, 128). Often, as discussed below, nomadic Samoed households would set their deadfalls before leaving the area for the winter and would return to check them several months, or even a half-year later.

Deadfall traps were also used by some Russian hunters who lived along the coast. Hunting households in the area of the Ness´ village council managed, on average, almost 18 *kulemy* per household. The 143 settled Russian households in Mezen´ *volost´* had 1,127 *kulemy* in total, 8 traps per household on average (table 7.4). The traps were located near the villages, making it possible to check them at least once a week. Trapping along the coast was often very profitable, especially during the years when the 'ice' Arctic fox (*ledianyi*) came. This was a local name for an Arctic fox which ventured out on the sea ice in February in order to hunt Greenland seal puppies. The 'ice' fox were hunted when they returned to the mainland from the sea. These animals were very fat (which must have made it difficult to process the skins) and their fur was often seri-

Table 7.4. The number of Arctic fox traps in the north of Arkhangel´sk *guberniia* (GAAO 760-1-28: 1–48)

Volost'	Village and tundra council	Type of household	Kulemy per household		Leg-hold traps per household			Total	
			Russian	Samoed	Komi	Russian	Samoed	*Kulemy*	Traps
Dorogory	El´kin	settled	0	0	—	3.9	3.8	0	203
	Moseev	settled	0	—	—	1.5	—	0	94
Kaninsko-Timan	Kanin	nomadic	0	21.2	1.5	0.0	4.4	3010	657
	Timan	nomadic	—	0	2.7	—	4.7	0	258
Mezen	Ness´ (partly)	settled	17.8	30.0	0.0	4.6	5.0	190	46
	Oma	settled	11.6	0.0	—	4.6	5.0	872	353
	Pesha	settled	1.6	0.0	1.2	1.7	2.3	95	142

ously damaged against ice hummock in the process of travelling (Zhilinskii 1925: 74–79).

Tolara hunting was more common on the Timan and Bol´shezemel´ tundras than in the Kanin tundra. In his report, the enumerator P.I. Barskii mentions that the Samoeds of the Timan tundra often use this method of rounding-up Arctic fox and red fox (GANAO 5-1-3: 28). The method involved gathering 30 to 50 sledges together in one place before spreading out in different directions and then forming a circle. The sledge drivers would then begin closing in towards the centre of the circle, gradually making it smaller. Dogs ran between the sledges and quite often the first circle of sledges was followed by a second, outer circle. Animals trapped in the middle of the circle had no escape. Besides Arctic fox, red fox and sometimes wolves were hunted in this way. When the circle was narrow enough, Samoeds chose the best hunter to kill all the surrounded animals.

Tolara hunting lasted the full duration of daylight hours, usually about eight hours. Anybody who was able to drive reindeer, including women, old men and teenagers, could participate. As soon as the hunt was over, the animals were shared out, with shares determined by the number of sledges provided by each tent owner, regardless of his role in the hunt as hunter or chaser. This type of encirclement only took place in winter. On the Timan and Bol´shezemel´ tundra ambush hunting involving 40 to 60 people on reindeer sledges could surround an area of 20 and even up to 50 *versta* in diameter. In order to increase the coverage in autumn, when the sea was free from ice, people undertook this type of hunting near the coast or on separate capes (Mikulkin, Oma, Barmin, Sviatoi, Zakharvin and others). In successful years there could be 50 to 100 animals hunted in a single ambush. Sometimes animals could escape from the circle if some chasers were inattentive. In the winter of 1924 a group of Samoeds of the Kanin Peninsula chased 17 wolves into a circle but all of them escaped (Zhilinskii 1925: 74–79).

P.I. Barskii (GANAO 5-1-3: 27–28) describes in detail how Samoeds encircled Arctic foxes. He describes how, on a bright sunny day, a hunter followed traces of what was called a 'silly' animal on a reindeer sledge. Having noticed an Arctic fox from far away, the hunter started to circle it. The animal, probably thinking that the hunter would just go past, continued to lie down with no fear of danger. Meanwhile, the hunter kept surrounding the animal in smaller and smaller circles while never directing his reindeer straight at the fox. When the animal was close, the hunter either got off the sledge or drove up as close as possible hoping to remain unnoticed, and shot the animal. Hunters used the same method when hunting on skis.

Hunting Arctic fox from a shelter called a *karaulka* was practiced mainly by the Russians and was considered to be one of the most civilized and successful methods. *Karaulky* were constructed on the banks of rivers and streams and looked like small log-houses half dug into the ground, or simply dugouts. A deep ditch covered with turf or planks led to the entrance of each hut. Sometimes these ditches measured 10 to 15 *sazheny* [23.4–35.1 metres] in length in order to prevent the hunted animal from smelling the hunter. The front wall of the *karaulka* faced the ice from the bank and contained a small hole for shooting, covered with a special shutter. A hunter sitting in *karaulka* could not smoke or even move very much. Bait such as the corpse of a dead sea animal (*raushka*) or any other animal was put 10 to 15 *sazheny* away from a *karaulka*. On a moonlit night a hunter could kill 6 to 10 animals including Arctic fox, red fox and sometimes wolves (Zhilinskii 1925: 74–79).

In 1927, the year associated with particularly high numbers of migrating Arctic fox, Russian hunters invented an elaboration on the *karaulka*. A camouflaged net would be strung at an angle across the animals' track at a site along the coastline very close to the water. A deep hole was then dug at the end of the net. A string would connect the net to a *karaulka* where a hunter was sitting. An Arctic fox on the run would either run into the net and became entangled or would be diverted along the net falling into the hole. The hunter was alerted by movement of the rope and would come out of the *karaulka* to kill the animal (Migratsiia pestsa 1927: 69).

The seasonal rearing of Arctic fox pups was a widely used strategy that was practiced in a variety of different ways by differing territorial groups. This special type of fox called a *kormiazhka* [literally 'the little one that was fed'] is perhaps one of the best examples of the intuition that went into what I refer to here as the sustaining landscape. The small differences between regional and ethnic groups likewise show the subtleties in this intuition.

Russian colonists in the tundra villages of Mezen *uezd* located along the rivers Vizhas, Oma, Pesha and Snopa reared Arctic fox puppies in small log huts with a method they called *perederzhka* [literally 'maturing']. They made narrow perches inside the huts where the animals liked to lie in a way that did not damage their fur. The animals were killed by suffocation in February when their fur was ready and new stock hunted in summer. One household could rear 6 to 10 animals. The *kormiazhka* fur could be sold at a price 25 per cent less than that of a wild animal.[6] The rearing of *kormiazhky* was an established tradition and the warren from which puppies were taken was distributed among households and inherited (GAAO 187-1-892: 753–768). Incoming settlers had to seek their own warren far away on the tundra or buy cubs for rearing from other people.

Solov'ev (1927), who participated in a government expedition charting the forest resources in the Pechora River valley, gathered detailed information about methods of rearing Arctic fox among two groups: the settled population among the Usa and Kolva River valleys (including the *kolvinetses*, other settled Samoeds, and Komis), and among nomadic Samoed reindeer herders.

He called the Usa basin a 'centre for Pechora animal breeding' where local hunters developed a systematic rearing system by trial and error in the early years of the twentieth century. According to Solov'ev's estimations, inhabitants of the Usa basin hunted 756 Arctic fox per year on average. Of that number 700 were transported to the villages and 665 of these were successfully reared. On average, a Usa 'fur rearer' would get an income of 41 roubles from one reared Arctic fox.

In order to get cubs for rearing, Usa hunters undertook long boat trips lasting from six weeks to two months along tributaries of the river Usa such as the Kolva, Rogovaia and Adz'va northwards and deep into the tundra. Villagers went hunting for warrens in groups of three to fifteen people. The groups set off as soon as the ice broke up on the rivers. People travelled day and night with 3 to 4 hours of rest per day. Under favourable conditions, the trip from Ust'-Usa to the upper reaches of the river Adz'va and Vatushkiny lakes (about 300–500 *versta*) took 10 to 15 days; whereas in a headwind it could take 20 to 30 days. Each group tried to go as far onto the tundra as possible. When the first warren was found, groups would leave one boat there and continue their trip with the rest of the boats occupying new places. Sometimes the boats belonging to one party stretched out over 40 *versta*. A central camp was set up in the middle and hunters returned to that camp when they were finished with their warren.

Hunters usually knew the location of Arctic fox warrens from previous trips to the tundra. Having reached their hunting places, Usa people often met Samoeds there who claimed rights over the warrens. In these instances, Usa hunters bought the right to the warrens from Samoeds for approximately 10 roubles. This price was usually paid in-kind in food or equipment. Ten roubles was then was equal to 1 *pud* [16 kilograms] of flour or dried bread in the Upper Adz'va, while the price at a trading post would be two-thirds less. Solov'ev (ibid.), records how a group of hunters reimbursed a Samoed family for seven inhabited warrens (from which they took 35 *krestovatiki*) with food and the following second-hand items: a pair of high-waders, 5 sections of seine, 2 *pudy* of flour, 3 *pudy* of salt, an empty barrel, 3 pairs of woollen stockings and a padded jacket.

Upon finding a warren, the hunters made sure it was inhabited, in which case they filled in all exits with brush and stones except two or three near which they watched for emerging animals. At the open exits they set up traps. These were tied to pegs so that a *krestovatik* did not pull the trap into the warren. Several rods were stuck into the ground on both sides of the trap to prevent the animal from going sideways. Hunters used small ermine traps for this, wrapping the curves in cloth or grass to reduce the damage to an animal's paw. Small traps with soft springs were particularly valued.

Groups that came late bought additional *krestovatiki* from Samoeds. The prices for live Arctic fox were as follows: *norniki* [very young cubs] cost from 3 to 5 roubles and *krestovatiki* 6 to 7 roubles on the tundra. The prices were much higher in the village of Ust´-Usa where *norniki* cost 10 to 13 roubles, and *krestovatiki* 13 to 30 roubles depending on their size, condition and how tame they were. Hunters were reluctant to sell Arctic fox that were already brought to the village and did this only in cases of financial need.

The importance of this activity is illustrated by the fact that the return of hunters with Arctic fox pups was treated as a holiday. In order to let the villagers know whether the trip was successful in advance, the hunters fired their guns when approaching the village and decorated the masts of their boats with flowers and flags (ibid.).

Once in the village, the Arctic fox were most often placed in attics above the living areas and more rarely in sheds or small storehouses constructed specifically for this purpose, as recorded in the village of Kolva. One attic could contain from 2 to 17 animals. *Norniki* were separated from *krestovatiki* with partitions. Sometimes people kept tame animals free inside their houses. Arctic fox responded to the calls of their owners, played with domestic cats and entertained their keepers. Animals were given fresh milk, sour milk with pieces of brown bread or potatoes, and so called *shchi* (cabbage soup) which was, in fact, barley porridge with milk added. Prior to slaughter, the animals were kept half-starving and sometimes were even driven to death from hunger as it was assumed that it would make their fur better. Arctic fox were killed between the end of November and the end of February depending on their state of shedding (ibid.).

Holding Arctic fox in captivity was very common among the nomadic Samoed population as well. However if this activity was refined to considerable efficiency among the Usa and Kolva settlers, among the nomadic Samoeds it was practiced mainly by poorer families and it was often criticized for its inefficiency by observers of the time. For example, Solov´ev criticized Samoed nomadic families for using whatever traps they had on hand to retrieve the cubs from the warren, which sometimes could break the cubs' paws.

Samoed strategy revolved around taking advantage of the habits of the animals and observing their behaviour carefully. It can be described as a type of domestication in the wild. Some families would regularly place food near their warrens. Before they left the area on their autumn migration, and the Arctic fox had grown a little older, the Samoeds would retrieve them with traps. Hunters hardly ever dug out a warren in order to get to cubs as they wanted to save the warren for the future. On rare occasions, hunters smoked animals out of their warrens when they wanted to hunt as many warrens as possible, of if the requirement to move their reindeer herds meant that they no longer had time to watch the warrens. Arctic fox did not return to a smoked out warrens for a minimum of three years.

During their travels, the captured Arctic fox were transported on sledges and kept on tethers in the camps. People used small chains of one *arshin* long to tether the animals. Chains were highly valued in the tundra, and the thinner they were the better. In the absence of a chain people constructed a *zhazhel*, a piece of reindeer horn six to seven *vershok* long [26.4 to 30.8 centimetres] with a hole in one end through which a small strap was passed and tied to a peg. A swiveling shackle was attached to the other end of the horn and fastened to a leather collar. A *zhazhel* could also be made out of two or three smaller pieces of horn that were fastened together with leather rings so that they stayed mobile. The chain or *zhazhel* would be tied to a peg three quarters of an *arshin* long with two crossbars between which was a ring that moved freely around the peg. Pegs were stuck into the ground near the tent. Arctic fox spent all their time outside and could run in circles. If possible, they were kept in sandy places where they could dig out small warren, though this did not protect them from bad weather. Those Samoeds with few reindeer who spent their summers near lakes and hardy migrated at all made special turf shelters for hand-reared Arctic fox.

Samoeds considered fresh fish to be the best food for the Arctic fox. They also fed them with lemmings which they hunted with the help of dogs, sometimes catching up to 100 lemmings in a day. In the absence of other food, they fed them reindeer liver and meat. It was forbidden to give Arctic fox anything salted.

As reindeer herders knew the tundra well and moved around it in different directions, they took many Arctic fox from their warrens. According to Solov'ev, most of these animals died because of hard conditions during travel. He presents an example of six Samoed tents near Vashutkiny lakes which had an average of 30 Arctic fox cubs each in July. After several days of cold rains, however, only 6 cubs were left alive in each tent. According to his estimations, Samoeds managed to successfully rear one or two Arctic fox per tent and Izhemetses three or four per tent on average.[7] It was mainly women who reared the animals.

Many other authors besides Solov'ev noted that holding Arctic fox in captivity was widespread among Samoeds. Zhilinskii (1925) wrote that Samoeds sometimes kept Arctic fox on a leash near their tents but did so mainly for fun. The animals often became tame and ran around the tent free, going to tundra for mice and coming back. Bulyzhnikov (1926: 6–7) notes:

> Nomads, with and without reindeer, with very few exceptions, watch Arctic fox warrens trying not to miss the moment when the offspring appear. When this happens, they start digging out the warren in spite of the issued [1922] law, set up traps, and finally take the whole offspring out of the broken warrens.

In his report for the Polar Census, El'kin says that, in spite of the ban, all reindeer herders were involved in rearing Arctic fox and that it was hardly possible to stop the practice because of the income it provided as well as the fact that for Samoeds, who migrated to the forest in winter, this was the only practical way of hunting the animals (NARK 1341-1-11: 62–74). In good years every tent reared five to eight Arctic fox, and in bad years, two to three. The catching and rearing of *krestovatiki*, as well as trade in their fur, were carried out in secret due to the ban.

When conducting the Polar Census on the Bol'shezemel' tundra, Babushkin saw ten to twenty Arctic fox puppies tied near every tent (1930: 15). These animals had been either trapped or taken from broken warrens. Most of them died before they reached maturity.

When we compare the strategies of rearing Arctic fox by nomadic Samoeds and settled villagers of the Kolva and Usa Rivers (settled Samoeds, Komis and mixed Komi-Samoeds) we can find an important distinction. For Usa and Kolva River people, rearing was their main economic activity which in turned defined the temporal and spatial structure of activities within their sustaining landscape. It developed into sophisticated, economically efficient and ecologically balanced technology of human-animal relationships that could be described like a type of domestication. In this case, the 'wild' cubs were brought into the settled domestic space of the villagers. In contrast, the rearing methods of nomadic Samoeds was efficient in terms of time and effort but inefficient in their results if one calculates the fact that most of the cubs died and the skins produced from the surviving cubs were of poor quality and therefore fetched a low price. For them, it was a subsidiary activity that could not disturb the seasonal migrations of the reindeer herds. Nevertheless it also showed signs of a different type of 'domestication' whereby the cubs were tamed in their own homes, out on the tundra, and the later brought into the mobile households of the Samoeds.

The Moral Economy of Arctic Fox-Hunting Strategies

Reflecting on the differences in Arctic fox-hunting strategies between the different groups of the population, it is difficult to explain these differences solely in terms of economic expediency or a particular geographic locale that suggested a certain strategy. Differences in hunting strategies seem clearly related to different cultural values and perceptions of the environment. This study of the history of Arctic fox hunting provides a particularly rich case study due to the moralistic way that observers of the time judged the value or 'culturedness' of one method over another.

Two examples can illustrate the way that judgements and strategies sat at cross-purposes in the 1920s.

As already discussed, the first controversy concerned the case of the mass hunting of immature Arctic fox (*nedopeski*) during the peak cycle of 1926–27. The accounts of Samoed hunting practices of the time repeatedly label this strategy as 'predatory'. However, given what we know of the population dynamics of the species, during an expanding phase of their population cycle the cubs run out of forage triggering long migrations in the aftermath of which most die. One could make the argument that the mass culling of animals in the autumn and at the beginning of winter actually helps to stabilize the population by reducing pressure on local food resources. In the 1920s, it would seem that neither local Samoed hunters nor early Soviet observers thought about population ecology in these terms. For example, the local Samoed hunters on Vaigach Island in the autumn of 1926 were observed to 'mercilessly extirpate' Arctic fox which had not finished changing their coats on the grounds that as soon as Iugor Shar Strait froze, the animals would escape to the mainland and the hunters would lose them entirely. Russian administrative workers assumed that such hunting would harm the population and tried to stop the hunters. Their attempts to persuade the hunters were unsuccessful and produced only the anxious inscriptions left behind today in the archival record (Pestsovyi pitomnik 1926: 84–85).

The second controversy surrounded the use of *kulemy* deadfall traps by Samoed hunters on the Kanin Peninsula, which many Russians also found to be 'barbaric' and 'predatory'. While the use of deadfalls was optimal in terms of saving hunters' efforts, it could be ecologically 'irrational' depending on the competing demands on a reindeer herder's time. The traps were usually set up during the first snowfall before Samoeds left their summer pastures for their winter homes, moving to the forest zone along the rivers Kuloi, Peza, Vizhas and Oma. The traps were checked only in March and April after reindeer herders came back from their winter camps (AGSK 1924: 22). Most furs could not be preserved for such a long time and were spoiled by other Arctic fox, wolverines, red fox and other animals. Community diaries indicated that wolverines ate 50 per cent of the Arctic fox caught in *kulemy* (GAAO 187-1-892: 395–410). In the case of an early spring or an unexpected delay of the reindeer herders' return from winter places the prey could be spoiled and was thrown away. Zhilinskii (1925) notes that in the year 1922 some Samoeds lost between 30 and 50 Arctic fox in *kulemy* in the Kanin Peninsula. According to his estimations, during the 1923–1924 season wolverines and wolves destroyed at least 500 Arctic fox in *kulemy* on the Kanin tundra.[8]

These two examples from nomadic Samoed practice illustrate two 'archetypes' that the ecologist Iamskov (2005) attributes to pre-agrarian societies. The first archetype is demonstrated by the lack of any consciously articulated restrictions on the consumption of natural resources, as in the first example above. The second archetype is illustrated by the impulse to minimize the expenditure of effort, such as the use of *kulemy* deadfalls to catch Arctic fox over a longer period of time.

By contrast, the then-contemporary social criticisms of Samoed hunting practices implied that two alternate ecological models were better. Each of these had their moral and symbolic challenges. The best strategy was that of the settled Samoed *kolvinetses* who reared Arctic fox pups after an elaborate process of retrieving them from warrens. The *perederzhka* practice involved inscribing onto the tundra alternating property regimes. The warrens and their cubs were private property in the season of their use, but over time were subject to a sort of collective property regime. Such a system ran the risk of the well-known analytical limiting factor known as the 'tragedy of the commons' when individual entrepreneurs could dig up warrens for a quick instant profit (Hardin 1968; Iamskov 2005). The examples described here, however, provide a powerful counter-example to this negative archetype. The Usa people and the *kolvinetses* perfected the rearing of pups to an art, keeping a sensitive eye to the survival of a large number of the pups to maturity and the continued productivity of warrens passed down by group by group. It demonstrates that economic profit did not necessarily lead to the destruction of natural resources but could also mean balancing social needs with ecological cycles.

A second 'cultured' strategy was promoted by the new Soviet administration which tried to blend techniques or alter property relationships in order to improve the well-being of certain social groups. El'kin, for example, suggested that poorer reindeer herders without sufficient herd animals to organise a collective *tolara* round-up could be taught to use Russian greyhounds (NARK 1341-1-11: 62–74). The state also tried to rationalise local models of animal rearing by trying to control the breeding process as well as through the establishment of an Arctic fox farm on Kolguev Island (Pestsovyi pitomnik 1926, 84–85; GAAO 760-1-39: 287–293; 297).[9] Both ideas, although intended to ra-

tionalise and expand existing techniques, required significant external investment which led to their demise. It would not be until the 1950s and 1960s that
mechanised transport and a more interventionist type of state structure would
lead to the construction of successful breeding farms in the region.

From this overview, it is possible to describe three interlinked hunting strategies which together made a 'sustaining landscape' in the region as mediated
by differing ecological opportunities, local values and rules governing access.
The first strategy, best illustrated by the two controversial Samoed examples
above, showed a preference towards reacting to biological cycles which over
time maintained a balance in the numbers of animals on the tundra, allowing
these predominately small-scale nomadic households to pursue a subsistence
lifestyle. The second strategy, best illustrated by the market-oriented settled
Komi-Izhemets and settled *kolvinets* households, showed a concern for reg-
ulating access to warrens through various combinations of communal and
private property. In the third strategy, often suggested by early Soviet modern-
isers, bureaucratic institutions took responsibility for measuring population
cycles and access to Arctic fox warrens in order to achieve certain social-politi-
cal objectives such as 'equality' or 'efficiency'.

Conclusion

In this chapter I have tried to demonstrate the variety of ways in which population groups of the European North approached the Arctic fox as a hunting
resource, as well as the range of meanings that hunting Arctic fox had for these
groups' subsistence.

On the one hand, these differences were determined by natural factors such
as the layout of Arctic fox holes, the peculiar rhythms of its population dynamics and resulting mass migrations. On the other hand, such factors as property
relations and other economic activities, especially reindeer herding, which
required people's migrations over long distances, also played their role. As a
result, hunting practices were adapted to fit into a complex set of environmental relations and social practices. This adaptation was achieved by developing
a unique economy within which every activity took place at a certain time of
year and in a certain geographical place.

The resulting 'sustaining landscape' was comprised of a complex web of interactions and inter-dependant relations. For example, the impact that people
had on the Arctic fox population depended on hunters' property relations in
hunting territories, certain cultural traditions, current price levels, opportunities for marketing Arctic fox furs, and the seasonal migrations related to
reindeer herding. At the same time natural processes such as the Arctic fox's

migration patterns and population dynamics influenced, via income from hunting, people's abilities to settle in a particular territory, the character of a settlement's layout and a nomadic household's migratory routes.

As a result, it is possible to talk about the development of a particular ethnic and geographical division of labour in which each ethnic and territorial group specialized in using a particular range of resources, at a particular time of year, in a particular part of the ecosystem. Several ethnic groups with different strategies, economies and ways of nature management built up a complicated spatial structure within the ecosystem of the European North.

Acknowledgements

The research for this chapter was a collective effort co-ordinated under a research grant from the Research Council of Norway and directed by David Anderson. Iurii A. Stupin and Igor V. Semenov co-ordinated the collection and digitization of the archival manuscripts and regional publications. Anna Naumova and Arina Bil'diug digitized and organized the manuscripts. The interpretations and conclusions in this chapter are my own.

I would like to thank Joseph Long of the University of Aberdeen for doing the first copy-editing of the chapter and especially for suggesting the English term 'sustaining landscape'.

Translated by Maria Nakhshina

Notes

1. Editor's Note: The taking of Arctic fox was described most often in this chapter as *promysel* – a difficult word to translate into English – which implies hunting, trapping and gathering of animals, plants and minerals. In this chapter the words hunting and trapping are used interchangeably.
2. The first group lived on the islands of Vaigach (12 families), Novaia Zemlia (105 families), Kolguev (9 families) and Morzhovets (36 families). Of these, only twelve families on Novaia Zemlia, two on Vaigach and two on Morzhovets hunted fur-bearers, their main energy being devoted to fishing, sea hunting and hunting wild reindeer (GAAO 187-1-865).
3. It should be noted that the Polar Census only surveyed part of this group of Russians (AGSK 1924: 17). There was only one family in Velikovisoch village council registered as involved in fur hunting. However, there were three Russian households in Nizhnepechora *volost'* who took high numbers of Arctic fox, each taking 26 animals on average, with 60 being the most taken by a single household. This group distinguished itself for hunting ptarmigan in winter. When the birds had turned totally white at the end of November or the beginning of December, hunters set their traps 10 to 15 *versta* [16 to 24 kilometres] from the settlement and then checked them every 3 or 4 days until the end of March. Every hunter set at least 150 and sometimes over 200 traps. One hunter could catch up to 2,000 birds on average during winter.

4. The enumerators on the Kanin tundra conducted their work from the end of September 1926 until January 1927. Census-taking on the Malozemel´ tundra was conducted by K. Korelin from the end of November 1926 until January 1927. Korelin organised his expedition to compensate for the unsuccessful summer expedition of Petr Khatanzeiskii.
5. The references to specific Samoed communities using deadfall traps are in the following community diaries: GAAO 187-1-892: 266–426; (Sal´nitsa) 411–426v; (Malaia Kiai) 427–442v; (Elovinskie) 459–474v; and (Ust´e Sobachiikh) 364–379v.
6. The average price of an Arctic fox in Arkhangel´sk *guberniia* varied from 40 to 42 roubles in continental tundra, and up to 50 roubles on the islands of the Arctic Ocean (TsSU 1929 Appendix 2: 236).
7. Apparently, this difference was related to the fact that Samoed families each lived in separate tents whereas Komi-Izhemtsy usually had two families living in one tent.
8. The situation started to change in the middle of the 1920s. Due to high fur prices, Samoeds started to check their traps not only in spring but in the middle of winter too. Some of them travelled hundreds of *versta* in order to check their traps several times during winter. Later, under collectivization, the special reindeer herders' brigades that were created spent their winter on the tundra and checked traps regularly during the whole hunting season. This version of hunting combined with using deadfall traps became widespread across the Russian North and was one of the most ecologically sound ways of hunting. It provided a higher level of fur preservation and quality than hunting with metal traps.
9. The enterprise, which was organized by the state trade company Gostorg, aimed to allow specially imported Arctic fox free range access to the entire island. The fox would be domesticated through the provision of feed in certain places. To make the system work the company imported two hundred Arctic fox and exterminated all red fox in 1927. The state also compensated local Samoeds for the loss of their traditional hunt with money equivalent to 150 furs at average prices. The attempt was a failure due to the expense of importing 35,000 *pudy* of forage, the fact that the fox migrated very easily to the mainland, and problems with the design of the specially constructed houses (GAAO 760-1-39: 291, 297).

8 | The Origin of Reindeer Herding as a 'Sector' on the Kanin Peninsula

Stanislav Kiselev

The twentieth century was a century of dramatic and yet cyclical change for reindeer herders across the Russian North. At the beginning of the Soviet period, when the new Soviet state was consolidating its power in the north, reindeer herders were forced to subsist in a state of complete independence, relying upon their own resources and whatever trade they could freely arrange. At the end of the Soviet period, a similar economic condition was imposed on high Arctic reindeer herders by a state that had decided to detach itself from the lives of its rural citizens. In between these periods, starting from the 1930s, the state displayed a keen interest in incorporating even the most geographically remote reindeer herding families into a national economy through collectivised institutions, a fixed and reliable set of prices, new travel technologies, and a social welfare system. To a great degree these changes can be linked to the idea of reindeer herding as an economic 'sector' [*olenevodstvo*], which still survives today in the newly subsistent economy.

The statistical instruments of the Polar Census of 1926/27 captured the start of this cycle in great detail. Inspired by the original sets of questions in the household cards and the community diaries, the Northern expedition of St. Petersburg University decided to reapply the exact same survey instruments in 2007 in order to test the way in which they measured the subsistence and trade economies of the North. The Kanin Peninsula was chosen for its remoteness from urban centres as well as for its relatively strong reindeer-breeding economy which was reputed to be flourishing because of the collapse of central state subsidies in the late 1990s. This chapter documents methodological problems and advantages of working with the Polar Census instruments and also compares the state of the economy in 2007 with that documented at the start of the Soviet period. At first glance, it would seem that Kanin reindeer-herding economies in 1927 and 2007 were both, in their 'natural' state, free of distortions and ideologies introduced by a centralizing state. However as this chapter will show, the legacy of the reindeer-herding 'sector' made the situation in 2007 look and feel different than its counterpart in 1927.

Unfortunately, as documented in the chapter by Igor Semenov in this book, the primary Polar Census manuscripts for the Kanin Peninsula did not survive in any of the regional and central archives. This chapter uses regional literature based on the primary materials of the census by Geidenreikh (1930), Saprygin and Sinel'nikov (1926) and also uses some comparative material from the household cards of Komi reindeer herders preserved in the NARK. During our fieldwork on the Kanin Peninsula in July and August 2007, my colleagues and I collected information on the contemporary economy using computerized versions of the original household cards and the community diaries lightly adapting the questions for use in the twenty-first century. In this experiment of re-applying the methodology of the Polar Census, we changed only the questions that pertained to geographical regions (*raiony* vs. *volosty*) and altered the names of some commodities (gun shells vs. powder and shot). The measurements recorded were in metric units rather than in Imperial measurements. We preserved the main thrust of the instruments – for example the manner in which they measured the relative monetary importance of different economic spheres (fishing, gathering and reindeer herding).

From the outset, it became clear that some of the questions on the original forms had lost their relevance. Questions about specific types of fish caught or fur-bearers trapped caused some confusion for our informants. We associated these problems with a change in the way that subsistence was structured then compared to now, and specifically with the growth of reindeer herding as a sector, which now dominates the attention of people. On the whole, the information that informants provided on reindeer herding was far more detailed than the forms designed in the 1920s allowed us to record. Informants were happy to comment upon the structure of their reindeer herds, going well beyond cells of the gender-age structure pre-printed on the form [cells 79–109]. Further, they had at their fingertips details of the economic rouble indicators and qualitative information on the organization of pastures and nomadic itineraries that were far more detailed than those asked in 1927. At the same time, there was also an interesting loss of detail. For example, our informants were unable to comment on any difference in reindeer herding strategy between Komi-Izhemetses and Nenetses as it seems that since 1927, reindeer herding itself has become a standardized set of practices between these groups. Informants also provided far less detail on hunting than did their ancestors in 1927. The practice of hunting sea mammals completely disappeared during the Soviet period. The monetary importance of the fur trade also declined dramatically. The only exception to this general rule was the notable increase in the subsistence hunt of waterfowl and gathering eggs and berries. However, it is important to note that the wide variety of active and passive techniques for hunting birds in 1927 has been replaced by a single strategy of using shotguns today. Fishing remained an important source of food in 2007 and informants provided fine detail on this activity for these sections of the forms. However it was striking that in 2007 there was no longer a group of nomadic families who spent most of their time fishing.

In posing questions we ran into some of the same problems that our colleagues faced in 1927. Some informants had difficulty putting a monetary value on the commodities that they consumed. One of the reasons for this is that often these commodities were bartered to them as a proxy for a monetary wages they were supposed to receive from their local institutions (and therefore they were not too sure what the real cost of the goods were). Although we received very rich commentary on the structure and economics of reindeer husbandry it was very difficult to get exact numbers of how many private reindeer there were. We also had difficulty getting information on the number of hunting weapons since, we suspect, many of these weapons were not properly registered with the authorities.

We also made some changes to the way that the surveys were carried out. In 1926–27 the work was done by one enumerator, Aleksandr Kuroptev (GAAO 187-1-897: 105), who arrived at the mouth of the river Kiia by the sea in the beginning of September 1926 and finished his work by 1 March 1927 (AGSK 1927). In contrast, our work in 2007 was conducted by fourteen people over the period of one month. Moreover, our expedition did not aim at an exhaustive survey of the whole reindeer-herding population of the region but instead selected certain families as being representative of the most typical production units ('brigades'). Here, we stood on the shoulders of our colleagues from 1926 by identifying brigades which specialized in main economic strategies that were identified at that time. I have used these ideal economic types to organize the field material and to structure my comparison. The data that we have gathered allows a comparison of the economies of the local population in the 1920s and at the start of the twenty-first century, in terms of their orientation towards market or domestic consumption, the role of different activities in the local economy, and peculiar economic features of different groups of reindeer herders.

The Cycle of Private and State-Mediated Trade

Today, the reindeer herders of the Kanin Peninsula form a mixed regional society (see Semenov, this volume). They include both Nenetses and Komi-Izhemetses and are distinguished from both the local Russian population and other neighboring Nenets and Komi-Izhemets groups in dialect, material culture and their nomadic round.

According to the oldest records, the economy of the nomadic population of the peninsula had always combined reindeer herding with other activities such as fishing and fur hunting. However by the end of the nineteenth century, the marketing of meat, fish and furs gradually came to form a more important part of the regional economy (Babushkin 1930). In the Imperial era, reindeer herders sold meat and fur to private traders who used to travel into the tundra during summer months up until the beginning of the 1920s. Nomadic herders would also travel to special fairs that were held in settlements close to the open tundra. For example, the St. Nicholas fair in Pinega used to play a major role in trade between nomadic and settled populations of Arkhangel´sk *oblast´* at the beginning of the twentieth century (Iz torgovoi 1911: 63). Reindeer herders were also involved in an unlicensed 'grey' trade with Norwegian sailors who bought furs from them on the coast (VSNKh 1927: 10). I will be referring to these personal transactions, which characterised all trade on the tundra in the beginning and end of the twentieth century, as 'private', since it was characterised by direct exchanges between known individuals from the settled and reindeer-herding communities. The extent to which that trade was 'private' or was mediated by the state will be shown to be one of the great differences when comparing these two periods.

From the 1920s onwards, tundra areas in the Kanin Peninsula witnessed the active development of a co-operative movement. New co-operatives were both producer- and consumer-oriented. Members of co-operatives brought all their produce to the storehouse. After that, one member was nominated to take the goods to the market, redistributing the profit upon his return. This strategy of pooling expenses allowed shareholders to limit expenditures on transportation (Chaianov 1925). People also bought necessary goods such as grains, kerosene, tobacco in the same centralized way, which reduced the cost of goods. The main aim of co-operatives in this region was to arrange for the advantageous sale of meat, reindeer skins, fish and furs. To maximise income for the group, a co-operative bought up all the produce from its members at a minimum delivery price and tried to sell it to settler consumers or middlemen at a higher price. After paying for their costs, they would return the balance to their members (Na s˝ezde 1926: 102). By the middle of the 1920s, the village of Nes´ hosted two locally organised co-operatives ('Promyshlennik' and 'Kochevnik') and the village of Pesha hosted one. It is interesting that state organisations also mimicked the co-operative structure. By the same time, the state agencies Gostorg, Sevkoryba and Severopushnina began operating with a similar strategy of delivery and final prices (Torgovlia 1926: 104). The competition between co-operatives and state procurement agencies in the region led to a change in market structure. By the time of the Polar Census, the amount of trade organised privately by individuals fell to 23 per cent of the total number of transactions, whereas the share of cooperatives and state organizations made up 35 per cent and 41 per cent respectively (Geidenreikh 1930: 44–60). However, this liberal period did not last long. By the 1930s, the state gradually closed down the activity of locally controlled co-operatives and became a monopolist in the local market, fixing prices for local products as well as consumer commodities. As I shall show, this was an important stage for the definition of a reindeer-herding sector.

As is well-known, the Russian European North went through a process of collectivization from the mid 1930s onwards when most reindeer became property of collective farms and only a small proportion of the herd was allowed to be held in private ownership by individuals. Strictly speaking, the local nomadic population ceased being independent reindeer herders and became a reindeer-herding labour force hired by the state. All profit and investment into local regional economy was organised directly by the state. More importantly, the budgets of local collective farms came to depend on the biannual audit of reindeer numbers, eclipsing the visibility of other types of economic activity such as fur-trapping or fishing. It is perhaps significant for this chapter that several generations of herders became comfortable with using numbers to describe reindeer herds. The situation began to reverse at the end of the 1980s when the state stopped subsidising reindeer-herding collective farms as a result of the general economic crisis in Russia. This led to a break in this state-centred division of labour. Bankrupt collective farms delayed or ceased paying salaries to their workforces. The state ceased investing in equipment and in buildings for workers involved in reindeer herding. In desperation, the local population started to return to local models of subsistence that dated back to the beginning of the twentieth century. Workers involved in the reindeer-herding industry became reindeer herders again. Their privately arranged trade with the local settled population helped them survive during the first half of the 1990s when there was no support from the state. These autarkic techniques now characterise the newly stable economy of the beginning of this century.

The Commune Kanin

On the ruins of the centrally planned reindeer-herding industry, herders organised a new type of collective institution called a reindeer herding 'commune' (*obshchina*). On the Kanin Peninsula, the tundra population became a member of the commune 'Kanin' in 1993. Until 1994, the population worked in a state farm (*sovkhoz*) known as 'The North Pole' which had been created at the start of the 1960s out of several collective farms. The collective farms were created at the end of the 1920s after the Polar Census survey. Within the commune, a number of 'brigades' (*brigady*) occupied different parts of the peninsula. Unlike at the start of the twentieth century, today it is virtually impossible for people to travel and to practice reindeer herding outside of the commune due to their need for access to land which is controlled by the commune. Within the commune 'Kanin', there were 11 brigades consisting of four to eight interrelated members in 2007. Across the brigades there were 65 brigadiers and herders in 2007, and an unspecified number of people acting informally as tent-workers or apprentices. Apart from reindeer herders, who are always men, and tent-keepers who are usually women, children and elderly people also reside within the commune but do not count as its members. In this sense the commune today serves as a total social institution. As soon as children start going to school they only visit their parents in the commune during holidays. Most children after they graduate from school start working for one of the brigades as apprentices earning 50 per cent of an average wage. They become herders after a year, or leave the region for the obligatory military service. There are not many elderly people living in the brigades. Most pensioners choose to remain in the village of Nes' upon reaching the age of 55 or 60 when the local administration provides them with housing.

The 'brigade' is not a stable organisational form and only serves as shorthand for a complex set of relationships mediated by kinship. The term itself originates from the previous state-mediated collective farm when the unit might have been more directly controlled by a collective farm's director. The core of a contemporary brigade is most often comprised of one or two groups of relatives who are then joined by several non-related families. In the example of brigade 8, the majority of its membership is made up of families of Petr Ivanovich Niurov and Aleksandr Alekseevich Kaniukov and their children (fig. 8.1). In addition, two other unrelated families with children worked with the brigade in the period of 2006–07. Such 'unattached' families often move across brigades. Their reassignment may be caused by inner conflicts, a marriage followed by a transfer to another brigade, or a temporal secondment of a herder to another brigade due to the lack of men there. It should be noted that secondments were more common in the 1990s, when the commune organisation was new, than they are at present.

The leader of a brigade, a brigadier, is currently appointed by the chairman of the commune 'Kanin'. In the 1990s this position was formally elective, but in reality the position is rarely rotated. A brigadier was expected to serve for several years and at least four brigadiers at 'Kanin' have served in this capacity for several decades, having begun their careers in the Soviet period. The main duties of a brigadier are the day-to-day organisation of work as well as the biannual reporting to the commune 'Kanin' on the number of reindeer in a brigade, amount of procured meat, antlers etc. The main regional decisions are taken by all brigadiers together at general meetings that take place twice a year. The first meeting is held during the Reindeer Herder's Festival on the 2nd of August usually in the north of the peninsula. The second meeting takes place in the village of Nes' in March. Between meetings, affairs are managed

Figure 8.1. Brigade 8, Kanin Commune, with the author. Adults from right to left: Boris Ivanovich Latyshev, Konstantin Aleksandrovich Kaniukov, Igor′ Aleksandrovich Kaniukov [holding an infant], Arkadii Aleksandrovich Kaniukov, Sergei Petrovich Niurov [with a backpack], Irina Aleksandrovna Kaniukova [with a headscarf], Rimma Petrovna Kaniukova [white jacket], Aleksandr Petrovich Niurov.

Children from right to left: Sergei Igorevich Kaniukov, Viktorina Igorevna Kaniukova [an infant], Dmitrii Igorevich Kaniukov, Svetlana Igorevna Kaniukova [in a skirt], Svetlana Kaniukova. The author of the chapter, Stanislav Borisovich Kiselev, is standing in the middle of the last row.

Photograph by Igor Semenov.

by the chairman of the commune who resides in the city of Arkhangel′sk and regularly visits brigades by travelling in a helicopter. The chairman is elected once every few years by all members of the commune. There is no fixed time interval between the elections.

I consider such a commune an intermediary form between a cooperative in its initial form and a collective farm of the high Soviet period. On the one hand, it provides for centralized marketing of reindeer skins, meat and antlers and procures everything that the reindeer herders require, much like the early co-operatives. Further, all members of the commune equally take part in the election of the chairman. On the other hand, the commune owns part of a reindeer herd and members of the commune earn a wage, both of which are features associated with a collective farm. The latter is a significant factor. In 2007, 70 to 80 per cent of meat and furs produced in the region were sold via the commune, providing an important source of income for low- and middle-income families. The rest is sold privately to the settled population of the region. However, the situation is reverting gradually back to an increase in private trade as the largest and strongest households try to sell reindeer meat independently in the cities of Nar´ian-Mar and Arkhangel´sk (ASE Fieldnotes Kiselev 2007: 28). One must also note the fact that often these wages are not paid but are instead offset through the bartering of consumer goods, making the state enterprises again look a little more like co-operatives.

If we look at the structure of the regional economy from the point of view of a reindeer herder today we can identify further similarities with the late 1920s. First, the absence of restrictions on trade make this period (and that of the 1920s) considerably different from the high Soviet period between 1930 and 1980. Second, the growing importance of private trade between reindeer herders and the settled population is much like in the early 1920s when herders could choose between different spheres of exchange. Despite these structural similarities, fieldwork based on the Polar Census questionnaires revealed a significant difference in the way economic relations were perceived. In the 1920s, reindeer were recorded and spoken of almost as a set of resources that local nomadic people could use to facilitate their access to fish, berries and fur-bearing animals. Following several generations of state organized reindeer husbandry, reindeer herding itself was clearly marked as an industry in its own right that able to form relationships with other sectors. This consciousness of reindeer herding as a sector is a conspicuous marker of a social change.

In the sections that follow I will focus upon the 'sectoral' aspect of economic organization by reporting on how informants spoke about 'reindeer herding', 'fishing' and 'other gathering' in the conditions of 2007 and reflect upon how this differed from 1927.

Reindeer Herding in 2007

In 2007, the commune 'Kanin' had approximately 30,000 reindeer (of which 12,500 were communal), 11 brigades and 65 employees involved directly in herding. This number represents a marked change from approximately 13,000 which were held in 2004 (of which 42 per cent were communal) and 25,000 reindeer in possession in 1994 (of which 68 per cent were animals belonging to the collective farm). In trying to understand how relationships to reindeer are structured, I adapted a distinction from the analysis of reindeer herding in the 1920s by dividing the brigades on the peninsula into two types (AGIK 1924: 29). I classified 'herding' brigades (*olenevodcheskie*) as those that kept between 5,000 to 8,000 reindeer and spent most of their time tending to their animals.

I saw 'foraging' brigades (*promyslovo-olenevodcheskie*) as those with 2,000 to 3,000 reindeer, which invested much more of their time into hunting and fishing. In adapting this distinction to twenty-first century conditions I have already made a 'sectoral' adjustment in that I have classified groups of families in brigades as having similar strategies. In the 1920s these labels would have applied to specific nuclear or extended families.

As in 1927, the structure of the two types of reindeer herds is also different. A herding brigade will keep up to 40 per cent of the herd as cows, while in a foraging brigade 60 per cent of the herd will be cows, 18 per cent bulls, 8 per cent young male reindeer, 8 per cent barren cows and 6 per cent breeding bulls. The productivity of a reindeer-herding household depends directly on the number of female reindeer. There is one breeding bull per 25 to 30 female reindeer in a herding brigade, whereas the correlation is 1 to 18 in a foraging brigade.

Unlike in the 1920s, there is a distinction of the property status of reindeer between the two types of brigades. A reindeer-herding brigade would collectively tend a small proportion (25 per cent) of its herd as communal property. However, a foraging brigade might hold up to 75 per cent of its stock as communal property.

The difference in the structure and property status of reindeer herds in turn implies that the economic structure of each brigade is also different.

Brigade number 8 in the 'Kanin' commune is an example of a foraging brigade. I surveyed this brigade from 14 to 19 July 2007. As recorded above, it was made up of 33 Nenetses belonging to six families (of which two were dominant) and held 2,800 reindeer. In 2007, the brigade sold 4 tons of meat, 150 skins (including the valued skins from the top of the reindeer's head), 1 ton of ossified antlers and 150 kilograms of velvet antlers.

Reindeer are also slaughtered for the brigade's own consumption. According to herders, an average family of 5 to 7 people requires 37 reindeer per year. Seventy per cent of slaughtered reindeer go to cover family's immediate needs such as food and clothing, whereas the rest of the animals are used in exchange with the settled Russian population and to help the extended family in the village. One family slaughters about one ton of meat on average per year, from which 500 to 700 kilograms are consumed and the rest is sold or exchanged. Both ossified and velvet antlers are valuable commodities that bring 60 to 70 and 150 roubles per kilogram respectively. The herders hardly ever use ossified antlers to make tools any more, since they have switched to other materials. Therefore, about 150 kilograms of ossified antlers are sold per year, which provides about 10,000 roubles of income. Velvet antlers are sold in much smaller quantities in volumes of not more than 10 kilograms per family per year, providing 1,500 roubles of income. About 150 kilograms of meat are sold per year. As one kilogram of meat costs 100 roubles in the village, this makes up 15 thousand roubles of income per year. It is important to note that often meat is bartered for fish, vegetables and other commodities. The market value of other reindeer-herding produce is relatively small. Reindeer herders use most of the skins for making clothes. Skins are sold only occasionally.

Reindeer commodities made up about 20 to 25 per cent of the budget of a family in a foraging brigade. The total value of sale of their reindeer products was approximately 25,000 to 30,000 roubles per year. The wage of a reindeer herder in brigade number 8 ranges from 30,000 to 40,000 roubles per year (but can often be paid out in-kind in bartered products).

Brigade number 10 serves as a clear example of a herding brigade. The brigade was made up of 31 Nenetses organized loosely into 7 families. The brigadier in 2007 was Vasilii Ivanovich Kaniukov. The brigade traveled primarily along the route Nes´ – Chizha – Kiia – Shoina – Kanin Nos (fig. 6.4). It was located near our camp and was thus surveyed by all members of the expedition over the entire length of our stay on Kanin in July and August 2007. In 2007, brigade 10 had 7,500 reindeer, of which 60 per cent were private reindeer. In 2007, the brigade sold 10 to 15 tons of meat slaughtered from private reindeer. The share of meat in a family's diet is much higher in this type of brigade, as subsidiary activities such as hunting and fishing are less developed. An average family slaughters 50 reindeer per year but consumes about 800 to 1,000 kilograms of meat per year (or 30 per cent more than a foraging brigade). Because of the higher number of animals slaughtered, the amount of ossified and velvet antlers available for sale is also 30 per cent bigger. The sale of antler products provides 17,000 to 18,000 roubles of cash income per year. The amount of meat exchanged to villagers is nearly the same as for foraging brigades (approximately 500 to 700 kilograms) due to the limited market in the village. This means that the proportion of meat sold by a family is in turn smaller. The wage of a reindeer herder in brigade number 10 can be up to 90,000 to 110,000 roubles.

Table 8.1. A comparison of the income structure for families living in two types of brigades, 2007

Family averages	Brigade 8	Brigade 10
Average number of reindeer slaughtered	37	50
Average amount of meat slaughtered	1,000 kg	1,500 kg
Average amount of meat consumed	500–700 kg	600–800 kg
Average amount of meat exchanged or sold	300–500 kg	700–900 kg
Average amount of antlers sold	150 kg ossified, 10 kg velvet	Does not sell ossified antlers since they earn enough profit on meat. Velvet antlers were not collected to recently in order to improve the reindeer's health)

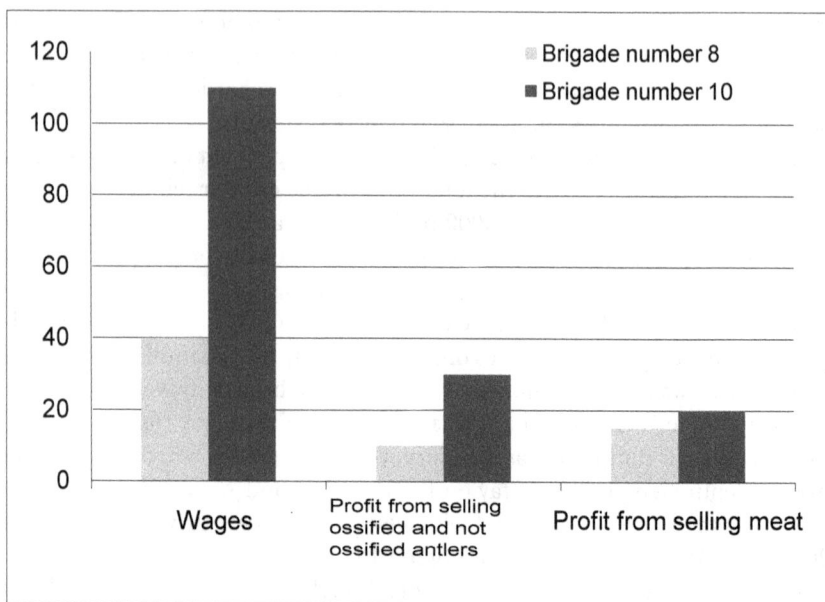

Figure 8.2. Comparative rates of income from reindeer herding in two types of brigades per year

Reindeer Herding in 1927

In 1927 there were 38,853 reindeer on the Kanin Peninsula (Geidenreikh 1930: 41). Approximately 169 households (925 people) lived on the tundra at that time (GAAO 187-1-852: 269–270). A number of authors reported the differentiation of reindeer-herding households into two types based on size, although it should be noted that this differentiation was controversial. Using an article published before the Polar Census (AGIK 1924: 29) and field notes, it would be possible to define a small 'foraging' herding household as having up to 150 reindeer. The same source defined a large herding household as having upwards of 150 reindeer. Economists here, as elsewhere in Russia, were under some pressure to use models of stratification that divided households into three categories. Thus Geidenreikh (1930: 42) defined 53 per cent, or 79 of the 149, households in the region as being poor since they held less than 150 reindeer. He saw 38 per cent of the households (with 100 to 150 reindeer) as 'middle' status and 8 per cent as prosperous with more than 500 reindeer.

Other commentators confirmed the division of reindeer-holding families into two types depending on how they sold their produce. Households of the first type used reindeer mainly for transportation purposes, whereas those of the second, larger type made their income directly from selling reindeer-herding produce such as meat and skins. These economic characters had an impact on other spheres of reindeer herders' lives. The two types based their choice of pastures on different criteria. For households with big herds, the quality of forage resources was most important, whereas households with small herds looked for pastures situated close to lakes and rivers that were rich in fish.

According to Saprygin and Sinel'nikov (1926), only 15 per cent of the households holding less than 50 reindeer could afford to sell any produce derived from reindeer – and this was limited to reindeer skin rugs and skins from the forehead of a reindeer. By contrast, 60 to 70 per cent of households holding between 40 and 150 reindeer were involved in marketing of rugs and skins (Bunakov 1936: 58). Households with more than 150 reindeer were completely involved in selling reindeer produce and their income came predominantly from selling meat. The very few larger households provided 30 per cent of skins and 60 per cent of meat to government procurement agencies (Geidenreikh 1930: 70). Geidenreikh (ibid., 42) also confirmed the boundary of 150 reindeer as the level beyond which a household became a reindeer-herding household. According to Geidenreikh (ibid., 43), the 149 households in the region held 34,323 animals and produced 235.4 tons of meat. Unfortunately, he does not report how much meat each group of households sold.

In the neighbouring Komi Republic, where a large set of household cards was preserved, roughly three-quarters of the 495 Komi-Izemets reindeer-herding families were also recorded as having some reindeer related production (394 families). Of those, just over half (231) reported producing or selling some meat. Omitting those 18 cards where the amount of meat was missing or illegible, the average amount of meat produced was 103 *pudy* by families who held, on average, 297 reindeer. However, as one might expect, this ratio changes radically when reindeer ownership is analysed. Families holding 150 reindeer or more, on average, produced 195 *pudy* of meat while those with less than 150 reindeer produced only 45 *pudy*. The upper end of the distribution heavily weighs the averages with those 95 households holding 500 reindeer or more producing nearly 300 *pudy* of meat. One of the top meat producers, a family with 13 adult members and 2,900 reindeer, produced 1,707 *pudy*. Komi families with less than 150 reindeer were more likely to report the sale of rugs and fur products exactly as the secondary literature reports for the Kanin Peninsula.

The difference in herd structure between the two types of enterprise was similar in 1927 as in 2007. A herding household would keep up to 70 per cent of its herd as breeding females while a smaller 'foraging' household with less than 150 reindeer would keep 43 per cent of its population as breeding females, 2 per cent as breeding bulls and 20 per cent as castrated transport bulls (Geidenreikh 1930: 41).

An important ethnohistorical footnote was the existence of approximately 7 Nenets households in the 1920s who did not depend on reindeer herding at all but who were commercial fishermen. They gave their reindeer (usually not more than 20 animals) to more prosperous Nenetses to pasture during summer-autumn period while they went fishing in the mouths of the rivers Torna, Kambal'nitsa and others.

Fishing, Hunting and Gathering a the turn of the 21st century

In contrast to reindeer herding, which our informants in 2007 called an industry in its own right, fishing, hunting and other forms of gathering were generally spoken of as extra activities that improved the subsistence basis of a household or provided some additional income. In general, the 'foraging' type of reindeer brigades engaged more enthusiastically in these activities. Comparing these activities to the records from 1927, it seems that one can point to the rise of reindeer herding as an industry supplanting that of the fur trade which has become insignificant 80 years later.

The fishing season in the Kanin Peninsula starts in the middle of July when the floods pass and lasts until the middle of September or beginning of October. Fishing usually takes place in lakes and at the mouths of rivers. The main species that are fished include loach, salmon, peled, grayling, plaice and chum salmon. Out of these, only loach has a market value and that is mainly in August and September. Sea fishing is hardly practiced here at all. Only brigade number 10, whose migration route takes it close to the coastline, fish for salmon in the sea when they happen to camp for several days or a week.

Fishing as an activity falls within the dualistic typology that we applied above. While members of reindeer-herding brigades are opportunistic fishermen, members of foraging brigades deliberately plan to stop at places where they also can fish. For example, brigade number 8 would plan to fish at the confluence of the rivers Modakha and Ianei and near Bol'shoi and Malyi Niuder. The camps set at these places would last for 3 weeks, 2 weeks and a month and a half respectively.

The age and gender composition of people that are involved in fishing also depends on the number of reindeer in a brigade. The more reindeer a brigade has in possession, the more the brigade relies on women and children to fish since the men are constantly busy with reindeer. On the contrary, it is mainly men who do fishing in foraging brigades. For example, women from only one family out of the six in brigade number 8 are involved in fishing.

In total, foraging brigades procure 65 kilograms of fish per one adult in a family per year, whereas reindeer herding brigades procure only 18 kilograms of fish per person. The latter even buy fish to supplement their catch often by bartering meat. Members of foraging brigades might sometimes buy or barter fish, but to a much lesser extent. About half the families living in foraging brigades do not buy any fish at all and consume only what they catch themselves.

Accordingly, the market value of fishing varies in different types of brigades. Foraging brigades procure 110 kilograms of salted fish per family per year while each family consumes only 40 kilograms per year. They have three strategies for exchanging the surplus fish. The fish can be sold to villagers, in which case the price for 1 kilogram of salted loach can reach 100 roubles. Or, they can exchange fish through middlemen, which is less profitable but more reliable. The risk involved with selling directly to villagers is that most of them are involved in fishing themselves. The third method is to give fish to relatives who reside permanently in villages.

The total income from fishing, in absolute terms, including the market value of barter, can reach up to 7,000 roubles per year for foraging brigades. By contrast, a reindeer-herding brigade might spend the equivalent of 2,000 to 3,000 roubles per year to cover the shortage of fish.

Hunting plays a similar role in the local economy of the two types of brigades. In contrast to the families recorded during the Polar Census, in 2007 reindeer-herding families living in both types of brigades preferred to invest their hunting efforts in the spring and summer hunt of migratory waterfowl such as geese and ducks. Very few families hunted barnacle goose and wood grouse in winter. Unlike in the past, people hunt today exclusively with guns. Passive instruments, such as the use of traps and snares have fallen out of use. Waterfowl hunting is a subsistence activity. The meat, down, feathers and goose fat is consumed within the family and is not sold. A family living in a foraging brigade consumes up to 200 kilograms of bird's meat per year, whereas a family in a reindeer-herding brigade consumes up to 70 kilograms. The demand for feathers does not depend on the number of reindeer since it is purely linked to the needs of a particular household in one or the other type of a brigade.

Members of foraging brigades also engage in the opportunistic hunting of moose, hares and other animals. For example, brigade number 8 hunted three moose in 2006. The procured meat (400 kilograms) was divided among all members of the brigade. Members of reindeer-herding brigades, however, are rarely involved in hunting of hares or wild ungulates. Members of both brigades only hunt predators if they start threatening reindeer or destroying storage platforms in the tundra. For example, the last time members of brigade number 8 hunted a bear was in the beginning of the 2000s, when the animal started to destroy a storage platform near the confluence of the rivers Bol'shoi and Malyi Niuder.

Fur hunting is almost extinct today. People hunt foxes and Arctic foxes occasionally. Arctic foxes are also hunted in spring when they threaten newborn calves. However, their fur is of a very low quality at this period and hunters do not procure it. The most likely reason for the decline in fur hunting, in comparison with its predominance in 1927 is the lack of a market for fur in the region today.

There is another problem which places limits on people's ability to hunt at the start of the twenty-first century. Within the Russian Federation, hunters have to obtain a hunting license and permission for having a weapon every year. This is troublesome for reindeer herders who are often unable to leave their herds to travel to the cities to obtain such documents. In the Soviet period, by contrast, these documents and the weapons themselves would have been provided by the collective farm. Despite these problems, every reindeer-herding family carries 1 to 2 small-caliber rifles, and every hunter expends up to 300 cartridges per year.

The two types of reindeer brigades are also engaged in the gathering of food and other resources from the tundra. In general, the foraging types of brigades more enthusiastically gathered edible products, while both types of reindeer herders collected the same raw materials that they each needed to make tools and other things necessary to make tundra life comfortable.

For example, one family in a foraging brigade would pick up to 90 kilograms of berries per year (mainly cloudberry). Further, members of a foraging brigade could be expected to gather up to 300 eggs of wild birds a year (and as a rule no less then 100). By contrast, members of a reindeer-herding brigade would gather no more than 20 kilograms of berries or a minimum of 20 bird eggs. In their adaptation to the tastes of settled Russian communities, members of foraging brigades would procure up to 30 kilograms of mushrooms for sale while members of reindeer-herding brigades would pick none at all.

Members of both types of brigades were equally proficient at gathering inedible resources. Both would gather the Norwegian nets that are washed up by the tides. Plastic buoys (for kindling), plastic cans, iron barrels, and even metal from the discarded stages of Russian rockets would be collected by all reindeer herders. Driftwood and willow wood was of course equally used by all for cooking and heating.

Fishing, Hunting and Gathering in 1927

According to the published results of the Polar Census, fishing was economically significant for Komi-Izhemetses holding very small numbers of reindeer. It was carried out in summer and autumn near camping sites. As mentioned earlier, some Nenets reindeer herders gave their reindeer to more prosperous herders to pasture during the summer-autumn period while they went fishing. Households with few reindeer often united together during the summer and assigned several people to look after the herd, while the rest went fishing in the rivers' mouths. Plaice was the most important fish caught, but people also fished loach, pike, peled and other fishes.

Selling fish was economically significant for more than 50 per cent of households who held up to 100 reindeer, but for those households keeping 100 to 500 reindeer, fishing was a significant activity for only one-third. Households with large herds did not fish for sale at all and got involved in fishing only occasionally (Saprygin and Sinel'nikov 1926: 82).

It is unfortunate that the household cards were not preserved for the Kanin Peninsula. That would have allowed us to better understand how 'economic significance', which implied converting the value of production into roubles, related to gross production. If we return to the neighbouring Komi Autonomous *oblast'* it is interesting that both reindeer-rich and reindeer-poor households caught roughly the same proportion of fish. The richer families tended to support larger numbers of people and thus had a larger gross production.

As one would expect, most of the Komi reindeer herders of that time did report some fishing (299 households). Of the 161 families holding 100 reindeer or less, 119 were recorded as involved in fishing. They would produce, on average, 23 *pudy* of fish, or 78 kilograms per person – a number very similar to the foraging brigades of today. Among these, there were approximately six specialist families fishing upwards of 90 *pudy* of fish. The poorer families as a whole reported catching poorer fish (pike, herring and Arctic cisco (*omul'*)) but approximately one-tenth of families reported up to two-thirds of their catch as being higher quality whitefish or sometimes bulltrout (*kumzha*).[1] Aside from these specialist households the next most significant cluster of households caught only around 45 *pudy*. In contrast to the sector-driven reindeer-rich brigades of today, the larger reindeer-holding families of 1926–27 reported a similar relative level of fishing to the smaller reindeer-holding families. Of the 95 families with 500 reindeer and upwards, half (50) reported some fishing activity. Their average catch was 54 *pudy* or 82 kilograms per person – essentially the same ratio as for the poorer families. Interestingly, eight families reported extremely high volumes of fishing upwards of 105 *pudy* (although the exact amounts that they fished is open to a debate).[2] These 93 individuals produced approximately 160 kilograms of fish per person suggesting that in this region some of this fish found its way to market. Almost all of these 8 families caught pike, herring and Arctic cisco with only one reporting half of its catch (50 *pudy*) in whitefish (NARK 140-2-210: 006–007). If the specialist households are excluded, the average for the 42 remaining families was a smaller amount of 23 *pudy* (or 167 kilograms per person) – the same as for the smaller reindeer-herding families. In this group there was one family of 13 with 3,500 reindeer who reported producing 50 *pudy* of lower quality perch and pike (NARK 140-2-211: 139–140).

The data on gross fish production for the reindeer-herding families of the Komi Autonomous *oblast'* suggest that in 1926–27 there was a significant difference in reindeer-herding strategies between households with many reindeer and those with less, but that all households carried out some fishing, generally not surpassing 25 *pudy* or 400 kilograms per year. It would seem that in the days before reindeer breeding became a sector, the sale of fish was one of the reasons for keeping reindeer in this region. Unlike in the Kanin Peninsula, it seemed that here a very small number of large reindeer-herding families did carry out some intensive fishing.

The main type of hunting in the 1920s was the hunting of animals for pelts. Arctic fox made up 70 per cent of the catch, while people also hunted marten, fox, ermine, hare and wolf. As discussed by Klokov in this volume, fox hunting was done mainly with the help of *kulemy*, deadfall traps that reindeer herders set up along animal trails before they left the region for their winter pastures, retrieving the fur in the spring. People would also surround game with the help harnessed reindeer and guns. Hunting summer Arctic fox called *krestovatik* was widespread until 1924. It was easy and productive to hunt it despite the fact that the *krestovatik*'s fur was of little value. The state prohibited this type of hunting completely in the 1920s. One hundred per cent of fur-hunting produce was sold, out of which 50 per cent was sold to the state and 50 per cent to co-operatives (Geidenreikh 1930: 55). Unlike fishing, fur hunting was important for all types of households. I assume that this was due to the stable demand for furs.

Seal hunting was also practiced in the peninsula in the 1920s. However, it was significant mainly for the Russian population, whereas reindeer herders were involved in it only occasionally.

The published secondary literature does not put any emphasis on the gathering of berries or eggs for Komi-Izhemets of Nenets households in 1927. In the nearby Komi Republic, however, the household cards report five reindeer-herding households gathering eggs (with one holding 621 reindeer reporting 250 eggs gathered [NARK 140-2-210: 058–059]). Most Komi households (378) were recorded collecting cloud berries and both types of cranberries, but only in small amounts (average 5.4 *pudy* with no one household reporting more than 20 *pudy*). This fact seems to speak to the value of consulting the primary records, where they exist. It would seem that as with fishing subsistence, small-scale gathering among reindeer-herding families was not such a significant activity to be reported in the published literature of that time.

By contrast, the secondary literature does speak about the importance of transport services for Komi households on the Kanin Peninsula. Many households with 100 or more reindeer would hire their transport reindeer out to transport navaga caught by Russians to market. According to Sakharov (1909:

19), a household could earn 45 kopecks per *pud* in 1909 (and similar prices were in place in the 1920s).

Conclusion

Between 1927 and 2007 the reindeer-herding families of the Kanin Peninsula experienced a full cycle from being complete autarkic to being incorporated into a state-centered division of labour, and then to being autarkic once again. Komi and Nenets families living with reindeer adapted to these changes with a similar set of strategies. Those families holding large numbers of reindeer in both periods of time would tend to specialize in the sale of reindeer products, spending far less time on hunting and fishing. By contrast, those families with smaller number of reindeer in both time periods would have a broader range of activities. Perhaps more importantly, the rhythm of life of those families holding large herds is also dictated by the needs and imperatives of reindeer. By contrast, foraging brigades would alter their nomadic movements in order to take into account the opportunities offered by fishing, hunting or gathering.

The main differences between 1927 and 2007 can be described as sectoral. What is striking is the complete absence of fur hunting today. This seems to be connected to the collapse of the market for Arctic fox but also to the restrictions placed on hunting, and on accessing hunting weapons. By contrast, fishing has become a much more important activity for smaller reindeer herders. This has been partly encouraged by the fact that people living in settlements fish far more infrequently today than they did in the 1920s.

Despite the fact that a dualistic typology of reindeer households is still relevant, it would be wrong to conclude that Kanin reindeer herders have simply returned to a 'natural' pre-Soviet economy. Our interviewing results made it clear that reindeer herding today is seen as a coherent activity – a sector – in its own right. This can been seen in both the way that the economic health of a brigade can be measured through reindeer as a proxy and the fact that families today collectively live in groups (brigades) that have a collective economic strategy. The rise of reindeer herding as a sector has some disadvantages. Although the quality of life of reindeer-herding households has improved, there is today considerable pressure on pastures which do not have time to recover from over-grazing. The situation is complicated by the fact that 'plant association and particularly the lichens that comprise pastures are low efficient, intolerant to external impacts such as over-grazing, fires or anthropogenic mechanical damages and are virtually incapable of natural recovery' (Khrushchev 1991: 35). If the same tendency continues it is possible that there may be a crisis in this sector in the future.

Nevertheless the growth in private, opportunistic trade at the end of the Soviet period has made some elements in the regional economy similar to that of the time of the Polar Census of 1926/27. It was a surprise to all members of our expedition at how relevant the survey instruments of 80 years ago were to a new economic climate. The structuring of questions along certain types of economic activity (hunting, fishing, reindeer herding) in particular have brought forth an interesting set of data that allows regional economies of today to be compared to those of the past.

Acknowledgements

The Northern Expedition of St. Petersburg University conducted a collective expedition to the Kanin Peninsula in July and August of 2007. There were fourteen members of this expedition including seven researchers: Igor Semenov, Konstantin Klokov, Valdis Pilats, Digna Pilats, Din Khun and Roman Sen'ko and myself; and seven students: Aleksandr Mazin, Dmitrii Khapaev, Polina Sergeeva, Ol'ga Veselovskia, Arina Bil'diug, Marina Anokhina and Elena D'iakova. The funding for the fieldwork and for the archival work on the Polar Census records was provided by the Research Council of Norway under a standard research grant titled 'The Polar Census in Western Siberia'. I am grateful for the help of Igor Semenov, Konstantin Klokov and David Anderson for comments on this chapter. The comparative material from the Polar Census in the Komi Republic was digitised by Konstantin Klokov and Anna Naumova and was analysed by David Anderson.

Translated by Maria Nakhshina

Notes

1. For whitefish-dominant households, see NARK 140-2-209: 51–52 [25 *pudy*]; NARK 140-2-202: 41–42 [80 *pudy*]. For salmon, see NARK 140-2-211: 119–120 [70 *pudy*]; NARK 140-2-204: 195–196 [60 *pudy*]).
2. In some of the NARK household cards representing large-scale reindeer enterprises, the enumerators took advantage of the fact that the cells representing fishing were split between the top and the bottom of page 4 of the card. Often data representing reindeer production (meat, skins, etc) spilled over into cells 345–349 representing fish. Unfortunately they did not always cross out the pre-printed labels.

9 | The Spatial Demography of the 'Outer Taiga' of the Zhuia River Valley, Eastern Siberia

David G. Anderson, Evgenii M. Ineshin and John P. Ziker

Introduction

A census is often associated with the accounting of people; however people always live in places – and place is usually a silent partner in demographic research. In this chapter we present our interim results of a project reconstructing the cultural landscape of what is today a remote resource extraction outpost of Irkutsk *oblast'*. Our project used traditional ethnographic field research, ethnohistorical interpretation, and environmental archaeology to understand the intersecting environments of Evenki, Iakut, Russian Settler and Russian Industrial inhabitants. Here we focus upon the meaning of certain transitory spaces often described as 'encampments' [*stoibishche*] in official Soviet archival records but today are often called 'meadows' [*poliana*] or 'seasonal or overwintering cabins' [*zimov'e*] by local people. The Polar Census enumerator A. T. Samokhin wrote of these transitory spaces in his manuscripts with great energy and yet with great difficulty since they complicated the official distinction between 'nomadic' and 'sedentary' populations. Here we argue that a sufficient understanding of the interaction of people and place forces a broader understanding of the 'built environment' which includes meadows, trails and culturally modified trees as material signs of a flexible and autonomous hunting and herding culture. We propose that the material artefacts of what Samokhin described a 'chaotic' and 'semi-nomadic' [*polukochevoe*] existence can be better described as an adaptation focussed upon the use of a 'river valley' [*reka*] as a territorial unit. Instead of concurring with older arguments that these 'not-yet' settled adaptations were signs of the half-completed pressures of cultural evolution and the incipient extinction of ancient nomadic forms, we argue that this semi-settled use of place is finely attuned to exploit the hunting and trade opportunities that mining and the fur-trade created. Our ethnographic work demonstrates that these adaptations are still viable today in the post-Soviet period. This chapter underscores the importance of the Polar Census archive for providing a frame for the project around which other types of data – such as landscape – can be arranged.

The heart of the project was planned by Dr. Evgenii M. Ineshin of the Laboratory of Archaeology, Irkutsk State Technical University. Responding to Prof. David Anderson's request to retrieve and digitise a set of three community diaries from the State Archive of Irkutsk Province (GAIO 1468-1-2) which matched a set of household cards held in the state Archive of Krasnoiarsk (GAKK 1845-1-78), he came upon Samokhin's exacting description of the Zhuia River valley. Dr. Ineshin is an archaeologist with a strong interest in Upper Holocene geology and the reconstruction of ancient climates. He has worked in the lower Vitim region since 1985 as a state archaeologist ensuring that gold-mining operations do not erase the cultural heritage of the region. One of his portfolios is the protection of graveyards. The community diary for Lake Tolondo made passing reference to a previously unknown aboriginal (*tuzemets*) cemetery located near 'an island' at this alpine lake (GAIO 1469-1-2: 35v). Dr. Ineshin was already aware of this lake in a different context. Created by the retreat of an ancient glacier, the lake is a geographic oddity for being a large, relatively deep body of standing water (43 metres) in a rugged mountainous region. The river cuts into the middle of the lake allowing the lake to become a sort of reservoir for fish when the river falls in the summer and winter. The census records for 1926/27 record 229 *pudy* of fish caught including taimen, grayling and whitefish. The five-metre terraces surrounding the lake, initially formed by the nearby Zhuia River, are very old and have seemingly been stable for 9,000 years. Knowing that the Vitim-Patom plateau in general is characterised by ancient overlays of organic material sealed by permafrost, this combination of long-term occupation and climate alerted his instincts to a potentially interesting site for an archaeologist to find marks of ancient human occupation.

Prof. Anderson suggested adapting certain Swedish landscape archaeological techniques to try to untangle the history of human occupation in the Zhuia valley. The work of Kjell-Åke Aronsson (1991, 1994) demonstrated that forest meadows in Northern Sweden often begin their lives as the sites of ancient reindeer corrals. They then, in turn, can be taken over by other incoming populations for use as hay meadows for other types of animals. Aronsson's work shows that what may at first glance look like a forest meadow might be a complex artefact created through generations of different types of cultivating strategies. The Polar Census documents suggested that the landscape of forest, meadow, log buildings and trails was very similar to Aronsson's documentation of an area that collectively belonged to Forest Sami and Swedish farmers. At first, this was a surprising idea since this region at the beginning of the twenty-first century is popularly thought to be empty – both in the sense of being 'unbuilt' and being thoroughly 'erased' by the placer gold-mining operations of the last 150 years. The longer history of occupation of Evenki, Iakut and Russian Settler populations in the region, which we conservatively estimate at 800 years, is not widely acknowledged by residents today.

We were fortunate to arrange an ambitious programme of ethnographic and oral history research in the summer of 2007 (John Ziker) and in the summer of 2009 (David Anderson, Konstantin Klokov and Elena Volzhanina). This work was designed to recover the history of 'local' hunting and herding adaptations in the region. We were all struck by the categories of the *iakuty* and *russkie*. These local words, which stand respectively for 'indigenous people' and for 'long-term [Russian] settlers' at first glance seem to sound like nationality markers for 'Iakut' and 'Russian'. Through interviews it turned out that the *iakut* stood for a person of Iakut and/or Evenki descent who lived with domestic reindeer and that the term *russkii* often signalled a 'long-term dweller' [*starozhil*] who was different from the shift-work miners of the current industrial area but who was not necessarily 'Russian'. In describing their lives, there was not much to separate the settler from the indigenous person. Indeed the later Imperial history of the valley was characterised by a cosmopolitan and creolised type of land use, where ancient hunting techniques for wild reindeer and moose are combined with relatively recent strategies for forage management to support small herds of cattle and horses. Dr. Ziker's preliminary work played an important role in demonstrating the robustness of a lifestyle that it seems has left very old traces in the environment. This chapter, therefore, summarises our collective work in bringing together archival and environmental clues with oral history to draw attention to an environment built not by foundations and structures but by a cultivated forest space of meadows, roads, and trees. Here we trace the ethnogenesis not of blood-lines and lineages but of the places that harbour life for many different types of local people.

Our project was designed to work over three summer field seasons. The Polar Census documents were digitised first in Krasnoiarsk in 2002 and then in Irkutsk in 2004. In August of 2006 a small group travelled to Lake Tolondo to discover the site of the former village 'on the island at Tolondo' as well as the aboriginal cemetery and to use excavations and field survey to recover cultural markers. Along the way the group made valuable contacts with individuals who began to narrate the complex history of the region and suggest other sites. In June of 2007 a second group travelled from Tolondo along the Zhuia valley excavating more sites and documenting examples of modern land use. A key part of this second expedition was the retrieval of paleoecological data from several pits at Tolondo. A final expedition took place in July of 2009 to refine the paleoecological techniques and to speak once again to elders in the region. The detailed data from the paleoecological research is being published separately (Ineshin et al. 2009). Although the two seasons of archaeological work were inconclusive, it directed the attention of our team to the material signatures of the use of space, which is the subject of this chapter.

The Zhuia River Valley and the Polar Census

The Zhuia River is a left tributary of the Chara River, which in turn, after merging with the Olekma River, drains into the Lena River – one of the central arteries of Northern Eurasia. For half of its course, the Zhuia is a high-energy mountainous stream which floods twice a year as snow and rain collect in the high plateau that separates its course from the Vitim River. It calms sufficiently to be reliably navigated only at the point that another tributary – the Khomolko – joins it. Indeed the valley is not remarkable at all in the literature. The region is better known simply as the 'Upper Lena' or by the almost mythic ring of two of its tributaries – the Khomolko (where placer gold was discovered in 1846); and the Vacha (made famous in a song by the dissident bard Vladimir Vysotskii). Most Western and Russian historians, and many Russian school children, will know of this place not by its hydrology but as the site of the famous Lena Massacre. The mass execution of striking mining labourers and porters in Lenzoloto's Bodaibo River gold mines in 1912 was one of the events that fuelled the second Russian Revolution and civil war (Melancon 1994; Rosenberg 1996). In the local language, the valley is called the 'Outer Taiga' [*dal'niaia taiga*] by the hard rock and placer miners working out of the new regional centre in Bodaibo – a small city located one watershed over on the Vitim River (Leshkov 1996).

Today the Zhuia valley is one of the outer frontiers of Irkutsk *oblast'*. It forms the watershed that defines the Northern boundary of Bodaibo *raion*, which in turn is the northernmost district of this large Eastern Siberian province. The river hosts one major population point – the community of Perevoz – a mixed Russian, Iakut, and Evenki village of 1,261 subsistence-plot farmers, hunters, reindeer herders, and affiliated employees of the many gold-mining operations still in the region. Upstream from Perevoz is the small similarly mixed community of Svetlyi (57 to 62 people), dominated today by a hard rock operation of the Greenfields Ltd. mining company. At the height of the Soviet period, Svetlyi was a busy settlement of upwards of 12,500 people largely employed by the Svetlyi gold-mining company (which still operates in other areas of the region). Svetlyi Ltd. still relies on one farming operation in the small village for fresh meat, milk, and vegetables for the kitchens of its shift-work camps.

To arrive on the upper Zhuia today one has to fly to the regional capital Bodaibo on the Vitim River, and then make arrangements to travel inland with one of the regular mining shift transports that service the many mining opera-

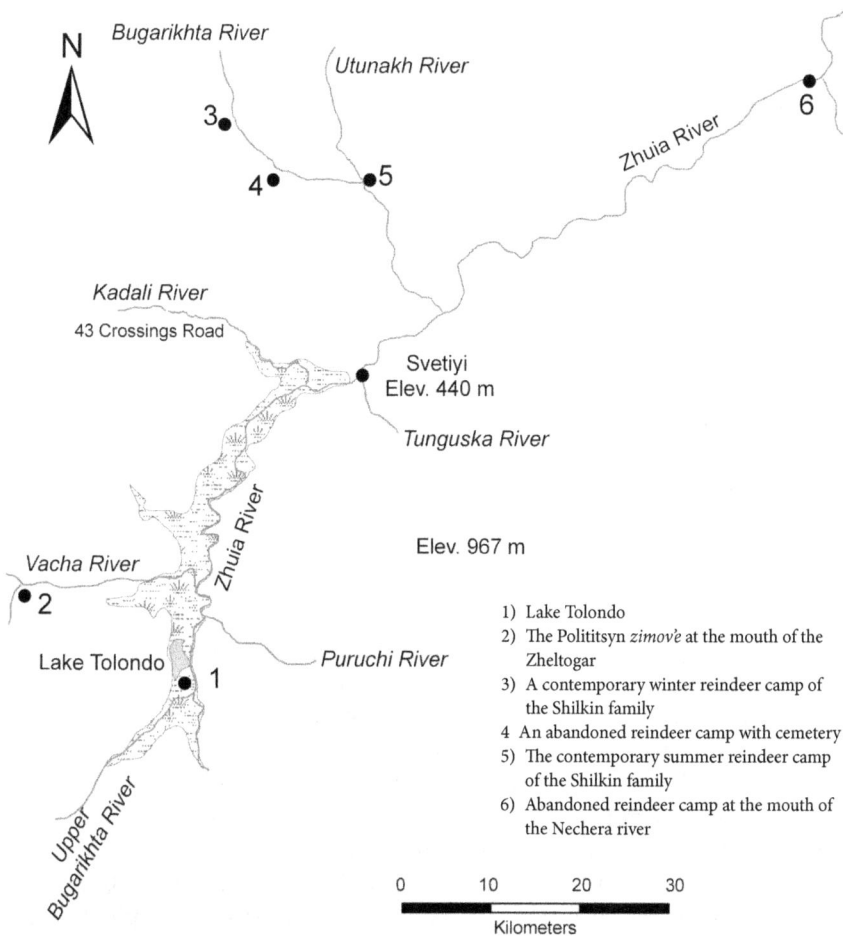

Figure 9.1. Map of the Outer Taiga along the Upper Zhuia River, Bodaibo region. Cartography by Chris Willson.

tions in the plateau region at Kropotkin. There is a rough all-terrain trail that connects Kropotkin with Svetlyi located in the next watershed. Local people travel the river with aluminium boats and outboard motors. There is an interesting local adaptation of these boats to travel upstream from Svetlyi in the shallow summer waters of the Zhuia. The *tiunnel'* is a type of homemade jet boat made by mounting a regular outboard motor high within an aluminium boat and constructing a conduit to bring water from under the boat to the propeller, which in turns shoots the stream through a pair of home-made dividers allowing one to steer the boat. Others use the more traditional transport of horse and reindeer, or they simply walk.

Table 9.1. Contemporary Aboriginal Population of selected settlements in Bodaibo region (2002–2008) by nationality

Date	Community	Evenkis	Iakuts	Total Pop.
	Svetlyi	9	[2]	60
	Perevoz	24	38	1,281
	Kropotkin	4	[<30]	1,775
2008	Bol'shoi Patom	2	52	70
	Mamakan	5	0	2,150
	Bul'bukhta	[2–4 families]		
	Bodaibo City			15,220
2002	Bodaibo Region (2002) Rural Population	89	202	27,321

Source: The 2008 data are from the administration of Bodaibo Region for 01 January 2008 [our estimates are in square brackets]. The 2002 data are from the Russian Federal Census.

It does not take a very long interview with local residents to realise that this 'outer taiga' to Bodaibo was not very long ago the centre of logistical supply routes. Elders today speak of the Lena River village of Macha as the regional centre (Leshkov 1999). One of the best visual illustrations of this shifting centre of activity is in the archaic 1866 topographical map by Petr Kropotkin (1873). This pioneering map shows an exact description of the valleys and tributaries of the Lena River, criss-crossed with trails, but a wonderfully distorted representation of the Vitim River drainage which at that relatively late date was still unknown territory. This old frontier – what one might describe as the 'Central Taiga' – was the main provisioning route for the global fur-trade economy through the Cossack fur-tribute posts built first at the mouth of the Olekma in 1643 and then at the mouth of the Zhuia on the Chara River in 1648, and later across the plateau at the Patom River in the1670s (Dolgikh 1960: 480–82). The Upper Lena region was firmly incorporated into the Russian Empire through the creation of an Imperial postal route in 1743 (Sokolov 2002; Mainov 1912: 136ff). This route consisted of a set of provisioning posts located 15 to 20 kilometres from each other where horses would be kept and traded to allow commerce and communication to flow seamlessly from Irkutsk to Iakutsk. The central postal *trakt* soon sprouted a system of subsidiary routes throughout the region which at least one historian cites as one of the major material factors of colonisation (Safronov 1978: 99–100, 121). Following Kropotkin's expedition of 1866–67, the southern leg of this route shifted through the headwaters of the Upper Zhuia valley to link with Imperial centres at Chita and Irkutsk. Parts of this supply route are still in use today as rough gravel roads. The Central Taiga became the food basket for the new placer gold-mining operations opened at first at Persi on the Upper Khomolko in 1843. These pre-California gold operations distinguished themselves for their massive reliance on manual labour for extracting this precious metal (Rosenberg 1996) and hence the need for a massive provisioning effort of meat, flour and other staples, which in turn required huge caravans of hundreds of domestic animals – both horses and reindeer. The animals, in turn, required their own lines of provisioning for forage – mostly hay and oats creating a unique economic opportunity:

> The gold mines created a demand for bread, butter, meat, hay, oats and labour power. Connected with this the traditional government [postal] freight created a new economy: the transport of freight for the mines from the [settlement] Vitim and from Macha. The freight was floated down to these settlements on the Lena river and then shifted to the main centre of the mining world at Bodaibo on winter roads. (Mainov 1912: 94–95)

Mainov (1912: 99) describes this economy in all of its exploitative detail, from the effect that it had on the creation of a 'Iakut bourgeoisie' to the diminishing returns that led to eventual impoverishment of the porters who staked their entire estate of 3 to 5 horses in the hope of gaining some monetary income (ibid., 136ff, 253 ff.). Despite the small scale of the pastoral estates of the porters, and average Iakut contractor from Macha would shift 6,000 *pudy* (ibid., 157) requiring a fleet of 180 horses and 20 sub-contractors (each pulling 6 horses) (ibid., 285). Today a local elder remembers this economy through the words of his grandfather as a picture of 'thousands and thousands of horses and reindeer'. According to A. Sokolov (2002: 81) between 1860 and 1894, over 85,000 horses served to supply the gold mines. In Soviet times, the transport economy was routinised with the establishment of collective farms which were given a profile of keeping horses and reindeer for cargo transport. The farms in the Zhuia valley – 'Red Khomolko', 'The Trusted Trail', and 'The Chara Hunter' – kept herds of between 50 to 370 reindeer and 6 to 30 horses to shift freight into the rugged highlands of the valley.[1] Parallel to the collective farm economy, the nationalised mining company of the time – Lenzoloto – was documented as holding its own herd of 1,273 reindeer in 1934 (BGGA 26-1-4: 50). It is also significant to our research that a large number of local families also kept large herds of private reindeer which were never collectivized. In this case, the hunters were incorporated into fur-hunting brigades through the *koopzveropromkhoz* which was not interested in socialising their reindeer estates. Oral history suggests that during the 1930s a 'tag-team' system was developed of delivering freight to warehouses in the lower Zhuia valley by horse (roughly marked by the boundary of the Khomolko and Nechera tributaries) and then carrying the freight onwards and upwards into the mountainous highlands with reindeer. This distinction between 'lower' and 'higher' will be important when discussing the spatial demography of the cultural landscape below.

It is important to mention the impact of Christianity on the region, even if its direct effects on the population were muted. In what is still today one of the best summaries of archival Orthodox church data on the region, Mainov

Figure 9.2. An Evenki-Tungus transport reindeer camp in the region of the Lena Goldfields at the turn of the twentieth century (IOKM 11912-1)

(1898: 50ff) only finds records relating to Olekma Iakuts and makes no mention at all of the Zhuia River Tunguses. Despite the fact that there were only 4 churches serving the huge Olekma district at the start of the twentieth century (Mainov 1927: 377), the enumerator A. T. Samokhin in several places in his manuscripts classifies both the Zhuia River Evenkis and Iakuts as Christians due to their burial practices, their names, and most importantly the integration of church holidays into their yearly round.[2] If Christianity was not an active faith, it nevertheless left its mark on the way that the landscape was used and most obviously on the burial practices of the people living in the valley. Long-term stopping places in the valley are more often than not associated with a cemetery with grave monuments either in imported carved marble or built wooded structures with a cross placed in an Orthodox Christian manner.

The published literature suggests that local peoples of the central part of the Zhuia valley have been living, trading and provisioning the lives of others with domestic animals for at least 350 years. The key parts of this economy were a trade of fur (sable, squirrel) and meat (wild reindeer, domestic reindeer, moose) for commodities; the supply of transport services; and, of importance to this chapter, the provisioning of hay to the animals that for such a long time formed the lifeline of this region.

Despite the long history of contact and settlement, by the summer of 1927 the Zhuia River valley was a place that seemed isolated from the centres of civilisation. The Siberian Statistical Administration was late in sending an enumerator to this valley. The region was then an extraterritorial fragment of Irkutsk Okrug, perched on the boundaries between the Far Eastern Territory and Iakutsk Okrug, within the sprawling Siberian Territory based in Novosi-birsk. The Polar Census enumerator A. T. Samokhin spent June, July and August of 1927 negotiating his way through the uplands above Bodaibo into what then seemed the remote interior of the Zhuia valley. His sketch map (GAKK 769-1-310: 4) is an ironic inversion of Kropotkin's map of only 66 years earlier. It shows the places closest to the Vitim River in relatively exact detail and only the vaguest understanding of the supply trails and rivers that look towards the Lena River valley. Mainov (1912: 150) records the gradual shift in the geography of trade from the Lena to the Vitim drainage from 1893 onwards with the technological improvements that led to river navigation as far as Bodaibo.

Samokhin's census manuscripts are a richly documented yet interstitial set of texts which were never analysed due to the dislocations of a rapidly changing early Soviet institutional structure. The detailed set of index tables, household cards, community diaries, hygiene cards and sketch maps were designed to be read as an integral whole representing the middle range of the Vitim valley, the Zhuia valley, and portions of the Olekma valley. However the collection was divided between the relevant statistical administrations and sent to Irkutsk, Krasnoiarsk, and Iakutsk where they lie divided to this day.[3] Samokhin published a preliminary summary of his work in 1929. That article gives a very good prosaic reflection of the type of information collected in his community diaries as it mimics the organisation and classification of the polar census forms themselves. What is distinctive in his published and unpublished work is his keen interest in documenting space – a question which was linked to an implicit evolutionist agenda of whether or not the indigenous Evenki-Tunguses exist or have been assimilated. The article gives a very clear summary of his impressions that 'strangely' Tungus cultural traditions are best preserved in only a few *versty* from the headquarters of Soviet mining operations in Bodaibo but seem especially weak in the Zhuia valley farthest from the mining. He attributes this to an 'evolution' of Tungus cultural patterns into the 'higher' culture of Iakut horse pastoralism. To illustrate this implicit agenda his manuscripts carefully document the dimensions and internal conditions of conical moose skin lodges, with sketches, and approvingly the architecture of log cabins and structures built with imported timber. As this chapter will demonstrate, his interest in the relation between culture, structure and space can be reassembled into a detailed account of a semi-sedentary subsistence strategy that combines trade and transport with hunting and herding.

Population and Territory in 1927

Taken as describing a single population, the household cards compiled the Zhuia valley in June and July of 1927 present an intermarried population of

40 Tungus and Iakut families with a total population of 151 individuals. The decision of the Siberian Statistical Committee to do a partial census of the region, focussing only on the indigenous people, has produced a skewed picture of the population dynamics. The ragged age-sex pyramid in figure 9.3 shows an imbalance of men and women in almost every cohort except the oldest and the youngest. The ratio of men to women in Samokhin's sample is 128.4 – a number which speaks to significant under-enumeration. The noticeable lack of women in their late teens to their 30s may speak also to out-marriage with settled Russian populations. The enumerator, guided by early Soviet transportation corridors, includes the Evenki people of the Vitim drainage as part of the same grouping as the Zhuia valley. However both oral history and a reading of the archives show that kinship links and local geography have traditionally made this population look northwards towards the Lena valley and the Iakut republic.[4] Samokhin (1929: 6) himself records the hearsay existence of a minimum of 350 individuals in valleys towards the Patom plateau who were missed in his survey.

Population records are a highly politicised topic in this region. Although data on lifestyle and economy of the indigenous peoples of the Upper Lena valley are particularly sketchy, counts of the tax-paying male population are surprisingly prolific. Using published sources it is possible to trace the crude demographic history of the *zhuintsy* as far back as 1640 dating right back to the arrival of the first Tsarist *torgovye liudi* from Mangazei and Eniseisk (table 9.2). The history of the population of the Upper Lena valley is a history of gold rushes. In the words of the eminent Siberian historian Sergei Bakhrushin (1922: 35), the newly opened 'Great' [Lena] River valley became a 'dizzying'

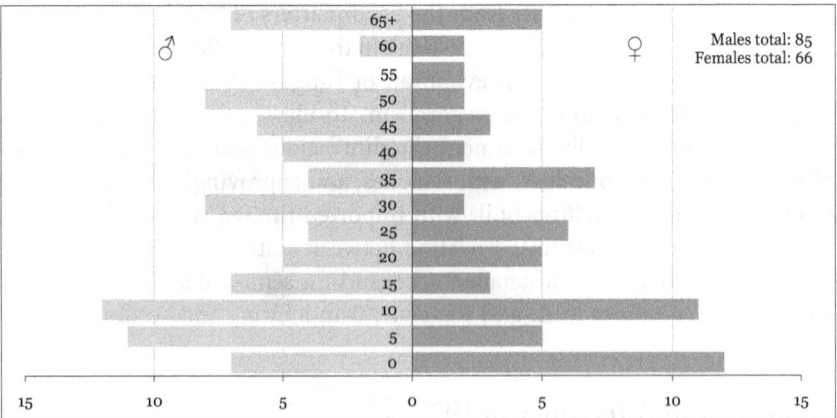

Figure 9.3. Age-sex distribution of the aboriginal population of the Zhuia valley from 1926/27 census results

Table 9.2. A summary of Imperial-era populations for the Zhuia Administrative Clan, Olekma Region

Year	Population Male	Female	Total	Imputed total*	Source
1652	92			[368]	Dolgikh (1960: 483) 'Chara and Patom zimovii'
1665	116			[464]	Dolgikh (1960: 483) 'Chara and Patom zimovii'
1672	120			[480]	Dolgikh (1960: 483) 'Chara and Patom zimovii'
1681	157			[628]	Dolgikh (1960: 483) 'Chara and Patom zimovii'
1691	129			[516]	Dolgikh (1960: 483) 'Chara and Patom zimovii'
1700	72			[288]	Dolgikh (1960: 483) 'Chara and Patom zimovii'
1712	94			[376]	Dolgikh (1960: 483) 'Chara and Patom zimovii'
1767	64			[256]	'Delo o postroike pochtovykh domov' in Mainov (1898: 11)
1782	98			[392]	'Delo o postroike pochtovykh domov' in Mainov (1898: 11)
1796	123			[492]	Mainov (1898: 20)
1798	123			[492]	'Delo o postroike pochtovykh domov' in Mainov (1898: 11)
1824	166			[664]	'Vtoraia iasachnaia komissiia' in Mainov (1898: 12)
1835	210			[840]	'Vtoraia iasachnaia komissiia' in Mainov (1898: 14)
1858	178	161		339	'Desiataia reviziia' in Mainov (1898: 36)
1859	497		895	895	Patkanov (1906: 96)
1895	174	138		312	'Desiataia reviziia' in Mainov (1898: 36)
1897	244		476	476	Patkanov (1906: 95–96) [includes Vitim drainage]
1927	97	75	172	[522]**	Samokhin (1929: 6) [includes Vitim drainage]
1927	86	67	153	[503]**	Samokhin (GAKK 1845-1-78) [restricted to Zhuia drainage]

* Iasak total populations in square brackets are imputed at a ratio of 4.
** Samokhin (1929: 6) states that some 350 Patom River-area river Tunguses were not surveyed in his census according to local government records.

magnet for immigration of peasants searching for 'soft gold' starting from the second half of the seventeenth century. Official representatives of the Russian state were obliged to keep accurate taxation records of the indigenous peoples upon whom they relied to bring in a regular intake of furs. However the richness of the paper archive led to a debate, mediated by some of the great names of late Russian and Soviet historical ethnography, on whether or not the original population of the region was *tungus* or *iakut* (Mainov 1898; Tokarev 1945; Dolgikh 1960). Mainov (1927: 392) credits the first tribute being taken from Tunguses by the Cossack Dem′ian Mnogogreshnyi in 1673 and cites documents stating that Iakuts came to the Iasak post at Olekminsk in 1675 from the north. It is often remarked, in some accounts, that the 'wandering' Evenki-Tunguses were 'pushed away' to 'remote' parts of the river drainages suitable only for hunting, leaving better hay pastures to settled pastoralist peoples like Iakuts (Mainov 1898: 28–29; Mainov 1927: 73; Dolgikh 1960: 482, 490; Samokhin 1929: 6). Indeed there are interesting written complaints by Tunguses concerning their lands being occupied by Iakut horse pastoralists without paying respect to what Mainov (1898: 31; 1912: 243) describes as an indigenous land tenure system involving annual payments of rent for leasing pastures over a long term period of time. Iokhel'son (1896: 130–31) has perhaps the most colourful representation of the process:

> After bloody battles with the Iakuts...the Tunguses surrendered their outer territories and [retreated] to the mountainous forests rich in fur, or to the barren tops of the mountain ridges and to the moss-covered tundras rich in birds. In these places...they were left in peace.

It is striking when reading these accounts today that little data is produced to illustrate this common-sense fact that nomadic Evenkis were removed from their lands and that settled Iakuts assumed all of the places suitable for horse pastoralism. As this chapter will show, the relation between settled pastoralism and remote hunting outposts is not so clear-cut. As will be seen below, relatively remote taiga areas, in this case in the 'Upper Zhuia', were fashioned to create new hay-producing meadows suitable for both reindeer and horses, and these new upland meadows were strategically located closer to the intersection of fish, fur and meat and the hungry mining populations. It would seem that local people had more options than a simple choice of following either 'cultured' pastoralism or 'wild' fur hunting.

What is remarkable about the list of population numbers in table 9.2 is the consistency in the total population numbers for the valley for several centuries.[5] Most estimates show a population ranging between 300 to 400 individuals (with high estimates of 900 over a slightly larger territory). Although micro-level statistics are only available for the 1926/27 Census, it would seem that general age/sex proportions and total population numbers have been stable, pointing in turn to a stable economic system.

Samokhin, surveying the region in 1927, invested a great deal of energy in trying to identify a territorial focus for the population moving across the valley. Being more conservative than some, he identified only two focal points for the population: Lake Tolondo in the Upper Zhuia (GAIO 1468-1-2: 21–36), and the Mouth of the Khomolko River [Khomolko] in the Lower Zhuia (GAIO 1468-1-2: 47–58). This strategy of identifying rather tight orbits of people led to interesting anomalies in his work. It is interesting that he crossed out the title 'nomadic' on many of the cards and often inserted the words 'semi-nomadic' for 14 households. The notations in the community diary affirm that the movements of the population are 'regular' or 'planned' (*pravil'no*) for the range at Lake Tolondo. However the movements of the population at Khomolko are described as travelling 'within a specific region but within this region

they travel chaotically' (Samokhin 1929: 10). In the study of nomadic populations anywhere, the word 'chaotic' is often a good clue that an outside observer
does not fully understand a rather complex pastoral system. An analysis of the
place names that Samokhin associated with each family on the first page of
his household cards shows 18 unique place names. Of these two are properly
settlements (*priisk* Svetlyi; Ust´-Khomolkho). Fifteen are all small tributaries
of the Zhuia River. One is Lake Tolondo. The places along the fifteen rivers are
distinguished with crude identifiers of 'mouth', 'middle' and 'headwaters'. Local
people then undoubtedly associated these relational identifiers with specific
places which are good to hunt, good to pasture animals, or a 'high dry moraine
where it is good to set a tent' (*aian* – Evenki), as they do today.

As is well remarked in the literature for the region, the unit of a 'river' is a
very old and robust unit for marking territory. Mainov (1912: 243) remarks
that the word 'river' is a proxy in the local dialect for an area where one hunts
or fishes (i.e. 'territory' or 'range'):

> … within each clan there was a common clan territory. It served as a commons for
> pasturing animals (*dlia vsekh rodovichei obshchim vygonom*) in the summer season.
> However natural hay fields from which each family prepared winter reserves of hay
> for their [cattle and horse] herds were usually kept in constant use by these very
> families. The ancient measure of land for Iakuts it seems was the naturally-bounded
> meadows (*urochishcha*). In fact the Tunguses still today call the same measure a
> 'river [valley]' (*rechka*). The inherited use rights of these meadows from a long time
> back has come to a situation that access to them produces a quality like sovereignty
> (*dominium* Latin). The hay-producing meadow could be rented out by the holder
> for money, could be gifted, or could even be sold to Russian [settlers].

In another work, Mainov (1898: 31–32) cites a well institutionalised system
of the exploitation and leasing of 'rivers' such that one *tungus* family rented
out a system of twelve rivers for cash while saving for themselves another 100
rivers for their own use. In the urban folklore of gold mining in the region, it
is said that the Tungus elder Afanasii Iakomin 'sold' the rich Upper Khomolko
to Russian gold miners for 'a mere' 40 roubles in silver (Gulevskii 2007). Whatever the status of this transaction in the mid nineteenth century, two Iakomin
descendants were still using at least some of the Upper Khomolko tributaries
for autumn hunting in 1927.

It is interesting that the Imperial geographer Serafim Patkanov (1906: 95–
96) in his summary of the 1897 census results for the Zhuia Tunguses of Olekma *okrug*, also describes them as a group of 476 individuals occupying using
a set of eight rivers over a somewhat larger territory.

Unfortunately, the household cards are not specific enough to reconstruct
the yearly round in all of its detail. Specific examples of movement are nevertheless interesting. An extensively migrating family, like that of Gavril Zakha-

rov (GAKK 1845-1-78: 91–92) moved right from the mouth of the Zhuia in winter up to its headwaters beyond Tolondo in the spring (a distance of over 150 kilometres) – a strategy that would have combined the needs of tending herds with that of subsistence fishing. Eight other households circled around the placer mining operation at Svetlyi, moving into the gold-mining community in September and then switching to a nomadic rhythm up and down the Zhuia valley from October to January and then from May to August.

Examples such of these cast doubt on whether the population can really be summarised as being based around two specific population points (or that indeed these population points were slowly becoming dominant). It would seem that the presence of a collection of built wooden structures at both Tolondo and Khomolko attracted the enumerator's attention. However, reading the community diaries carefully, it seems that the built village at Tolondo cannot be understood without including hay meadows and hunting areas along the Vacha and Zhuia River valleys. Similarly the Khomolko diary speaks to smaller established and named settlements at Nechera, Chenga and Bolochzhik.[6]

The language used by Samokhin, and indeed many other government enumerators of this period, betrays a predilection to classify economies in this region as either nomadic or settled. His scribbled-in notation of the semi-nomadic and lists of place names, which stand in exception to the tight description of settled focal points, speak to the existence of an economy organised on a broader scale such as that of an entire river valley. The word Samokhin uses for place – the *stoibishche* (literally a stopping place) – treats these settled spots as exceptions to a nomadic rule. However it would seem that regularly occurring winter and summer places were in fact the keystone of the economic strategy – and nomadism the exception.

Samokhin (1929: 11–12) chose to analyse Iakut and Tungus households separately, following a long tradition of ethnological separatism. What is striking about the Polar Census survey was the presence of only one Russian woman marrying into a Tungus household. Six partnerships were entirely Iakut; eighteen were entirely *tungus;* and a five were a mixture of Iakut and Tungus. Our oral history work in 2006 and 2007 showed evidence of what in other parts of the world would be described as a mixed-blood settler population. As mentioned above, mixed marriages of this type were likely coded as Russians (as indeed these individuals self-identify today). However this problem of identification leads to a broader problem of the identity of households. Ten individuals are recorded in the cards as being sole householders, but the notes on the cards and in the community diaries link most of them by descent or mutual aid to one of the other families. Here, as in many cases across Siberia, the strict definition of the household in the census forms did not capture the way that the extended family worked in this region. The population is perhaps best described by its dwellings with 19 cabins (*zimov'e*) and six conical tent systems (moose leather and bark lodges) housing 151 individuals with their associated meadows, storage structures, and fishing areas. It is significant for this chapter that most sets of dwellings (17), whether a cabin or a set of conical tents, had a hay pasture (*pokos*) recorded as being assigned to it with an average size of 2 *desiatok* (approx 3 hectares). Information is missing on Russian-headed households which may have been related by blood to indigenous households but our oral history work shows that these Russians also maintained a system of cabins, pastures and domestic reindeer and spoke a language that mixed Russian, Iakut and Evenki.

A Pastoral System of Dwellings and Roads

If we disaggregate the two community diaries and link together the single households cards from Samokhin's 1926/27 survey, it is possible to build an interpretation of people in a space that captures elements of a traditional pastoral economy which is in use today and which has left a long-term archaeological signature. Rather than placing the focus upon household heads (*khoziain*) and settled communities (*poselennye*), a focus on the so-called 'stopping-places' (*stoibishche*) creates a different frame through which the data can be organised.

On all vernacular maps of the region, in addition to rivers, there are certain semi-settled places that every observer has found notable. Prince Kropotkin, in 1866, used the words of his Evenki guides to mark 27 'winter-cabins' and storage structures in the Lower Zhuia and neighbouring Molbo drainage. Even Samokhin, in his sketch map, indicated significant collections of lodges on the Vacha and Nechera Rivers.

In the worlds of the Russian 'old-settler' elder Iurii Konstantinovich Polititsyn, the winter cabin *zimov'e* was more than a timber-frame structure. It was a moral undertaking well integrated into a regional economy:

> … my uncle kept a winter-cabin on the Zheltogar [a tributary of the Vacha river in the 'Upper Zhuia']. He had a big meadow and a big winter cabin there. Up to 100 people could spend the night and they lived there [as well]. The meadow was created by hand. Before, everything was cultivated by hand. They could service up to 1000 horses [over a season(?)]. Now everything is overgrown there. Many years have passed. … Before, there were no trains, no roads, there was nothing here. … Before everything only came by transport – by horses, reindeers; and by *karbaza* – the big boats that were floated down to the mouth [of the Zhuia]. … People from Chara [shifted freight] to the collective farms. … They farmed and hunted, they had big herds of cattle and made butter and so on. … People from the Nizhnee Vuliui [river region] brought meat, lard and other things – everything. … Flour and sugar came up from the Lena. All these products were brought by transport caravan. …

The caravans (*transport*) worked with the power of 1500–2000 horses. Then, four days later, a caravan of 1500–2000 reindeers would follow. They arranged for the road not to be used at the same time. [The different caravans] needed a place to spend a night. They travelled in intervals of two to three days. One caravan came, spent a night. Rested. Three days later the second group came, also spent a night and rested, and then the third came.

The *zimov'e* was centred around a built log dwelling, but attached to it was a meadow carved from the forest and maintained through constant use. Given the severe shortage of forage recorded in the historical literature of the region, these cultivated places were certainly valuable. Mainov (1912: 273) records how in the nineteenth century, native portage contractors working for the gold mines kept a network of local people based in such *zimov'e* to supply and refresh their caravans:

> In Olekma *okrug*, the richer peasants build in convenient places (if they have access to these places) small *zimov'ia* and employ there some kind of resident or watch-keeper [to look after the place]. On the plot of land next to the winter-cabin over the winter a good supply of manure collects which serves to create an *utug* [a Buriat word meaning a meadow specially created over several years by deliberate manuring]. The peasants of the Iakut *okrug* usually take the porter into their homes for pay. They receive payment not in money but almost always in frozen milk, butter and frozen and whipped butter (*khaiak*).

An anonymous overview of agricultural strategies in pre-revolutionary Iakut Province also underscores the complex way in which pastoralism, architecture and hay production were interlinked in the Olekma region:

> Iakuts, at first, seed hay on the *otekhakh*. These are cultivated (*usadvenye*) places near old dwellings (*iurty*) where for a long time there was a corral for horses or for cattle. ... In extremely remote locations one can still find this type of economy. The Iakuts also can cast up to 7 *pudy* of rye on the marshy banks of a retreating lake (or on a lake peninsula), but they harvest very little. (K voprosu 1896: 67)

None of the historical literature confirms there being 'thousands' of horses and reindeer in discrete caravans as cited by Polititsyn's grandfather and uncle. However the question of scale aside, the intertwining of a dwelling with a regional economy of reindeer and horse transport is an important clue to the interpretation of the landscape.

Samokhin's 1926/27 census survey only records 14 instances of literal *zimov'e*, but as mentioned above, there were 17 meadows held in association with various systems of timber cabins (*izbushki*) and winter and summer skin (or bark) lodges (*chum*). Unfortunately, the exact location of these dwelling-meadow systems is not always possible to reconstruct from the cards. However three abandoned residential meadows were investigated by our archaeological team in 2006 and 2007 (Ineshin et al. 2009). As the old-dweller Polititsyn predicted, they all showed signs of colonisation on the outer edges by dwarf birch (*Betula nanae*) but nevertheless even after 30 to 40 years of disuse their meadows were still visible and stuck out sharply from a landscape otherwise characterised by thick forests of tamarack. Our botanist, Oksanna Vinkovskaia, estimated that elements of what she described as a 'meadow plant community' (*lugovoe soobshchestvo*) created by the trampling and fertilising effects of domestic animals, could persist for up to 300 years in this region.[7] Our archaeological team dug three pits at the intricately referenced meadow-dwelling system at Lake Tolondo and two pits at the mouth of Nechera River – both places at the gateway to the 'Upper Zhuia'. Although their detailed results will be the subject of other publications, it is sufficient to say that fossil pollen shows signs of continuous human disturbance and the presence of some semi-settled form of domestication at both sites for at least 350 years. This time frame would correspond to the arrival of tax-collecting Cossacks at the mouth of the Zhuia River, and what may have been an initial re-organisation of the local economy into one that supplied fur to these visitors.

Our team intensively analysed the site at Lake Tolondo, which initially attracted us to this region. According to the Polar Census household cards, at least two log cabins and one summer bark conical lodge were present at the site in 1927, as well as a system of 6 subsidiary hunting cabins in the immediate vicinity. The household cards record 10 hectares of hay-producing meadows around the dwellings. A visual inspection of the territory of the site showed several deeply inscribed trails approaching the lake (and undamaged by mechanised vehicles) which may represent fragments of overland transportation corridors. There was also a system of pits along the banks of both the lake and the river as well as inland, which may have been used for storing fish. Across from the peninsula on which the cabins once stood we discovered the 'aboriginal' cemetery consisting of one marked grave and two stone heaps which might represent an older type of burial. Although the region was heavily transformed by logging in the 1930s and by forest fires in the 1960s and 1970s, we also found evidence of culturally modified trees such as stumps carved with a one-sided axe-adze and imperial-era forestry markers. Oral history from elders at Svetlyi speaks to the regular tending of the meadows and even the seeding of grass at Tolondo in Soviet times. The old cabin was still used as a hunting way-post into the mid 1990s when it was destroyed by fire.

Our archaeological research at this important site showed a much longer picture of occupation. The stratification of the trenches revealed a 10-centimetre deep soft soil layer which may point to a history of occupation starting approximately 850 years ago.[8] The presence of fossil pollen from dwarf birch (*Betula Nanae*), goosefoot (*Chenopodiaceae*), dandelion (*Taraxacum*) wild rhubarb (*Rumex*), and wild sage (*Artemsia*) in the upper 5 centimetres in various trenches points to a more intensive history of occupation which, again inconclusively, may point to the presence of corrals and even types of seasonal gardening corresponding with the arrival of Russian tax-collectors.

It is difficult to link the community at Tolondo directly with a network of trade. Three of the eight families at the site in 1926–27 used their reindeer to ship logs for the gold-mining operation at Svetlyi which was then in decline. The documents record these families as then unemployed. Tolondo is visible on both Kropotkin's map and Samokhin's map, but both put it somewhat to the side of the main overland transportation corridors which went from the Zhuia River up the Vacha valley some 30 kilometres downstream. Patkanov (1906: 95) listed five individuals living on the 'Zhuia Peninsula' in 1897. The presence of a well-marked cemetery with several monuments mark the site as an important place at least at the end of the nineteenth century (one grave for a 29-year-old member of the Zhuia Tungus clan is marked to 1910). It is unlikely that the site served as a major staging post for 'thousands' of reindeer and horses, but given the evident richness of the lake and the close location of important moose and wild deer-hunting areas, it may have been a stable provisioning post of meat, forage and fish for the families of the region for a very long time.

This picture of a system of rivers characterised by certain fixed points with cultivated meadows can be filled out by the data collected on domestic animals in 1926–27. In contrast to the discussion above on the history of population records, Samokhin's census manuscripts provide one of the only sources in existence on the subsistence economy of the region (see also Gibel'man 1925). Most of the 40 households held small estates of domestic animals. Only 6 households were recorded as having no animals whatsoever, and of those only one was a large multigenerational family (implying that some other family was looking after the interests of the single elderly individuals or young families without animals). In contrast to the prosaic herds of Turukhansk *krai* these herds were typically small with the majority holding between 4 and 6 head of reindeer and horses together. Only 7 households held more than 6 reindeer or more than 4 horses – a number which Mainov (1912: 154) identifies as the minimum number of animals in order to offer oneself for portage work. The total population of animals for the valley was 121 reindeer (of which 82 were used for transport), 49 horses and 86 head of cattle. The average herd size by census household, or by households-in-dwellings, was 8 head of reindeer, 2 head of horses, and 7 head of cattle. It is interesting that no Iakut-headed families held any reindeer. Mainov records only 20 per cent of all Iakut households in Olekminsk *uezd* having more than 5 head of horses (ibid.). Indeed, as remarked above, these small-sized herds were constant through the Soviet period and, as we shall see below, are typical even today.

Although the statistics from this community are small it is possible to see a division of subsistence strategy between Iakut and Tungus households. Tungus households were far more likely to have all-reindeer operations or to combine horse herding with reindeer. Although Iakut-headed households were few, they were more likely to combine horses with cattle as is noted in the literature (Seroshevskii 1993: 156ff; Mainov 1912). The choice of a herding strategy is significant for this chapter since once a family keeps a horse or a cow it is bound to also to have access to a meadow for preparing forage for the winter. It is interesting that at Ust'-Khomolko, seven Tungus-headed households seem to have adopted an Iakut pattern by keeping hay pastures. In the community dairy for Ust'-Khomolko there is a record of feeding hay to reindeer (GAIO 1468-1-2: 46v). Reindeer cows were milked (even if there were not very many of them). Almost all households (35) had at least one hunting dog and three kept more than two.

It is significant that in the community diaries for the region the enumerator states strongly that Tunguses 'as a general rule' do not employ themselves as porters (despite some evidence to the contrary in that same enumerator's household cards) (GAIO 1468-1-2: 51v). Instead he says that Russian peasants from Macha are much more engaged in contracts for delivering goods to the mining camps. He does note a significant tradition of hauling wood with reindeer for the local gold-mining operation and notes that by 1927 with the decline in the use of the mining interest at Svetlyi that this source of income is declining (GAIO 1468-1-2: 22; 51v–52v). Iokhel'son (1896: 133), writing of a period one generation earlier, associates Olekma Tunguses exclusively with the pattern of hauling timber for the mining companies.

According to the community diaries for Tolondo and Khomolko, reindeer were pastured together. In the summer, herds were gathered together for collective defence against insects with a small group of people hired to tend the smoke smudges. The smudges were prepared for them under a shelter which shaded the reindeer from the sun. The shelter could be built or the herders could take advantage of the overhanging branches of large larch trees to create shade for the animals. This typical strategy for taiga forest reindeer herding is significant for the creation of the meadows described above. A contemporary illustration of this process is described and documented with photographs in the recent doctoral dissertation of Yoshiko Abe (2005) on an Evenki hunting and herding camp at nearby Lake Nerchatka in the Olekma River drainage. In the winter the animals would be used for fur hunting and for transporting goods. A close reading of the occupational data held in the household cards show that those households with large numbers of animals would be employed for wages as porters in October and November or March through June. Of the 16 households reporting a money income, wages could be as a high as 1,000 roubles per year but averaged at 370 roubles (which was still a large sum –

equivalent to an income from fur trapping). The largest reindeer herder in the region, with eighteen head, had nine members to his family and many young children. He distinguishes himself from others by concentrating on shooting squirrel (700 furs) and hunting moose, roe deer *iziubr* and other ungulates (18 head) but only bothering to catch 24 *pudy* of fish. By contrast, a smaller family with 5 head of reindeer at Lake Tolondo would catch 55 *pudy* and a large quantity of waterfowl. In the community diaries, the enumerator singles out the hunt for squirrel, bear and fox as the most profitable sources of income. Squirrels functioned as a money proxy at the rate of 10 skins to 1 *pud* of rye flour (at 15 roubles being approximately double the monetary rate for store-bought flour). Rye flour was sometimes fed to reindeer (up to 4 *pudy* per year) (GAIO 1468-1-2: 47v). There was a commercial market for fish at the mining camp at Svetlyi with taimen (15 roubles/*pud*) and Arctic char being especially valued (GAIO 1468-1-2: 49). The commercial sale of wild meat and fish still continues today in the post-Soviet period.

Territory and Population in 2007

Eighty years after the Polar Census expedition to the Bodaibo region, we still find Evenkis and Iakuts living together with Russians engaged in small-scale hunting and trade using small herds of domestic reindeer. The numbers of families holding reindeer have declined greatly. Instead, transport is provided more commonly by the diesel-powered all-terrain vehicles owned by the mining companies and in the summer by the outboard motors that individuals may own. In the summer of 2007 there were two reindeer-herding families travelling around the community of Svetlyi and two families travelling around the mouth of the Nechera River at the Zhuia (fig. 9.1). The heart of the reindeer-herding culture was north of Perevoz where 24 families still keep small herds on the Molbo, Patom and Gorbylakh Rivers.

Very little remains today of the 150-year-old direct alliance between reindeer herding and gold prospecting in the high alpine areas above the Zhuia River. The two brothers who hold reindeer at Svetlyi today worked for geological expeditions until about 1997. Aleksander and Veniamin Shil'nikov worked from May through October transporting explosives up to the highlands and returned to base camps with samples of rock (up to 50 kilograms). They were paid 5 roubles per reindeer per day. They explained that their job was to use reindeer to reach places where horses could not travel. It seems that even at the end of the twentieth century, the reindeer maintain their economic advantage in that they could forage locally and not have to be provisioned with forage (unlike horses). The fact that reindeer are generally useful in extreme conditions is one of the reasons these families cite in 2007 for keeping them.

However in the context of a community wracked by unemployment and the absence of a regular supply of cash, the fact that they provide cost-effective transport that allows these families to hunt is no doubt a second important reason.

The use of domestic reindeer for odd jobs in the modern mining economy continues a long tradition of using harnessed reindeer transport to mediate the divide between the Lower and Upper Zhuia valley. Elders in the village of Perevoz recalled their former jobs in the 1950s as reindeer porters who would take freight brought to the mouth of the Nechora tributary by horse and then would be taken onwards by reindeer caravan through the Vacha drainage to the heart of the mining operations. The elder Pavel Feoderov fondly recalled working with geological exploratory parties in the mid 1970s high in the headwaters of the Zhuia River when his herds were brought to the needed site by transport helicopter.

The main connection today between the mixed Evenki, Russian and Iakut community at Svetlyi and the gold-mining operations at Kropotkin is in the provision of food – much as in the past. Svetlyi is blessed with rich soil and abundant water, making it the closest source of fresh vegetables. The community may host up to sixty permanent residents all year round, but its numbers double in the summer as Kropotkin residents return to tend their subsistence plots. It is very difficult to draw an ethnographic line around these market-garden activities, as indeed with the history of mixed reindeer and horse pastoralism in the region. One finds Evenkis and Iakuts equally engaged in planting potatoes much as one finds the label 'Iakut' being applied to Evenkis and Russian elders who were very good reindeer herders in their time. The Zhuia River valley has developed a very distinctive and diversified subsistence economy based on market gardening, small-scale pastoralism, and the sale of wild meat, fish, berries and sable pelts.

In 2007 our team made a case study of one reindeer-herding family at Svetlyi, including a visit to their herding operations up a small tributary from the community. The Shil'nikov family includes Sasha, his wife Lena, and their son Sasha. Their elder daughter studies in Bodaibo and had plans to go to college in Irkutsk. The family has 30 to 40 reindeer with 11 calves. Five calves had been killed by bears by the time of our visit. Their economic activities include reindeer herding and milking, small-game hunting (especially capercaille), fur trapping, gathering herbs and nuts, fishing and big game hunting. The family, like everyone else, keeps a potato plot in Svetlyi. The Shil'nikovs also keep seven goats imported from Irkutsk which are tended by Lena's mother when the couple were out in the taiga. This family hunts moose and wild reindeer for meat for themselves and for sharing with the extended family, as well as for sale to villagers in Svetlyi and Kropotkin. Sables are hunted on foot with the aid of several dogs that the family owns and a small-calibre rifle. Pelts are turned in to the Bodaibo co-operative hunting administration (*koopzver'promkhoz*), which issues use-rights for certain valleys to hunt sable in exchange for a contracted minimum number of pelts. In the summer and fall the family collects wild blueberries, low-bush cranberries (*brusnika*), and cloudberries. In 2006, they collected 6 barrels (60 litres each) of berries for flavoured drinks and preserves for their own use and for sale. In the past they collected and froze up to 35 barrels of cranberry. The family also collects a small amount of wild red and black currents, wild grapes and wild mushrooms. They also gather several types of traditional medicine such as the *bogul'nik* (*Rhododendron spp.*) used by Russians and Evenkis as an expectorant, golden root (*adiola rosa*) used an energising plant, and a special type of petrified liquid found in cliffs in the winter known as 'stone fat' (*zhir kamen'*) – a medicine used exclusively by Evenkis. Fresh cow or reindeer milk is whipped to make a dish called *köchü*, which is sometimes mixed with the berries they gather.

The Shil'nikov family hold their 35 reindeer using an open pasturage system. It is interesting that they still preserve a system of 'river tenure' and speak of keeping their reindeer up the watershed of one small tributary (fig. 9.1). Each of the two interrelated reindeer-herding families at Svetlyi keep their herds in separate valleys. In the summer Sasha Shil'nikov maintains a summer camp 16 kilometres from the community up the Lower Bugarikhta River. This summer camp has been used for ten years by this family and featured a cemetery dating back to 1870. This cemetery, as the one at Tolondo, contained graves of Christianized Tunguses of the Zhuganskii clan from the 1870s, three of which are complete with wooden grave houses and stone monuments carved with their information. The Bugarikhta summer camp was noted on the above mentioned map by Kropotkin as a *zimov'e*. The old cabin is a characteristic low-ceiling log structure with a support log down the middle and an open attic. It is said that an old Iakut used to live there before this family moved in (fig. 9.4).

As a somewhat ambiguous symbol of their alliance with gold miners today, the camp had been partially destroyed by gold prospectors who bulldozed part of the traditional bark and wood structures to make room for their own structures and machine shops between 2002 and 2005. Characteristically, the Shil'nikovs use these structures in an assemblage that combines their own vernacular architecture. The heart of the summer camp is an uncovered reindeer corral of approximately 1,400 square metres. However the gates to the corral are kept open since it seems that the reindeer preferred to rest during the day in the cool shade of the old machine shop left by the miners. In addition to setting up small smudges in buckets within the corral, Sasha sets up a larger smudge in the hearth of an old metal stove, just outside the machine shop to improve the environment for the reindeer. As Sasha says, the reindeer know where their home is and there is no need to keep a close eye on the herd. He

Figure 9.4. The Shilkovs separating cows from their calves at their summer camp on the Lower Bukharikhta in 2007 to prepare them for milking. Photograph by John P. Ziker.

maintains the smudge to remove the insects, provides salt, and comes to milk the cows regularly.

The family has two other camps located up and down the valley where they have a more traditional set of vernacular structures. The family follows their herd as it migrates up and down the Lower Bukharikhta River valley in an annual cycle. The animals move up the valley in the fall and into the highlands in the winter, where winds blows the snow off the surface making it easier for the reindeer to find forage. Their favourite summer forage was bamboo grass (*sibikhta*) and mushrooms. As spring approaches, the reindeer moves closer to the Zhuia River where the snow melts first along the riverbanks and at the various meadows that one finds along its banks. Unfortunately, we were not able to map the expansive meadows along the river, but it is possible that the yearly return of the herds to these sites has kept them open over a long period of time. In the spring, the reindeer change their diet to one of young grass and buds off of birch and larch trees. This migration scheme is convenient for the family in that they can trap and hunt efficiently in the higher elevations in the autumn, winter and spring. As a cultural marker of this yearly round one can find a well-worn path running parallel to the Lower Bukharikhta River. Along the river one can find other signs of habitation. For example, two kilometres downstream from the current summer camp, there is an abandoned reindeer-herding camp site featuring semi-subterranean structures and a conical lodge that was partially destroyed by the road built by the gold-mining company at the start of the twenty-first century. Sasha suspected this site had been abandoned for at least 50 years.

This small reindeer herd is also used to hunt wild ungulates now as in the past. Wild reindeer migrate through the valley from the northwest (Khomolko River and Patom uplands) just before the domestic deer go into rut in the fall. Occasionally, the domestic reindeer in rut are used to attract wild reindeer as prey. The wild deer are present until their springtime migration in small valleys (*kliuchi*) as well as the highlands. The herders also kill roe deer (*iziubr*) and moose (*sokhatyi*). The family needs three domestic reindeer to move a wild reindeer carcass, four to five reindeer to transport an elk, and eight to ten reindeer to carry a moose back to Svetlyi.

It is interesting that both reindeer-herding families in the region are called *iakuty* by locals in the villages of Svetlyi and Perevoz. The genealogies, surnames and language of both families are clearly Evenki. As mentioned above, this local identity seems to have more to do with their role as porters and as reindeer-people than their so-called ethnic identity. This brings up an interesting question of how skill and identity are related in this region – a question which could bear more research. By far the strongest identity category in the valley is the difference between a Russian settler (*starozhil*) and that of a newly arrived Russian working in the mines, a category we define as 'Industrial Russian'. The Russian settlers speak of their knowledge of place and of skill in a way that approaches what anthropologists usually associate with indigenous people.

One of the best examples of this tendency is the elder Iurii Konstantinovich Polititsyn who describes himself as a 'private famer'. Aged 70 years, Polititsyn is a tough, hardworking and highly opinionated pensioner with a total of 350 hectares of land in and around Svetlyi. He has lived in the same house in the village since 1951 and identifies himself as a Russian. However, his great passion is for speaking about the taiga and the exploits of his family. His great-grandfather came to the Zhuia River as a *katorga* exile at some point in the mid nineteenth century. He survived by building a *zimov'e* downstream from the Nechera River confluence and provided sleeping quarters and food for travellers and animals on the Macha-Vacha-Bodaibo trade route. Although it was left unclear in the interview if he married a local Evenki woman or not, it was made clear that he was fluent in Russian, Evenki, Iakut and Chinese. Indeed his great-grandson's interviews are interspersed with Evenki terms that he uses to describe geographical features. In some of the more colourful stories, his great-grandfather is described as wearing Evenki reindeer skin leggings, of setting self-shooting arrow traps for wolves, and managing a large herd of domestic reindeer. His reindeer herd were literally gathered from the taiga as the stragglers (*padezh*) which were cut loose from impatient porters rushing to meet deadlines at appointed freight warehouses. It seems that the old man's reindeer estate was a solid one for it was passed down to his grandson. Iurii Konstantinovich speaks proudly of his own reindeer herd of 300 head that he used for trapping and hunting wild reindeer at the headwaters of the Zhuia. He used his own herd well into the 1990s when age drew him to the comfort of the village and the relative luxury of relying on horses for hunting. Iurii still keeps several reindeer saddles that he used when he rode reindeer to hunt. His account of a creolised tradition of skill and knowledge of the environment serves as an appropriate conclusion to this chapter which has emphasised the importance of places in a regional economy not necessarily monopolised by one or another ethnic group.

Conclusion

As a preliminary study, this chapter has used a particularly evocative set of digitised household and community records from the 1926/27 Polar Census to make an argument about the way in which population, domestic animals and space can be combined to build a long-term social and economic adaptation that is not the property of one or another cultural group. To make this argument, we have critically analysed the categories of the 1926/27 Polar Census – namely those of household and community – to suggest that the local categories of 'river', *zimov´e*, 'stopping-places' and meadow (*poliana*) create objects which have their own history. We have tried to represent this history in three ways. First, by consulting oral history, we have shown that the populated places in the taiga are not limited to rich agricultural sites along the banks of major rivers but can be carved out of the taiga and cultivated by use of domestic animals. Second, by adapting the methods of environmental archaeology, we have shown that certain named places have a long-term signature that might pre-date the arrival of Russian fur-tax collectors by as much as 500 years. Third, by conducting a critical analysis of the published literature on the region, we have shown that many of the categories in use by geographers and enumerators have assumed a model of cultural evolution that is not as nuanced as it might be to local ways of understanding the environment. Together this critique has shown that a combination of seasonal movement along rivers, together with knowledge of how to build attractive places for reindeer and horses, has created a flexible local economy that has survived in combination with major industrial development and also the collapse of the Soviet industrial state. In the terms of this volume, this chapter illustrates the way that the data of the Polar Census can be useful for guiding archaeological and historical research in the Siberian North.

Acknowledgements

This research is the product of a large team of people all of whom took part in the fieldwork and many of whom are writing up their results in separate publications. Oleg V. Kuznetsov of Chita State University helped with excavations in both field seasons. Elena G. Vologina of the Institute of the Earth's Crust, Russian Academy of Sciences assisted in excavations and co-ordinated core analysis of sediments from Lake Tolondo in 2006. Oksanna P. Vin´kovskaia of the Irkutsk Regional Museum directed botanical analysis of abandoned reindeer pastures. Natal´ia V. Kulagina of the Institute of the Earth's Crust conducted the species identification of pollen from excavations. Christopher Hill, of Boise State University, assisted with the excavations in 2006 and 2007 and commented generously on this chapter.

The research would not have been possible without the help of Iurii Konstantinovich Polititsyn, a lifetime resident of Svetlyi, who gave advice on sites of previous Evenki occupation and whose family helped us to navigate the river and organise the fieldwork.

This research was sponsored by grants from the National Science Foundation 0631970 and the Social Sciences and Humanities Research Council of Canada (SSHRCC MCRI 412- 2005-1005). The NSF grant is part of the larger BOREAS research programme initiated (but not funded by) the European Science Foundation. This chapter has benefited from two small seminars financed by the ESF EUROCORES programme under its BOREAS initiative.

The research could not have been carried out without the in-kind support, equipment and expertise of the Laboratory of Archaeology, Irkutsk State Technical University and the logistical support of the mining enterprise 'Svetlyi' based in Bodaibo. We are grateful to Iurii Vasil´evich Zharkov of the gold-mining company Vitim and his uncle Iurii Alekseevich Zharkov of Svetlyi Ltd for professionally and reliably arranging ground transport for us and our equipment to and from the banks of the Zhuia River.

Notes

1. Archival accounts show that between 1931 and 1939 the collective farm 'Red Khomolkho' kept on average 291 reindeer and 34 horses (BGGA 26-1-4: 2, 46; BGGA 26-1-5: 4, 6v; BGGA 26-1-49: 27–30). 'The Trusted Trail' in Svetlyi kept, on average, 152 reindeer and 6 horses (BGGA 26-1-27: 2; BGGA 26-1-45: 3; BGGA 26-1-49: 12, 29). The 'Chara Hunter' on average kept 63 reindeer and 10 horses (BGGA 26-1-33: 3; BGGA 26-1-37: 3). Individual families no doubt kept their own small private herds. This ratio of reindeer to horses contrasts sharply with the 'Bol´shoi Patom' collective located to the north on the Lena River which had 20 reindeer to 80 horses, illustrating a regional difference in the use of reindeer (BGGA 26-1-7: 2; BGGA 26-1-7: 36, 38; BGGA 26-1-49: 18).

2. Samokhin, in an unpublished essay, specifically mentions the respect for St. Peter's Day, the *Pokrov* Day and Easter as highly respected holidays for Evenkis in the region (GAIO 1468-1-2: 39). Interestingly in character with the overriding importance of trade relations, all three holidays are associated with certain public markets.
3. The household cards for the Olekma valley are in NARS 70-1-3355 and partially in 70-1-973. The household cards for the Upper Vitim, Lower Vitim and the Zhuia valley are in GAKK 1845-1-78; however, the corresponding community diaries and settlement total sheets are in GAIO 1468-1-2 with significant handwritten supplemental notes at ll. 39–44v. The four hygiene cards are in GAKK 769-1-460: 60, 80, 81, 87. There is a detailed sketch map for the Lower Vitim and Zhuia valley in GAKK 769-1-310: 4. Although the material was summarised in the regional publication (SKSO 1928) the data does not appear on Terletskii's 1938 map of the region nor in the published federal results.
4. The statistics are not much better if we take a regional population of all of the Evenki or Iakut people recorded in the Vitim, Olekma and Zhuia valleys in 1926–27 by Samokhin and Kuznetsov (working for the Far Eastern Statistical Administration). This composite survey of two census districts yields a total of 828 individuals with a ratio of men to women of 114.5, with many of the same cohorts missing.
5. Imperial fur-tax *iasak* records record only male 'souls'. Historical demographers use different coefficients to estimate the total population based on the number of men presenting themselves to pay tax. Patkanov (1906: 96), based on his analysis of 1898 census data, recommends a coefficient of 4.3. Mainov (1927: 394), based on his comprehensive analysis of archival records in Olekma and Irkutsk (many of which are now destroyed), recommends 6. Dolgikh (1960: 14), based on his analysis of the summary data for the 1926/27 Polar Census, uses the coefficient 4 across Siberia and the figure of 5 for the Tungus horsebreeders of Zabaikal´e. Our analysis of the Polar Census records based on the microlevel household records indicates a figure of 3.8. A coefficient of 4 was used to construct table 9.2.
6. There are seven named 'rivers' associated with fishing spots in the immediate vicinity of Ust´-Khomolkho (GAIO 1468-1-2: 48v) and thirteen named places associated with fur hunting over a much larger radius in both the Zhuia and the Lena drainage (GAIO 1468-1-2: 49v).
7. Oksanna Vin´kovskaia describes the 'meadow plant community' in the Zhuia valley as being characterised by the plant families *Fabaceae, Poaceae, Ranunculasae, Saroylphyllaceae, Rosaceau* and *Polygonacaea.* These plants distinguish themselves from the background communities of larch, and over time are gradually colonized by a series of bushes.
8. The pollen diagrams created from two trenches at Tolondo show a rise in *Fabacea* and *Poaceae,* and a drop in *Superaceae* at this time, which, according to our botanist, speaks to there being a clearing in the forest at this site.

10 | Identity, Status and Fish Among Lake Essei Iakuts

Tatiana Argounova-Low

Introduction

The Polar Census of 1926/27 was an exercise aimed at creating a complete description of the households in the Russian North. The records from the north of Turukhansk *krai* are some of the richest in the collection. The surviving manuscript community diaries, household cards, diet cards, kinship cards and enumerators' diaries are almost certainly one the most comprehensive data sets on Lake Essei Iakuts, a little known diasporic group of people living today in the northeast corner of Ilimpea *raion* in Krasnoiarsk *krai*. They are closely related to the Iakuts (Sakha) in central Iakutiia, sharing the same language and, according to their own legends, the same origin. According to several scholars, the ethnogenesis of this group was also strongly influenced by the neighbouring Evenki culture and economy (Dolgikh 1950, 1960; Gurvich 1950, 1952, 1977, 1982; Vasilevich 1951). The appellation of this ethnic group shifted for many centuries. In early records they were referred to as the Dolgan-Essei tribe (Berg 1927: 4) and as Tunguses in the 1897 Census. The designation as Essei Iakuts was used consistently only in the manuscript household cards collected by Boris Osipovich Dolgikh during the 1926/27 Polar Census expedition.[1] The Lake Essei Iakuts identify themselves today as *sakhalar;* however, in communication with Russian speakers this is often translated as 'Iakut'. The term used in the manuscript records seems to reflect this shorthand used at that time. This group was recorded by the missionary Suslov (1884), and studied by a number of scholars, including Ostrovskikh (1904) and Vasilevich (1951), but more comprehensive studies were conducted by Dolgikh (1950, 1960) and Gurvich (1950, 1952, 1977).

The census data on Lake Essei Iakuts fills gaps in the history of this unique group but also provides us with an opportunity to take a cohesive and systematic overview of their society and economy. In this chapter I analyse only a small part of the Polar Census archive directly related to 84 families at Lake Essei. This chapter also incorporates data from the fieldwork that I carried out in the village of Essei in the summer of 2002 and spring of 2003. The census materials used for this paper were located in the Krasnoiarsk Regional Museum (KKKM), the State Archive of Krasnoiarskii Krai (GAKK) and the National Archive of Sakha-Iakutiia (NARS). Some of this material has already been published in Russian (Argounova-Low 2005).

Northern Reindeer-Herding Iakuts or Fishermen?

Gurvich, the author of *The Culture of the Northern Reindeer-Herding Iakuts* (1977), coined the term 'northern reindeer-herding Iakuts' for the population living around Anabar, Essei and Olenek. Using archival records, he developed a story of their ethnogenesis beginning with the migration of cattle-herding Sakha (Iakut) from Iakutiia to the northern areas of Olenek and Essei, where they adapted a reindeer-herding economy from the Tungus people. According to Gurvich (ibid., 5), the newcomers not only retained their language and Iakut identity but also assimilated a large part of the local population. Gurvich's conclusions on the ethnic origin of this cultural group were questioned by Terletskii (1951), one of the organisers of the Polar Census. Terletskii argued that the history of local ethnonyms suggest that the population in this corner of Eastern Siberia is better described as Tungus. In this chapter, I wish to shift the focus to a different side of Gurvich's well-known definition – the economic quality of identity. Here, I will argue that the mainstay of people's lives both symbolically and economically was not connected to reindeer but instead to fishing. Based on my own fieldwork in the region I have become aware of a complex relationship between Lake Essei Iakuts and what was, for Russians, a low status food: fish. I will argue that fish play a rich symbolic role in Essei Iakut culture. Even relatively common and low-fat species of fish were also valued as so-called 'black food' – a concept that I will introduce in order to explain some of the marginal comments that one finds in the manuscript records. The Polar Census questionnaires were designed to bring information together on economic measures of status but also the details of everyday life. In this chapter, I will draw out the implications of the symbolism linked to fish and fishing and thereby question the way that economic activity is linked to identity. By highlighting fishing as the main form of occupation, economy and subsistence for the majority of Lake Essei Iakuts, I offer an independent foundation for their identity separate from the regional economic group described as the 'northern reindeer herder'.

The data for this study comes mainly from two Polar Census sources that provided information indirectly linked to diet. One of them, the hygiene card (*sanitarnaia kartochka*),[2] included 25 questions on both sides of a form enquiring about the sanitary conditions of the living premises and overall health of the occupants. This form represents an interest in diet-related issues that were covered in section 2, 'Food':

1. Sources of water supply, water quality.
2. Means of water delivery to the place of living and water containers.
3. What food is mainly used (types of food) according to various seasons?
4. Are food surrogates used and which exactly?
5. Are any spices used (particularly salt)?
6. Is food procured in advance and for what length?
7. Times of food intakes during the day, number of intakes.
8. Ways of cooking the food: containers used for that.
9. Medicinal practices (how often and which members of the family use medicines).
10. Alcohol.
11. Tobacco.

The more elaborate household card (*pokhoziaistvennaia kartochka)* consisted of more than 400 cells.[3] The card had an extensive list of questions concerning hunting and fishing, including terms for snares and tools. Of specific interest for the purpose of this chapter were questions related to the tools used to procure food and the species of animals caught.

The comments of enumerators are of particular interest. These were often written down in a special section for comments on page three of the household cards. Yet, at Lake Essei, the enumerator also filled the margins of the cards with additional observations. This additional information revealed an emotional side and provided a poignant insight into the communication between an enumerator and an informant that was otherwise concealed by the rigidity of the questionnaire. The choice of words, emphasis, and construction of the sentences help to expose and recreate a fuller picture.

The Polar Census Expedition to Lake Essei

The Polar Census enumerator Andrei Lekarenko recorded census sector XI which included the area of Lake Essei. An artist by occupation, Lekarenko had an eye for detail, a photographic memory, and an artistic way of depicting his surroundings. He also had an excellent way of extracting information and used a logical approach to ordering his observations that resulted in eloquent conclusions in his remarks in the margins of the census cards.

Andrei Lekarenko, with assistance from Dolgikh and Naumov, covered the entire territory travelled by Lake Essei Iakuts. Descendants living today at

Lake Essei identify very few missing names from the manuscript records. The material collected represents the most complete archive of household data on this area, since no equally detailed enumeration was conducted before or after the Polar Census.

Andrei Lekarenko kept a personal diary in which he recorded his impressions and observations and which provided an important addition to the statistical data (KKKM 7626-110). From this diary we can get a sense of the difficulties that Lekarenko and other enumerators experienced. Working for the census became a sort of heroic deed for many of the enumerators (Makarov 2005: 48). However, the local tribal council (*rodovoi sovet*) provided all possible cooperation and assistance to the enumerators of the Polar Census. They organised and summoned people, typically to the house of the former 'clan prince' of the Imperial era, where the enumerator stayed (KKKM 7626-110: 107).

At the time of the census, the Lake Essei Iakuts were caught in the middle of a struggle over authority that put them in a unique position relative to the other Evenki (Tungus) households in the region.

> And tomorrow we should be in Essei, the centre of the Essei republic, so to say. Interesting to know how the work will go there. I should take the correct strategy that will be comfortable for the Essei people and Ilimpiia. I don't know if this is possible – but I will try. First of all I should compile a list of migration areas on Essei, then I need to get a list of names from the Tribal Council, to have an idea of the residents. (KKKM 7626-110: 82)

The director of the Census Adam Petrovich Kurilovich briefed Andrei Lekarenko about the special approach needed when working with residents at Essei:

> Lake Essei belongs to the territory of the Siberian region, but is populated by Iakuts, nationally drawn to the Iakut Republic. On these grounds there are misunderstandings in this area. The Iakuts do not want to acknowledge the power of the Turukhansk RIK [regional executive committee] and only obey the representatives from Iakutiia. It is probable that they even do not let you work there. In any case, use all opportunities to list this region. (GAKK 769-1-307: 33–34)

According to Soviet government officials, Lake Essei Iakuts were reputedly better off than Tunguses due to their large reindeer herds and the fact that they were thought to be often involved in long-distance trade. However the Polar Census data demonstrate that a significant section of the population had few or no reindeer at all (table 10.1). With the exception of 11 families who had upwards of 100 head of riding reindeer, the majority of 84 families settled around the lake held an average of 46 adult reindeer. Although classified formally as a 'nomadic' people on the household cards due to their extreme distance from the nearest officially registered settlement, the vast majority of the population travelled in orbits near the lake, perhaps centred at Lake Essei but not entirely settled. Their adoption of a lake-centred fishing lifestyle may have been part of a larger regional process. In his overview of the indigenous nationalities of the area, Terletskii (1951: 91) argues that by 1926 (in comparison with the 1897 census) over half of the Evenki population of the area had become 'sedentary' fishermen. It would seem that many Lake Essei Iakuts were affected by the same process.

Most of the household heads were classified by the enumerator into three general categories of *bogatyi* or *zazhitochnyi* (rich), *seredniak* (well-off or of average means), and *bedniak* (poor). This categorisation was both economic and social, but most of all ideological; it was obvious that one of the aims of this census was to reveal the relationship between the exploiters and those being exploited (Anderson 2006: 15). The most decisive factor in the enumerator's classification seemed to be the number of reindeer owned. People with herds of over 50 and up to 5,000 were categorised as 'rich' or 'wealthy'[4]; those with medium herds of domestic reindeer (usually over 20) were categorized as *seredniak*. Households with no reindeer or up to 20 were categorised as 'poor' (*bedniak*) with different degrees and shades of poverty indicated in the comments fields.[5]

Out of 84 households, 54 were classified as poor (*bedniaks*) with up to 20 reindeer, and among those, six households had no reindeer at all, and three had only one reindeer. Seventeen households had from 21 to 50 reindeer and were considered *seredniaki* and only 13 households had herds of 100 to 1,500 reindeer and were considered rich (*zazhitochnyi*). The large majority of people in the Essei area were thus poor people who did not rely on reindeer husbandry in their economy.

The degree of poverty and deficiency was also expressed on the household cards in marginal notes by the following phrases: 'he eats fish all the time'; 'he fishes a lot, almost all the time eats fish'; 'does not have anything except for fish'; 'he eats nothing else but fish', 'they have been eating fish for ages' (GAKK 769-1-406: 17). In the case of the family of Evdokiia Vasil'evna, an elderly resident of the area of Essei, the enumerator states: 'poor people, living poorly – in need of everything' (GAKK 769-1-406: 39). The notes in the margins run: 'they eat

Table 10.1. Reindeer ownership by households around Lake Essei

	'Bedniaki' – poor residents			'Seredniaki' – residents of average means		'Zazhitochnye' – wealthy residents		
Adult reindeer per household	0	1–10	11–20	21–30	31–50	51–200	201–500	501–1,500
Number of households	6	33	15	11	6	4	6	3

only fish all the time'. It is notable that the construction of the sentence emphasises the extreme poverty of that particular family. However not only poor people (*bedniaki*) lived off fish; among the records one can find commentaries like this: 'Seredniak – eats fish all the time' (GAKK 769-1-406: 23).

There is some evidence that people tried to conceal their property when confronting a representative of a powerful state machine. In many cases, Lekarenko had to assign the category of 'rich' or 'poor' on the basis of secondary signs. This is what Lekarenko wrote in his diary when listing the family of one of his informants: 'When recording I felt that they were lying, even their noses were sweating from tension. I spent time till lunch when meat was served, silver spoons, forks, meat with fat, such can be encountered only in rich families… Forest stretching again, small hills, snow trampled to a shine, that saliently speaks for large herds of reindeer' (KKKM 7626-110: 99). The reliability of the Polar Census data regarding the number of reindeer owned was undermined by the owners to a significant extent and therefore required, in his view, upward adjustment. On the unreliability of this data Lekarenko wrote in his diary when registering one household: 'so we are in the family of a *seredniak*, who has many more reindeer than he acknowledges during the survey' and 'I suppose, I did not get all the data from this *seredniak* man – I have written down almost half less than he has' (KKKM 7626-110: 91–92). The reasons for misinformation were numerous, yet one of the main reasons was the habitual caution of reindeer herders and their fear of the new powerful authorities. Another reason might be the way that an extensive bilateral kinship system distributed reindeer estates across a large number of the nuclear families who were the focus of this particular census (Anderson, 2011). According to Sakha belief, boasting was also a punishable trait that could lead to reductions in the size of herds through the malignant eye of watchful spirits. Reducing the number of reindeer meant complying with beliefs and served as protection of one's luck.

Rather than casting doubt on the honesty of informants at Essei, I would like to suggest that one reason why reindeer were 'missing' might be due to a bifurcation in the way that different households arranged their economy. My analysis of the household cards suggests that there was a division between people who practiced reindeer husbandry and people who lived by fishing. In this region, reindeer were kept as a means of transportation to facilitate hunting fur-bearers and for long-distance trade. The possession of a reindeer estate required regular movement. This was indicated on the card on the first page in the table listing 'stopping sites'. The so-called impoverished families, whose household economy was predominantly based on fishing, listed the laconic 'Lake Essei' (or its characteristic peninsulas) as their only stopping sites. Out of 84 households, 57 listed Lake Essei as their only site of migration over the four seasons. The average number of adult reindeer they held was 10 (ranging from

1 to 35 head). By contrast, those 24 with more elaborate itineraries could range hundreds of kilometres away in nearby riversheds. They on average held 133 adult reindeer (ranging from 7 to 1,500 head). Andrei Lekarenko describes this bifurcation in his diary: 'Those who own reindeer go further away from the winter pastures; those who do not own reindeer are busy fishing – in the summer they procure a lot of fish. Yet rich people fish very little – they are all the time occupied by the reindeer' (KKKM 7626-110: 98).

Another indicator of this delineation between reindeer herders and fishing people evident from the household cards is the difference in the variety of fish caught (table 10.2). People who relied essentially on fish would declare several species of fish on their cards (cells 313–344). Whereas when Savva Botulu, the legendary rich reindeer herder, declared catching only four species of fish, the added commentary ran: 'they fish very little' (GAKK 769-1-406: 95–96). This implies that people who relied entirely on fish had a better knowledge of fish, could distinguish between various types of fish, and the varieties of fish caught did matter for them.

Table 10.2. The percentage of households at Lake Essei catching specific species of fish in 1926–27

Fish Species	% of households (N=84)
whitefish (*Coregonus lavaretus*)	91.6
chir (*Coregonus nasus*)	85.5
taimen (*Hucho taimen*)	84.3
peled (*Coregonus peled*)	78.3
pike – *shchuka* (*Esox lucius*)	77.1
grayling – *kharius* (*Thymallus arcticus*)	71.1
perch – *okun'*(*Perca fluviatilis*)	13.3
peled – *baranatka* (*Coregonus lacepede*)	9.6

Fish Subsistence, Status and 'Black Food'

In the section above, I argued that marginal notes on the Polar Census cards used diet (specifically a diet of fish) as a proxy for describing degrees of poverty. In this section I wish to argue that eating fish – even poor quality fish – need not necessarily imply a poor diet. There are several sides to this idea.

First, eating fish did not mean eating poorly for local people, even if the enumerator might have thought so. The card describing the household of Marfa Petrovna states: 'In the summer the diet is better, there is plenty of fish, up to ten fish per person. In the summer they catch 50–100 fish every day. The nets are checked 2–3 times a day, in the morning and at noon – sometimes they get 10 and more fish at each check. For winter time they procure 4 *pudy* (16.3 kilograms) of *pursa* and *iukola*' (GAKK 769-1-405: 7). The last line runs: 'If they do not catch fish, they eat meat', revealing the significance of fish as a staple food, as well as the food of retrenchment that intentionally prolongs the supply of provisions.

Second, many 'not-so very wealthy' reindeer herders also relied on fishing. This is illustrated in many comparative ethnographic examples from the circumpolar north (Eidlitz 1969: 27). The reliance on fish by Koriaks was described by Jochelson (1908: 575): 'Those who own small herds of reindeer and do not tend the herds of wealthy herd-owners, but wander about alone, must procure supplies of fish for winter, since they cannot afford to kill many reindeer. These poor reindeer-breeders go out in summer to the mouth of some river or to the sea-coast, and there dry fish for winter use'. Fishing, even if it was regarded as an inferior activity to reindeer husbandry or hunting, was a 'reserved occupation and was in many ways a livelihood for the poor and sick' (Eidlitz 1969: 29). At Lake Essei wealthy Iakuts resorted to fish at times when hunting of wild reindeer failed, as they slaughtered domestic reindeer only in exceptional cases. It would seem that fishing might be an 'embedded activity' within some forms of reindeer herding (see Kiselev, this volume).

This base-line reliance on fish as a type of everyday food is evocatively illustrated by the Sakha concept of 'black food' (*khara as*). The concept is considered to be somewhat archaic and obsolete, yet the residents of Lake Essei still often employ this concept when they refer to certain foods as 'black'. The definition of 'black food' varies according to social context, but in general it refers to foods that are in steady supply, and remain available most of the time. Here I argue that the definition is not the same as food of the poor but rather denotes a type of food which is 'not-exceptional'.

Semantically, one of the direct translations of the word '*khara*' is 'the colour black'. Yet colour designation has little to do with the colour of food in this case, as the colour in culture is the 'process of relating, not of recognizing' (Sahlins 1976: 9). The Sakha-Russian dictionary gives further elaboration on translations of *khara* as 'vague, unattractive'; 'something just made, but not given shape or polished'. *Khara* also was used to denote anything plain and ordinary, e.g.: *khara kihi*[6] – an ordinary man, a common person, as opposed to a man of aristocratic origin; or *khara syerga* – an ordinary sledge without ornaments (Pekarskii 1917: 3,329). It is the connotation of something plain and basic that offers an opportunity to extend semantic analysis of the 'black food' concept to subsistence food.

The economic context is a significant indicator in the definition of the concept of 'black food', which implies variability according to the sources of reliable supply as I discovered during my fieldwork. For many Lake Essei Iakuts who have a large enough supply of fish and meat due to fishing and hunting, black food denotes predominantly meat and fish, in other words 'something that is plentiful', 'something that one has all the time', 'something that can be cooked quickly'. Those who reside in the village and hunt very little if at all, depend in their diet on fish and food from the local store. Their concept of black food implies fish from nearby lakes or macaroni and bread. Thus *black food* in this case denotes ordinary, plain food for everyday occasions.

In order to make this definition I would like to contrast 'black food' with true emergency food that Sakha people turn to out of desperation. A good example of emergency food is the inner bark of pine and larch trees. There is much evidence for the tree inner bark being used by the native peoples as a main source of food in times of famine from Chukchi and Eskimo at one end of the Arctic stretch to Lapps and Swedes at the other (Eidlitz 1969: 54–59; Bergman et al. 2004). People in the Arctic used pine and larch inner bark to bulk up their food. It was also used as candy for its sweet taste (Bergman et al. 2004: 4). The inner bark was known to many Arctic cultures practising retrenchment: 'The use of Scots pine inner bark is commonly associated with famine in agricultural economies. Indeed, Nordic and Finnish farmers used the inner bark to make bread as emergency food during years of famine' (ibid., 5). The provision of bark took place in the summer when the tree was full of juice. The bark was detached from the tree, and the inner layer was scraped, dried and chopped into small pieces. The inner bark was stored in large quantities and was consumed all year round. The Sakha were known to rely on the inner bark of the pine tree as a subsistence food (Savvin 2005: 185–86). According to Maak, the Sakha consumed so much of the inner bark that he referred to them as 'tree eaters' (*dendrophages*) (N. Popov 1926: 8). A very similar variation of this staple food was in central Iakutiia: pickled fish porridge mixed with the inner bark of the pine tree (*Pinus sylvestris L.*) (Gurvich 1977: 77). In the Essei area, where pines did not grow, Iakuts adjusted to use the inner bark of the larch tree (*Larix L.*).

There are instances in the hygiene cards where Lekarenko noted the use of inner bark. The hygiene card for Khristofor Maimago at Essei explains how bark helped his family to eke out resources sparingly: 'they sometimes use larch bark as a surrogate, especially in winter, when the fish catch is low. They mix it with boiled fish' (GAKK 769-1-459: 19). The interview with Stepan Ivanov links fish bark with a subsistence diet: 'All year round they eat fish. They almost never see flour. They use powdered larch [surrogates] mixed with [illegible] fish' (GAKK 769-1-459: 20). In both of these cases Lekarenko also makes reference to richer families who provided additional food to these families.

What we might call the 'black food economy' did involve some matter of forward planning and preparation. At Lake Essei, summer and autumn were the busiest months for fishing and preparation of fish for storing. The household cards have detailed lists of fishing gear. Among many listed the most popular ones were pull-nets, sweep nets and snouts. The Lake Essei Iakuts wove large fishing nets – up to 250 square metres – from horsehair (fig. 10.1). Horsehair was one of the most desirable and valuable items of merchandise. Because of the lack of horses in the Essei area horsehair had to be regularly

Figure 10.1. A horsehair net from Lake Essei collected by Lekarenko during the Polar Census Expedition. Photograph from KKKM.

delivered by merchants from Viliuisk in central Iakutiia. Pull nets were widely used by Lake Essei Iakuts, according to the Census data, for they were used for fishing in the summer, as well as through the winter for under-ice fishing.

The most prestigious fish were large white fish. However, the fish that were often specified in the household cards, the smaller fish, were more characteristic of the economy: grayling, herring and perch (table 10.2). Prejudice against small fish is explained by their low calorific and nutritious value and their prolific bones. More likely than not small fish that were caught in the net together with the larger ones were considered a side product of fishing for large, noble fish. Although small fish, like carp and perch, were not favoured by the Essei people, it was precisely these small fish that constituted the staple diet of Lake Essei Iakuts. Small fish caught in winter were frozen in blocks and used throughout the winter to make soup or porridge. Although household cards did not record a variety of fish dishes, they referred to a few ways of cooking and preserving fish. *Iukola* remains the most popular way of preserving fish by drying and smoking. Reasonably sized fish were scaled, cut in two and then the flesh was incised (fig. 10.2). They were dried and smoked above the fire.

Figure 10.2. Fedos′ia Egorovna Miroshko prepares *iukola*, July 2002. Photograph by Tatiana Argounova-Low.

This was a popular between-meals snack and often accompanied tea instead of bread. *Iukola* was often ground to the consistency of powder (*pursa, buorcha*), and when boiled or mixed up with the larch inner bark it would make a soup of thick consistency.

Fresh fish caught in winter could be stored for eating frozen (*tong balyk*). But most often fresh fish were grilled in front of the fire or boiled. Frying was not practised at all; fat and grease, being precious ingredients, were reserved as a separate food item and for making flat breads. The data from the Polar Census does not have any record of preserving fish by salting, the cells (183–187) requiring information on salting equipment remained empty. Recent enquiries revealed that salt production was established nearby Lake Essei only after 1927, when salting was introduced to Lake Essei Iakuts. In the summer excess fresh fish was pickled by oxidation. Although pickling was practised less in this area where fish were available in large quantities all year round, it was a known way of preserving them. In order to preserve fish by pickling, large pits were dug in the ground where fish were collected and left for oxidation and, despite their strong pungent smell, reportedly had a pleasant taste. This was a popular way of preservation until salting entirely replaced the pickling of fish (Gurvich 1977: 77).

According to the observations of the enumerators, the winter diet was more modest and food intake took place 2 to 4 times a day, whereas the summer food intakes occurred more often (GAKK 769-1-459: 17). This could be explained by the long-light evenings during the summer season which enabled greater physical activity and required a larger calorific intake facilitated by the availability of fresh food. So this was a natural way of practising economy and retrenchment. Although the obvious months for procurement were the summer and autumn seasons, when fish were plentiful and bark collection was easier, the procurement of black food in advance was an on-going process throughout the year.

If practicing a black food diet was the mainstay of the economy, even the poorest family set aside a stock of good or luxury food that could be served on a special occasion like receiving a guest. Of the 57 households 'restricted' to fishing at the lake, almost all households kept flour, sugar and tea, and several kept butter (from cow milk). In wealthier households festive food was accumulated in anticipation of a big celebration, for instance a wedding, after which the family would return to a black food diet.

Economising and storage were important elements in the economy of the Lake Essei Iakuts and their subsistence, but food is a code and 'the message it encodes will be found in the pattern of social relations being expressed' (Douglas 1972: 61). Despite black and white being obvious opposites, I have demonstrated that when related to food, the concept of black is not based on colour identification; indeed what is called black is white in colour. I argue that for Sakha and Iakuts in Essei 'black food' is an illustration and reflection of the hierarchy of social relations. The semantic antithesis for 'black food' is not 'white', as I observed, but good or festive food (*maany as*). This antithesis also underlines the special social relationship between the donor and the recipient, implying the generosity and humbleness of the giver in front of the honour and potential reciprocity of the guest. Levi-Strauss (1966) referred to boiled food as 'endo-cuisine', consigning domestic consumption and more elaborate ways of cooking, such as roasting, to 'exo-cuisine'; the principal foundation in the concept of black food is analogous. According to the same principle based on the tightening or loosening of familial and social ties, black food refers to 'endo-' or internal consumption, whereas non-black, festive and celebratory food is aimed and directed at guests, people from beyond the immediate family or close circle. The analysis of 'black food' elucidates an understanding of the social boundaries for Sakha that '[t]he grand operator of the system is the line between intimacy and distance' (Douglas 1972: 66). Black is thus reserved for the closest circle of immediate family and ordinary meals, whereas festive food, including meat with a higher nutritional value, is related to outside of the family, honourable guests and for occasions related to ritual offerings and ceremonial food. Black is a code for ordinary and is consumed internally, whereas non-black, either of a different colour, ornate, or festive and special in terms of food, sends a code to the external recipients, who could include supreme deities. It sends a message to outsiders of willingness to co-operate, to make an alliance whether political or economic; it lets the spirits know of the virtuous nature of a donor requesting their benevolence. Black food is at the core of the centre, whereas special food constitutes peripheral food that is used on rare occasions. The following section will emphasise the significance of fishing as a means of procurement of reliance food in the Essei area, for fish had a distinctive symbolic meaning to Lake Essei Iakuts.

Fish and Its Symbolism

Despite relatively few 'obvious points of resemblance with human beings' fish are often used as metaphors for human society (Palsson 1990: 119). Otto Von Sadovszky (1995), basing his studies on archaeological and linguistic findings, analyses fish as a major aspect of the ancient people's world view and revealed that there are many conceptual associations of fish as related to human beings. For Lake Essei Iakuts, fish, as a significant element of everyday diet, held appropriate obvious symbolic signification. For them, fish continue to be a valuable resource – a food that saves in hardship times and therefore possesses special qualities.

The lakes providing an abundance of fish are treated with veneration and respect by Iakuts; similar to many indigenous people's relationship with their environment. The lakes are often likened to a matrilineal ancestor, and construction of a child-ancestor relationship is undisguised (e.g. Turner 1967: 48–58). Local people refer to Lake Essei as *Ebe* (Grandmother). This is a respectful name by which Iakut people refer to lakes and rivers of significance as a source of food, drinking water and a vital transportation link. This respectful attitude is expressed also by tossing small offerings of tea, tobacco, food or alcohol into the water and by the often-used phrase: 'Our Granny feeds us, Granny saves us' (*Ebebit ahatar, ebebit abyryr*). Lake Essei is often ascribed human-like qualities, for instance, getting cross and angry at someone's behaviour, being moody and possessing the ability to punish. The belief that anything in the world which is created by a higher order than a human being has a soul bestows lakes and rivers with power over a fisherman or a hunter. A fisherman thus has to communicate with spirits by making offerings and behave according to certain ethical standards. Luck and chance, a profound concept of Lake Essei Iakuts and an element of the everyday life of hunters and fishermen, are requested from deities. The landscape around fishing lakes was mapped with small wooden statues, representations of the fish spirit. It is believed that this spirit, appropriately called Fish Grandpa (*Balyk Ehekene*), is there to assist and protect the fishermen and hunters. The wooden statues of Fish Grandpa can still be found by lakes, close to the former fishing grounds.

The significance of fish as a source of reliance and subsistence is amplified by the study of toponyms around the area where Lake Essei Iakuts reside. The names given to lakes reflect the knowledge of Lake Essei Iakuts and communicate this knowledge to the community. Keith Basso writes that topographic representations are 'most revealing of the conceptual instruments with which native people interpret their natural surroundings' (1996: 73). It is through the engagement with landscape and its features – through activity – that the people become familiar with places, create their knowledge and experience that then is forged in a characteristic place-name, a toponym. The names of places thus become 'accounts and observations of the landscape that consistently presuppose mutually held ideas of what it actually is, why its constituent places are important, and how it may intrude on the practical affairs of its inhabitants' (ibid., 74). Knowledge related to fish and the water medium is reflected on the landscape around Lake Essei. Places, rivers and lakes are given characterization according to the people's knowledge about them and qualities of lakes and rivers related to fishing: Carp Lake (*Sobolookh*), Pike River (*Sordonnookh*), Net Fishing Lake (*Ilimnir kyöl*), Sig Lake (*Bökchögördöökh*), Fishing Hook Cape (*Sittir Tumuhakh*), and even Skinny Carps Lake (*Kötökh sobolookh*). By naming lakes and giving them a characteristic that reflected their adaptation to the physical environment, Lake Essei Iakuts created knowledge and their philosophy, which merged the landscape and the water medium into one whole.

After Palsson (1990: 119), who stressed the importance of studying symbolic expressions in a context of development over time, I suggest that we address the philosophy of life expressed by Lake Essei Iakuts. According to them, human existence is not static, but can flow and take different forms. People are not stuck in their human bodies and mind frames for the rest of their living time, but rather they transform throughout their physical or spiritual existence into different beings: animals, birds and fish. Lake Essei Iakuts have a documented clan affiliation to birds. The clan Maimaga has a swan (*kuba*) as a sacred bird, and the Botulu have an eagle (*khotoi*); Osogostok has a crow (*suor*); Chordu has a duck (*andy*); Espek, a jay (*hökchöki*) and Beti, a loon (*kuogas*). These birds are considered sacred. And although fish is so much further from humans in the representation and associative connection, it is still believed that fish can be one of the links in the long chain of the metamorphosis of people during the course of their existence. The concept of human-animal relationships has immense educational value, so from an early age children learn the values of the animalistic significance in the overall philosophy and understanding of their world where a human being undergoes multiple transformations throughout his or her existence on the earth. Associations with fish are engaged on the level of social ranking. A remarkably hierarchical society, the Iakuts have a clear division between the families of distinction and poorer families. A husband from a poor family, not of a noble origin, is reminded from time to time by his in-laws that he is a perch (*khakhynai*), not a prestigious fish. Often on the subject of their background people refer to themselves as fish: 'We are just fish people' or 'Our parents always lived on the lake; they were poor fish people'.

In the course of life, whether in story-telling, metaphorical expressions, dreams or desires human beings are transformed into different living creatures. They can turn into a bear, a raven and a fish, to name a few links in the long chain of metamorphosis. Fish become a part of human existence, a transformed human being itself. This is a philosophy and vision of the world where every living creature, be it a human being or other, live equally and no man can be superior to other living creatures, as tomorrow he can turn into a different being, be that in a dream, a story, communication with the spirits, or hunting. He will be undertaking this eternal journey all the time he exists in this world, because life is continual birth (Scott 1989: 195).

Conclusion

The Polar Census data helped to reveal that the majority of Lake Essei Iakuts relied on the produce of their fishing as a main source of their subsistence diet. A majority of the people in Essei, according to the census data, did not have enough reindeer, if they had any at all. They could not support themselves by produce from domestic reindeer herding, nor had they an opportunity to engage fully in hunting due to the lack of transportation. Lacking domestic reindeer also prevented them from being involved in trading, another important source of income in the well-off families. The main diet of these people thus was based on year-round fishing. The importance of fishing and fish in the life of Lake Essei Iakuts finds its signification in place-names and symbolic representation, as I have shown in this chapter. By examining the notion of 'black food' that is used by Lake Essei Iakuts, the concept that was and is still used by the local residents of Essei, I re-instate the importance and significance of fishing as food of subsistence in the economy of the Lake Essei Iakuts.

Returning to the definition proposed by Gurvich of 'northern reindeer-herding Iakuts', in the light of the analysed data from the Polar Census it becomes obvious that emphasising reindeer herding as the main occupation of Lake Essei Iakuts presents an ostensible difficulty. Unlike the pastoralists of diary cattle, reindeer-herding Lake Essei Iakuts could not sustain themselves with a range of milk products; a reindeer cow can only produce 50 to 100 grams of milk per day. Nor could they rely on meat from their domestic reindeer – domestic animals had great value and their slaughter was rather exceptional. It is this evidence from historical records that provides the opportunity to question whether Gurvich's coined definition of 'northern reindeer-herding Iakuts' which he ascribed to Lake Essei Iakuts, is appropriate. However, what can be helpful in overcoming this representational obstacle is a suggestion proposed by Sirina, who observed that in the case of the Katanga Evenkis, the traditional economic system presented a 'northern triad' of hunting for meat and fur, fishing, and tending reindeer (2006: 63). In fact, in 1950 Il´ia Samoilovich Gurvich himself remarked that '[a]long the rivers of Olenek and Anabar there were several types of reindeer herding economies with various combinations of herding, hunting and fishing corresponding to certain zones' (1950: 165). Indeed, it was common for the northern inhabitants, hunters and reindeer herders, to have no fixed share of these activities, for food procurement represented a continuous process of switching from one source to another. Therefore it would be incorrect to single out one economic aspect as the main occupation, since in their economic sustainability Lake Essei Iakuts had to diversify their sources of food, employing opportunistic hunting-gathering strategies. The data from the Polar Census clearly demonstrates that the poorer Lake Essei Iakuts, who constituted the majority of the population, in their everyday diet relied on fish. However, fishing was universal for all social categories of the Essei residents: 'Fishing was practiced in one way or another by all the groups of Iakuts-reindeer herders. This occupation, very seasonal, was of important consumption significance. In the summer time, when hunting for wild reindeer was difficult or not productive, and slaughter of undernourished domestic reindeer was not practical, fishing was the main source of food' (Gurvich 1977: 44). We thus might question whether all Lake Essei Iakuts were herders of reindeer, but we can state with confidence that all of them were fishermen.

Acknowledgements

I would like to thank The Leverhulme Trust for sponsoring my research in 2003–05 as a Special Research Fellow. Most of the data was collected within the 'Baikal Archaeology Project' financed by the Social Sciences and Humanities Research Council of Canada (MCRI 412-2000-1000). One expedition was financed by The British Academy Small Grant 'Remembering lost connections: past and present of two native villages'. I would like to thank Antonina Alekseeva and Aleksei Beti and many other residents of Essei for their assistance during my fieldwork.

Notes

1. The term 'Iakut' was used to classify household heads for almost all the cards collected at Lake Essei by Lekarenko. A number of individuals were classified by B. O. Dolgikh as 'Essei Iakuts' living in communities to the north and west of the lake itself. For the purpose of clearer designation in English, I adhere to 'Lake Essei Iakut' in this chapter.
2. The manuscript archive of the primary Polar Census documents for the community of Lake Essei is split between GAKK and NARS. Ten kinship cards for the people immediately at Essei and five hygiene cards are held in GAKK (GAKK 769-1-446: 64–73; GAKK 769-1-459: 16–20). A further hygiene card is in NARS at (NARS 70-1-1024: 11). Additional seven hygiene cards for Essei Iakuty living beyond the lake on the Aiakli drainage near Kamen´ are held in Krasnoiarsk and Iakutsk (GAKK 769-1-459: 48, 49, 72; GAKK 769-1-452: 89; NARS 70-1-1024: 6–10).
3. There are two sets of household cards for Lake Essei. GAKK holds 77 cards in dela (GAKK 769-1-405; 406; 441 and 424). NARS holds a duplicate set (70-1-1004) of which five are not held in GAKK. The complete set analysed for this study is for 84 households. Another 138 cards hold data on Iakuts who were born at or who migrated to Lake Essei but who at the time of the Polar Census were surveyed at different places. These cards were not used in this chapter.
4. Although a rich reindeer herder Savva Botulu (Savva Egorov Botulu in the Polar Census records) registered 1,500 reindeer, the notes ran: 'according to the Tungus people of the Chirinda area, where Savva Botulu travels to trade, he is the richest reindeer owner of the Essei district, owning up to 5,000 reindeer' (GAKK 769-1-406: 95). Some

contemporary informants in Essei have anecdotal accounts of Savva Botulu possessing up to 11,000 reindeer.

5. This classification conflicts significantly with data obtained during the 1934 collectivisation, where families with 300 to 400 reindeer constituted *seredniaki*. The category of wealthy reindeer herders possessed between 800 and 1,500 reindeer (Gurvich 1977: 236).

6. Compare with the Mongolian expression '*khar khun*' (literally, 'black person') denoting a common or secular person.

11 | Subsistence and Residence in the Putoran Uplands and Taimyr Lowlands in 1926–27

John P. Ziker

This chapter investigates the ecological history of the Putoran uplands and Taimyr lowlands as reflected in the hunting and migration strategies of a unique local community of Iakut and Tungus hunters and herders. Here I make extensive use of the primary materials of the 1926/27 Polar Census, as well as my own ethnographic work in this region. This material helps us to refine ideas about indigenous settlement and subsistence patterns, travel and economic relationships in the region (Dolgikh 1960, 1962, 1963; A. Popov 1934, 1937, 1964). The chapter will discuss seasonal migration, the daily movement associated with resource use, demographic changes, annual movements associated with the coming-together and fissioning of residential groups, and travel to and from trading posts and distant communities.

The relationship between the Putoran uplands and Taimyr lowlands is also an important applied issue for the native people who live in Taimyr today. Although few, if any, people travel to the uplands from their homes in the lowland villages today, the upland region is still very much alive in memory. Further, contemporary indigenous entrepreneurs still hope to reclaim this area. The present residential shift to the lowlands was sealed by a change in technology wherein motorized transport replaced reindeer for short- and long-distance travel. The uplands have become now logistically difficult to reach since the traveller must provision his or her own fuel on such trips. This has lead to a situation where many people assume that all indigenous people have always lived in the lowlands in small, relatively compact villages. The records from the Polar Census help us to dispel this myth and are useful in proving a history of occupation.

In the next section I outline the historical importance of community movements in the uplands, and why we know little about them. I develop the perspective of political ecology which aims to consider the complex social factors that govern hunting and pastoral societies. In the third part of the chapter, I interpret a set of household cards and a community diary for the Kamen´ region

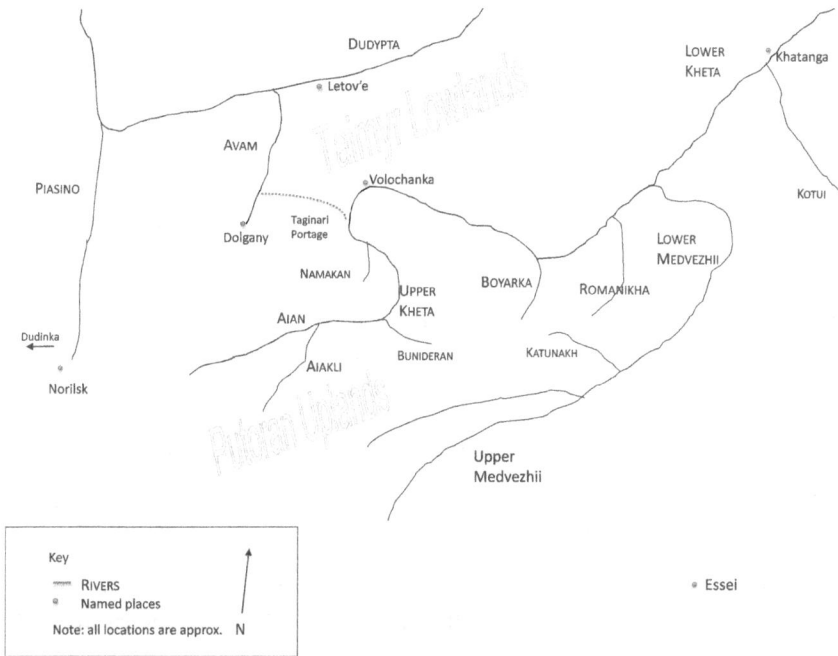

Figure 11.1. The Kamen´ region showing the major watersheds, the uplands and lowlands

focusing on seasonal movement, settlement patterns, and resource use. In the fourth part of the chapter I return to ecological theory and consider continuities and changes through the present. Finally, I document how the uplands figures in the establishment of new clan communes in the region.

The Political Ecology of Central Siberia

The Putoran is a complex of high flat-topped mountains that span central Siberia. The highest elevations are on the northern and western ranges near Noril´sk. Characteristic of this sub-Arctic landscape are wide-stepped canyons and deep, narrow lakes (Lake Lama, Lake Keta, Lake Glubokoe, Lake Khantaiskoe, Lake Aian). Vegetation includes larch taiga, sparse forests and mountain tundra. To the north of the plateau are the Ari-Mas (Dolgan, 'northern forest') and the central Taimyr lowlands. To the south and east is the vast forest-tundra of Ilimpiia, marked by the settlement of Iakuts at Lake Essei (see Argounova-Low, this volume). Wild reindeer migrate from the uplands through the central lowlands twice a year to and from birthing and summer feeding grounds in the north. For wild reindeer there is an important ecological connection between uplands and lowlands ecosystems. Human existence in the region historically has been connected largely to reindeer, and to this extent, the ecological dynamics of reindeer and other local renewable resources, including fish, fur-bearing animals, and large predators, have implications for human subsistence and settlement.

The model represented in figure 11.2 combines the three interacting factors discussed in archaeological approaches to human subsistence and residence (Jochim 1976) – dynamics of resource use, demographics and settlement patterns – with explicit consideration of the social environment discussed in political ecology (Borgerhoff Mulder and Coppolillo 2005: 157) and anthropology (Steward 1977; Chagnon 1997). I will use this complex model, which explicitly frames both the social and the physical environment, to interpret the fragmentary oral history and documentary record of the Putoran uplands. The chapter analyses the structure of certain named 'encampments' (*stoibishche*) identified in the archival record as the centres of subsistence activity, seasonal movement and political organization.

We know, through information recorded in the Polar Census and later ethnographic interviews, that there were numerous families who used the uplands as part of a trade route or for seasonal subsistence activities at least as far back as the nineteenth century and through the 1960s. David Anderson (2000: 134–38) maps the nineteenth century overland trading routes across the western Putoran Mountains and the lower Enisei River areas. In that work he focuses on how political factors, such as the avoidance of *iasak* tax collectors, may have affected the timing and direction of movements. At the same time he shows that local knowledge of where to find migratory wild reindeer and

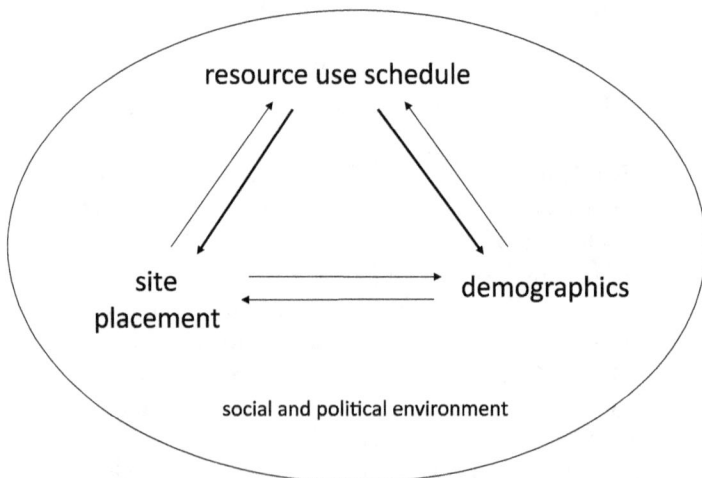

Figure 11.2. A model of subsistence and settlement with explicit consideration of the social, political and physical environment

fish added an element of flexibility to the long-distance movements. He uses these maps to demonstrate how Soviet territorialisation policies beginning in the 1930s slowly tied hunters and herders into orbits around fixed settlements, leading them to abandon upland areas.

The enumerator of the Kamen´ region, the famous Soviet ethnographer Boris Iosofich [Osipovich] Dolgikh, conducted his interviews between 28 December 1926 and 7 January 1927 (fig. 11.3). He wrote a heavily annotated community diary (NARS 70-1-789: 305–321 [duplicate diary on folios 356–372])

Figure 11.3. Boris Osipovich Dolgikh preparing for his Taimyr enumeration (KKKM 7930-1-01: 11.6)

which gave a clear picture of the political reason for the formation of the large Kamen´ encampments in the 1920s.[1] Noting that the Second Letnie Tunguses are the 'indigenous' (*korennye*) inhabitants of the region, he observes that the dominant Iakut population arrived just '5–8 years ago' [c. 1919] from Lake Essei and that they are 'a completely distinct group of the Essei population of rich reindeer herders who brought with them their workers and relatives' (folio 321). Dolgikh continued:

> They abandoned the Lake Essei region for reason of the political disorder that dominated that region. There were attempts by certain individuals to divide off portions of the herds of the rich and to force them to shift freight free of charge. In order to save their private herds, these Iakuts abandoned their homeland and began to establish themselves here. But they have not lost political contacts with Essei and once a year travel there for a yearly gathering [*skhodka*] (folio 321–321v).

From this account it would seem that the political context of settlement in Taimyr was a strong element continuously throughout the nineteenth and twentieth centuries.

According to my research, we can identify three relevant scales of movements among native hunters, fishers, trappers and their families in central Taimyr: 1) long-distance movements for trade, education and political/military reasons; 2) seasonal movements associated with the demands of reindeer herding and/or migratory prey; and 3) local daily and weekly movements associated with hunting, fishing, trapping and herding activities, and fuel gathering. All three are relevant if one wishes to find habitation sites on the landscape or analyse the degree to which subsistence and settlement patterns coincided in the colonial and prehistoric past.

Long distance travel in the region has been documented archaeologically as far back as the Mesolithic. Then, as now, wild reindeer hunting, fishing, and hunting of migratory birds and small game were important to the ancient residents of Taimyr. Data from the Iron Age suggests two different cultural traditions entering the region from east and west (Khlobystin 2005). Long-distance movements of families can take place over generations. The most recent migrations led to the identification of the Dolgan nationality (Anderson 2000; Dolgikh 1963; Ziker 2002a).

Individuals, families and sometimes whole communities would establish seasonal trading and hunting routes between and within the uplands and the lowlands. For example, the large *chir* whitefish descended the major rivers in late September, and families would move to camp along rivers to harvest this resource, as they still do today at Letov´e (Russian for 'summer place') on the Dudypta River. Recorded place names are therefore often evocative of seasonal movement (see Jordan, this volume). On the household card, evocative place names are presented in a special section on the header page of the household card listing the 'nomadic round' (*kochevye mesta*) which was distinguished by the season in which they were occupied. These are explored in the rest of this chapter. Such movements and accompanying economic activities would be expected to be closely tied to subsistent resource use, as suggested by Jochim, along with any additional reasons for travel arising from the political or economic situation.

Although the table on nomadic rounds gives a clear picture of seasonal movements, the household cards were not designed to provide direct data on localized daily movements. There is only indirect information on daily cycles. Daily or weekly subsistence movements (i.e. herding reindeer, checking trap lines, fishing and wood gathering) can by inferred from the lists of commodities and tools documented on the cards for one season. We can extrapolate from Dolgikh's 1926–27 winter observations using contemporary field data with Dolgan hunters to break lists and tasks into conjectural local movements.

For example, on the 19 surviving household cards of Iakuts, Dolgikh records that there were 18 metal traps and 1,283 wooden deadfall traps. I know from my own fieldwork that if trap lines existed, people in this region would travel to check them at least once a week. Further, contemporary fieldwork tells us that hunters and herders in the Putoran region often organized their subsistence into task-groups. These groups would travel some distance from a main camp to extract a particular resource. In 1996 I participated in a thin-ice fishing trip to the Bol'shoi Avam River in the Putoran foothills, during which six men caught 800 kilograms of fish in a day and a half. Such short-term migrations might last from less than a day to several days or weeks. More likely than not, the results of these brief logistical travels would be associated with the name of the base camp, which might be recorded on a document like a census card. Today, with the benefit of motorized transport, these task-based movements are organized out of urbanized settlements. Our understanding of task-based movement in the region can further inform our understanding of demography. Certain logistical forays can temporally alter the gender composition of a camp for a week, or even for several months. Therefore, when making generalizations about localized demographic structure in cultures such as this, we have to be aware of the effect that seasonality and subsistence behaviour might have on the presence of men and women when an enumerator comes to visit.

In the following sections, I look at these three types of movements of people in the Putoran-Taimyr area documented in the 1926/27 Polar Census. In considering such movements, I will direct my attention to records of resource use, demographics and settlement locations. I then use my own insight gained during ethnographic research in the region since 1992 to provide further interpretation of this information. Finally, I make comparisons and contrasts in order to highlight any continuities and changes identified.

The Encampments of the 'People of the Mountain' (*Tasdegilar*)

The people originating from the Kamen´ region are today known as the *Kamen´skie* (Russian, 'of the Mountain')[2] or *Tasdegilar* (Dolgan, 'of the Mountain'). Although Kamen´ became a permanent settlement on the Kheta River only in the 1950s, Dolgikh grouped together 27 households in 1926–27 to produce a single community diary titled 'Kamen.''

The collection of encampments defining the Kamen´ region includes the broad region of the Aiakli, Aian, and upper Kheta Rivers to the Kheta's confluence with the Namakan River approximately 75 kilometres from the contemporary village of Volochanka (fig. 11.1). In the community diary, the 27 households (157 individuals) were grouped into three nationalities by the identity of the household head (19 Essei Iakuts, 3 Ilimipei Tunguses, and 5 Second Letnie Tunguses) (NARS 70-1-789: 305). From these 27 households, the team digitizing the historical records has discovered only 19 household cards documenting six Iakut encampments (in NARS 70-1-1004 & 1005). Each of the six encampments also has a Household List indexing the cards. In addition, there are six hygiene cards (NARS 70-1-1024: 8–10; GAKK 769-1-459: 48–50) and two kinship cards (GAKK 769-1-446: 1–5).[3] It is interesting that the 19 surviving household cards give information only on Essei Iakuts, and that there are no surviving household cards on Tunguses (although there are fragments of information about them in the diary and in the hygiene and kinship cards).[4]

In this section I have chosen to analyse the four named encampments within the Kamen´ area. In the community diary, Dolgikh included a handwritten sheet (NARS 70-1-789: 306) which describes the locations of 9 winter and 12 summer encampments. Each encampment supported between 2 and 5 households. On the surviving household cards there is complete information on six Essei Iakut winter encampments named after the dwelling of a significant person (*balagan* Poiba, *chum* Maimaki, *balagan* Davyda, *golomo* Espek, *balagan* Tasbai, *chum* Psikhasa).

The naming of each encampment after the dwelling is a remarkable detail of this particular region of Taimyr. A *chum* is a conical tent often made of several overlapping panels of either moose or reindeer skin and is designed to be transported on cargo reindeer (Anderson 2007). A *balagan* is a wooden house made of unfinished timber in the shape of a lopped pyramid (Sokolova 1998) (fig. 11.4). A *golomo* is a four-sided wooden structure covered with earth that is often submerged (fig. 11.5). The latter two dwellings are stationary but may be inhabited seasonally. The 19 surviving cards also recorded the presence of log cabins (*zimov´e*). Families living in each of the encampments reported at least one winter conical lodge (10 total) and one summer conical lodge (16 total). It is striking that only two *balki* – the ski-mounted mobile caravan typical of Dolgans – are reported. Four *balagany* were reported. In his short history

Figure 11.4. A *balagan* at the mouth of the Kochechum River in 1926–27 in contemporary Evenkiia at the southern border of the Putoran uplands. Photograph by N. P. Naumov (KKKM 7930-1-09: 8) (The photograph contains the annotation 'A Iakut balagan')

Figure 11.5. A *golomo* at Ekondakon at the far eastern borderlands of the Putoran region. Photograph by N. P. Naumov 1926–27 (KKKM 7930-1-09: 2)

of the region, Dolgikh states that the Essei Iakuts began building the *balagany* in 1925 with the goal of creating a semi-permanent settlement between Essei and Dudinka (*zatundra*) in order to exploit trading opportunities (NARS 70-1-789: 321v). This gives us our first important clue to the relation between resource use, travel and residency.

In table 11.1 I have provided a list of the basic subsistence resources and tools in three of the six encampments.

Encampment 1: Davyd's Balagan

The first encampment was named after Davyd Stepanovich Buatulu (NARS 70-1-1005: 10–11), a Essei Iakut from the Katyginskii clan. At age 70, Davyd Stepanovich's card listed 5 sons aged 2 to 24 (the eldest adopted), a wife Olga (aged 35), and 3 daughters aged 5 to 20 (the middle one, an adopted orphan). Davyd Stepanovich's seasonal movements are mapped on figure 11.6. In springtime, he was recorded as travelling 'along the Bunideran River'. In the summer, his camp moved down the Bunideran (presumably) to 'the Kheta river, near the confluence with the Bunideran River'. In the autumn, he moved up the Kheta to the 'confluence of the river Aiakli', the major eastern tributary of the Kheta River. In the winter, they moved further into the uplands to live 'along the Aiakli River, 20 *versty* above the confluence on the right bank'. Davyd Stepanovich's household was recorded as having 700 reindeer. Dolgikh noted that his '*ambar* (an elevated log cache) was on the Essei River. He did not live in a winter *chum*, but used the *balagany* of relatives. His earnings were paid in kind for supplying sleighs to traders'. Lake Essei is 400 kilometres to the southeast.

Four other households were also living at Davyd's *balagan* on New Year's Eve in 1926. The seasonal encampments on these four household cards were listed exactly as Davyd Stepanovich. This suggests that these five households travelled together and were likely functioning as a residential unit for some time. The household heads of the other four households were listed as: Ivan Khristoforovich Buatulu, Afanasii Khristoforovich Ogostok, Mikhail Nikolaevich Espek, and Il'ia Afanas'evich Ogostok.

Ivan Khristoforovich, aged 35, was a widower with a 5-year-old son and 100 reindeer. Dolgikh wrote that he 'owed various people 20 roubles. He shared a table with Davyd'. Ivan was only partially able to work because he has rheumatoid arthritis.

Afanasii Ogostok, also was 35 years old and a widower, had a teenage son and daughter. With 35 reindeer, 60 deadfall traps, and an *ambar* at Essei, Afanasii 'did not buy consumer goods, but was supported by Davyd'.

Mikhail Espek, 25 years old along with his 25-year-old wife Akulina, and their 4-year-old daughter and infant son, came to Davyd's encampment the

Table 11.1. Table of subsistence resources of three Essei Iakut encampments at Kamen´ in 1926–27

Label	*balagan* Davyda	*balagan* Tasbai	*balagan* Paibala
Number of Adults Older than 14 years	11	10	6
Selected Fish Species (*pudy*)			
whitefish	140	110	26
grayling	60	85	10
chir	26	112	1
Arctic cisco (*omul´*)	37	63	
perch		50	2
nel'ma	11	59	
belok	10	50	
pike	2	23	10
Total – all fish species	290	571	56.5
Hunting (count)			
squirrel		113	
hare	10	39	3
ermine	19	45	1
Arctic fox	5	4	
black bear		3	
mountain goat			5
Reindeer products (count)			
wild reindeer	7	10	12
reindeer meat (*pudy*)	273	325	200
pelts – blankets	74	98	54
vyportok	10	10	9
calf skins	20	18	3
leg skins			
Birds (count)			
wild goose		200	2
ptarmigan		100	15
wild duck	20	120	2
Gathering (*funty*)			
cloud berry			
mammoth ivory		140	
Fishing equipment			
salting Equipment			
zabory – fenced rivers	6	9	
pushchal'ni – nets	27	27	12
Hunting equipment (count)			
guns (all types)	9	8	5
mechanical traps	4	3	15
deadfalls	260	150	60
dogs	2	1	2
Reindeer – selected types			
transport (male and female)	323	228	172
breeding cows	267	267	212
Total – all reindeer	901	643	782

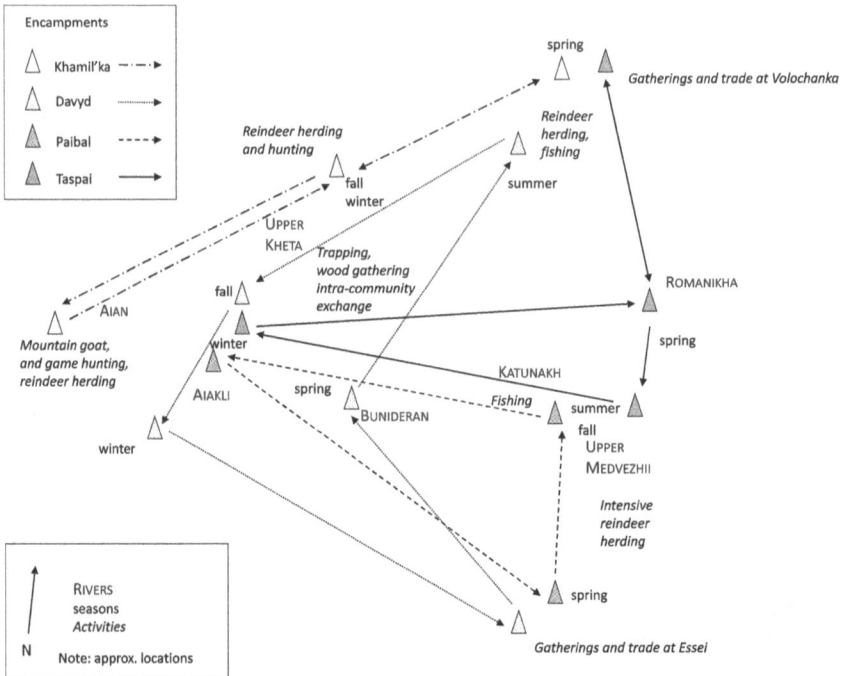

Figure 11.6. The seasonal movements of four sets of households in the Kamen' region in 1926–27

previous year from the Essei River. According to their kinship card (GAKK 769-1-446: 1), they were married for 6 years and both declared their 'clan' and that of their parents was Katyginskii. Mikhail had one brother and one sister, but it was not clear if they lived at Essei or at Davyd's encampment. This young family supported themselves living through the support of relatives, and was paid in kind working as a reindeer herder for Davyd. One wonders if his unpaid work was not a form of bride-service. He also did not purchase consumer goods according to these records.

Il'ia Afanas'evich Ogostok, 42, along with his wife, 45, and three children, 14 to 22, only owned 15 reindeer, and had 100 deadfall traps. Dolgikh noted that he 'lived with Davyd in his *balagan*. Arctic fox and ermine were sold to a Iakut'.

Unfortunately, neither the household cards nor the single kinship card went into any direct detail on the relationships between these households, or the kinds of goods and services shared (except food at meals). What is clear is that they lived and worked together throughout the year and had a largely subsistence-based economy and trade with outsiders managed chiefly by Davyd. In the community diary Dolgikh made reference to relatives and others serving as 'workers' to service large reindeer herds, and this subservience may have characterized the status of some of these families. However, this group of households travelled frequently and occasionally long distances (to Lake Essei), each family owned at least one summer *chum*, winter *chum* or winter *balagan*, and three families had household *ambary* and a network of deadfall traps (*pasty*) and some metal traps (*kapkany*). This group of households could have exhibited egalitarian relations in most of their activities with Davyd acting as front man in relations with outsiders.

During the year prior to the census, Davyd purchased 20 *pudy* of crackers and toast, 10 *pudy* of wheat flour, and 30 *pudy* of rye flour. On Ivan Buatulu's census card, a note was made that 'Davyd's *balagan* was in charge of buying groceries'. Obviously, he shared out what he purchased with the other four families. What about goods for which remuneration was received? The census noted a total of 19 ermine and 5 Arctic fox pelts sold. Beyond furs, Davyd alone reported catching 102 *pudy* of fish and 200 *pudy* of meat (over 3 tons). Two other families caught a total of 183 *pudy* of fish. All together, the *balagan* produced almost 4.5 tons of fish. The household cards were silent on what happened exactly to all this meat and fish. We know from current ethnographic research that meat and fish is consumed commonly in summer, fall, and winter, and is often gifted or traded in both processed (smoked and salted) and raw (frozen) forms. Fish, along with the wild reindeer meat, comprises an important aspect of the contemporary sharing economy in the region (also important for other hunter-gatherers) (Ziker 2002a, 2002b). According to current studies, hunters prefer to use everything, including rotten fish which is kept for bait in fur-bearer traps or to feed dogs. With the lack of any record of salting facilities for this family we can only assume that this large amount of fish was either smoked or dried in a traditional manner for consumption and used to bait the family's network of 1,203 deadfall traps.

Encampments 2 and 3: Taspai Buatulu and Paibal Buatulu

These two encampments were led by two brothers, Taspai (Nikolai) and Paibal (Pavel) of the Katyginskii family. According to the surviving cards, four other households were co-resident with Taspai's camp. Paibal's camp lived with a third brother, Platon. As with Davyd's encampment, each of these separate territorial encampments were recorded as having the same seasonal round, but the pair of brothers moved in a slightly different orbit as described below.

These Buatulu (Katyginskii) brothers are remembered well in the region today. In 1992, I met Stepan Nikonovich Katyginskii in Dudinka where he told me an interesting story about his grandfather, Taspai, who was a large-scale reindeer herder from Kamen´. Stepan Nikonovich told me that his grandfather had 5,000 reindeer at one time. His herd was confiscated in 1934. Taspai's brother, Paibal did not give up his reindeer, and he was never seen again.

In 1995, during an interview with Dmitrii Andreevich Antsiferov (b. 1931) in Ust'-Avam, I heard another story about the Katyginskiis:

> Oksin'ia married Nikolai, brother of Nikon. Nikon killed a bear with a knife. He lost an eye. He died with his gun in his hand, aimed at a bear. Tasmai [Taspai] lived near Kamen'. Before the village [was built], he travelled all by himself [i.e., not in a brigade]. He had 5 or so helpers. He drove into [the village of] Dolgany for marriage. They killed reindeer for marriage, and picked dark ones with good furs to sew clothes, about 15 head. They separated their deer from the Antsiferovs' deer. He didn't leave any of his deer. He left some for his son. He moved to Dolgany. [There were] a lot of deer then. Kostia Katyginskii, son of Tasmai, [was called] Kosto. He died that year, 1939, on the way back from Dudinka from alcohol poisoning.[5]

The Katyginskiis had a tough and independent reputation, as did many families and native people today in the Taimyr. Dmitrii's account mentions inter-community social connections between the villages of Kamen' and Dolgany, giving another clear example of long-distance movement. It appears that Taspai's (Tasmai) deer and the Antsiferovs' deer had intermingled, since they needed separating. It is likely the Antsiferovs provided a dowry (reindeer meat and, importantly, dark reindeer hides). The Antsiferovs traditionally travelled around Tungusy station, just west of Dolgany on the Chopko River, but were moved into Dolgany after a period of *kolkhoz* consolidation in the 1930s according to the family oral history. As the name of this station (Tungusy) indicates, this was an Evenki-speaking area. Dmitrii also indicates the extent of social problems being experienced as a result of integration with the Soviet state. Kosto's death was symptomatic of these difficulties that continue on to the present.

The information from Stepan Nikonovich and Dmitrii Andreevich is corroborated to some extent by historical information in the household cards. Between 30 December 1926 and 3 January 1927, Paibal (NARS 70-1-1004: 26–27) and Taspai (NARS 70-1-1009: 18, 25) were recorded as being household heads in their mid-to-late thirties in two separate *balagany*. The kin relationship between Paibal and Taspai was confirmed on the cards, as were the names of their children mentioned in the stories above. Paibal was recorded as having 739 reindeer, and Taspai was recorded as having 497 reindeer (40 of which are leased) (table 11.1). Paibal migrated with his younger brother, Platon, and his small family. Platon owned only 43 reindeer. The three other households migrating with Taspai had a total of 146 deer (10 were leased).

To what extent were Paibal and Taspai co-operating as part of a larger kinship network? Some hints can be gleaned from the household cards (fig. 11.6). Paibal's migration pattern was documented as beginning in the region between the upper Medvezh'i River and Lake Essei in the spring. His household moved to a tributary of the Medvezh'i, called Katukakh River, for summer and autumn, and in the winter they moved to the upper Aiakli River on the left bank. Taspai's household began in the upper Romanikha River in the spring, moved to the sources of the Medvezh'ii River for summer and autumn, and spent the winter on the Kheta River, 15 to 20 kilometres west of the confluence with the Aiakli. Paibal spent the spring farther south than his brother (fig. 11.6). In the summer and autumn they were in the upper Medvezh'i River area, and in the winter they were either near or on the Aiakli River. Paibal moved from the Lake Essei area in the spring, northwest to Aiakli River in the winter. Trade with Essei likely occurred after a winter's trapping and hunting. It seems that Taspai moved farther north (downriver) during the winter than his brother, but that they came to the same areas deep in the Putoran (upper Medvezhi'ii River) during the summer. This arrangement could have facilitated connections and communication between the brothers and cooperative herding during the summer, as well as differing sets of social and economic connections between the two *balagany* in two different areas (Paibal with Essei Iakuts and Taspai with Kheta Dolgans).

The data on subsistence in the household cards provides some information explaining the different nomadic strategies of the three brothers (table 11.1). The encampment of Paibal did not produce much fish – a total of 57 *pudy* of fish (predominately whitefish) for the two households. The encampment of Taspai produced substantially more – a total of 571 *pudy* – for five households. They caught substantial amounts of whitefish but also other kinds of fish such as pike, lake cod and perch in lakes. The hygiene card for Paibal (GAKK 769-1-459: 52 [duplicate in NARS 70-1-1024: 10]) recorded his family as eating boiled meat often (with a lot of tea) often unsalted and without much flour. Fish was recorded as being cooked from frozen stocks. The hygiene card for Taspai (GAKK 769-1-459: 48) recorded fish being consumed in equal quantities as meat and the fact that bread was rare. The fish used was recorded as being frozen and dried.

This difference in subsistence is undoubtedly linked to the difference in the seasonal movements of the two *balagany*. Further, it is possible that the two interrelated *balagany* traded fish and reindeer products with each other.

Encampment 4: Golomo Khamil'ka (and Other Tungus Encampments)

An important part of the story of the Kamen' settlement was the role of the 8 Tungus households in the community. Unfortunately, no cards were discovered for these households. However, fragmentary evidence in the community diary suggested that they practiced a slightly different nomadic round. Dolgikh stated that the three Ilimpei Tungus families were 'refugees' from the Essei-Chirinda region, implying that they kept large herds and moved in a similar way to their Essei Iakut colleagues (NARS 70-1-789: 321). It may be possible some of the Tungus families may have served as workers to the richer Kamen' herders. More subtle and egalitarian relations may have also been supported. One Tungus woman was recorded as being intermarried into the Tasbai encampment on a Community Index (Tat´iana Ivanovna Buatulu [Khukogir]) but the same index records that no card was filled out for her (NARS 70-1-1005: 17). At least one Ilimpei Tungus family, Anufrei Ivanovich Ioldogir, was associated with a group of Essei families called Maimaki's *chum* (NARS 70-1-1004: 30). Aside from knowing that Dolgikh filled out his detailed community diary in the *golomo* of a Tungus named Khamil´ka, the only direct record of any household in this community is one hygiene card for the same (GAKK 769-1-459: 49).

Demographically, Khamil´ka's *golomo* comprised 5 adult males, 2 adult females, and 1 child (under age 15). Physically, the *golomo's* dimensions were impressive: 10 by 10 *arshin* [50 square metres] and 2 *sazhen's* [4.2 metres] high. The card indicated an open fire, as well as an iron stove, used for heat and light. According to the hygiene card, Khamil´ka's group made smoked fish filets (*iukola*) during the summer, and dried reindeer meat, moose meat, and occasionally, mountain goat as well. In contemporary communities, long strips of smoked and dried fish known as *iukola* are made from large whitefish (*chir*), implying the group was fishing on the larger river during the summer. Dolgikh noted that Kamil´ka's *golomo* members ate, in large part, meat and fish, drank tea, and consumed pancakes in smaller quantities.

In his community diary, Dolgikh wrote that Tunguses migrated over a smaller range than Iakuts. Nevertheless, they utilized both highland and lowland resources during the summer and fall along the Aiakli and Kheta Rivers. In figure 11.6 I have used Khamil´ka's name to stand for the fragmentary records of all of the Tungus encampments. According to Dolgikh, 'the Tunguses had a smaller area of migration and hunt wild reindeer, mountain sheep, and moose' (NARS 70-1-789: 307) in contrast to the wide-ranging Iakuts who spent the winter with the Tunguses. In the summer the 'households broke up and wandered over a large area between the Kotui river and the Namakan river, where the interests of reindeer herding force the Iakuts to separate' (ibid.). Dolgikh mentions that Tunguses once affected long-term travel to Volochanka in the spring but that this pattern was no longer common. One wonders if the large reindeer herders from Ilimpei and Essei might have started providing them with groceries. Dolgkih wrote that the 'Tunguses were dependent on the Iakuts and their households, and others, as if they mutually supplement one another' (folio 307a). Additional information from the Polar Census on the Tungus households of Kamen´ was scant.

Dolgikh linked the process of seasonal expansion and contraction in range to architecture. He stated 'a part of the population [lived] in *balagany* and *golomo;* the other part lived in *shestovoi chumy* [caribou-skin lodges]' (folio 307). One wonders if Tunguses were more often found in association with *chumy*, but Iakut encampments such as Mamaika utilized the *chum* dwelling type, and others such as Davyd's, all had *chumy* as well as *balagany*. The use of *chumy* by all households of Kamen´ was more likely a seasonal strategy for those time periods of highest mobility (spring and summer).

Dolgikh added that the 'Tunguses are continually interested in wild-reindeer- and mountain-sheep hunting, while the Iakuts were mostly rich reindeer herders, bringing trade goods to the area to exchange with the Tunguses' (folio 307a.). Thus, it is implied that the Tungus families had smaller reindeer herds and locally practiced a lot of hunting like other Evenki communities in Siberia to the present-day. At the same time, the Iakuts had larger herds requiring more intensive herding, which enabled transport of consumer goods and required travel over great distances to trade.

Long Distance Travel and Trade

The above overview of four encampments raises certain general questions about the relation between subsistence activity, settlement pattern and movement. As noted above, the Essei Iakuts settled in the upper Aiakli valley for political reasons, in order to exploit trading relations with other regions. In this section I evaluate the evidence for long-distance trade.

Dolgikh wrote the 'Essei Iakuts rode to a gathering of kin to Lake Essei. To Lake Essei they travelled 300–400 *versty* from the upper Aiakli. They went across [the mountain] Kamen´ on reindeer 10 days … usually … in the middle of January, returning at the beginning of March' (folio 307a). One of the household cards analysed below, mentioned that trips to Essei were mentioned, but it did not specify the time of year. Long-distance travel in late winter and early spring was likely connected to the end of the main hunting and trapping seasons. The continued snow cover made travel and carrying freight by reindeer sleigh possible.[6]

While the Iakuts travelled south, the community card stated 'the Second Letnie Tunguses go [north] to Volochanka, although a significant retreat from that pattern was observed' (folio 307a). Without explaining that comment, Dolgikh wrote that 'both the Essei Iakuts and Tunguses also travelled to Volochanka and even to Letov´e [approximately 50 kilometres north of Volochanka on the Dudypta River]' (ibid.). Although he did not write when this occured exactly, he stated that 'the Kamen´ population's winter spots were from 2 to 5 days travel from Volochanka, and that there was a direct road to Station Belen´kii [on the lower Kheta River]' (ibid.).

Trade in the 1920s was an activity that required travel over greater distances and the ability to haul the goods to be sold and purchased. As indicated earlier, trading activities appear to have taken place in the late winter and spring.

In table 11.1, we can see that reindeer pelts are one of the significant trade resources of the community, with 3 encampments generating 226 pelts per year. Under the section of other economic activities, Dolgikh wrote that Iakuts sewed parkas from reindeer pelts and sold them to the *faktoriia* (trade posts) 'simply in order to sell reindeer raw material' (folio 314a). Following this underhanded comment on the motivations of the Iakuts, he wrote that there really were three destinations in the north to which they travelled to trade: 'Merchants were located at stations along the Khatanga tract. Natives from Kamen´ came out to them there' (folio 314). In addition, 'they rode from Kamen´ mainly to Volochanka. The rich reindeer households travelled [much farther] to Dudinka' (folio 315a).

While it sounds like everyone was travelling to some locations for trade, it appears that two segments of the population (rich and poor) had somewhat different long-distance migration patterns. Dolgikh stated that 'insufficiencies in availability of foodstuffs in Kamen´ were not felt. It was impossible to purchase imported goods summer and fall, when the *faktoriia* ceased to function and the reserves of the rich Iakuts became more important (*ismoshchevaiutsia*)' (folio 317). The families with more reindeer appear to be travelling greater distances and hauling more. Those who have fewer reindeer travel to regional gatherings or trading posts, but at times are dependent on those who travel more for consumer goods.

Seasonal Movements and Division of Labour

Dolgikh wrote that in the 1920s, 'hunting rock ptarmigan was a regular springtime activity, but goose hunting remained more or less incidental' (folio 312a). Rock ptarmigan are currently caught largely in lowland riparian settings along major rivers and tributaries. I have observed adolescents and young adults, adult women, and some adult males active in rock ptarmigan procurement in the springtime using snares. It is likely rock ptarmigan hunting was conducted in a similar manner throughout the region in the 1920s.

Rivers including the Dudypta and the lower Kheta are abundant in fish during the late spring, summer and early fall. Fishing under the ice was a distinct possibility in the 1920s. The household cards documented the ownership of nets. Additionally, relatively simply, self-fashioned tools could have been used to make holes and set up nets. Such tools are still made in the Avam community. The tributary rivers coming out of the uplands also have abundant fish during the summer, and we know that the Kamen´ community caught a lot of fish, so it is likely that fishing was a major activity in the seasonal round. That being said, the demands of fishing may not necessarily coincide directly with the demands of large domestic reindeer herds which utilized upland biomes and frequent, if not daily, movement. Regarding fishing, an important summertime activity, Dolgikh stated that 'the natives considered fishing to be the most reliable (*vernyi*); diminishment of it has not been noticed' (folio 312).

Commenting on the organization of reindeer herding in Kamen', Dolgikh noted 'in the summer, the smaller herds united into one big herd' (folio 310). Dolgikh also states that the 'reindeer were herded by *pastukhi* (herders) along with owners... Owners of large herds had their own migration paths, and herders with fewer deer grouped around the larger owners' (ibid.). Thus, at least some members of different household groups co-operated and shared in the herding of their united reindeer, contributing to an economy of scale. This seems particularly relevant for the Iakut herd owners. Mountain sheep hunting is summer activity according to Dolgikh, practiced largely by Tunguses, and most likely as an individual procurement activity.

The work of a reindeer herder is known to be difficult, especially in the summer. During an ethnographic interview in Ust'-Avam about reindeer herding, Boris Elogir' said that it was usually adolescent and young men who worked in small groups as *pastukhi* during the summer. They had to run practically the entire 24-hour-plus shift to keep up with the deer because of insects. It follows that the Essei Iakut households put together task groups involved in summer herding duties. Answering a question (number 16 under reindeer herding)

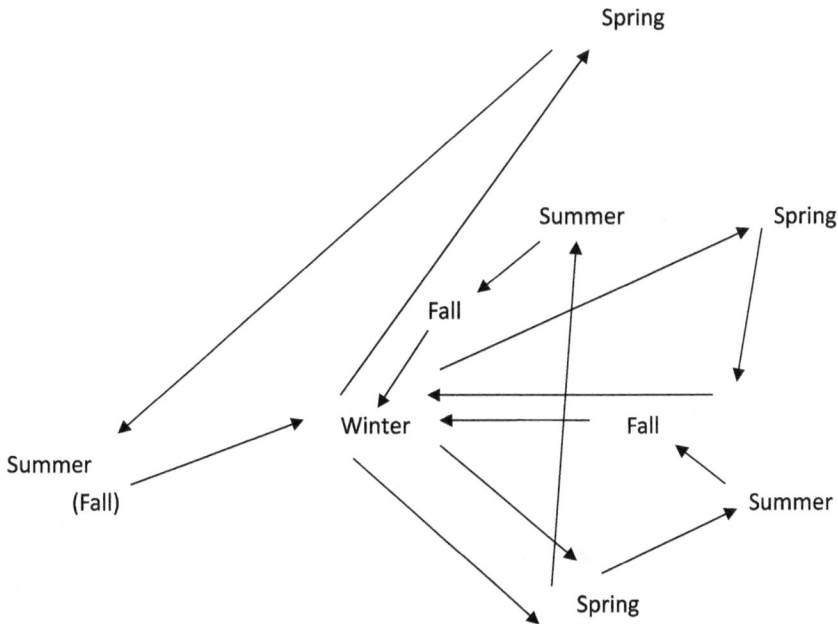

Figure 11.7. A schematic representation of the seasonal movements of the four sets of Kamen' households represented in Figure 11.6.

about the frequency of movement of campsites and the distance reindeer were kept from campsites, Dolgikh stated that 'during summer and spring they migrated (*argish*) almost every day' (folio 310a). This statement corroborates Boris Elogir's explanation of the work involved in summer reindeer herding, and implies that some family members did not necessarily accompany reindeer every day. Thus, regarding location of the herd relative to household campsites, Dolgikh wrote, 'during the summer reindeer were pastured not more than one day's travel from the *chum*, and during the winter they were held closer to *chumy*; spring and fall the reindeer herds were also farther from camp' (ibid.). In addition to being further from camp in spring and fall, Dolgikh reported that the 'herders constructed wooden corrals for the reindeer in the spring and fall' (folio 310v). As reindeer herds were farther from encampments in spring and fall, and herders weare using corrals, a division of labour would have been highly advantageous. It follows that fall and winter hunting spots garnered important benefits, and selection of location important. Dolgikh made this point stating 'they rarely moved their chum spots in the fall; in the winter, the camps stayed at one spot longer, especially those living in *balagany*' (ibid.).

Under the community diary's question on 'hunting and small-game activities', Dolgikh stated there was 'systematic hunting for Arctic fox, red fox, wild reindeer, mountain sheep (*chibukun* and *diago*), moose, ermine, and Arctic hare; incidentally wolverine, wolf, bear, and lynx were procured' (folio 312v). Except for mountain sheep, the large game, as well as foxes, ermine, hare and the incidental game were most likely to be hunted in fall and winter. Historic and contemporary data indicate that hunters occupied specific areas for hunting in the fall and winter – during the main caribou migrations and best hunting for other game (Ziker 2002a). Today, hunting reindeer in the early fall, before the rivers freeze, is usually conducted in small groups. Traditionally, hunters used small canoes and spears to surround a herd as it crossed the river, but now small aluminium boats with small motors are used. As hunters tend to man spots known to be crossing points, often with a high shoreline for good observation and hiding, who is included and excluded from such groups is a major consideration in informal property rights. This would have been especially important in Kamen' in the 1920s, considering the contraction of settlement patterns for the fall and winter into the upper Kheta River valley of people of various families and ethnic groups (fig. 11.7). Today, hunting later in the season after the freeze-up is usually conducted on land by individuals using shotguns or rifles. The household records for 1926–27 indicated the purchase of at least one long firearm in Taspai's group, so hunting reindeer on land was a distinct possibility. During the late fall and winter, trapping fur-bearers is the major activity today and property (in the form of traps and trap lines) again comes into consideration here. In the 1920s at least one reindeer team would have been required for a hunter to check his trap line.

In the year of the census there was measles epidemic in the region. Accord-ing to Dolgikh, 'During the epidemic of *kora* in 1927 a doctor and *fel'dsher* (nurse practitioner) came in an expedition of Narkomzdrava. This was the first incidence of medical personnel visiting Kamen'. In the 1927 epidemic 22 people died' (folio 320a). This epidemic was likely a significant blow to this small population, which could explain some of the observations that the poor were clinging to the relatively successful.

A demographic crisis occurred in Kamen' with the epidemic deaths Dolgikh reported in the 1920s. In a regional sample of 100 households in the 1926/27 household cards[7] the general fertility rate (GFR) was 0.070, also indicating a population under fundamental stress.[8] The 1926/27 GFR was nearly identical to the rate (0.071) I documented in Ust'-Avam in the mid-1990s, another time period of economic change and high mortality (Ziker 2002a).

In this regional sample of 100 households the most common woman's oc-cupation in 1926-27 was processing hides. Fishing was second. This finding may shed some potential light on the question of who was doing the fishing in the Kamen' area discussed above. In some areas, women were been doing a considerable amount of the fishing. While processing hides, berry-gathering and fishing are mentioned in ethnographic works as female occupations (e.g. Popov 1966), the Polar Census data and recent interviews show women were not excluded from predominantly male occupations. More specialized occu-pations, such as workers in co-operatives or transportation services, are absent in the Kamen' area household cards.

Discussion of the Model

Resource-use schedules throughout the Kamen' region in the mid 1920s en-tailed site placement in upland and lowland locations, depending on season and various production strategies (fig. 11.6 and 11.7). In addition, demographic adjustments were found to relate to resource use for reindeer pasturing, fish-ing and hunting. Demographic adjustments allow for division of labour and economy of scale, which both have implications for site placement and activi-ties, and the ability to be seasonally mobile and sedentary at the same time. Beyond the predominant factor of the physical environment and the highly seasonal resources provided by the central Siberian Arctic, surrounding hu-man population centres provided opportunities for trade that enabled some families to specialize in more intensive reindeer-herding activities and intra-community exchange. The upper Kheta River provided a political and ecologi-cal niche for Essei Iakut refugees, allowing use of varieties of natural resources and locations for a mobile population, while affording a strategic location midway between the Khatanga Tract in the north and Lake Essei in the south.

This location facilitated the development of middle-man strategies by particular household groups.

With regard to site placement the Kheta River valley itself provided abundant wood for fuel and construction of *balagany* and *golomo,* and became the
area of highest population density, especially in the winter. While a formal
or customary system of property was not documented in the 1920s – a likely
result of the influx of Essei Iakuts – competition over trap lines was documented as a significant point of contention: 'The Second Letnie Tunguses
complained that the Iakuts place their *balagany* next to their trap lines and
they spoiled fur trapping', according to Dolgikh (folio 314). Particular areas
were utilized by sets of more closely related kin along with their in-married
and adopted relatives and, to a lesser extent, hired labourers. These use areas
comprise an informal system of property that was being worked out in the
tumultuous 1920s.

The uplands provided vast mountain tundra suited for herding domestic
reindeer, along with supplementary subsistence opportunities. The expansion
of sets of households out of the Kheta River for the spring and part of the summer implies that human sites were more ephemeral at that time of the year and
indicate as well that task-specific sites were created. The development of task
groups entails a demographic adjustment through division of labour. Ethnographic interviews in the 1990s indicated that as late as the 1950s and 1960s
such a division of labour occurred every year: some group members focused
on herding reindeer in the higher elevations of the Putoran or the northern
tundra of the peninsula, and other family members stayed at camps on rivers,
occupied by fishing and household matters, and boat traffic along the river.
In the 1920s, similarly, a significant effort at fishing appears to have occurred
contemporaneously with intensive reindeer herding. Dolgikh mentioned that
the population spent part of the summer in the upper Kheta River valley. If
households with larger herds split into task groups for fishing and herding,
they would be able to manager their reindeer during the time of year they
are most susceptible to dispersal by insects and still be able to check fish nets
and process the catch. In fact, Dolgikh documented at least a small number of
Kamen' families visiting locations as far as the Dudypta River, famous for the
fish needed to make *iukola.*

The seasonal use of riparian habitats in the region was well documented in
the Polar Census and through recent ethnographic interviews. On the Dudypta
River I observed rich evidence of human habitation, including several *golomo,*
graves and other abandoned sites alongside contemporary camps, cabins and
former state farm facilities. Closer to the Kamen' area human habitation in
the Taginari portage (between the Kheta River and the Avam River drainages)
is evidenced by hunter-gatherer sites going back the Mesolithic (6000 years
before present) (Khlobystin 2005).

With regard to external social and political environments, the production of surplus in the Kamen´ area became an advantage in obtaining trade goods that some families had been able to sustain. Spring was the point in the annual cycle in which keeping large herds of reindeer paid off in the ability to harness the power of castrates and use hauling deer to transport trade goods. Trade goods could be purchased after the fall and winter hunting and trapping seasons provided hides and meat that could be exchanged for imported products. These products were transported back to the core area of Kamen´ and exchanged with families for whom travel to distant trading places was not feasible. The Kamen´ area provided meagre subsistence opportunities (i.e. snare lines) for those who were not travelling. This process speaks to the importance of connections between non-local political and economic processes and local subsistence and settlement patterns, following Julian Steward (1977), Robert Carneiro (1988) and Napoleon Chagnon (1997: 75), and modelled as the context in figure 11.2.

The core of the model assumes that resource-use schedules, demographics and site placement influence each other, while the influence of resource use is the overarching factor. Although Jochim (1976) developed this model to better understand archaeological materials using ethnographic analogies, the version of the model used here has been useful for analysis of historical demographic materials and to project what types of sites would be expected in lowland and upland ecological zones, including expectations about activity types, seasonality, temporal intensity and demographic characteristics. Resource-use schedules appear to have influenced site placement (lowland or upland) and demographics (high density, dispersion, task groups) with opportunities for trade being a significant force bearing back on resource use, demographics and site placement. Demographic insults, such as the 1927 epidemic, are compensated for through traditionally flexible roles in local social organization. Alongside demographics, social organization among the Tasdegilar showed a division of labour and flexibility of roles. Like extant hunter-gatherers in other parts of the world, women were significant contributors to the subsistence economy in the 1920s. They also played crucial roles in the mercantile trade through processing and sewing hides. Many of the hunting activities, the importance of women in the subsistence economy, non-market sharing (Ziker and Schnegg 2005; Ziker 2007) and production of surplus for trade goods continue to the present day in the region.

The Taimyr Lowlands Today

I heard about Kamen´ during my first visit to Taimyr in 1992 (in a meeting with Eduard Tumanov on 19 August). In 1969–70 the Taimyr agricultural bureau consolidated two *kolkhozy*, 'Taimyr' and 'Iskra' (Kamen'), to create *sovkhoz* 'Khantaiskoe Ozero'. As a part of the plan to create the *sovkhoz*, the whole population of Kamen' was sent to Lake Khantaiskoe, including the reindeer herders and their families. It interesting that they did not join the *sovkhoz* in Volochanka, a larger town much closer to Kamen'. They migrated by reindeer and on foot to join a similarly-sized population of Khantaiskie Evenkis that had been living in the lowland and adjoining Putoran uplands of Lake Khantaiskii, hundreds of kilometres to the southwest (Tugolukov 1963; Anderson 2000).

Living in Talnakh, a satellite town of Noril'sk, Stepan Katyginskii (grandson of Taspai) was trying to privatize part of the Kamen' area to set up a family/clan holding in 1992. In order to justify their claim, he, his Aunt Ira, and one other elder person were going to Kamen' that fall to hunt and fish. Stepan told me that the former director of the Volochanka *sovkhoz* received a very large hunting territory (*ugod'ia*). He claimed that it was easier for Russians to privatize land in the area. Stepan, working through the Association of Native People of Taimyr, understood the need for balance with nature, and wanted to go back to the land. He was successful with his claim in 1994, but his claim fell into disuse later in the 1990s, due to the loss of budgetary supports for the regional agricultural economy.

Despite the massive political changes occurring in the time since the Communist Revolution, traditional subsistence activities, such as springtime snaring, summer/fall fishing, fall reindeer hunting and winter hunting and trapping, continue to the present day in central Taimyr. Reindeer herding, which provides an ability to travel independently of combustion-powered engines, has disappeared from the Taimyr lowlands. The result is an increase in political and market elements in the local resource ecologies. An example is the organization of hunting mountain sheep (*Ovis nivicola borealis*), which are listed as an endangered species with uncertain status living on the isolated slopes of the Putoran. Hunting is conducted strictly by regional authorities. A Dolgan friend of mine from Volochanka has worked as a guide for mountain-sheep hunters in the Putoran, but has only been hired a few times. His clients were international hunters, paying the Russian government tens of thousands of dollars for the license, transportation and guide services. Between 2003 and 2007 he had not seen any business. Nevertheless, the Putoran uplands are alive in the discussions of the Dolgan in central Taimyr. Several families have made land claims in areas that adjoin Kamen', and discussions of events and rituals that occurred there still can be heard in local discussions. This chapter shows how Polar Census records can become important for native people in the region in reclaiming their history and archaeological monuments.

Acknowledgements

I would like to thank my friends in Taimyr for their assistance in document-ing the details of history in the region. This material is based upon work sup-ported by the National Science Foundation under Grant No. 0631970. I also express my gratitude to David Anderson and his team for the work involved in digitizing the Polar Census, and for comments from Christopher Hill and Mark Plew.

Notes

1. Editor's Note: In this chapter, Dolgikh's community diary is analysed in considerable detail. From here on only the folio page reference will be provided.
2. In modern Russian, *kamen* translates as 'stone'. It is usually translated as 'mountain' or 'escarpment' in older Russian. *Tas* means stone in Dolgan. 'Kamen'' in these doc-uments is usually written with a superfluous soft-sign reflecting pre-Revolutionary orthography.
3. Editor's Note: As this book goes to press a single folder of 50 kinship cards for this region was discovered in Iakutsk at classmark NARS 70-1-943. These have not been digitised or analysed.
4. Editor's Note: Although material on Kamen' can be found in both GAKK and NARS, by far the most complete archive is in NARS. The diaries and cards in Iakutsk read as if they were the first copy records, with the duplicates being filed in Krasnoiarsk. The Iakutsk collection is exclusively about Iakuts living within Turukhansk *krai* as if the authorities there had made a special collection of information about the Iakutsk dias-pora. There is some evidence that only 19 cards were sent to Iakutsk in an annotation in red pencil on NARS 70-1-789: 356 and that only 19 cards were present.
5. Interview with Dmitrii Andreevich Anstiferov, 26 September 1995.
6. Dolgikh (folio 308) notes important climate information and notations on the ease of travel. Snow fell in the mountains beginning in early September of 1926, and rivers and lakes froze over by 23 September. Travel by sleigh became possible from the end of September. In the spring of 1927, widespread melting began at the beginning of May, and travel by sleigh was no longer possible by the end of June. Between the end of June and the end of September travel would have to be accomplished by riding reindeer, walking by foot, or by boat.
7. Two Boise State University graduate students (Nikki Gorrell and Taiana Arakchaa) selected 50 households from Dudinskaia *volost'* (district) and 25 households each for Ilimpeiskaia and Khatanskaia *volosty*. This random sample of households was created by beginning at a random number and then selecting every fifth household listed in the census until reaching the target number (Bernard 2006).
8. The general fertility rate (GFR) is the number of live births divided by the number of women aged 15 to 49. There were 128 women aged 15 to 49 and 9 births in the year preceding the Polar Census in our random sample. Comparative data from Hern (1995) indicate this fertility rate is lower than what is considered normal by the World Health Organization, according to which the GFR's normal range is 0.088–0.305.

1 | The Manuscript Archives of the Polar Census Expeditions

David G. Anderson

The emphasis of this volume has been on the dialogues between enumerators and respondents as recorded in the manuscript archives of the Polar Census of 1926/1927. However, documents also have their histories. After the interviews were done, the forms circulated through a number of hands before being bound, catalogued and re-catalogued in the places where today they lie fragmented in a number of cities across Russia. Indeed, the first impetus for experimenting with digital photography for this archive came in 2000 when we tried to bring together on one computer screen manuscripts for one settlement which were curated in five archives in four different cities. The purpose of this appendix is to give an overview of the manuscript archive that survives and the steps we have taken to make parts of this archive available digitally. This appendix is supplemented by a publically available online catalogue of the existing records which also provides examples of the forms and some simple tools for producing statistical summaries from selected the data of the surviving household cards (Anderson 2008). This appendix draws from several earlier chapters and articles in Russian on the history of individual Polar Census expeditions (Anderson 2006; Glavatskaia 2007; Klokov and Semenov 2007; Klokov and Ziker 2010).

The Geography of Inscription

As the introduction to this volume outlines, this particular survey of northern populations was governed by a unique geographical limitation. It was undertaken in a *pripoliarnyi* 'North facing' set of communities. Although this adjective was used officially for only a short period of time it very succinctly captured an aspect of Russian colonial practice. At times, the term *pripoliarnyi* seems to have been used in an attempt to replace the Imperial Russian concept of a 'tributary alien' (*iasachnyi inorodets*) by replacing a status and taxation classification with a geographical concept. This is most evident in the string of questions that one finds on the header of the household card which tried to specify both the newly coined Soviet designation of the place where the people lived as well as their older 'administrative clan' affiliation. In general, there is an interesting tendency for the crisp Soviet designations to fade as one moves from west to east. In Murmansk *okrug* one generally finds all surviving cards correctly registered with the new Soviet language of districts [*raions*], and household heads' names unambiguously appear with Russian surnames, given names and patronymics. As one moves towards Iakutiia, the Soviet designations become rarer and often contradictory while tributary *iasak* designations become more common and more authoritative. In parts of the Obdor Peninsula, Taimyr, and northern Iakutiia surnames are often left out and only native designations [*prozvishche*] are filled in. A similar process is evident with the new idea of nationality [*natsional'nost'*] which was much more confidently applied in the European part of Russia than in Eastern Siberia.

The unevenness with which answers were provided to the categories preprinted on the census instruments also corresponds to a map of the strength of Soviet govermentality. If in Murmansk Okrug the Revolution and the Civil War were settled by 1920, in parts of northern Turukhansk Okrug and Western Iakutiia the Civil War ended late in 1925. With this history in mind, some of the questions asked by the enumerators were truly exploratory statements aimed at trying to understand the regions that had only recently come under Soviet influence.

The strength of Soviet hegemony was also reflected by the map of regions where the census results were considered to be more or less complete (fig. 1.1). Large areas of the Komi Autonomous *oblast'* [region 15], the Iamal Peninsula [region 18], and the eastern part of Kolyma Okrug [region 38] were officially reported in the central publications to be incompletely surveyed. The regional literature, published by provincial statistical agencies, also reported smaller areas of incomplete work. The reasons for the incomplete work varied. Often, there were not enough skilled enumerators with a knowledge of the region who could cover the extremely large distances involved. Some of the census districts extended for more than 5000 kilometres. This problem was reported in the Komi *oblast'* and in the Iakut Republic specifically. However, other districts were declared as being incompletely surveyed (such as the region of the Khantaika River in Turukhansk *okrug*) when in fact there was a full set of household cards with only a set of matching community diaries missing. In an extreme example, the enumerators of the Komi Republic returned three times as many household cards as were finally processed since they took advantage of their own local knowledge to fill in cards when the members of the household were not present. All of these factors make the manuscript archive a somewhat complex source yielding unique material that with careful attention can be useful in historical research.

The Polar Census Instruments

The standard questions asked by all enumerators were contained on two main forms: the household card [*pokhoziaistvennaia kartochka* - PK] and the community diary [*poselennyi blank* - PB]. Each of these main instruments will be described in greater detail below. In addition, many regions introduced supplemental forms designed to gather detailed information on a specific topic. The supplemental forms more often than not gathered information about prices, trading practices and family budgets, but some regional expeditions also collected additional information on diet, health, living conditions, hygiene, architecture and clothing. Beyond the pre-printed forms that one usually associates with the word 'census' most expeditions generated a rich archive of memoranda, reports, field diaries, correspondence and often photographs and drawings. Although these types of documentation were informal and often depended upon the enthusiasm of individuals, they enrich the manuscript archive considerably by often allowing scholars to reconstruct a relatively rich picture of life in these regions.

The best way to understand the relationship of the manuscripts to each other is with a diagram which organises the forms according to the types of information they recorded (fig. A1.1).

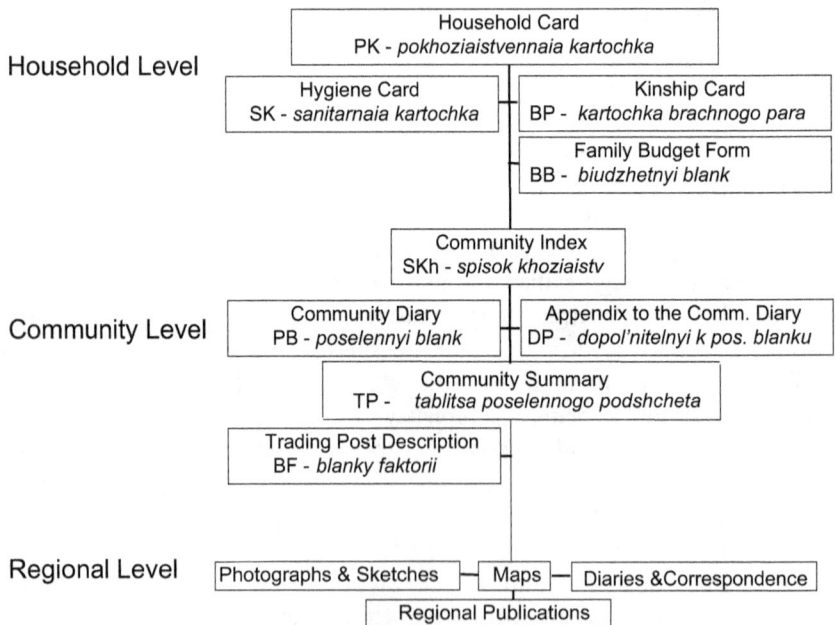

Figure A1.1. Polar Census documentation organised by information types

The information most coveted in its time was information organised at the community level, such as the community diary, and in specific regions, information on specific trading posts [*faktornyi blank*] in the Tobol'sk *okrug*. These documents tended to give an overview of living conditions and public services in small communities and, as described below, tended to have a higher survival rate in archives presumably since they were of greater use to policy makers.

The class of documents which generate more excitement today are those compiled at the household level, or which contain questions documenting data at the individual level. With modern databases these documents can now be used to generate nuanced statistical portraits or even be linked to other registries in order to trace individual biographies over time. The household card, with its large sections for recording individual-level information (and with spaces to record comments on specific households), is the primary instrument of ethnohistoric research today. However the documents collected by specific expeditions such as the hygiene card (*sanitarnaia kartochka* [SK]) and the kinship card (*kartochka brachnykh par* [BP]) for Turukhansk, Irkutsk and Iakutiia, or the family budget card (*biudzhetnyi blank* [BB]) of Tobol'sk, also give rich family-level information that is easily extended to the individual level. Often specific sections of each of these instruments give longitudinal snapshots recording household-level data from 1925 that give an impression of change.

The informal classes of information, such as the field diaries, correspondence archives or sets of glass-plate photographs, offer information at the variety of levels. Both the field diaries and the photographs provide sketches of specific individuals, but often it is extremely difficult to put names to many of these sketches even after extensive fieldwork in the host communities (see Ehrenfried 2004). Thus often these sketches work at the community or even regional level to given an impression of life in the region at that time and often contribute to interpreting information on housing, architecture, household tools, and the use of space which might be recorded at the individual level on particular cards.

In general, our group has found that using information from a variety of sources and levels of documentation helps to create a richer picture of a particular family or a particular place. The on-line public catalogue accompanying this collection is designed to display and sort the archival classmarks of the surviving Polar Census manuscripts by community and then by individual families to give researchers an idea of where there are clusters of different types of documentation. In the subsections below, we now turn our attention to the details of interpreting the main type of documentation that one finds in manuscript archive.

The Household Card

The household card, while objectively a single instrument, is in fact a composite collection of different survey projects rather cleverly compressed into the space of one A3-sized sheet. Looking at a card is an overwhelming experience. On the standard version of the card there are 403 numbered questions, some of which can support up to five rows of data. There are also another 25 unnumbered questions and 11 cells for totalling data. If any card existed with all of the questions answered it could contain over 1,200 points of information, assuming that there were only 3 people in the family. In practice only a small proportion of the questions were answered, and of those, not all of the intricate rows of data were filled in. The exact questions answered, of course, differ from region to region. An average card would have approximately 300 points of information at both the level of the individual and the level of the household.

Much like the library of Polar Census manuscripts themselves, the household card is best understood when it is broken apart into its component tables, many of which, we suspect, represented the projects of different early Soviet agencies (fig. A1.2). Two tables are extremely important in this figure: the header table and the table of individuals. As rule, both of these tables on the first page of the card were always completed.

The header table presents a series of standardised question that allow one to place a head of a household both in terms of his or her location(s) in space and in terms of his or her identities. The cards were arranged by the household head, and as chapter 3 explores, aggregate data could vary depending on whether or not it was taken from the header, or from a different table. The header presents space for a full list of Soviet and Imperial administrative territorial classifica-

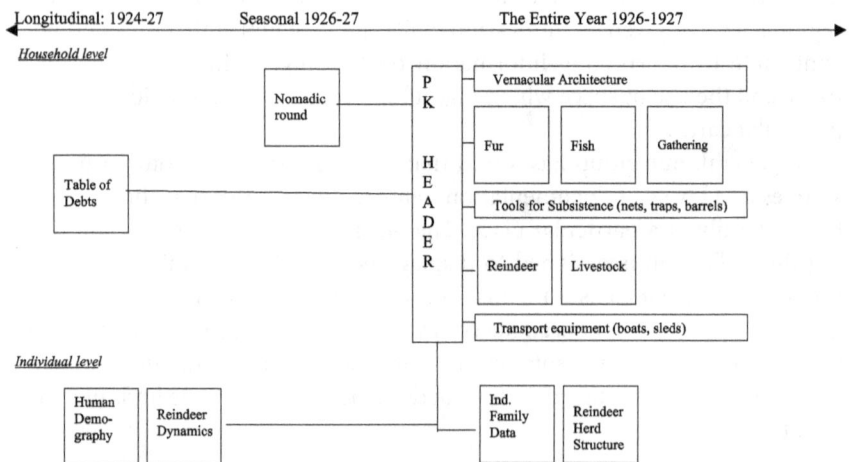

Figure A1.2. Information types within the household card

tions, spaces for a full set of Orthodox-style names for the household head, spaces for a native 'nickname' and 'tribal name', as well as a space for the new concept of 'nationality' and the older statistical category of mother tongue.

Following the territorial and identity variables, the header has a very important table documenting the yearly round of the family, broken up by season. This table was used often by the authors of this collection.

The table of individuals gives a range of basic demographic information on each member of the family including name, relation to the household head, age, nationality, marital status and literacy. This is followed by a set of rather specific entries on occupation. To the surprise of many enumerators, some individuals would have up to seven occupations in different seasons (graphically appearing on the form as if they became different persons in each season). The form had space to record the month or season of each task.

Following these two key tables, there then follows a large tier of tables containing household-level data. It would be impossible ecologically or culturally for all of these tables to be completed since no household could simultaneously hunt sea-mammals and carry out cereal agriculture. However when looking at the entire surviving archive of manuscripts one finds that almost always the tables recording trade goods, fishing and fur trapping are completed.

The tables on subsistence (fur trapping [cells 249–282]; gathering [304–312]; and fishing [cells 313–344]) were clearly set up by administrators interested in the terms of trade. The tables record subsistence action in four groups according to whether the goods in question were sold (and then if they were sold to private or state agencies), or then the total (which could include subsistence resources). On many cards a fifth field was scribbled-in indicating prices in that particular valley at that particular time. Data on consumer goods [cells 380–404] recorded quantity (in a large number of various Imperial era units of measurement) and often price. On many cards the total amount harvested, and the rouble-value of the total harvest, was indicated in a set of special summary fields on page 3 of the card.

The subsistence data provides one of the more intimate levels of analysis of praxis and economy in the collection and it was only partially used in this particular volume. Data on the amount of various animals and fish harvested can be cross-referenced to occupational data on individuals [cells 11 and 31] (and thereby indirectly to gender), as well as to lists of the tools used in the harvest [cells 133–162]. Households which followed a subsistence lifestyle would more likely be to report categories of tools that were homemade or which even had local names in indigenous languages (requiring the enumerator to add an additional field).

Following the data on subsistence, the final most evocative sub-table was that recording domestic livestock. This table documented horses [cells 53–58], a range of domestic farm animals [cells 59–77], and perhaps most importantly, reindeer [cells 79–109]. For the most part, the livestock tables recorded animals borrowed or 'leased', animals given out for lease, and the animals held by the family. A field for the total number of animals had to be calculated by our team by hand. The fields for traditional Russian livestock (horses, cows, pigs) distinguished stock by a small number of age and sex classes. However the cells for reindeer recorded such a wide variety of reindeer classes by age, sex, and function that this table is nearly as complex as the table recording the age, sex and occupation of people. The level of detail specified here may be a result of inexperience with reindeer societies but it certainly captures the importance of this animal for northern households, for many of which reindeer are just like people. It is important to add that the reindeer tables asked the enumerator to make a double count of animals (first by age and sex class, and then by function) allowing statisticians to cross-reference the numbers. All of the livestock tables can be further cross-referenced with data from the table recording equipment. For example, households reporting reindeer would almost always report equipment relevant to reindeer husbandry, dwellings relevant to living with reindeer, and often hired-in labour to look after the herd. Many reindeer-holding households would report fur trapping and fishing, but very few would report cereal agriculture or cattle pastoralism. Similarly households reporting forestry or even the gathering of cedar nuts tend also to report other miscellaneous wage labour and some forms of haying or cereal agriculture (with their accompanying tools), but very rarely reindeer pastoralism.

It is impossible here to summarise the content of all of the household-level tables. Table A1.1 gives an annotated list of the table headings on the household card. There is digital library of cards from the Turukhansk expedition, with a translation into English of every field, available online (Anderson 2008). The same database has an edited and coded web version of the subsistence data for the surviving household cards.

While the household card with its rich, nominal-level data is perhaps the most coveted archival resource today, it was not always viewed in that way. Although the protocols of the census expeditions asked that a copy of each card be filed with three different government agencies, our research has discovered only a partial set. After eight years of work we have catalogued and digitised 6,649 cards (including duplicates) out of a total possible population of some 33,641 households (TsSU 1929: 2). There is no one region with a full collection of the cards, but the collection of the Turukhansk expedition curated in Krasnoiarsk is by far the largest.

A map showing the quantity of cards discovered by region is in figure A1.3.

Concerning the administrative boundaries, the map shows the boundaries of the subdivisions of each *okrug* as they existed at the end of the Polar Census enumerations in approximately June 1927. Each subdivision would refer to a *raion* or an *ulus* depending on the region. The map follows the one in TsSU

Table A1.1. Index of sections within the household card

Cells	Table Name	Description
Card header	General Information	Administrative districts (Imperial and Soviet), name of household head, mother tongue, nationality, tribute status
Card header	Nomadic Round	Named places within a 4 season round
001–052	Population	Name, age, nationality, marital status, literacy, occupation, military service
040–052	Demography	Births and deaths since 1925
053–078	Livestock	Horses, cattle, sheep, goats, pigs by age and sex
079–092	Reindeer	Reindeer by age, sex and function
093–110	Reindeer Herd Dynamics	Reindeer births, deaths, sales, reasons for loss
I–VIII	Notes	Reserved space for regional tallies (often used for prices)
110–120	Hired Labourers	Names, age and nationality of employees including payment details
111–120	Hired Labour	Nationality
121–127	Day Labour	Description of activities for which people are hired
128–132	Hired Animals And Equipment	Description of the quantity and types of equipment hired, and from whom
133–139	Agricultural Equipment	Quantity and type of agricultural equipment (open fields)
141–161	Hunting Equipment	Quantity and type of hunting equipment (coded and open fields)
162–166	Bird Hunting Equipment	Quantity and type of bird traps (open fields)
167–187	Fishing Equipment Nets	Quantity and type of fishing equipment (coded and open fields)
188–199	Boats	Description and quantity of boats (coded and open fields)
200–216	Other Transport Equipment	Description and quantity of miscellaneous transport equipment, mostly sleds, skis and carts
217–230	Stationary Dwellings	Description and quantity of fixed dwellings (cabins and storage structures)
231–234	Mobile Dwellings	Description and quantity of mobile dwellings (tents) (with open fields)
235–238	Tillage	Quantity and description of tilled fields
239–248	Dogs And Poultry	Quantity of dogs, hens, geese (with open fields)
249–282	Fur-Trapping	Quantity, value and sale-point for fur (coded and open fields)
283–293	Marine Hunting	Quantity, value and sale-point for whale and seal (coded and open fields)
294–303	Fowl Hunting	Quantity, value and sale-point for grouse, ducks, geese (coded and open fields)
304–312	Other Gathering	Quantity, value and sale-point for berries and nuts (coded and open fields)
313–349	Fishing	Quantity, value and sale-point for salt and fresh water fish (coded and open fields)
350–354	Reindeer Commodities	Quantity and description of reindeer commodities (skin, meat) (open fields)
355–363	Cereal Crops	Quantity and description of the area cultivated with cereals (coded and open fields)
364–370	Fields	Description of agricultural areas (marsh, forest, meadow) (coded and open fields)
371–373	Trading Organisations	List of trading organisations with quantity of labourers
374–379	Credit And Debt	List of loans and debts specifying the amount and to whom
380–404	Consumer Goods	Quantity, value and price of consumption goods (flour, tea, etc.)

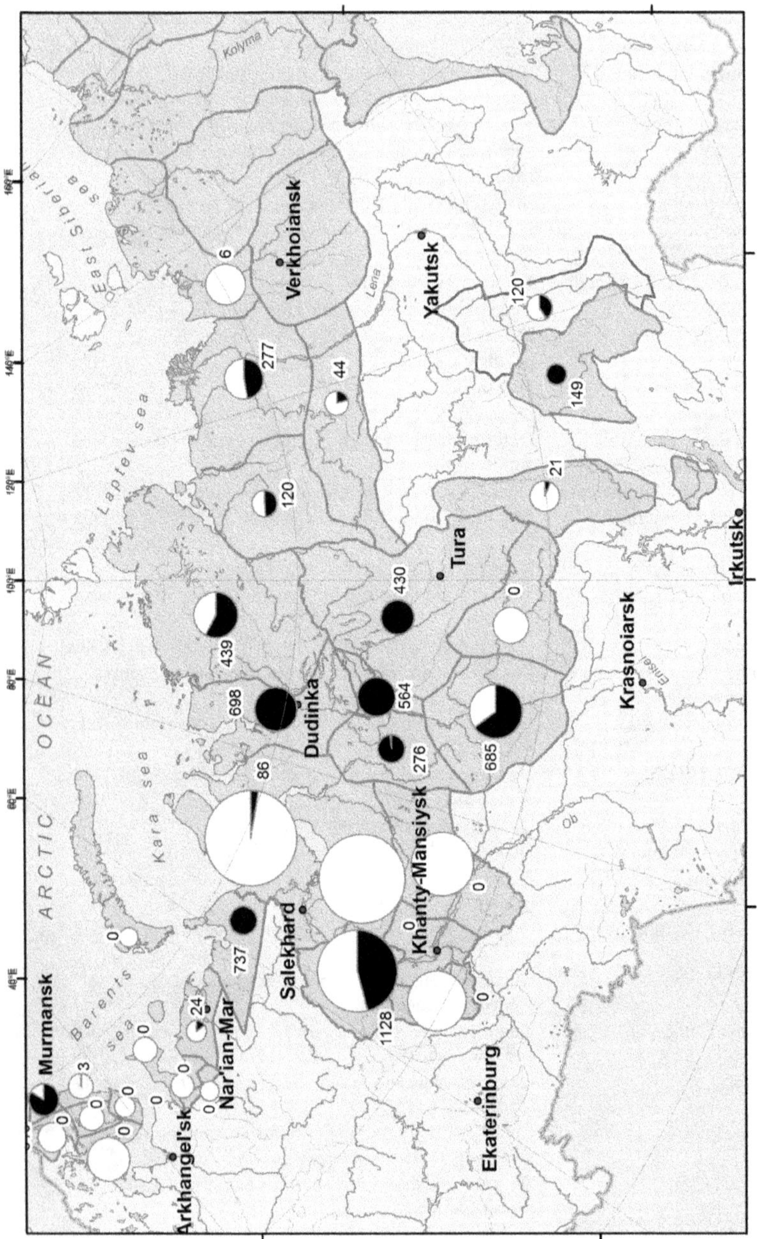

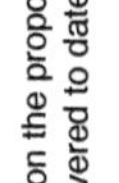

The size of each circle represents for each region the proportion of household cards submitted to the total number of cards. The fraction represents the proportion that have been discovered to date. The number next to the fraction indicates the exact number. The data for the Iakut republic is approximate.

Note on administrative boundaries. The map shows the boundaries of the subdivisions of each *okrug* as they were at the end of the Polar Census enumerations in approximately June 1927. Each subdivision would refer to a *raion* or an *ulus* depending on the region. The map follows that in TsSU 1928. The boundaries of Olekma *okrug* [south Iakutiia] are an exception in that this area was not included in the official list of regions where the Polar Census was conducted (although an archive of cards does exist). This *okrug* is not shaded in this map.

Figure A1.3. Map of Russia showing the quantities of household cards digitised by region

1928. The boundaries of Olekma *okrug* [south Iakutiia] are an exception in that this area was not included in the official list of regions where the Polar Census was conducted (although an archive of cards does exist). This *okrug* is not shaded in this map.

The Community Diary

Unlike the household card, the community diary was cared for much more consistently across most regions of Russia. Large complete sets of documents can be consulted for many regions of Russia (fig. A1.4). The community diary is a large ledger-sized booklet of 32 pages which reported on social and environmental conditions common to a group of households. The list of topics is similarly exhaustive, covering 22 themes (table. A1.2) and over 150 open-ended questions. The style of the document is unique. Reaching back to very old forms of Russian statistical practice, the document is based on a number of direct questions such as 'What rituals are performed during births, baptisms, weddings, and funerals' (Question XXI.2) or 'During what season do people hunt squirrel' (Question IX.14a).

The size of each circle in figure A1.4 represents for each region the proportion of household cards submitted to the total number of cards. The proportions are represented in three sizes: 1 – less than 50 diaries; 2 – 50–99 diaries; and 3 – 100 or more diaries. The numbers next to each circle represent the exact number of diaries found. The dark fraction represents the number found as a proportion of the total. The map shows the boundaries of the subdivisions of each *okrug* as they were at the end of the Polar Census enumerations in approximately June 1927. Each subdivision would refer to a *raion* or an *ulus* depending on the region. The map follows that in TsSU 1928.

The community diary was meant to be read in conjunction with a specific set of cards. On the header page there is a space for the index numbers of the cards to be cross-referenced to the diary. The header page also gives a summary of the identity and demographic structure of each community. The third page also gives an exacting description of seasonal movements, often by specific households. The middle pages also provide a detailed listing of consumer goods and prices for specific communities. Therefore to some degree the community diary can be used as a proxy for places where cards are missing.

The value of the community diary, of course, hinges on the definition of 'community' which, as stated many times in the book, was not clear in 1926–27. In parts of the European North and Western Siberia communities might be specific Saami *pogosty* or Khant *iurty*; however in Central and Eastern Siberia communities might be defined as 'Around mouth of the Kochechum river 15-20 *versty* in either direction' (GAKK 769-1-354: 1). This ambiguity about the meaning of people and place gives this document some its value by enabling researchers to

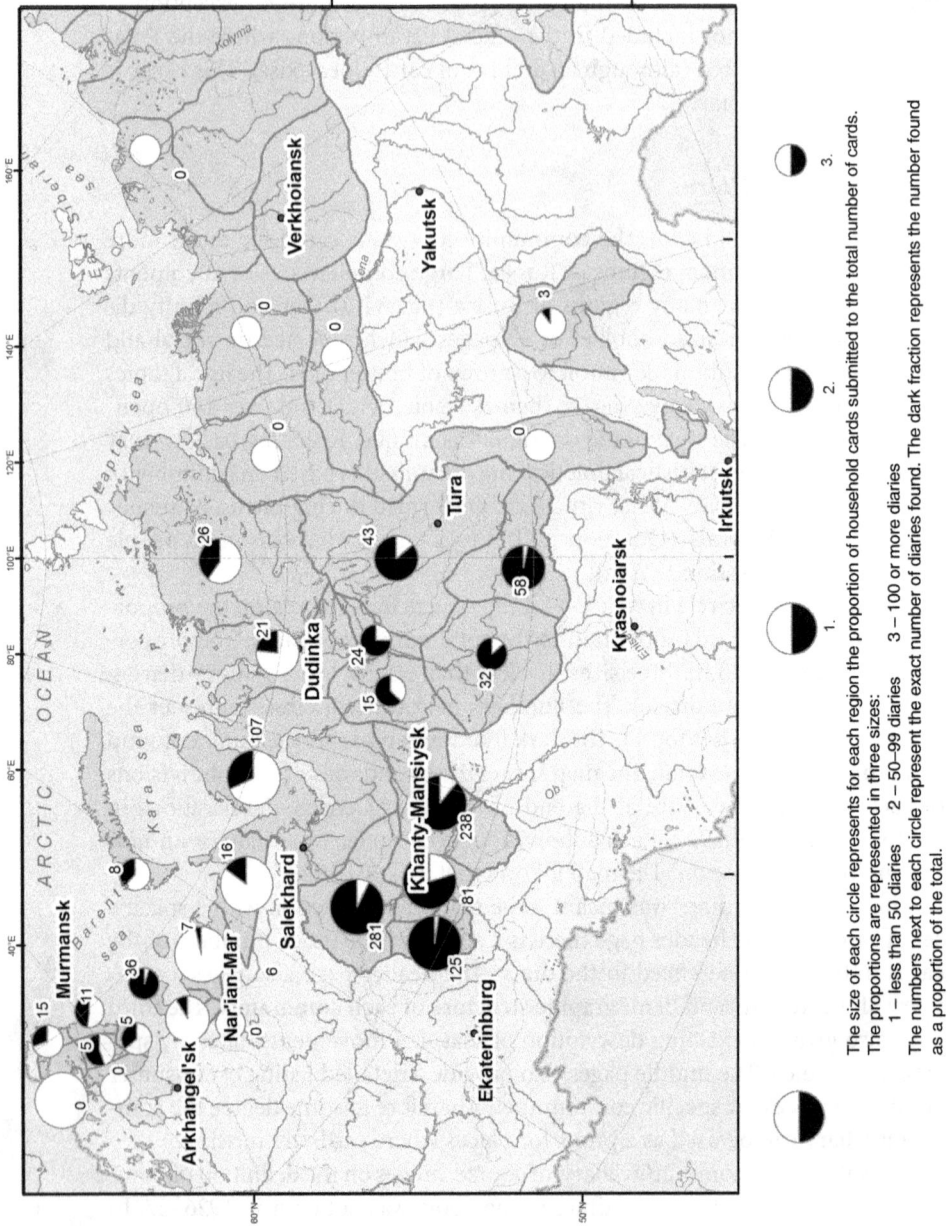

The size of each circle represents for each region the proportion of household cards submitted to the total number of cards. The proportions are represented in three sizes:

1 – less than 50 diaries   2 – 50–99 diaries   3 – 100 or more diaries

The numbers next to each circle represent the exact number of diaries found. The dark fraction represents the number found as a proportion of the total.

Note on administrative boundaries. The map shows the boundaries of the subdivisions of each *okrug* as they were at the end of the Polar Census enumerations in approximately June 1927. Each subdivision would refer to a *raion* or an *ulus* depending on the region. The map follows that in TsSU 1928. The boundaries of

Figure A1.4 Map of Russia showing the quantities of community diaries digitised by region

Table A1.2. Index of sections within the household diary

Section	Page	Title
Cover page	1	Information on Location, Nationality and 'Clan' Community
I	3	Nomadic Round
II	4	Physical Geography
III	5	Meteorological Data Over the Past Year
IV	5	Land Use (Land Ownership, Size of Plots, Disputes over Property)
V	7	Cultivation and Gardening
VI	8	Domestic Animals (Excepting Reindeer)
VII	9	Reindeer
VIII	12	Fishing
IX	14	Hunting
X	17	Roads and Road-Service Tax
XI	18	Miscellaneous Crafts And Occupations
XII	19	Trade and Exchange
XIII	21	Cooperatives (Locally-Run Trading Institutions)
XIV	22	Debts
XV	23	Access to Consumer Goods and Diet
XVI	24	Purchase and Delivery Prices for Local Goods and Consumer Goods
XVII	28	Hired Labour and Prices for Hired Labour
XVIII	29	Taxes and Duties
XIX	29	Administrative Units
XX	30	Public Services, Hygiene and Cultural Advancement
XXI	20	Customs and Way of Life
XXII	31	Extra Comments

better analyze the picture that may be visible in one particular season (see Jordan; Semenov; Anderson, Ineshin, and Ziker; and Ziker, this volume).

Not surprisingly, the complexity of this document meant that not every enumerator had time to fill out every page. It is not uncommon to find 'regional' community diaries which are filled out in fine detail. Diaries for neighbouring communities then ask the reader to consult the data in the 'main' diary for that region.

The Indices

As indicated figure A1.1 there were a number of indices created to help enumerators and their administrators to compile and sort information when submitting the raw data, and while preparing information for publication. These aggregate forms also tended to have a better life expectancy than the nominal data and survive in great numbers in most regional archives. Their scientific value is greater in places where, as in Arkhangel´sk *oblast´*, a regional summary of the material was never published. However in other regions such as Murmansk (MOI 1929), Ekaterinburg (USU 1928) and Krasnoiarsk (SKSO 1929) often these indices are simply unpublished copies of the final work. However in areas where collections of household cards have not been found, the intermediary index material has proven to be of great importance as proxy material for the nominal records (see Semenov; Volzhanina, this volume).

Closest to the enumerator, the Community Index (*spisok khoziaistv*) provides a list of every household card gathered for each community. It provides a key to the numbering system used on the cards, gives a short description of how many people there are in each family, and provides an inventory of the other types of documentation given to that community.

In each regional office, when the household cards were being organised, a large A5 ledger sheet known usually known as a Community Summary (*tablitsa poselennogo podscheta*) was prepared summarising all of the economic and trade data on the cards. In most regions, these sheets summarised the data on a community level. However in some archives it is possible to find rough sheets where counts are conducted on the level of the household or on groupings of households that are different than those published. These cumbersome sheets can often be of use where household level data is missing (see Volzhanina, this volume).

A final form, which is not strictly an index, provided one of the most important summaries of the data on individuals. The Personal Form (*lichnyi listok*) was a small A5 sheet on which regional officials extracted basic demographic data on individuals within families (age, sex, nationality occupation). This form was a standard instrument used in the 1926 general population census and thereby formed the first step in re-coding and interpreting the data before publication by the federal statistical agency. It is important to stress that the information extracted and coded here can often be different than that compiled and coded when variables associated with the household head are used (see Volzhanina, this volume). In general, the range of national identities and occupations were reduced, eliminating some of the variety of expression that makes the household cards evocative today.

Supplemental Types of Documents

Many of the regional census agencies devised their own supplemental forms in order to collect data that was of interest to local administrators. These local forms are often the most interesting, but none of these elaborated forms were collected on a universal basis. Two expeditions, the Turukhansk Census expedition and the Ural Census expedition were the most creative in devising their own forms.

The Turukhansk census expedition introduced at least two unique forms: the hygiene card (*sanitarnaia kartochka* [SK]) and the kinship card (*kartochka brachnykh par* [BP]). Fragmentary archival evidence suggests that there may have been further cards monitoring trade goods and trading posts, but this has not been confirmed by archival research. According to the instructions, every fifth household was to be questioned with these forms, but it often seems that only one household in each settlement was questioned. The forms were used by the Iakutsk census expedition and by the enumerators in Irkutsk working under the direction of Krasnoiarsk.

The hygiene card was a single ledger sized sheet containing questions in four sections (see Argounova-Low – this volume). The card surveyed the household head but also recorded the other members of the family. The first question surveyed the dwelling of the household, often describing the dimensions and architecture in great detail. The second section queried diet and especially the supply of clean water and access to basic consumer products such as salt, sugar and bread. The third section recorded sanitary habits and the frequency and technique of washing. The final section has two short questions about the history of illness. There are 304 unique hygiene cards in the collection. Although we have found no documents on the source of the questions for this form, the style of the questions bears a close resemblance to that of the Committee of the Red Cross which was active in the region at that time (Kytmanov 1927; Malysheva and Poznanskii 1998).

The kinship card, also on a ledger sized sheet, collected supplementary information on the personal histories of a married couple. Although unlikely to satisfy anthropologists, the card does document the birth clan of each partner, some very basic information about their parents, and the total number of children in their history (including deceased children) (see Ziker this volume). There are not many of these forms surviving (519, excluding duplicates) which would make it impossible to use the information for any statistically meaningful fertility study, but they do provide valuable information often for families in areas where household cards do not survive.

The Ural Census expedition, based in Sverdlovsk [Ekaterinburg] was a second centre of innovation with respect to local surveys (see Glavatskaya, this volume). Not only did the authorities introduce supplementary surveys, but they also collected basic household information on non-standard household cards. The two surviving collections of household cards for Berezovskii *okrug* (almost 100 per cent complete) and for Obdor *raion* (fragmentary) were each collected on their own specially designed forms which included most of the questions of the basic card, but as a rule altered the names of the pre-printed hunted species and tools, and added questions on trade relationships and trading posts.

The Ural Census expedition added two additional forms for a partial survey of the population. The family budget card (*biudzhetnyi blank* [BB]) was an extremely complicated instrument which collected data on the delivery of and consumer prices for a large basket of goods and tried to establish consumption patterns over a year. The forms were administered to a handful of families (28), each of which was thought to represent a socio-economic class of rich, poor and middling households of the regions.

The survey of trading posts (*blanki faktorii* [BF]) was also a complex document intended to help enumerators understand the volume and the prices of every trading post in the Ural district and perhaps even to gather evidence of unfair pricing. As with the family budget card there were not many forms (113). They are significant for this region of Siberia for their potential to be cross-referenced to the almost complete collection of community diaries for the region which also capture pricing information (see Glavatskaya, this volume).

Archival Histories

Although the Polar Census expeditions were designed to generate a holistic set of data nested at different levels of human experience, the history of these artefacts turned out much differently than many of the enumerators expected. It is clear from the memoranda and the first wave of publications that the enumerators were motivated by a sense of exploration and patriotism. Almost every census expedition had planned a series of multi-volume publications. Some, as with the Turukhansk and Ural expedition, left extensive unpublished manuscript versions of these publications. Indeed many of the young enumerators later became prominent scholars in a variety of fields. Others might have become prominent had they not been murdered during the repressions. Why was this material not analysed fully in its day?

There is a strong argument to be made that the material of these expeditions fell between the expectations of authorities and scholars as political and scientific priorities shifted in the tumultuous times of the early 1930s. On the one hand, the entire archive of the Polar Census could not be used to generate a general picture of the entire Soviet North due to significant gaps in the registration of some regions. On the other hand, there was no patience in those days for a detailed qualitative study of particular regions. In the published criticism of the Polar Census, it became quite clear that the material was far too rich for a state that was intent on simplifying its accounts of social relationships and making stark generalisations about its population (Anderson 2006). This indifference to the detail of these archives led to a peculiar fate for the documents.

Without a single master, the collection which was designed to be integral was often carved up regionally by different agencies and even individuals who had an interest in it. In general, the household cards tended to move from the files of the regional statistical agency into the hands of the rural economists conducting the territorial formation expeditions of the 1930s. Their nominal level data on migrations and movements were an important source of information in the building of collective farms. Indeed this is probably the most tangible artefact of the Polar Census today.

Any material which could be described as qualitative or even artistic was more often than not claimed by different archives. Maps and travel accounts tend to be found today in the files of regional local history *kraeved* organisations. The Russian Geographical Society, and its regional affiliates, claimed part of the material. Glass-plate negatives, photographs and sketches tend to be found in the archives of regional museums. The Krasnoiarsk Regional Museum today still has a fine collection of clothing and artefacts collected by the enumerators in 1926–27.

As mentioned above, much of the household-level data is simply missing. In our extensive work across the Russian Federation we have found that more often than not material is not so much missing as sitting uncatalogued. Some of the material of both the Ural and Arkhangel´sk expeditions was formally indexed as part of this project. It is possible that further material is sitting in storerooms, especially in the Far East where archives were transported several times over during World War II.

Digital Collections

This book would not have been possible if it were not for the work of dozens of archivists who assisted us in digitising the surviving manuscript record of the Polar Census. When this project began, archival digitisation was a new concept. Over the last eight years this project has similarly embraced successive innovations in digital technology.

The heart of the digital collection is a database index of every manuscript and artefact that can be associated with the Polar Census expeditions. While seemingly a straightforward task, it proved extremely complicated to come up with an indexing system which would allow the user to find the material that he or she was interested in. Since the logic of the instrumentation was to link households to a single place, the heart of the index system was a two-part numeric code which specified both the district (*okrug*) and the settlement from which a community diary or set of household cards was taken. In most regions of Russia, provincial statistical agencies published lists of population points. These names, and their original numbered system, were taken as the basis for a single list of population points. Needless to say the single list of population points is not flawless. Some manuscript collections, notably those from Turukhansk and Iakutsk were organised according to a much finer set of 'encampments' than the central agencies permitted – which necessitated creating a decimalised version of the authoritative published numbers. Other sets of households cards, such as from parts of Olekminsk *okrug* Iakutiia were never analysed as part of either the Polar Census or the general All-Union census. For them, new categories had to be created.

Beyond the single list of population points, the digital index also records heuristic labels for nationality, the date of enumeration, the name of the enumerator, and the name of the household head. Again, in many cases this information had to be attributed from correspondence or other memoranda. Given that nationality was a new idea in 1926, we retrospectively constructed national identifiers using data from the fields of *natsional'nost'*, mother tongue, and administrative clan. This variable is a heuristic variable which only gives a guide to the more nuanced data contained in the record.

The digital index is described in greater detail online (Anderson 2008).

The second level of digitisation was accomplished through the use of digital photography. We have collected digital photographs of 46 per cent of the collection of household cards and 53 per cent of the collection of community diaries, as well as all of the accessory instrumentation of kinship cards, hygiene cards, etc. Due to the development of digital technology the earlier images came in many parts in order to preserve the quality and detail of the originals. The later proxies, done in Western Siberia, tended to be made from a single image. These images are knitted together with the classmarks from the digital image embedded as metadata allowing a user to search the library by place, 'heuristic' nationality, date and surname.

Since digital photography was not permitted in all archives, or was too costly, the third level of digitisation consisted of creating proxies by retyping the information from the original manuscripts. All of the existing household cards (excluding duplicates) were entered into a specially designed MS ACCESS database allowing a very skilled user to make keyword searches and to construct exploratory queries across all of the raw manuscript data. This data is gradually being coded and cleaned to allow average users to perform numeric queries. Parts of this data have been exported to a simple online database.

Approximately half (56 per cent) of the known community diaries have also been entered on a specially designed Adobe Acrobat form which has allowed us to export the material in a file based in extended mark-up language (XML), making it possible to read these forms, in Russian, online. The only community diaries that have not been either photographed or typed into the special form are the sets from Tobol'sk *okrug* representing Konda, Surgut and Samar districts (228 diaries).

The proxies created by entering the data into new databases has advantages and disadvantages. One of the great advantages is that it makes these sources legible to a greater number of people, and further makes it much easier to distribute the source electronically. However the decisions of the person keying-in the material reduce ambiguities as spelling is standardised or by leaving corrections to the material unreferenced. The proxies serve only as an introduction to the material which should be followed by work with the primary manuscripts.

Conclusion

As stated in the introduction to this volume, the value of this collection lies in its nuanced and detailed annotation of individual lives at a particularly evocative period in the history of the Russian North. Our hope in recovering the primary manuscript data was to create an easily accessible archive which will allow Northerners and researchers to gain an overview of social life at the beginning of the Soviet period. The data collected is rich. As with the history of the documents that form this archive, the fate of which has been affected by personal biographies of concrete researchers, the purpose of this collection is to introduce the archive and invite researchers to use it.

2 | Table of Measures

Transliterated label	Ratio to SI	Type - SI Unit
kilogram	1	mass – kg
funt	4	mass – kg
pud	16	mass – kg
desiatina	1.45672	area – ha
litr	1	volume – L
chetvert´	6.56	volume – L
vedro	12.299	volume – L
bochka	491.96	volume – L
sack	1	unit
sack of flour	72	volume – kg
sack of dried bread	40	volume – kg
sack of sugar	16	volume – kg
metr	1	length – m
arshin	0.71	length – m
diuim	0.254	length – m
sazhen´	2.13	length – m

Archival References

Abbreviation

References to specific documents within archives are made in-text with a simplified system beginning with the abbreviation of the archive, and followed by all of the separate classmarks separated by hyphens. In most Russian archives, the classmarks are placed in the following order: *fond - opis´ - delo* (or *edinitsa khraneniia*). A unique folio (or its verso) is indicated following a colon. Thus GAKK P769-1-306: 15 represents the document Gosudarstvennyi Arkhiv Krasnoiarskogo Kraia *fond* R769 *opis´* 1 *delo* 306 *list* 15. If a reference is made to an entire series of folders (*dela*) these are indicated with an tilda, i.e. GAKK P769-1-306~308.

The State Archive of Sverdlovsk *oblast´* often has folders (*papki*) within *dela*. These are indicated with decimal, such as GASO 1812-2-181.01.

The Archive of the Northern Expedition of St. Petersburg University simply used surnames to classify field diaries. These references are in quotation marks to distinguish them from ordinary in-text references.

Abbreviation	Russian Title	Translated Title
AKKKM	Архив Красноярского Краевого Краеведческого Музея	Archive of the Krasnoiarsk Regional Museum
ASE	Архив Северной Экспедиции Санкт-Петербургского Государственного Университета	Archive of the Northern Expedition of St. Petersburg State University
BGGA	Бодобайдинский Городской Государственный Архив	Bodaibo City State Archive
GAAO	Государственный Архив Архангельской Области	State Archive of Arkhangel´sk Province
GAIaNAO	Государственный Архив Ямал-Ненецкого Автономного Округа	State Archive of the Iamal-Nenets Autonomous District
GAIO	Государственный Архив Иркутской Области	State Archive of Irkutsk Province

Abbreviation	Russian Title	Translated Title
GAKK	Государственный Архив Красноярского Края	State Archive of Krasnoiarsk Territory
GAMO	Государственный Архив Мурманской Области	State Archive of Murmansk Province
GANAO	Государственный Архив Ненецкого Автономного Округа Архангельской Области	State Archive of the Nenets Autonomous Okrug of Arkhagel'sk Oblast'
GARF	Государственный Архив Российской Федерации	State Archive of the Russian Federation
GASO	Государственный Архив Свердловской Области	State Archive of Sverdlovsk Province
GASPITO	Государственный Архив Социально-Политической Истории Тюменской Области	State Archive of Social-Political History, Tiumen' Province
GUTOGAT	Государственное учереждение Тюменской области 'Государственный Архив в г. Тобольске'	The State Institution of Tiumen' Oblast, 'State Archive of the City of Tobol'sk'
GU IaNOMVK	Государственное учережедение 'Ямало-Ненецкий окружной музейно-выставочный коплекс им. Шемановского'	The State Institution 'Iamalo-Nenets district museum and exhibition comples named after I.S. Shemanovskii'
NARK	Национальный Архив Республика Коми	National Archive of the Komi Republic
NARS	Национальный Архив Республики Саха (Якутия)	National Archive of the Sakha Republic
PFARAN	Питерский Филиал Архива Российской Академии Наук	St. Petersburg Division of the Archive of the Russian Academy of Sciences
RGAE	Российский Государственный Архив Экономики	Russian State Archive of Economics

Archive of the Krasnoiarsk Regional Museum // Arkhiv Krasnoiarskogo Kraevogo Kraevedcheskogo Muzeia [AKKKM]

KKKM 7626-110: 82, 91–92, 98–99, 107. Dnevnik A.P. Lekarenko ot 9 sentiabria 1926 po 8 sentiabria 1927 gg.

Archive of the Northern Expedition of St. Petersburg State University // Arkhiv Severnoi Ekspeditsii Sankt-Peterburskogo Gosudarstvennogo Universiteta [ASE]

Bildiug A. B. Fieldnotes. 2006: 54v–55.

Kaninskii sel′sovet. 1972-1975. Materialy pokhoziaistvennogo ucheta administratsii MO 'Kaninskii sel′sovet' za 1972–1975.

Kaninskii sel′sovet. 2002-2006. Materialy pokhoziaistvennogo ucheta administratsii MO 'Kaninskii sel′sovet' za 2002–2006.

Kiselev S.B. Fieldnotes. 2007: 28.

Semenov I.V. Fieldnotes. 2006: 48–50.

Terent′ev, Egor Ivanovich. nd. Stranitsy iz knigi zhizni komi-izhemtsa Terent′eva Egora Ivanovicha [manuscript]. Oral History Archive of the Village library of Nes′,

Nenets Autonomous Okrug [copy in the Archive of the Northern Expedition of St. Petersburg State University]. 2006.

Vokuevykh, Dinastiia. nd. Dinastiia Vokyevykh [manuscript]. Oral History Archive of the Village library of Nes´, Nenets Autonomous Okrug [copy in the Archive of the Northern Expedition of St. Petersburg State University]. 2006.

Bodaibo City State Archive // Bodaibinskii Gorodskoi Gosudarstvennyi Arkhiv [BGGA]

BGGA 26-1-4: 2. Otchet o deiatel´nosti Tuzsoveta za period s 1 ianvaria po 1 iiunia 1931 g.

BGGA 26-1-4: 46, 50. Godovye otchety kolkhozov 'Krasnyi Khomolkho', 'Imeni Pamiati rasstrela Lenskikh rabochikh' po osnovnoi deiatel´nosti i dokumenty k nim za 1931–1934 gody.

BGGA 26-1-5: 4, 6v. Proizvodstvennyi plan i finansovyi raschet kolkhoza 'Krasnyi Khomolkho' na 1932 g.

BGGA 26-1-7: 2, 36, 38. Godovye otchety po sel´skomu khoziaistvu kolkhoza 'Imeni 1-go maia' i dokumenty k nim za 1932–1934 gody.

BGGA 26-1-27: 2. Proizvodstvenno-trudovoi plan Svetlovskogo kolkhoza 'Vernyi put´' na 1936 g.

BGGA 26-1-33: 3. Godovoi otchet kolkhoza 'Chara-okhotnik' za 1936 g.

BGGA 26-1-37: 3. Proizvodstvenno-finansovyi plan arteli 'Charskii okhotnik' sela Ust´-Zhuia na 1937 g.

BGGA 26-1-45: 3. Godovoi otchet Svetlovskogo kolkhoza 'Vernyi put´' za 1937 g.

BGGA 26-1-49: 12–30. Godovye statisticheskie otchety po zhivotnovodstvu i prilozheniia k nim.

St. Petersburg Division of the Archive of the Russian Academy of Sciences // Piterskii Filial Arkhiva Rossiiskoi Akademii Nauk [PFARAN]

PFARAN 135-2-17: 35 Skematicheskaia karta sezonnykh peredvizhenei i olennyh kochevii lopari, izhetsev i samoedev.

State Archive of Arkhangel´sk Province // Gosudarstvennyi Arkhiv Arkhangel´skoi Oblasti [GAAO]

GAAO 6-8-153: 1. Svedeniia ob inorodtsakh Arkhangel´skoi gubernii, imenuemykh samoedami (1892 g.).

GAAO 6-8-168. Posemeinyi spisok samoedov Kaninskoi tundry (1895 g.).

GAAO 6-8-168: 18v–19. Primechanie k spisku.

GAAO 6-19-87: 1–429. Pervaia vseobshchaia perepis´. Mezenskii uezd Arkhangel´skoi gubernii. Spetsial´nyi uchastok po perepisi kochevogo i osedlogo naseleniia Kaninskoi i Timanskoi tundr Mezenskogo uezda (1897 g.).

GAAO 6-19-87: 6–9v. Podschet naseleniia samoedov osedlogo i kochevogo naseleniia po Kaninskoi tundre.

GAAO 6-19-87: 128–129v. Perepisnoi list sem´i Nikolaia Ivanovicha Ardeeva.

GAAO 187-1-848. Resheniia, doklady i perepiska po perepisi naseleniia – kochevnikov v 1926 godu.

GAAO 187-1-848: 17. Pros´ba k zaveduiushchemu Arkhangel´skim Gubstatbiuro Plandovskomu V.V. 1925.

GAAO 187-1-848: 26–26v. Vypiska iz protokola N24 Zasedaniia Biuro Gubplana. 27 ianvaria 1926g.

GAAO 187-1-848: 27. Arkhangel´skoe gubernskoe statisticheskoe biuro. Perepis´ naseleniia ostrovov Ledovitogo okeana i kochevnikov tundr 1926 goda.

GAAO 187-1-848: 27v. Obshchie svedeniia o khoziaistve i ego peredvizheniiakh.

GAAO 187-1-848: 28. Soobshchenie v Arkhangel´skoe Gubstatbiuro ot chlena Severnogo Komiteta Shal´kova. 9 fevralia 1926.

GAAO 187-1-848: 29–35. Spisok samoedskikh chumov Kaninskoi i Timanskoi tundr, zaregistrirovannykh v 1926 godu.

GAAO 187-1-848: 36–36v. Podvornaia karta dlia tuzemnogo naseleniia severnykh okrain.

GAAO 187-1-848: 45–77v. Skhema poselennogo blanka.

GAAO 187-1-852: 21. Instruktsiia v Arkhangel´skoe Gubstatbiuro o formuliarakh perepisi. M. Krasil´nikov. 1926.

GAAO 187-1-852: 74–91v. Instruktsiia k zapolneniiu formuliarov khoziaistvennoi perepisi v pripoliarnykh raionakh severa Sibirskogo Kraia. 16 maia 1926g.

GAAO 187-1-852: 209–210v. Pis´mo A. Kuropteva tovarishchu D´iachkovu. 24 ianvaria 1927g.

GAAO 187-1-852: 269. Pripoliarnaia perepis´ v 1926 godu v Arkhangel´skoi gubernii.

GAAO 187-1-852: 270–270v. Otchet Gubstatotdela v TsSU SSSR. D´iachkov. 3e avgusta 1927g.

GAAO 187-1-857: 52–53. Spisok kochevnikov naselennykh/kochevykh punktov po Porech´iu.

GAAO 187-1-857: 56–59. Kratkie poselennye itogi Pripoliarnoi perepisi 1926 goda po Arkhangel´skoi gubernii. Kaninsko-Timanskaia volost´.

GAAO 187-1-857: 60–63v. Spisok naselennykh mest Kaninskogo poluostrova i spisok domokhoziaev i chumo- khoziaev.

GAAO 187-1-857: 74. Spisok naselennykh punktov i domokhoziaev Malozemel´skoi tundry, sostavlennyi pri perepisi kochevogo naseleniia 92 goda. Kuloi.

GAAO 187-1-865. Proekt razrabotki materialov perepisi, poselennye itogi, spiski domokhoziaev.

GAAO 187-1-888: 240–274v. Poselennye spiski domokhoziaev. Kaninsko-Timanskaia tundra. Mezenskii uezd.

GAAO 187-1-891. Perepisnye listy dlia zhitelei ´mertvoi zony' (ostrovov Severnogo Ledovitogo Okeana i kochevnikov v tundrakh) v predelakh Arkhangel´skoi gubernii. Uezdy Pechorskii, Mezenskii, Arkhangel´skii.

GAAO 187-1-891: 268–283v. Perepisnye listy. Pechorskii uezd. Domokhoziaeva Laptander, Taleev, Ledkov, Taleev (Khyrta), Apitsyn, Ledkov (Sytovich), Iavtysyi, Taibaroi, Lageiskii.

GAAO 187-1-891: 677–678v. Perepisnoi list. Mezenskii uezd. Domokhoziain Semen Timofeevich Vaniuta.

GAAO 187-1-891: 683–684v. Perepisnoi list. Mezenskii uezd. Domokhoziain Ivan Rodionovich Terent´ev.

GAAO 187-1-891: 687–688v. Perepisnoi list. Mezenskii uezd. Domokhoziain Egor Andreevich Vokuev.

GAAO 187-1-891: 693–694v. Perepisnoi list. Mezenskii uezd. Domokhoziain Filipp Egorovich Khatanzeiskii.

GAAO 187-1-891: 699–700v. Perepisnoi list. Mezenskii uezd. Domokhoziain Gavril Egorovich Khatanzeiskii.

GAAO 187-1-891: 701–702v. Perepisnoi list. Mezenskii uezd. Domokhoziain Iakov Timofeevich Vaniuta.

GAAO 187-1-892. Poselennye blanki perepisi v raionakh Pripoliarnogo Severa po Arkhangel'skoi gubernii i Komi oblasti. 1926.

GAAO 187-1-892: 266–442v. Poselennye blanki dlia naselennykh punktov Shomoksha, reka Chizha, reka Mestnaia, Vst'e reki Gubistoi, Verkh. reki Gubistoi, reka Peza, Verkh. reki Sobach'ikh, Ust'e reki Sobach'ikh, Novaia doroga, reka Sobach'i, Versh. reki Sal'nitsy, Versh. reki Malaia Kiai.

GAAO 187-1-892: 459–474v. Poselennyi blank. Naselennyi punkt Elovninskie.

GAAO 187-1-892: 607–654. Poselennye blanki dlia naselennykh punktov Indigskie ozera, Gornostaeva Guba, Sviatoi mys.

GAAO 187-1-892: 753–768. Poselennyi blank. Naselennyi punkt derevnia Vizhas.

GAAO 187-1-897: 105. Spisok lits, uchastvovavshikh v provedenii Pripoliarnoi perepisi 1926–27g. v predelakh Arkhangel'skoi gubernii. A. Pavlov. 1929.

GAAO 187-1-891: 268–283v. Perepisnye listy kochevnikov materikovykh tundr (1920 g.)

GAAO 760-1-6: 125–125v. Spisok grazhdan o. Kolgueva s ukazaniem kolichestva olenei (tablitsa).

GAAO 760-1-6: 129–129v. Spisok grazhdan o. Vaigacha s ukazaniem kolichestva olenei (tablitsa).

GAAO 760-1-6: 134–137v. Spisok grazhdan o. Novaia Zemlia s ukazaniem kolichestva olenei (tablitsa).

GAAO 760-1-6: 138. Svodka naseleniia po stanovishcham Severnogo Ledovitogo okeana (tablitsa).

GAAO 760-1-28: 1–48, 187–257. Poselennye itogi (tablitsy poselennogo podscheta) po sel'sovetam Mezenskoi, Kaninsko-Timanskoi i Dorogorskoi volostei.

GAAO 760-1-39: 287–293. Dokladnaia zapiska. A.G. Sazonov. 1928.

GAAO 760-1-39: 297. Akt ob osmotre korma dlia pestsov.

State Archive of the Iamal-Nenets Autonomous District // Gosudarstvennyi Arkhiv Iamalo-Nenetskogo Avtonomnogo Okruga [GAIaNAO]

GAIaNAO 12-1-4. Poselennye itogi Obdorskogo raiona Tazovskogo sel'soveta [in 6 folders].

GAIaNAO 12-1-5. Dannye Vsesoiuznoi perepisi naseleniia po Tazovskomu sel'sovetu Obdorskogo raiona za 1926 g.

GAIaNAO 12-1-6. Dannye Vsesoiuznoi perepisi naseleniia po sel'sovetu Lesnye samoedy Surgutskogo raiona za 1926 g.

GAIaNAO 12-1-51-56. Materialy perepisi naseleniia 1932–1933 g. Posemeino-khoziaistvennye blanki.

GAIaNAO 12-1-90-91. Pokhoziaistvennye kartochki Nadymskoi ekspeditsii za 1933–1934 g.

GAIaNAO 12-1-35. Pokhoziaistvennye kartochki Tazovsko-Purovskoi ekspeditsii Omskogo oblastnogo zemel'nogo upravleniia za 1935 god.

GAIaNAO 12-1-128. Poimennyi semeino-khoziaistvennyi spisok Verkhne-Purovskogo natsional'nogo soveta Purovskogo raiona.

GAIaNAO 12-1-189: 24–40. Dokladnaia zapiska po osedaniiu kochevogo i polukochevogo naseleniia Iamal'skogo okruga Omskoi oblasti.

GAIaNAO 34-1: 2, 66, 77. Statisticheskie otchety ZAGSa.

GAIaNAO 34-1-2: 135. Chislennost' naseleniia po polu, vozrastu i natsional'nostiam po Iamal'skomu raionu Iamal'skogo (Nenetskogo) okruga Ural'skoi oblasti na 1 ianvaria 1932 g.

GAIaNAO 34-1-2: 139. Chislennost' naseleniia po polu, vozrastu i natsional'nostiam po Purovskomu raionu Iamal'skogo (Nenetskogo) okruga Ural'skoi oblasti na 1 ianvaria 1932 g.

GAIaNAO 186-1-1: 39–40v Proekt khoiaistvennogo ustroistva Nydinskogo olenevodcheskogo sovkhoza Nadymskogo raiona Iamal'skog okruga Ob'-Irtyshskoi oblasti.

State Archive of Irkutsk Province // Gosudarstvennyi Arkhiv Irkutskoi Murmanskoi Oblasti [GAIO]

GAIO 1468-1-2. Poselennye blanki Irkutskoi gubernii.

GAIO 1468-1-2: 21–36. Poselennyi blank. Naselennyi punkt ozero Tolondo.

GAIO 1468-1-2: 37–58. Poselennyi blank. Naselennyi punkt ust'e reki Khomolko.

State Archive of Krasnoiarsk Territory // Gosudarstvennyi Arkhiv Krasnoiarskogo Kraia [GAKK]

GAKK 769-1-307: 33–34. Opisanie i marshrut dlia X uchastka perepisi registratoru A.P. Lekarenko.

GAKK 769-1-308: 1–86 Perepiska N.V. Sushilina s Kurilovichem.

GAKK 769-1-310: 4 [Skhematicheskaia karta reka Vitim i Zhuia].

GAKK 769-1-354: 1–16. Poselennyi blank. Naselennyi punkt ust'e reki Kochechumo.

GAKK 769-1-405-406, 424, 441. Pokhoziaistvennye kartochki. Turukhanskii krai.

GAKK 769-1-405: 7–8v. Pokhoziaistvennaia kartochka. Naselennyi punkt ozero Essei. Domokhoziain Marfa.

GAKK 769-1-406: 17–18v. Pokhoziaistvennaia kartochka. Naselennyi punkt ozero Essei. Domokhoziain Khristoforov Samson.

GAKK 769-1-406: 23–24v. Pokhoziaistvennaia kartochka. Naselennyi punkt ozero Diupkun. Domokhoziain Petrov Anofrii.

GAKK 769-1-406: 39–40v. Pokhoziaistvennaia kartochka. Naselennyi punkt ozero Essei. Domokhoziain Evdokiia Vasil'eva.

GAKK 769-1-406: 95–96v. Pokhoziaistvennaia kartochka. Naselennyi punkt ozero Essei. Domokhoziain Egorov Savva.

GAKK 769-1-446: 1–1v. Kartochki brachnykh par. Mikhail Espek.

GAKK 769-1-446: 2–2v. Kartochki brachnykh par. Khristofor Buatulu.

GAKK 769-1-446: 3–3v. Kartochki brachnykh par. Pronkin Trofim.

GAKK 769-1-446: 4–4v. Kartochki brachnykh par. Pronkin Spiridon.

GAKK 769-1-446: 5–5v. Kartochki brachnykh par. Espek Nikolai.

GAKK 769-1-446: 64–73v. Kartochki brachnykh par. Naselennyi punkt ozero Essei.

GAKK 769-1-452: 89–89v. Kartochka brachnoi pary. Naselennyi punkt Khatanga. Chupriny.

GAKK 769-1-459: 16–16v. Sanitarnaia kartochka. Naselennyi punkt ozero Essei. Afanasii Kuiukta.

GAKK 769-1-459: 17–17v. Sanitarnaia kartochka. Naselennyi punkt ozero Essei. Matveev Nikolai.

GAKK 769-1-459: 19–19v. Sanitarnaia kartochka. Naselennyi punkt ozero Essei. Konstantinov Khristofor.

GAKK 769-1-459: 20–20v. Sanitarnaia kartochka. Naselennyi punkt ozero Essei. Ivanov Stepan.

GAKK 769-1-459: 48–48v. Sanitarnaia kartochka. Buatulu Nikolai Gavrolovich.

GAKK 769-1-459: 49–49v. Sanitarnaia kartochka. Naselennyi punkt balagan Khalil´ki. Khristofor Khalil´ka.

GAKK 769-1-459: 50–50v. Sanitarnaia kartochka. Pereprygin Ivan.

GAKK 769-1-459: 52–52v. Sanitarnaia kartochka. Naselennyi punkt balagan Poibala.

GAKK 769-1-459: 72–72v. Sanitarnaia kartochka. Naselennyi punkt stoibishche mezhdu rekami Medvezh´ei i Romashikhoi. Ivan Vas.

GAKK 769-1-460: 60–60v. Sanitarnaia kartochka. Naselennyi punkt ozero Khomolko. Vlasov Stepan.

GAKK 769-1-460: 80–80v. Sanitarnaia kartochka. Naselennyi punkt ozero Tolondo. Fedorov Il´ia.

GAKK 769-1-460: 81–81v. Sanitarnaia kartochka. Naselennyi punkt ozero Tolondo. Iakomik Afanasii.

GAKK 769-1-460: 87–87v. Sanitarnaia kartochka. Naselennyi punkt ust´e reki Khomolko. Petrov Nikolai.

GAKK 827-1-18: 2–5. Biografiia A.P. Kirilovicha.

GAKK 1845-1-78. Materialy perepisi 1926–27g. v raionakh pripoliarnogo Severa. Pokhoziaistvennye kartochki.

GAKK 1845-1-78: 91–92v. Pokhoziaistvennaia kartochka. Naselennyi punkt ust´e reki Khomolko.

GAKK 2275-1-13 Spisok khoziaistv kochevikh sovetov po sostoianiiu na 1926–1936.

GAKK 2275-1-227. Ocherk korennogo naselseniaia Ilimpeiskogo raiona.

State Archive of Murmansk Province // Gosudarstvennyi Arkhiv Murmanskoi Oblasti [GAMO]

GAMO 536-1-74: 8–17. Instruktsiia po proizvodstvu sploshnogo obsledovaniia olenevodcheskikh i bezolennykh kochevykh khoziaistv v Izhmo-Pecherskom uezde Avtonomnoi Komi Oblasti.

GAMO 536-1-96: 1a–1d. Pokhoziaistvennaia kartochka. Naselennyi punkt Bol´shaia Ura.

GAMO 536-1-98: 7–8v. Pokhoziaistvennaia kartochka. Naselennyi punkt Medvezhii ostrov.

GAMO 536-1-98: 9–10v. Pokhoziaistvennaia kartochka. Naselennyi punkt Zelentsy.

GAMO 536-1-99: 3–4v. Pokhoziaistvennaia kartochka. Naselennyi punkt Bol´shaia Volokovaia izba.

State Archive of the Nenets Autonomous District // Gosudarstvennyi Arkhiv Nenetskogo Autonomnogo Okruga Arkhangel´skoi Oblasti [GANAO]

GANAO 5-1-3: 18–41. P.I. Barskii. Pripoliarnaia perepis´ 1926 goda.

GANAO 5-1-3: 42–49. Po Malozemel´skoi Tundre. Nekotorye zametki. 1927.

State Archive of the Russian Federation // Gosudarstvennyi Arkhiv Rossiiskoi Federatsii, Moskva [GARF]

GARF 3977-1-75: 5–11. Chumovaia kartochka.

GARF 3977-1-75: 12–12v. Protokol zasedaniia Kollegii Engubstatbiuro ot 4go sentiabria 1925g.

GARF 3977-1-75: 17–17v. Skhema obsledovaniia tuzemtsev Turukhanskogo Kraia Eniseiskoi gubernii [Rossiiskogo Krasnogo Kresta po Sibiri].

GARF 3977-1-87: 18–19v. Semeinaia Kartochka. 5-go vrachebnogo obsledovatel'skogo otriada Krasnogo Kresta RSFSR Upolnomochennoi po Sibiri.

GARF 3977-1-87: 34–35. Oprosnaia kartochka perepisi samoedskogo naseleniia Kaninskoi i Timanskoi tundr 1925 goda.

GARF 3977-1-87: 36–37. Oprosnaia kartochka perepisi Samoedskogo naseleniia Bol'she-Zemel'skoi i Malo–Zemel'skoi tundr 1924 goda.

GARF 3977-1-87: 38–39. Perepesnoi list dlia prozhivaiushchikh v tak nazyvaemoi 'mertvoi zone' (na ostrovakh Severnogo Ledovitogo Okeana i kochenvnikov v tundrakh) v predelakh Arkhangel'skoi gubernii [Vserossiiskoi perepisi naseleniia 1920 goda].

GARF 3977-1-153: 24–25. Zamechaniia k chumovoi kartochke, predlozhennoi Okrstatbiuro dlia proizvodstva perepisi v Turukhanskom Krae v 1926 godu.

GARF 3977-1-214: 61–91. Skhema obsledovaniia tuzemtsev Turukhanskogo kraia Eniseiskoi Gubernii.

GARF 3977-1-355: 31–41. Doklad upolnomochennogo SKSO po perepisi K.M. Nagaeva v Komitet Severa – Osnovnye polozheniia i plan razrabotki materialov Pripoliarnoi Perepisi v Turukhanskom i drugikh okrugakh Sibiri.

State Archive of Sverdlovsk Province // Gosudarstvennyi Arkhiv Sverdlovskoi Oblasti [GASO]

GASO 677-1-49: 169–171. Obshchie zamechaniia po povodu materialov perepisi.

GASO 1812-2-181.01: 1–2. Protokol zasedaniia po podgotovke k Vsesoiuznoi perepisi 1926 goda na Tobol'skom Severe. V.S. Nemchinov, 1925.

GASO 1812-2-181.01: 3–5. Protokol soveshchaniia o provedenii Vserossiiskoi perepisi na Tobol'skom Severe. Vlagovolin, 1925.

GASO 1812-2-181.01: 30–30v. Rody lesnykh samoedov v basseine reki Pura.

GASO 1812-2-181.01: 35–39. Protokol soveshchaniia po voprosu o provedenii Vsesoiuznoi perepisi na Tobol'skom Severe. Noiabr' 1925 goda.

GASO 1812-2-181.01: 44–48. Protokol soveshchaniia s predstaviteliami severnykh okrainnykh oblastei po voprosu ob organizatsii perepisei.

GASO 1812-2-181.01: 105–107. Protokol zasedaniia komissii po rassmotreniiu pokhoziaistvennoi kartochki. P.F. Nevolin, 1926.

GASO 1812-2-181.01: 210–210v. Doklad otvetstvennogo rukovoditelia perepisi Severa L. R. Shul'tsa v Ural'skoe Oblastnoe Statisticheskoe Upravlenie.

GASO 1812-2-181.01: 131–136. Organizatsionnyi plan perepisi Priobskogo severa, Ural'skoi oblasti.

GASO 1812-2-181.04: 1–13v. Otchet o provedenii perepisi pripoliarnykh raionov. L. R. Shul'ts, 1927.

GASO 1812-2-181.04: 15. Predvaritel'nye raboty po provedeniiu perepisi. L. R. Shul'ts. 1927.

GASO 1812-2-183. Kratkie opisaniia Samarovskogo i Kondinskogo raionov. Sostavleny po okonchanii Vsesoiuznoi perepisi 1926–27gg.

GASO 1812-2-184: 85–89. Tablitsa poselennogo podscheta (dannye dlia Obdorskogo raiona Tobol'skogo orkuga).

GASO 1812-2-187. Uralgostorg. Berezovskoe agentstvo i faktoriia berezovskogo raiona.

GASO 1812-2-187.15: 1–17. Faktornyi blank iz Obdorskoi faktorii.

GASO 1812-2-187.16: 1–17v. Faktornyi blank iz Muzhevskoi faktorii.

GASO 1812-2-187.19: 1–15. Faktornyi blank iz Khenskoi faktorii.

GASO 1812-2-187.20: 1–16. Faktornyi blank iz Norenskogo torgovogo punkta.
GASO 1812-2-188. Ob´trest. Berezovskoe agentstvo i faktoriia berezovskogo raiona.
GASO 1812-2-188.04: 1–23. Faktornyi blank iz Tsentral´noi Zimovki sela Khal´med Seda.
GASO 1812-2-188.05: 1–16. Faktornyi blank iz Shchuch'e-Rechenskoi faktorii.
GASO 1812-2-188.06: 1–16. Faktornyi blank iz Iamburgskoi faktorii.
GASO 1812-2-188.07: 1–17. Faktornyi blank iz Purovskoi faktorii.
GASO 1812-2-188.08: 1–18. Faktornyi blank iz Norenskoi faktorii.
GASO 1812-2-188.09: 1–19. Faktornyi blank iz Nydinskoi faktorii.
GASO 1812-2-188.10: 1–17. Faktornyi blank iz Khadyttinskoi faktorii.
GASO 1812-2-188.11: 1–17v. Faktornyi blank iz Kushevatskoi faktorii.
GASO 1812-2-188.12: 1–17v. Faktornyi blank iz Muzhevskoi faktorii.
GASO 1812-2-190.18: 1–24. Blank registratsii faktorii obdorskogo obshchestva potrebitelei 'Pripoliarnyi krai'.
GASO 1812-2-190.20: 1–25. Blank registratsii faktorii muzhevskogo obshchestva potrebitelei 'Olen´'.
GASO 1812-2-191: Biudzhetnoe obsledovanie Tobol´skogo severa.
GASO 1812-2-191: 2–6v. Instruktsiia po biudzhetnomu obsledovaniiu Tobol´skogo severa.
GASO 1812-2-191: 21–75v. Blanki biudzhetnykh opisanii Obdorskogo raiona.
GASO 1812-2-206.09´: 135–151. Perepis´ 1926–27gg. Poselennyi blank. Tobol´skii okrug, naselennyi punkt Kaiukovy *iurt*.
GASO 1812-2-214: 273–384. Perepis´ 1926–27gg. Poselennye blanki. Obdorskii raion, naselennye punkty: Karvozh, Pokhronkovskie, Russoimov, Tetliarskie, Mashpanskii, Azov and Terlemkinskie.
GASO 1812-2-216: 65–80. Perepis´ 1926–27gg. Poselennyi blank. Obdorskii raion, naselennyi punkt Sor-papavt.
GASO 1812-2-216: 145–160. Perepis´ 1926–27gg. Poselennyi blank. Obdorskii raion, naselennyi punkt Iugan-Gort.
GASO 1812-2-216: 209–224. Perepis´ 1926–27gg. Poselennyi blank. Obdorskii raion, naselennyi punkt Uit-kort.
GASO 2757-1-786. Manuscript. Novosilov.
GASO Kollektsiia Surina: 145 (101). Samoedskii poselok iz mnozhestva chumov okolo poselka Khe v Obskoi gube.
GASO Kollektsiia Surina: 785 (048). Sem´ia samoedov.
GASO Kollektsiia Surina: 787 (050). Ostiatskoe selo Polnovat.

State Archive of Social-Political History, Tiumen´ Province // Gosudarstvennyi Arkhiv Sotsial´no-Politicheskoi Istorii Tiumenskoi Oblasti [GASPITO]

GASPITO 23-1-258. Spravki ob ekonomicheskom sostoianii Iamalo-Nenetskogo okruga Obsko-Irtyshskoi oblasti, a takzhe raionov Iamalo-Nenetskogo okruga za 1934 god.

State Institution 'Iamalo-Nenets district museum and exhibition complex named after I.S. Shemanovskii' // Gosudarstvennoe Uchrezhdenie 'Iamalo-Nenetskii okruzhnoi muzeino-vystavochnyi kompleks imeni Shemanovskogo' [GU IaNOMVK]

[bez fonda] Poselennye itogi, Obdorskii sel´sovet, 1926–27. Dannye Vsesoiuznoi perepisi 1926–1927 gg. po Obdorskomu raionu, poluostrov Iamal. Svodnye poselennye itogi Pripoliarnoi perepisi.

State Institution of Tiumen' Oblast 'State Archive in the City of Tobol'sk' // Gosudarstvennoe Uchrezhdenie Tiumenskoi Oblasti 'Gosudarstvennyi Arkhiv v gorode Tobol'ske' [GUTOGAT]

GUTOGAT 690-1-36: 8–11, 35–38, 60–64, 70–73, 74–77. Postanovleniia, instruktsii, vedomosti o razvitii seti gosudarstvennykh khlebozapasnykh magazinov na krainem severe.

GUTOGAT 690-1-49. Pokhoziaistvennye blanki Obdorskogo raiona Tobol'skogo okruga.

GUTOGAT 690-1-49: 10–14. Pokhoziaistvennyi blank roda Iakhtin (samoedin).

GUTOGAT 690-1-49: 15–19. Pokhoziaistvennyi blank roda Solinder (osamoedivsh. ostiaki).

GUTOGAT 690-1-49: 76–80. Pokhoziaistvennyi blank roda Nerka-khy (Vyl poslinskikh iurt).

GUTOGAT 690-1-49: 81–84. Pokhoziaistvennyi blank roda Nerka-khy (ostiatskoe).

GUTOGAT 690-1-49: 85–88. Pokhoziaistvennyi blank roda Nerko-khy (ostiatskoe).

GUTOGAT 690-1-54. Pokhoziaistvennye blanki Obdorskogo sel'soveta po vershine reki Se-Iaga.

GUTOGAT 695-1-78: 28–96. Protokol zasedaniia Ural'skogo komiteta Severa ot 26 marta 1927 goda.

GUTOGAT 695-1-191: 5–6v. Vsesoiuznaia perepis' naseleniia 1926 goda. Nastavlenie o tom, kak pisat' otvety na voprosy lichnogo listka.

National Archive of the Komi Republic // Natsional'nyi Arkhiv Respubliki Komi [NARK]

NARK 140-2-198: 1–18. Instruktsiia dlia registratorov pri proizvodstve imi perepisei tundrovogo khoziaistva.

NARK 140-2-200. Poselennye blanki perepisi 1926–27 goda v raionakh Pripoliarnogo severa.

NARK 140-2-201-211. Pokhoziaistvennye kartochki perepisi 1926–27 goda v raionakh Pripoliarnogo severa.

NARK 140-2-202: 41–42. Pokhoziaistvennaia kartochka. Domokhoziain Rochev Mikhail Sergeevich.

NARK 140-2-203: 85–100. Poselennyi blank. Naselennyi punkt selo Petrun'.

NARK 140-2-204: 195–196. Pokhoziaistvennaia kartochka. Naselennyi punkt Otvar.

NARK 140-2-209: 51–52. Pokhoziaistvennaia kartochka. Naselennyi punkt Lar' Vaigach.

NARK 140-2-210: 006–007. Pokhoziaistvennaia kartochka. Naselennyi punkt Sigovoe ozero.

NARK 140-2-210: 058–059. Pokhoziaistvennaia kartochka. Naselennyi punkt Bol'shaia Our'ia.

NARK 140-2-211: 119–120. Pokhoziaistvennaia kartochka. Naselennyi punkt Mokhcha.

NARK 140-2-211: 139–140. Pokhoziaistvennaia kartochka. Naselennyi punkt Bakurinskoe.

NARK 140-2-212. Svedeniia o mestakh i marshrutakh kochevok kochevogo naseleniia Bol'shezemel'skoi tundry (po materialam Pripoliarnoi perepisi 1926–27 goda).

NARK 1341-1-11: 62–74. O polozhenii v Bol'shezemel'skoi tundre.

National Archive of the Sakha Republic // Natsional'nyi Arkhiv Respubliki Sakha (Iakutiia) [NARS]

NARS 70-1-789: 305–321v. Poselennyi blank. Naselennyi punkt Kamen'.

NARS 70-1-789: 356–372v. Poselennyi blank. Naselennyi punkt Kamen´.
NARS 70-1-943. Kartochki brachnykh par Krasnoiarskoi volosti
NARS 70-1-1004-1005. Spisok khoziaistv (domokhoziaev) Krasnoiarskoi volosti. Perepis´ 1926–27gg.
NARS 70-1-1004: 26–27v. Pokhoziaistvennaia kartochka. Naselennyi punkt balagan Poibala.
NARS 70-1-1004: 30. Spisok khoziaistv. Naselennyi punkt chum Maimaki.
NARS 70-1-1005: 10–11v. Pokhoziaistvennaia kartochka. Naselennyi punkt balagan Davyda.
NARS 70-1-1005: 17. Spisok khoziaistv. Naselennyi punkt balagan N. Tasbai.
NARS 70-1-1005: 18, 25. Pokhoziaistvennaia kartochka. Naselennyi punkt balagan Nikolai Tasbai
NARS 70-1-1024: 6–11v. Sanitarnye kartochki naseleniia Krasnoiarskoi volosti. Perepis´ 1926-27gg.
NARS 70-1-3355. Pokhoziaistvennye kartochki individual´nykh khoziaistv po perepisi 1926–27gg. v raionakh Pripoliarnogo severa IaASSR.

Russian State Archive of Economics // Rossiiskii Gosudarstvennyi Arkhiv Ekonomiki [RGAE]

RGAE 1562-336-39: 9–11. Protokol soveshchaniia s predstaviteliami severnykh okrainnykh oblastei po voprosu ob organizatsii perepisi ot 4 dekabria 1925 goda.
RGAE 1562-336-39: 24–24v. Pis´mo ot Soveta Truda i Oborony Gosudarstvennoi Planovoi Komissii v Sovet Narodnykh Komissarov ot 8 marta 1926 goda.
RGAE 1562-336-39: 26–27. Pis´mo ot Zamestitelia Uprvaliaiushchego Tsentral´nym Statisticheskim Upravleniem M. Krasil´nikova v Komitet Sodeistviia narodnostiam Severnykh Okrain pri Prezidiume VTsIKa ot 7 marta 1926 goda.
RGAE 1562-336-205: 25–34. Materialy k slovariu natsional´nostei po perepisi 1939 g.

Bibliography

Abe, Yoshiko. 2005. 'Hunting and Butchery Patterns of the Evenki in Northern Trans-baikalia'. Unpublished PhD disseration, Stony Brook University.

Abramov, Vitalii F., and S. A. Zhivozdrova. 1996. 'Zemskaia statistika – natsional´noe dostoianie'. *Sotsiologicheskie issledovania*, no. 2: 89–100.

AGIK [Arkhangel´skii Gubernskii Ispolnite´nyi komitet]. 1924. *Tundry Arkhangel´skoi gubernii i avtonomnoi respubliki Komi (Zyrian)*. Arkhangel´sk: Tsentral´naia tipografiia.

AGPK [Arkhangel´skaia gubernskaia perepisnaia komissiia]. 1896. 'Protokol zasedaniia Arkhangel´skoi gubernskoi perepisnoi komissii 12 sentiabria 1896 g'. *Arkhangel´skie gubernskie vedomosti*, no. 76: 2–4.

AGSO [Arkhangel´skii Gubernskii Statisticheskii Otdel]. 1927. *Predvaritel´nye itogi Vsesoiuznoi perepisi 1926 g. v Arkhangel´skoi gubernii sprilozheniem territorial´nylkh itogov Pripoliarnoi perepisi 1926 goda*. Arkhangel´sk, Glavnaia tipografiia T-va Prizyv.

———. 1929. *Statisticheskii sbornik po Arkhangel´skoi gubernii za 1927 god*. Arkhangel´sk: Izdanie Arkhgubstatotdela.

Alymov, Vasilii Kondrat´evich. 1928a. 'Perepis´ naseleniia i khoziaistv na Kol´skom poluostrove'. *Chelovek*, no. 1: 97–98.

———. 1928b. 'Poslednie fil´many'. *Chelovek*, nos. 2–4: 224–26.

———. 1930. 'Rozhdaemost´ i smertnost´ loparei Kol´skogo poluostrova'. *Kol´skii sbornik: Trudy antropologo-etnograficheskogo otriada Kol´skoi ekspeditsii*, ed. D. Zolotarev. Leningrad: Izd-vo Akademii Nauk.

Ames, Kenneth M. 2004. 'Supposing Hunter-Gatherer Variability'. *American Antiquity* 69, no. 2: 364–74.

Anderson, Benedict. 1991. *Imagined Communities: Reflections on the Origin and Spread of Nationalism*, rev. ed. London: Verso.

Anderson, David Dzh., ed. 2005. *Turukhanskaia ekspeditsiia Pripoliarnoi perepisi: etnografiia i demografiia malochislennykh narodov Severa*. Krasnoiarsk: Polikor.

Anderson, David G. 2000. *Identity and Ecology in Arctic Siberia: The Number One Reindeer Brigade*. Oxford: Oxford University Press.

———. 2006. 'The Turukhansk Polar Census Expedition of 1926–1927 at the Crossroads of Two Scientific Traditions'. *Sibirica* 5, no. 1: 14–61.

———. 2007. 'Mobile Architecture and Social Life: The Case of the Conical Skin Lodge in the Putoran Plateau Region'. In *Les civilisations du renne d'hier et d'aujourd'hui. Approches ethnohistoriques, archéologiques et anthropologiques*, eds. S. Beyries and V. Vaté. Antibes: Éditions APDCA.

———. 2008. The Soviet Polar Census of 1926–27: Photo Album, Database, and Digitised Material. www.abdn.ac.uk/polarcensus.

———. 2011. 'The Mystery of the Magnate Reindeer Herders'. In *Indigenous Peoples and Demography: The Complex Relation between Identity and Statistics*, eds. P. Axelsson and P. Skold. Oxford: Berghahn Books.

Appadurai, Arjun. 1993. 'Number in the Colonial Imagination'. In *Orientalism and the Post-Colonial Predicament*, eds. C. Breckenridge and P. van der Veer. Philadelphia: University of Pennsylvania Press.

Argounova-Low, Tatiana. 2005. 'Khoziaistvennye i dukhovnye aspekty zhiznedeiatel'nosti esseiskikh iakutov'. In *Turukhanskaia ekspeditsiia Pripoliarnoi perepisi: etnografiia i demografiia malochislennykh narodov Severa*, ed. D. Anderson. Krasnoiarsk: Polikor.

Aronsson, Kjell-Åke. 1991. *Forest Reindeer Herding A.D. 1–1800: An Archaeological and Palaeoecological Study in Northern Sweden*. Archaeology and Environment 10. Umeå: University of Umeå, Department of Archaeology.

———. 1994. 'Pollen Evidence of Saami Settlement and Reindeer Herding in the Boreal Forests of Northernmost Sweden - An Example of Modern Pollen Rain Studies as an Aid in the Interpretation of Marginal Human Interference from Fossil Pollen Data'. *Review of Palaeobotany and Palynology* 82: 37–45.

Babushkin, Aleksandr I. 1930. *Bol'shezemel'skaia tundra*. Syktyvkar: Izdanie Komioblstata.

Bakhlykov, Petr S. 1996. *Iuganskie khanty: istoriia, byt, kul'tura*. Tiumen: Softdizain.

Bakhrushin, Sergei V. 1922. 'Istoricheskii ocherk zaseleniia Sibiri do poloviny 19 veka'. In *Ocherki po istorii kolonizatsii Severa i Sibiri*. Petrograd: Tipografiia Komissariata Zemledeliia.

———. 1955. 'Ostiatskie i vogul'skie kniazhestva v XVI-XVII vv'. In *S. V. Bakhrushin Nauchnye trudy*, eds. A. A. Zimin et al. Vol. 3, part II. Moscow: Izdatel'stvo Akademii Nauk SSSR.

Balée, William. 2006. 'The Research Program of Historical Ecology'. *Annual Review of Anthropology*, no. 35: 75–98.

Basso, Keith. 1996. *Wisdom Sits in Places: Landscape and Language Among the Western Apache*. Albuquerque: University of New Mexico Press.

Beliavskii, Frants M. 1833. *Poezdka k ledovitomu moriu*. Moscow: Tipografiia Lazarevykh Instituta Vostochnykh Iazykov.

Berg, L. 1927. 'Istoriia Geograficheskogo Oznakomleniia s Iakutskim Kraem'. In *Iakutiia*, ed. P. V. Vittenburg. Leningrad: Izdatel'stvo Akademii Nauk SSSR.

Bergman, Ingela et al. 2004. 'The Use of Plants as Regular Food in Ancient Subarctic Economies: a Case Study Based on Sami Use of Scots Pine Inner Bark'. *Arctic Anthropology* 41, no. 1: 1–13.

Bernard, Harvey Russell. 2006. *Research Methods in Anthropology: Qualitative and Quantitative Approaches*. Oxford: AltaMira Press.

Bernshtam, Tatiana A. 1978. *Pomory. Formirovanie gruppy i sistemy khoziaistva*. Leningrad: Nauka.

Bogoraz-Tan, Vladimir G. 1932. 'Severnoe olenevodstvo po dannym khoziaistvennoi perepisi 1926-1927 gg'. *Sovetskaia etnografiia*, no. 4: 26–62.

Bogoraz-Tan, Vladimir G., and Lev Ia. Shternberg. 1925. 'K voprosu o priroste severo-sibirskikh tuzemnykh plemen'. *Severnaia aziia*, no. 4: 27–31.

Borgerhoff Mulder, Monique, and Peter Coppolillo. 2005. *Conservation: Linking Ecology, Economics, and Culture*. Princeton, NJ: Princeton University Press.

Borisov, Aleksander A. 1906. *U samoedov. Ot Pinegi do Karskogo moria*. Sankt-Peterburg: Izdanie A.F. Devriena.

Borisov, Vladimir A. 1987. 'Vmesto zakliucheniia'. In *Vosproizvodstvo naseleniia i demograficheskaia politika v SSSR*, ed. L. L. Rybakovskii. Moskva: Nauka.

Broch, Igvild, and Ernst H. Jahr. 1981. *Russenorsk: et pidginsprek i Norge*. Oslo: Novus.
Brodnev, Mikhail M. n.d. [c.1950] Ot rodovogo stroia k sotsializmu. Unpublished manuscript, Salekhard.
Bulyzhnikov [no initials provided]. 1926. 'Khoziaistvo Bol'shezemel'skoi tundry'. *Komimu*, no. 5: 6–7.
Bunakov, Evgenii V. 1936. *Nenetskii natsional'nyi okrug severnogo kraia*. Trudy poliarnoi komissii vyp. 29. Moskva i Leningrad: Izd-vo Akademii Nauk SSSR.
Cadiot, Juliette. 2000. 'Organiser la diversité: la fixation des catégories nationales dans l'Empire de Russie et en URSS (1897–1939)'. *Revue D'Études Comparatives Est-Ouest* 31, no. 3: 127–49.
———. 2004. 'Le recensement de 1987: Les limites du contrôle impérial et la représentation des nationalités'. *Cahiers du Monde russe* 45, nos. 3–4: 441–64.
———. 2005. 'Searching for Nationality: Statistics and National Categories at the End of Russian Empire (1897-1917)'. *Russian Review* 64 (July): 440–55.
Carniero, Robert. 1988. 'The Circumscription Theory: Challenge and Response'. *American Behavioral Scientist* 31, no. 4: 497–511.
Carrère d'Encausse, Hélène 1992. *The Great Challenge: Nationalities and the Bolshevik State, 1917–1930*. New York: Holmes & Meier.
Castrén, Matthias Alexander. 1853–1858. *Castren's Nordische Reisen und Forschugen*. Edited by A. Schaefner. 5 vols. St. Petersburg: Auftrage der kaiserlichen Akademie der Wissenschaften.
Chagnon, Napoleon A. 1997. *Yanomamö*, 5th ed. Fort Worth, TX: Harcourt Brace College Publishers.
Chaianov, Aleksander. 1925. *Kratkii kurs kooperatsii*. Moskva: Kooperativnoe izdatel'stvo.
Chernetsov, Valerii N. 1930. 'Natal'ia Aleksandrovna Kotovshchikova'. *Sovetskii Sever*, no. 1: 165–66.
Chirkova, Anna F. 1967. 'Pesets. Biologiia. Praktichsekoe znachenie' In *Mlekopitaiushchie Sovetskogo Soiuza*. T. 2, ch. 1., eds. V.G. Geptner and N.P. Naumov. Moskva: izdatel'stvo Vysshaia shkola, 208–65.
Cohn, Bernard. 1987. 'The Census, Social Structure and Objectification in South Asia'. In *An Anthropologist among Historians*, ed. Bernard Cohn. Dehli: Oxford University Press.
Curtis, Bruce. 2001. *The Politics of Population: State Formation, Statistics and The Census Of Canada, 1840–1875*. Toronto: University of Toronto Press.
Darrow, David W. 2001. 'From Commune to Household: Statistics and the Social Construction of Chaianov's Theory of Peasant Economy'. *Comparative Studies in Society and History* 43, no. 4: 788–818.
———. 2002. 'Census as a Technology of Empire'. *Ab Imperio*, no. 4: 145–76.
Dolgikh, Boris O. 1950. 'K voprosu o naselenii basseina Oleneka i verkhov'ev Anabary'. *Sovetskaia etnografiia*, no. 4: 169–73.
———. 1960. *Rodovoi i plemennoi sostav narodov Sibiri v XVII veke*. Trudy Instituta Etnografii, T. 55. Moskva: Nauka.
———. 1962: 'The Origins of the Nganasans: Preliminary Remarks.' In *Studies in Siberian Ethnogenesis*, ed. H. N. Michael. Toronto: Arctic Institute of North America/University of Toronto Press.
———. 1963: 'Proiskhozhdenie dolgan'. In *Sibirskii etnograficheskii sbornik V*, ed. B. O. Dolgikh. Trudy Instituta Etnografii im. N. N. Miklukho-Maklaia, Novaia seriia 84. Moscow: Izdatel'stvo Akademii Nauk SSSR.
———. 1970. *Ocherki po etnicheskoi istorii nentsev i entsev*. Moskva: Nauka.
Dopp, Mary. 1919. 'Geographical Influences in the Development of Wisconsin'. *Bulletin of the American Geographical Society* 45, no. 7: 490–99.

Douglas, Mary. 1972. 'Deciphering a Meal'. *Daedalus (Myth, Symbol, and Culture)*. Winter: 61–81.

Dunin-Gorkavich, Aleksandr A. 1904. *Tobol'skii Sever*. St. Petersburg: Tip V. Kirshbauma.

———. 1909. *Geograficheskoe opisanie nizov'ev r. Obi i usloviia sudokhodstva*. St. Petersburg: Tipografiia Morskogo Ministerstva.

———. 1932. 'Russko-ostiatsko-samoedskii prakticheskii slovar' naibolee upotrebitel'nykh slov'. In *Samojedische Worterverzeichnisse*, ed. K. Donner. Helsinki: Suomalais-ugrilainen seura

———. 1995. *Tobol'skii Sever. T. 1*. Moskva: Liberiia.

———. 1996. *Tobol'skii Sever. T. 2*. Moskva: Liberiia.

DVSU [Dal'nevostochnoe Statupravlenie]. 1929a. *Itogi perepisi severnykh okrain Dal'ne-Vostochnogo kraia (1926–27 gg.) s prilozheniem karty severnykh okrain DVK*. Blagoveshchensk: Dal'nevostochnii Kraievoi statisticheskii otdel.

———. 1929b. *Spisok naselennykh mest Dal'nevostochnogo kraia; po materialam Vsesoiuznoi perepisi naseleniia 17 dekabria 1926 goda i Pripoliarnoi perepisi 1926–27 goda*. DVSU: Khabarovsk.

Edemskii, Mikhail B. 1930. 'Samoedy i olenevodstvo v Kuloiskom krae Arkhangel'skogo okruga (Iz dorozhnykh zametok 1927g.)'. *Izvestiia gosudarstvennogo russkogo geograficheskogo obshchestva*. Tom LXII, vyp. I.

Ehrenfried, Aline. 2004. 'Meeting Ancestors In Population Statistics: The Soviet Polar Census 1926–27 And The Ethnographical Expedition of the Krasnoyarsk Museum Of Regional Studies 2004 – Report on an Ongoing Research'. In *Etnosy Sibiri. Proshloe, nastoiashchee. budushchee: Materialy mezhdunarodnoi nauchno-prakticheskoi konferentsii*, ed. N. P. Makarov. Krasnoiarsk: Polikor.

Eidlitz, Kerstin. 1969. *Food and Emergency Food in the Circumpolar Area*. Uppsala: Almqvist and Wiksells Boktryckert AB.

Emmons, Terence, and Wayne S. Vucinich. 1982. *The Zemstvo in Russia: An Experiment in Local Self-Government*. Cambridge: Cambridge University Press.

Engelen, Theo, and Arthur P. Wolf, ed. 2005. *Marriage and the Family in Eurasia: Perspectives on the Hajnal Hypothesis*. Amsterdam: Aksant.

Evladov, Vladimir P. 1930. *V tundrakh Iamala. (Etnograficheskie ocherki)*. Sverdlovsk: Gos. izd-vo Ural'skoe oblastnoe otdelenie.

———. 1992. *Po tundram Iamala k Belomu ostrovu. Ekspeditsiia na Krainii Sever poluostrova Iamal v 1928–1929 gg.* Tiumen': Institut Problem Osvoeniia Severa SO RAN.

Fedorova, Elena G. 2000. *Rybolovy i okhotniki basseina Obi: problemy formirovaniia kul'tury khantov i mansi*. St. Petersburg: Evropeiskii Dom.

Fedorova, Natal'ia V. 2000. 'Olen', sobaka, kulaiskii fenomen i legenda o Sikhirtia'. In *Drevnosti Iamala*, vyp 1, ed. A. V. Golovnev. Ekaterinburg-Salekhard: UrO RAN.

Freeze, Gregory L. 1986. 'The *Soslovie* (Estate) Paradigm and Russian Social History'. *American Historical Review* 91 (February): 11–36.

Gaponenko, L. S., and Kabuzan, V. M. 1961. 'Materialy sel'skokhoziaistvennykh perepisei 1916–17 gg. kak istochnik opredeleniia chislennosti naseleniia Rossii nakanune Oktiabr'skoi revoliutsii'. *Istoriia SSSR* 6: 97–115.

Geidenreikh, Lev. 1930. *Kaninskaia tundra*. Arkhangel'sk: GIZ.

Gibel'man, M. I. 1925. 'O tungusakh Olekminskogo okruga'. *Izvestiia Gosudarstvennogo Russkogo Geograficheskogo Obshchestva* tom. 62, vyp. 2: 33–51.

Gjessing, Gutorm. 1960. 'Circumpolar Social Systems'. *Acta Arctica* XII: 75–81.

Glavatskaia, Elena M. 2002. 'Khanty v sostave Russkogo gosudarstva'. In *Ocherki istorii traditsionnogo zemlepol'zovaniia Khantov (Materialy k Atlasu)*. 2nd ed. ed. E. Viget. Ekaterinburg: Tezis.

———. 2005a. 'Khristianskoe osvoenie Obdorskogo kraia'. In *Russkoe osvoenie Iamala do nachala XX v.*, ed. I. V. Poberezhnikov. Salekhard-Ekaterinburg: Bank kul'turnoi informatsii.

———. 2005b. 'Po sledam zabytoi ekspeditsii: pripoliarnaia perepis' v Severo-Zapadnoi Sibiri'. *Rodina*, no. 12: 16–19.

———. 2006. 'Ural'skaia ekspeditsiia Pripoliarnoi perepisi 1926–27 gg.: istoriia organizatsii'. *Ural'skii istoricheskii vestnik*, no. 13: 187–97.

———. 2007. 'Materialy Ural'skoi ekspeditsii Pripoliarnoi perepisi 1926-1927'. www.abdn.ac.uk/polarcensusdata (accessed 10 May 2008).

Glavatskaya, Elena M. 2004. 'Religious and Ethnic Revitalization among the Siberian Indigenous People: The Khanty Case'. In *Circumpolar Ethnicity and Identity*, eds. Takashi Irimoto and Takako Yamada. Senri Ethnological Studies, no. 66. Osaka, Japan: National Museum of Ethnology.

Gololobov, Evgenii Il'ich. 2004. 'Istochniki po istorii vzaimodeistviia prirody i cheloveka na Ob'-Irtyshkom severa (1923–1934).' In *Pis'mennye istochniki po istorii Zapadnoi Sibiri*, ed. E.I. Gololobov. Surgut: Surgutskii Gosudarstvennyi Pedagogicheskii Universitet.

Golovnev, Andrei V. 1993. *Istoricheskaia tipologiia khoziaistva narodov Severo-Zapadnoi Sibiri*. Novosibirsk: INU.

———. 1995. *Govoriashchie kul'tury: traditsii samodiitsev i ugrov*. Ekaterinburg: Uro RAN.

———. 2004. *Kochevniki tundry: nentsy i ikh fol'klor*. Ekaterinburg: Uro RAN.

Golovnev, Andrei V., and A. Iu. Konev. 1989. 'Obshchina u narodov Nizhnego Priob'ia vo vtoroi polovine XIX - nachale XX vv'. In *Obshchina i sem'ia v sibirskoi derevne XVIII-nachala XX vv*, ed. E. I. Solov'eva. Novosibirsk: Nauka.

Golubtsov, Nikolai A., comp. 1907. *Spisok naselennykh mest Arkhangel'skoi gubernii k 1905 godu*. Izdanie Arkhangel'skogo gubernskogo statisticheskogo komiteta.

Gorodkov, Boris N. 1924. *Zapadno-sibirskaia ekspeditsiia Akademii Nauk i Geograficheskogo Obshchestva*. Leningrad: Rossiiskaia gosudarstvennaia akademicheskaia tipographia.

Gray, Patty A. 2004. *The Predicament of Chukotka's Indigenous Movement Post-Soviet Activism in The Russian Far North*. Cambridge, NY: Cambridge University Press.

Gulevskii, Oleg. 2007. 'Pervootkryvateli rudnogo zolota'. *Oblastnaia gazeta* 84, no. 206. www.ogirk.ru/vp206/pervootkrivateli_rudnogo_zolota/view_3416.html (accessed 03 April 2008).

Gumilev, Lev N. 1993. *Etnosfera: istoriia liudei i istoriia prirody*. Moskva: Ekopros.

Gurvich, Il'ia Samoilovich. 1950. 'K voprosu ob etnicheskoi prinadlezhnosti naseleniia Severo-Zapada Iakutskoi ASSR'. *Sovetskaia etnografiia*, no. 4: 150–68.

———. 1952. 'Po povodu opredeleniia etnicheskoi prinadlezhnosti naseleniia basseinov rek Oleneka i Anabara', *Sovetskaia etnografiia*, no. 2: 73–85.

———. 1977. *Kul'tura severnykh iakutov-olenevodov*. Moscow: Nauka.

———. 1982. 'Severnye iakuty i dolgany'. In *Etnicheskaia istoriia narodov Severa*, ed. I. Gurvich. Moscow: Nauka.

Gurvich, Il'ia Samoilovich, ed. 1987. *Etnicheskoe razvitie narodnostei Severa v sovetskii period*. Moskva: Nauka.

Gurvich, Il'ia Samoilovich, and Boris Osipovich Dolgikh, eds. 1970. *Obshchestvennyi stroi u narodov Severnoi Sibiri XVII - nachalo XX vv*. Moskva: Nauka.

Habeck, Joachim Otto. 2005. 'Dimensions of Identity'. In *Rebuilding Identities. Pathways to reform in Post-Soviet Siberia*, ed. Erich Casten. Berlin: Dietrich Reimer Verlag.

Hacking, Ian. 1982. 'Biopower and the Avalanche of Printed Numbers'. *Humanities in Society*, no. 5: 279–95.

———. 1990. *The Taming of Chance*. Cambridge: Cambridge University Press.

Hansen, Lars I., and Bjørg Evjen. 2008. 'Kjært barn - mange navn: om forskjellige beteg-nelser på den samiske befolkningen i Nordland gjennom århundrene'. In *Nordlands kulturelle mangfold: etniske relasjoner i historisk perspektiv*, eds. B. Evjen and L. I. Hansen. Oslo: Pax.

Hardin, Garrett. 1968. 'Tragedy of the Commons'. *Science* (New Series) 162, no. 3859: 1243–1248.

Hern, Warren M. 1995. 'Micro-ethnodemographic techniques for field workers studying small groups'. In *The Comparative Analysis of Human Societies: Toward Common Standards for Data Collection and Reporting*, ed. E. F. Moran. Boulder, CO: L. Rienner Publishers.

Hirsch, Francine. 2005. *Empire of Nations: Ethnographic Knowledge and the Making of the Soviet Union*. London: Cornell University Press.

Iadrintsev, Nikolai M. 1892. *Sibir´ kak koloniia v geograficheskom, etnograficheskom i istoricheskom otnoshenii*. St. Petersburg: Izdanie I. M. Sibiriakova.

———. 2000. *Sochineniia. T.1. Sibir´ kak koloniia: Sovremennoe polozhenie Sibiri. Ee nuzhdy i potrebnosti. Ee proshloe i budushchee*. Tiumen´: Izd-vo Iu. Mandriki.

Iakobii, Arkadii I. 1891. Kaninskaia tundra. *Trudy Obshchestva estestvoznaniia pri Kazanskom universitete*. T. 23, Vyp. 1: 1–79.

———. 1893. *Ugasanie inorodcheskikh plemen Severa*. St. Petersburg: tipografiia doma prizrenia maloletnikh bednykh.

Iamskov, Anatolii N. 2005: 'Ekologicheski znachimye kul´turnye arkhetipy povedeniia cheloveka'. In *Etnoekologicheskie aspekty dukhovnoi kul´tury*, eds. V. I. Kozlov, A. N. Iamskov, and N. I. Grigulevich. Moskva: Izd. IEA RAN.

Ineshin, Evgenii et al. 2009. 'Late Quaternary Environments in Southern Siberia: Landscape Response to Climate Change and Human Activities in the Baikalo-Patom Upland'. Published Conference Abstract, Portland GSA Annual Meeting, 18–21 October.

INNOIK [Iamal´skogo (Nenetskogo) Natsional´nogo Okruzhkoma Ispolnitel´nogo komiteta]. 1935. *Otchet Iamal´skogo (Nenetskogo) Natsional´nogo Okruzhkoma Ispolnitel´nogo komiteta sovetov o rabote za 1931–1934 gg*. Salekhard: Izd-vo Oblispolkoma.

Iokhel´son, Vladimir I. 1896. 'Naselenie Iakutskoi oblasti'. *Pamiatnaia knizhka Iakutskoi Oblasti za 1895*. vyp. 1. Iakutsk: 109–51.

IRGO [Imperatorskoe Russkoe Geograficheskoe Obshchestvo]. 1858. *Etnograficheskii sbornik, izdavaemyi Imperatorskim Russkim Geograficheskim Obshchestvom. Vypusk IV*. St. Petersburg: Tipografiia Eduarda Pratsa.

Islavin, Vladimir A. 1847. *Samoedy v domashnem i obshchestvennom bytu*. St. Petersburg: Tipografiia Ministerstva gosudarstvennykh imushchestv.

Itkonen, Toivo I. 1958. *Koltan- ja kuolanlapin sanakirja. Wörterbuch des Kolta- und Kolala-pischen*. Lexica Societatis Fenno-Ugricae 15. Helsinki: Suomalais-ugrilainen seura.

Iurchenko, Aleksei 2005. 'Economic Adaptation by Colonists (mid 19th to early 20th century)'. In *In the North My Nest is Made: Studies in the History of the Murman Colonization 1860–1940*, eds. A. Iurchenko and Jens Petter Nielsen. St. Petersburg: European University at St. Peterburg Press.

[Iz Torgovoi]. 1911. 'Iz torgovoi i promyshlennoi zhizni'. *Izvestiia Arkhangel´skogo Ob-shchestva izucheniia Russkogo Severa*, no 1: 60–65.

Jentoft, Morten. 2001. *De som dro østover: Kola-nordmennenes historie*. Oslo: Gyldendal.

Jochelson, Vladimir. 1908. *The Koryak*. Memoirs of the American Museum of Natural History. Vol. X. Leiden: E.J. Brill Ltd Printers and Publishers.

Jochim, Michael. 1976. *Hunter-gatherer Subsistence and Settlement: A Predictive Model*. New York: Academic Press.

Jordan, Peter. 2003. *Material Culture and Sacred Landscape: The Anthropology of the Siberian Khanty.* New York: Rowman and Littlefield Inc.

Jordan, Peter and Andrei Filtchenko. 2005. 'Continuity and Change in Circumpolar Worldview'. In *Rebuilding Identities in Post-Soviet Siberia,* ed. E. Kasten. Berlin: Dietrich Reimer Verlag.

[K voprosu]. 1886. 'K voprosu o razvitii zemledeliia v Iakutskoi oblasti'. *Pamiatnaia knizhka Iakutskoi oblasti za 1895.* vyp. 1. Iakutsk: 1–167.

Karacharov, Konstantin G. 1999. 'Khoziaistvo naseleniia srednei Obi v period pozdnego srednevekov'ia'. In *Materialy II-go Sibirskogo simpoziuma kul'turnoe nasledie narodov Zapadnoi Sibiri: Obskie ugry,* ed. A. V. Golovnev. Tobol'sk-Omsk: Izd-vo OmGPU.

Karapetova, Irina A. 1999. 'Kollektsiia R.P. Mitusovoi po aganskim Khantam v sobranii REM'. In *Materialy II-go Sibirskogo simpoziuma "kul'turnoe nasledie narodov Zapadnoi Sibiri: obskie ugry,* ed. A. V. Golovnev. Tobol'sk-Omsk: Izd-vo OmGPU.

Kastren, Matias A.1999. *Laplandiia. Kareliia. Rossiia.* Tiumen': Izd-vo Iu. Mandriki.

Kertselli, Sergei V. 1910. Arkhangel'skie tundry. *Izvestiia Arkhangel'skogo Obshchestva izucheniia Russkogo Severa,* no. 23: 1–3.

Khariuchi, Galina P. 2001. *Traditsii i innovatsii v kul'ture nenetskogo etnosa.* Tomsk: Izd-vo Tomskogo universiteta.

Kharuzin, Nikolai. 1890. *Russkie Lopari: Ocherki proshlogo i sovremennogo byta.* Moscow: Tovarishchestvo skoropechatni A. A. Levenson.

Khlobystin, Leonid P. 2005. *Taymyr: The Archaeology of Northernmost Eurasia.* Washington, D.C.: Arctic Studies Center, National Museum of Natural History, Smithsonian Institution.

Khomich, Liudmila V. 1970. 'Sovremennye etnicheskie protsessy na severe evropeiskoi chasti SSSR i Zapadnoi Sibiri'. *Preobrazovaniia v khoziaistve i kul'ture i etnicheskie protsessy u narodov Severa,* I. S. Gurvich and B. O. Dolgikh. Moskva: Nauka.

———. 1976. 'Predstavleniia nentsev o prirode i cheloveke'. In *Priroda i chelovek v religioznykh predstavleniiakh narodov Sibiri i Severa (vtoraia polovina XIX - nachalo XX v.),* I. S. Vdovin. Leningrad: Nauka.

———. 1995. [1966.] *Nentsy.* St. Petersburg: Russkii dvor.

———. 2005. 'Semeinaia obriadnost'.' In *Narody zapadnoi Sibiri: Khanty, mansi, sel'kupy, nentsy, entsy, ngansany, kety,* eds. I.N. Genuev, V.I. Molodin, and Z.P. Sokolova. Moskva: Nauka.

Khrushchev, Sergei A. 1991. 'Ekologo-khoziaistvennaia ustoichivost' traditsionnykh otraslei pri promyshlennom osvoenii Severa. Raiony prozhivaniia malochislennykh narodov Severa'. *Geografiia i khoziaistvo,* no. 4: 32–49.

Kirikov, Sergei V. 1966. *Promyslovye zhivotnye, prirodnaia sreda i chelovek.* Moskva: Nauka.

Klokov, Konstantin, and Igor V. Semenov. 2007. Pripoliarnaia perepis' na Evropeiskom Severe: arkheografiia, metodologiia, interpretatsiia. International Conference Proceedings, 'Polevaia etnografiia–2006'. St. Petersburg, March.

Klokov, Konstantin, and John Ziker. 2010. *Pripoliarnaia perepis' 1926/27 na Evropeiskom Severe (Arkhangel'skaia guberniia i avtonomnaia oblast' Komi).* St. Petersburg: MPSS

Kodolov, Nikolai I. 2005. 'Uchastok IV: Dokumenty Nikolaia Ivanovicha Kodolova'. In *Turukhanskaia ekspeditsiia pripolarnoi perepisi: Etnografiia i demofrafiia malochislennykh narodov Severa,* ed. D. Anderson. Krasnoiarsk: Polikor.

Kol's, Roman E. 1930. *Reka Taz (Tasu-iam): Opisanie i poiasneniia k atlasu nizhnego techeniia reki Taza ot Khal'mer-sede do Sidorovskoi pristani ili zimov'ia V.V. Sedel'nikova.* Leningrad: Gosudarstvennoe russkoe geograficheskoe obshchestvo.

Konakov, Nikolai D. 1985. 'Etnicheskie stereotipy komi kak etnogeneticheskii istochnik'. *Trudy Instituta iazyka, literatury i istorii Komi filiala AN SSSR*, Vyp 36: 78–91.

———. 1991. Semeino-brachnye mezhetnicheskie stereotipy u severnykh komi. International Conference Proceedings, 'Problemy istoriko-kul'turnoi sredy Arktiki'. Syktyvkar, Russia, 16–18 1991.

Konakov, Nikolai D., and O. V. Kotov. 1991. *Etnoareal'nye gruppy komi. Formirovanie i sovremennoe etnokul'turnoe sostoianie.* Moskva: 'Nauka'.

Konev, Aleksei Iu. 1998. 'The State And The Peoples Of North Of Western Siberia from the 17th to the Beginning of 20th Centuries: Experience Of Legal Regulation And Land Relations'. International Conference Proceedings 'Indigenous Peoples. The Oil. The Law'. Khanty-Mansiisk, Russia, 23–25 March.

Kopylov, Dmitrii I., ed. 1994. *Sud'by narodov Ob'-Irtyshskogo Severa (Iz istorii natsional'nogosudarstvennogo stroitel'stva. 1822–1941 gg.). Sbornik dokumentov.* Tiumen': Upravlenie po delam arkhivov Administratsii Tiumenskoi oblasti, Gosudarstvennyi arkhiv Tiumenskoi oblasti, Tiumenskii oblastnoi tsentr dokumentatsii noveishei istorii.

KOSO [Komi oblastnoi statisticheskii otdel]. 1929. *Komi oblast': kratkii statisticheskii spravochnik.* Syktyvkar: Izdanie Komi obstatotdela.

Kostikov, Leonid V. 1930. 'Bogovy oleni v religioznykh verovaniiakh khasovo'. *Etnografiia,* nos. 1–2: 115–32.

Kotz, Samuel, and Eugene Seneta. 1990. 'Lenin as a Statistician: A Non-Soviet View'. *Journal of the Royal Statistical Society, Series A (Statistics in Society)* 153, no. 1: 73–94.

Kovalashchina, Elena. 2007. 'The Historical and Cultural Ideals of the Siberia *oblastnichestvo*'. *Sibirica* 6, no. 2: 87–119.

Koval'chenko, Ivan D. et al. 1988. *Sotsial'no-ekonomicheskii stroi krest'ianskogo khoziaistva Evropeiskoi Rossii v epokhu kapitalizma: istochniki i metody issledovaniia.* Moskva: MGU.

Kozlov, Victor I. 1969. *Dinamika chislennosti narodov. Metodologiia issledovaniia i osnovnye faktory.* Moskva: Nauka.

Krasil'nikov, Mitrofan Pavlovich. 1913. *Zemskie otsenki imushchestv v Ufimskoi gubernii.* Ufa: Ufimskoe gubernoe zemstvo.

———. 1926 . *Zadachi, programmy, organizitsatsionnyi plan proizvodstva i razrabotki materialov obshchesoiuznoi perepis' 1926 goda.* Moskva: tipografiia MKKH im Lavrova.

Kropotkin, Petr A. 1873. 'Otchet ob Olekminsko-Vitimskoi ekspeditsii'. *Zapiski Imperatorskogo Russkogo Geograficheskogo Obshchestva po obshchei geografii.* 3 (I-XI): 1–681.

Krupnik, Igor I. 1987. 'Demograficheskoe razvitie aziatskikh eskimosov v 1970-e gody (osnovnye tendentsii i ethnosotsial'nye usloviia)'. In *Regional'nye problemy sotsial'no-demograficheskogo razvitiia,* ed. V. V. Prokhorov. Moscow: Nauka.

———. 2000. 'Liudi v chumakh, tsifry na bumage. Russkie istochniki k demograficheskoi istorii Iamala, 1695–1992 gg'. *Drevnosti Iamala,* Vyp. 1: 122–51.

Kulemzin, Vladislav M., and Nadezhda. V. Lukina. 1992. *Znakom'tes': Khanty.* Novosibirsk: Nauka.

Kupriianova, Zinaida N. 1954. 'Terminologiia rodstva v ustnom narodnom tvorchestve nentsev'. In *Uchenye zapiski Leningradskogo gosudarstvennogo pedagogicheskogo instituta im. A.I. Gertsena* 101. Leningrad.

Kurilovich, Adam Petrovich. 1934. 'Gydanskii poluostrov i ego obitateli'. *Sovetskii Sever,* no. 1: 129–40.

Kurilovich, Adam Petrovich, and Nikolai Pavlovich Naumov. 1934. *Sovetskaia Tungusiia (Evenkiiskii natsional'nyi okrug Vostochno-Sibirskogo kraia).* Moskva: Gos. izd-vo standardizatsii i ratsionalizatsii.

Kuropiatnik, Marina. 2000. 'The Ter Sami According to the Russian Census of 1858: Ethno-Social Characteristics'. *Acta Borealia* 17, no. 2: 39–48.

Kytmanov, D. A. 1927. 'Tuzemtsy Turukhanskogo kraia'. *Sovetskii sever,* no. 2: 37–67.

———. 1930. 'Funktsional'nye nevrozy sredi tungusov Turukhanskogo kraia i ikh otnoshenie k shamanizmu'. *Sovetskii Sever,* nos. 7–8: 82–85.

Lar, Leonid A. 2003. *Kul'tovye pamiatniki Iamala. Khebidia ia.* Tiumen´: Izd-vo Instituta problem osvoeniia Severa SO RAN.

Lashuk, Lev P. 1972. *Formirovanie narodnosti komi.* Moskva: Nauka.

Laslett, Peter. 1983. *The World We Have Lost: Further Explored.* London: Routledge.

Lebedev, Feodor Nikolaevich, and A. A. Kolupaev 1929. *Smertnost' i prodolzhitel'nost' zhizni naseleniia Ural'skoi oblasti. Po dannym razrabotki Vsesoiuznoi perepisi 1926 g. i materialov estestvennogo dvizheniia naseleniia.* Sverdlovsk: Izdanie Ural'skogo Oblastnogo Statisticheskogo otdela.

Leinonen, Marja. 2008. 'The Filman Sami on the Kola Peninsula'. *Slavica Helsingiensia,* no. 32: 138–62.

Lepekhin, Ivan I. 1795. *Dnevnikovye zapisi puteshestviia doktora i Akademii Nauk ad"iutanta Ivana Lepekhina po raznym provintsiiam Rossiiskogo gosudarstva 1768 - 1769 gg.* t. 3, 4. St. Petersburg: Imperatorskoi Akademii Nauk.

Leshkov, Vladimir Grigor'evich. 1996. 'Istoriia starinnogo Lenskogo priiska'. In *Smirnovskii sbornik - 1996,* ed. V. I. Starostin. Moskva: RAEN. http://geo.web.ru/conf/CD_Smirnov/html_96/index.html (accessed 28 March 2008).

———. 1999. 'Macha - Taezhnoe selo na Lene'. In *Smirnovskii sbornik - 1999,* ed. V. I. Starostin. Moskva: fonda akademika Smirnova. http://geo.web.ru/conf/CD_Smirnov/html_99/index.html (accessed 28 March 2008).

Levi-Strauss, Claude. 1966. 'The Culinary Triangle'. *New Society,* no. 166: 937–40.

Lukina, Nadezhda V. 1985. *Formirovanie material'noi kultury Khantov.* Tomsk: Izdatel'stvo Tomskogo Universiteta.

Machinskii, Dmitrii A. 1986. 'Etno-sotsial'nye i etnokul'turnye protsessy v Severnoi Rusi'. In *Russkii Sever,* ed. D. A. Machinskii. Leningrad: Nauka.

Mainov, Ivan I. 1898. *Nekotorye dannye o tungusakh Iakutskogo kraia.* Iakutsk: tipolitografiia P.I.Marushina

———. 1912. *Russkie krest'iane i osedlye inorodtsy Iakutskoi oblasti.* St. Petersburg: tipografiia V.F. Kirshbauma.

———. 1927. 'Naselenie Iakutii'. In *Iakutiia sbornik statei,* ed. P. B. Vittenburg. Leningrad: Izd-vo Akademii Nauk.

Makarov, Nadezhda. 2005. 'A.P. Lekarenko v pripoliarnoi perepisi'. In *Turukhanskaia ekspeditsiia pripoliarnoi perepisi: etnografiia i demografiia malochislennykh narodov Severa,* ed. D. Anderson. Krasnoiarsk: Polikor.

Malysheva, M. P., and V. S. Poznanskii. 1998. 'Tragicheskoe polozhenie malykh narodov Sibiri v nachale 20-kh godov XX v'. *Gumanitarnye nauki v Sibiri,* no. 3: 107–8.

Martynova, Elena P. 1995. 'Obshchestvennoe ustroistvo v XVII-XIX vv'. In *Istoriia i kul'tura khantov,* ed. N. V. Lukina. Tomsk: Izdatel'stvo TGU.

———. 1998. *Ocherki istorii i kul'tury khantov.* Moscow: Russian Academy of Sciences Publishing House.

Matsak, Veronika. A. 2005. *Pechenga: opyt kraevedcheskoi entsiklopedii.* Murmansk: Dobrosmysl.

Medkov, Viktor M. 2002. *Demografiia.* Rostov-na-Donu: Feniks.

Melancon, Michael. 1994. 'The Ninth Circle: The Lena Goldfied Workers and the Massacre of 4 April 1912'. *Slavic Review* 53, no. 3: 766–95.

[Migratsiia pestsa]. 1927. 'Migratsiia pestsa'. *Severnoe khoziaistvo,* no. 1–2: 69.

Minenko, Nina A. 1975. *Severo-Zapadnaia Sibir' v XVIII-pervoi polovine XIX veka.* Novosibirsk: Nauka.

Mitusova, Raisa P. 1926. 'Aganskie ostiaki'. In *Ural. Tekhniko-ekonomicheskii sbornik, Vyp. 8. Ural'skii Sever. Chast' 1.* Sverdlovsk: Uralplan.

———. 1929a. 'God sredi lesnogo naroda'. *Vokrug sveta,* no. 9: 6–9.

———. 1929b. 'God sredi lesnogo naroda'. *Vokrug sveta,* no. 11: 10–13.

———. 1929c. 'God sredi lesnogo naroda'. *Vokrug sveta,* no. 12: 15–17.

———. 1929d. 'God sredi lesnogo naroda'. *Vokrug sveta,* no. 14: 12–15

———. 1929e. 'God sredi lesnogo naroda'. *Vokrug sveta,* no. 15: 6–8.

MOI [Murmanskii Okruzhnoi Ispolkom]. 1929. *Murmanskii okrug: statistiko-ekonomicheskoe opisanie.* Murmansk: izd-vo okrugispolkom.

Moring, Beatrice 1994. *Skärgårdsbor: hushåll, familj och demografi i finäöndsk kustbygd på 1600-, 1700-, och 1800-talen.* Helsingfors: Finska vetenskaps-societeten.

MOSO [Murmanskii orkuzhnoi statisticheskii otdel]. 1929. *Murmanskii okrug: statistiko-ekonomicheskoe opisanie.* Murmansk, izd-vo okrugispolkom.

MVD [Ministerstvo Vnutrinikh Del]. 1861. *Spiski naselennykh mest Rossiiskoi Imperii. Tom 1. Arkhangel'skaia guberniia po svedeniiam 1859 goda.* Sankt-Peterburg: Tipografiia MVD.

[Na s''ezde]. 1926. 'Na s''ezde promsoiuza'. *Severnoe khoziaistvo,* nos 2–3: 102–4.

Nielsen, Jens Petter. 2005. 'The Murman Coast and Russian Northern Policies ca 1855–1917'. In *In the North My Nest is Made: Studies in the History of the Murman Colonization 1860–1940,* eds. A. Iurchenko and J. P. Nielsen. St. Petersburg: European University at St. Petersburg Press.

Niemi, Einar. 1994. 'Den lange, lange sti over myrene og ind i skogene, hvem har trakket op den?' *Nordnorsk kulturhistorie,* vol. 2, eds. E. A. Drivenes, M. A. Hauan and H. A. Wold. Oslo: Gyldendal.

Nyyssönen, Jukka. 2005. 'The Finnish Presence on the Murman Coast – the Era of Petsamo 1920–1944'. In *In the North My Nest is Made: Studies in the History of the Murman Colonization 1860–1940,* eds. A. Iurchenko and Jens Petter Nielsen. St. Petersburg: European University at St. Petersburg Press.

Ostrovskikh, Petr E. 1904. 'Poezdka na ozero Essei'. *Izvestiia Krasnoiarskogo podotdela Vostochno-Sibirskogo otdela Imperatorskogo Russkogo Geograficheskogo Obshchestva,* no. 6: 21–33.

Palsson, Gisli. 1990. 'The Idea of Fish: Land and Sea in the Icelandic World-View'. In *Signifying Animals: Human Meaning in the Natural World,* ed. R. Willis. London: Unwin Hyman.

Pápay, József. 1988–1995. *Osztják hagyatéka.* Debrecen: Közzéteszi Vértes.

Patkanov, Serafim Keropovich. 1906. *Opyt geografii i statistiki tungusskikh plemen Sibiri. Na osnovanii dannykh perepisi naseleniia 1897 i dr. istochnikov.* St. Petersburg: tipografiia Slovo.

———. 1911a. *O priroste inorodcheskogo naselenia Sibiri. Statisticheskie materialy dlia osveshcheniia voprosa o vymiranii pervobytnykh plemen.* St. Petersburg: Imperatorskaia Akademiia nauk.

———. 1911b. *Statisticheskie dannye, pokazyvaiushchie plemennoi sostav naseleniia Sibiri, iazyk i rody inorodtsev (na osnovanii dannykh spetsial'noi razrabotki materialov perepisi 1897 g.). Zapiski Imperatorskogo Russkogo Geograficheskogo obshchestva po otdeleniiu statistiki.* T. XI. Vyp. 2. St. Petersburg: Imperatorskaia Akademiia Nauk.

Peabody, Norbert. 2001. 'Cents, Sense, Census: Human Inventories in Late Precolonial and Early Colonial India'. *Comparative Studies in Society and History* 43, no. 4: 819–50.

Pekarskii, Eduard K. 1917. *Iakutsko- Russkii Slovar'*. Vol. 3. Petrograd: Tipografiia Imperatorskoi Akademii.

Perevalova, Elena V. 2004. *Severnye khanty: etnicheskaia istoriia*. Ekaterinburg: UrO RAN.

Perevalova, Elena V., and Konstantin G. Karacharov. 2006. *Reka Agan i ee obitateli*. Ekaterinburg, Nizhnevartovsk: UrO RAN, Studiia 'GRAFO'.

[Pestsovyi pitomnik]. 1926. 'Pestsovyi pitomnik na o. Kolgueve'. *Severnoe khoziaistvo*, nos. 7–11: 84–85.

Plandovskii, Vladimir Vasil'evich. 1898. *Narodnaia Perepis'*. St. Petersburg: tipografiia Shtaba otdel'nago korpusa pogranichnoi strazhi.

Plotnikov, Mikhail. 1925. 'O priroste nekotorykh severnykh sibirskikh tuzemnykh plemen'. *Severnaia Aziia*, kn. 4: 9–27.

Poberezhnikov, Igor. 2005. 'Iamal v XII – nachale XX vv: Periodizatsiia russkogo osvoeniia'. In *Russkoe osvoenie Iamala do nachala XX veka. (Dokumenty i issledovaniia)*, ed. I. V. Poberezhnikov. Salekhard-Ekaterinburg: Bank kul'turnoi informatsii.

Popov, Andrei A. 1934. 'Materialy po rodovomu stroiu Dolgan'. *Sovietskaia etnografiia*, no. 6: 116–39.

———. 1937. Okhota i rybolovstvo u dolgan. In *Pamiati V. G. Bogoraza (1865–1936). Sbornik statei*, ed. I. M. Meshchanikov. Moscow: Izdatel'stvo Akademii Nauk SSSR.

———. 1964. 'The Dolgans'. In *The Peoples of Siberia*, eds. M. G. Levin and L. P. Potapov. Chicago: University of Chicago Press.

———. 1966. *The Nganasan: The Material Culture of the Tavgi Samoyeds. The Uralic and Altaic Series*, 56, Bloomington: Indiana University Publications.

Popov, Nikolai P. 1926. 'Pishcha Tungusov'. *Izvestiia Krasnoiarskogo podotdela Vostochno-Sibirskogo otdela Imperatorskogo Russkogo Geograficheskogo Obshchestva*. tom 1, no. 5: 3–34.

Portsel', Aleksandr K. 2005. 'The Norwegian Colonists in Murman during the Soviet Period (1920–1940)'. In *In the North My Nest is Made: Studies in the History of the Murman Colonization 1860–1940*, eds. A. Iurchenko and J. P. Nielsen. St. Petersburg: European University at St. Petersburg Press.

Prokof'eva, Ekaterina D. 1956. 'Nentsy'. In *Narody Sibiri. Etnograficheskie ocherki*, eds. M. G. Levin and L. P. Potapov. Moskva-Leningrad: AN SSSR.

[Promysly pestsa]. 1923. 'Promysly pestsa'. *Severnoe khoziaistvo*, no. 7: 103.

[Pushnoi promysel]. 1923. 'Pushnoi promysel v tundrakh Severa'. *Severnoe khoziaistvo*, no. 2: 111.

Rabinow, Paul, and Nikolas Rose. 2006. 'Biopower Today'. *BioSocieties* 1: 195–217.

Rantala, Leif. 1996. Ryska samer –material på västerländska språk. www.rovaniemi .fi/includes/file_download.asp?deptid=15790&fileid=16932&file=20060125094823 .pdf&pdf=1 (accessed 29 August 2008).

Ray, Arthur J. 1978. 'History and Archaeology of the Northern Fur Trade'. *American Antiquity* 43, no. 1: 26–34.

RHD [Registeringssentral for historiske data]. 2008. 'Documenting the Norwegian Censuses'. http://www.rhd.uit.no/nhdc/census.html (accessed 20 Nov 2009).

Rosenberg, William G. 1996. 'Representing Workers and the Liberal Narrative of Modernity'. *Slavic Review* 55, no. 2: 245–69.

Rostislavin, Anton F. 1926. *Promysly Mezenskogo poberezh'ia*. Arkhangel'sk: Assotsiatsiia po izucheniiu proizvodstvennykh sil pri Arkhangel'skom Gubplane.

Ruggles, Steve. 1987. *Prolonged Connections: The Rise of the Extended Family in Nineteenth-Century England and America*. Madison, WI: University of Wisconsin Press.

Rydving, Hakan. 1993. *The End of Drum-Time. Religious Change among the Lulle Saami. 1670s–1740s*. Uppsala: Acta Universitatis Upsaliensis.

Safronov, Fedot G. 1978. *Russkie na severo-vostoke Azii v XVII-seredine XIX v. Upravlenie, sluzhilye liudi, krest'iane, gorodskoe naselenie.* Moskva: Nauka.

Sahlins, Marshal. 1976. 'Colors and Cultures'. *Semiotica* 16, no. 1: 1–22.

Sakharov, G. 1909. 'Promysly i okhota v Dolgoshchel'skoi volosti Mezenskogo uezda'. *Izvestiia Arkhangel'skogo obshchestva izucheniia Russkogo Severa*, no. 13: 17–32.

[Samoedy] 1908. 'Samoedy Timanskoi i Kaninskoi tundr'. *Pamiatnaia knizhka Arkhangel'skoi gubernii na 1908 god.* Arkhangel'sk: Gubernskii Statisticheskii Komitet.

Samokhin, A. T. 1929. Tungusy Bodaibinskogo raiona. *Sibirskaia zhivaia starina.* vyp. 8–9: 5–66.

Saprygin, Nikolai E., and Mikhail F. Sinel'nikov. 1926. 'Samoedy Kaninskoi i Timanskoi tundr'. *Severnoe khoziaistvo*, nos. 2–3: 60–79.

Savel'ev, Aleksandr S. 1849. 'Poluostrov Kanin'. *Zhurnal Ministerstva vnutrennikh del*, Chast' XXVII: 385–86.

Savvin, Andrei A. 2005. *Pishcha iakutov do razvitiia zemledeliia.* Iakutsk: Sakhapoligrafizdat.

Schrader, Tatiana. 2005. 'Legislative Aspects of the Norwegian Colonization of Murman (1860–1915)'. In *In the North My Nest is Made: Studies in the History of the Murman Colonization 1860–1940*, eds. A. Iurchenko, and J. P. Nielsen. St. Petersburg: European University at St. Petersburg Press.

Schürer, K. Anke. 1989. 'A Note Concerning the Calculation of the Singulate Mean Age at Marriage'. *Local Population Studies* 43: 67–69.

Scoones, Ian. 1999. 'New Ecology and the Social Sciences: What Prospects for a Fruitful Engagement?' *Annual Review of Anthropology*, no. 28: 479–507.

Scott, Colin. 1989. 'Knowledge Construction among Cree Hunters: Metaphors and Literal Understanding'. *Journal de la Société des Américanistes* 75: 193–208.

Scott, James. 2009. *The Art of Not Being Governed: An Anarchist History of Upland Southeast Asia.* London: Yale University Press

Sergeeva, Jelena. 2000. 'The Eastern Sami: A Short Account of Their History and Identity'. *Acta Borealia* 17, no. 2: 5–37.

Sergeev, Mikhail A. 1933. 'K voprosu o narodo-khoziaistvennoi perepisi Krainego Severa'. *Sovetskaia etnografiia*, nos. 3–4: 9–28.

Seroshevskii, Vatslav L. 1993 [1896]. *Iakuty. Opyt etnograficheskogo issledovaniia.* Moskva: ROSSPEN.

Shatilov, Mikhail B. 1931. *Vakhovskie ostiaki (etnograficheskie ocherki).* Tomsk: Izdanie Tomskogo kraevogo muzeia.

Shavrov, Kirill B. 1929. 'Perepis' severnykh okrain Dal'nevostochnogo kraia 1926–27'. In *Itogi perepisi severnykh okrain Dal'ne-Vostochnogo kraia (1926–27 gg.) s prilozheniem karty severnykh okrain DVK*, ed. Dal'nevostochnoe Statupravlenie. Blagoveshchensk: Dal'nevost. krai statisticheskogo otdela.

Shavrov, Vasilii Nikolaevich. 1871. 'Kratkie zapiski o zhiteliakh Berezovskogo uezda'. In *Chteniia v obshchestve istorii i drevnostei Rossiiskikh pri Moskovskom universitete*, ed. V. Shavrov. kn. 2. St. Petersburg: Smes'.

Shiliaeva, Lilia M. 1967. 'K probleme izucheniia migratsii pestsa'. *Problemy Severa*, no. 11: 91–98.

———. 1982. *Ekologiia i osnovy prognozirovaniia chislennosti pestsa na primere severoevropeiskoi populiatsii.* Avtoref. kand. diss. Moskovskii oblastnoi pedagogicheskii institut im. N. K. Krupskoi.

Shimkin, Dmitri B. 1990. 'Siberian ethnography: historical sketch and evaluation'. *Arctic Anthropology* 27, no. 1: 36–51.

Shrenk, Aleksandr I. 1855. *Puteshestvie k severo-vostoku Evropeiskoi Rossii cherez tundry samoedov k severnym ural´skim goram, predpriniatoe po vysochaishemu poveleniiu v 1837 godu.* St. Peterburg: Tipografiia Grigoriia Trusova.

Simchenko, Iuri B. 1974. 'Terminologiia rodstva nentsev, entsev, nganasan i iukagirov'. In *Sotsial´naia organizatsiia i kul´tura narodov Severa. Posviashchaetsia pamiati B.O. Dolgikh.* Moskva: Nauka.

Sirina, Anna A. 2006. *Katanga Evenkis in the 20ᵗʰ Century and the Ordering of Their Life-World.* Edmonton: CCI Press.

Skalon, Vasilii N. 1931a. 'Olenevodstvo v basseine r. Taza (Turukhanskii krai)'. *Sovetskii Sever,* nos. 3–4: 70–87.

———. 1931b. 'Rybnye promysly v basseine r. Taza'. *Sovetskii Sever,* no. 9: 42–65.

Skrobov, Vasilii D. 1960. O nekotorykh voprosakh ekologii pestsa Bol´shezemel´skoi i Malozemel´skoi tundry i uluchshenie ego khoziaistvennogo ispol´zovaniia. Avtoref. kand. diss. Moskovskaia vetorinarnaia akademiia.

SKSO [Sibirskii Kraevoi Statisticheskii Otdel]. 1927. *Predvaritel´nye itogi demograficheskoi perepisi 1926 goda v Sibirskom krae.* Novosibirsk: Sovetskaia Sibir´.

———. 1928. *Materialy pripoliarnoi perepisi v Sibirskom krae,* vyp. 1. Krasnoiarsk: izd-vo Sibirskogo Kraevogo Stat. Otdel.

Slocum, John W. 1998. 'Who, and When, Where the Inorodtsy? The Evolution of the Category of "Aliens" in Imperial Russia'. *Russian Review* 57, no. 2: 173–90.

Smith, Richard Saumarez. 2000. 'Between Local Tax and Global Statistic: The Census as Local Record'. *Contributions to Indian Sociology* 34, no. 1: 1–35.

Sogner, Sølvi B. 1990. *Far sjøl i stua og familien hans: trekk fra norsk familiehistorie før og ne.* Oslo: Universitetsforlaget.

Sokolov, Anatolii D. 2002. *Po sledam gosudarevykh iamshchikov.* Iakutsk: Sakapoligrafizdat.

Sokolova, Zoia Petrovna. 1983. *Sotsial´naia organizatsiia khantov i mansi v XVIII-XIX vv: Problemy fratrii i roda.* Moscow: Nauka.

———. 1998. *Zhilishche narodov Sibiri (opyt tipologii).* Moskva: IPA 'TriL'.

Sokolova, Zoia Petrovna, and V. A. Tugolukov. 1983. 'Starye i novye nazvaniia narodov Severa'. *Sovetskaia etnografiia,* no. 1: 76–87.

Sokolovskii, Sergei V. 2001. *Obrazy drugikh v rossiiskikh nauke, politike i prave.* Moskva: Put´.

Solov´ev, Dmitrii K. 1927. 'O zverovodstve na Pechore'. *Komi-mu,* nos. 1–2: 3–13.

SØS [Statistisk sentralbyrå]. 1960. *Ekteskap, fødsler og vandringer 1856–1960* (SØS 13). Oslo: Statistics Norway.

Sosunov, P. I. 1931. 'Tazovskii raion k tret´emu godu piatiletki (khoziaistvenno-ekonomicheskii obzor)'. *Sovetskii Sever,* no. 10: 29–72.

Stagl, Justin. 1995. *A History of Curiosity: The Theory of Travel 1550–1800.* Chur, Switzerland: Harwood Academic Publishers.

Startsev, Georgi. A. 1930. *Samoedy (nencha). Istoriko-etnograficheskoe issledovanie.* Leningrad: Izdanie Instituta narodov Severa.

Steward, Julian H. 1977 [1968]. 'The Concept and Method of Cultural Ecology'. In *Evolution and Ecology: Essays on Social Transformation by Julian H. Steward,* eds. Jane C. Steward and Robert F. Murphey. Urbana: University of Illinois Press.

SUIaASSR [Statisticheskoe Upravlenie Iakutskogo ASSR]. 1928. *Spisok naselennykh zimnikh punktov 4-kh iuzhnykh okrugov Iakutii. Materialy vsesoiuznoi demograficheskoi perepisi naseleniia 1926 g. (predvaritel´nye itogi).* Iakutsk: Statisticheskoe upravlenie.

Suslov, Mikhail I. 1884. 'Poezdka Missionera Suslova k Ozeru Essei'. *Eniseiskie eparkhial´nye vedomosti,* no. 12: 89–107.

Susoi, Elena G. 1994. *Iz glubiny vekov.* Tiumen´: IPOS SO RAN.

Svavitskii, Nikolai A. 1961. *Zemskie podvornye perepisi: obzor metodologii.* Moskva: Gosstatizdat.

Tarasov, Vasilii N. 1915. 'Soobshchenie o poezdke na poluostrov Iamal s veterinarnoi ekspeditsiei S.I. Drachinskogo v 1913 g'. *Ezhegodnik Tobol'skogo Gubernskogo Muzeia,* Vyp. 24: 1–32.

Teren'tev, N. D. 1926. 'K voprosu o podniatii dokhodnosti tundrovogo khoziaistva. Utochnenie poniatiia "tundrovoe khoziaistvo"'. *Komi-mu,* no. 3: 3–10.

Tereshchenko, Natal'ia M. 1965. *Nenetsko-russkii slovar'.* Leningrad: Uchpedgiz.

———. 1966. 'Sobstvennye imena liudei u nentsev'. *Voprosy finno-ugorskogo iazykovedeniia,* Vyp. 3: 45–53.

———. 1967. 'Slova tabu v nenetskom iazyke'. *Sovetskoe finnougrovedenie,* Chast' 2: 123–29.

Terletskii, Petr. E. 1929. 'Predisloviia'. In *Pokhoziaistvennaia perepis' pripoliarnogo Severa SSSR 1926/27 goda. Territorial'nye i gruppovye itogi pokhoziaistvennoi perepisi,* ed, Tsentral'noe Statisticheskoe Upravlenie. Moskva: Statizdat TsSU SSSR.

———. 1930. 'Osnovnye cherty khoziaistva Severa'. *Sovetskii Sever.* No. 9–12: 42–85.

———. 1932a. 'Naselenie Krainego Severa (Po dannym perepisi 1926/1927 gg.)'. *Trudy nauchno-issledovatel'skoi assotsiatsii Instituta narodov Severa TsIK SSSR* T. 1, Vyp.1/2. Leningrad: Tipografiia Kominterna.

———. 1932b. 'Narodno-khoziaistvennaia perepis' Krainego Severa'. *Sovetskii Sever,* no. 6: 5–10.

———. 1951. 'Eshche raz k voprosu ob etnicheskom sostave naseleniia Severo-Zapadnoi chasti Iakutskoi ASSR'. *Sovetskaia etnografiia* 1: 88–99.

Thorvaldsen, Gunnar. 2007. 'An International Perspective on Scandinavia's Historical Censuses'. *Scandinavian Journal of History* 32, no. 3: 237–57.

———. 2008. 'Fra folketellinger og kirkebøker til befolkningsregister'. *Heimen* 4: 341–60.

———. 2009. 'Changes in Data Collection Procedures for Process-Generated Data and Methodological Implications. The Case of Ethnicity Variables in 19th Century Norwegian Censuses'. *Historical Social Research/ Historische Sozialforschung* 34, no. 3: 168–90.

Thuen, Trond. 1987. 'One community – one people? Ethnicity and demography in a North-Norwegian community 1865-1930'. *Acta Borealia* 1, no. 23: 65–83.

Tokarev, Sergei Aleksandrovich. 1945 . *Obshchestvennyi stroi iakutov XVII- XVIII vv.* Iakutsk: Iakutskoe knizhnoe izdatel'stvo.

Tokhole, Galina. 1996. 'Ob imenakh nentsev'. In *Narody Severo-Zapadnoi Sibiri,* ed. N. V. Lukina. Tomsk: Izd-vo Tom. universiteta.

[Torgovlia]. 1926. 'Torgovlia v tundrakh'. *Severnoe khoziaistvo.,* nos. 5–6: 104–5.

TsSK [Tsentral'nii statisticheskii komitet] 1899–1905. *Pervaia vseobshchaia perepis' naseleniia Rossiiskoi Imperii, 1897 g.* [St. Petersburg]: Izd. Tsentral'nago statisticheskago komiteta Ministerstva vnutrennikh del.

TsSU [Tsentral'noe statisticheskoe upravlenie.] 1920. Otdel osnovnoi promyshlennoi statistiki. *Vserossiiskaia promyshlennaia i professional'naia perepis' 1918 goda, predvaritel'naia svodka dannykh.* Moskva: 14-aia tipografiia Gossovnarkhoz.

———. 1926. Tsirkuliar po Vsesoiuznoi perepisi No. 10 ot 26 oktiabria 1926. [Reference copy in GAMO 536-1-80: 24–24v].

———. 1928–1933. *Vsesoiuznaia perepis' naseleniia 1926 goda.* Moskva: Izd. TS.S.U. Soiuza SSR.

———. 1929. *Pokhoziaistvennaia perepis' pripoliarnogo Severa SSSR 1926/27 goda. Territorial'nye i gruppovye itogi pokhoziaistvennoi perepisi.* Moskva: Statizdat TsSU SSSR.

Tugarinov, Arkadii Ia. and Dmitrii E. Lappo. 1927. *Tuzemtsy Prieniseiskogo Severa*. Krasnoiarsk: izd-vo Biuro Kraevedeniia pri Kras. Otdel. RGO.

Tugolukov, Vladillen A. 1963. 'Khantaiskie Evenki (ocherk istorii, khoziaistva, i kul'tura)'. In *Sibirskii Etnograficheskii Sbornik V, Trudy Instituta Etnografii im. N. N. Miklukho-Maklaia, Novaia Seriia 84*, ed. B. O. Dolgikh. Moscow: Izdatel'stvo Akademii Nauk SSSR.

Turner, Victor. 1967. *The Forest of Symbols: Aspects of Ndembu Ritual*. Ithaca, NY: Cornell University Press.

[Ustav]. 1999. 'Ustav ob upravlenii inorodtsev'. In *Soslovno-pravovoe polozhenie i administrativnoe ustroistvo korennykh narodov Severo-Zapadnoi Sibiri (Konets XVI-nachalo XX veka)*, ed. A. Iu. Konev. Tiumen': IPOS SO RAN.

USU [Ural'skoe statisticheskoe upravlenie]. 1928. *Spisok naselennykh punktov Ural'skoi oblasti. T.XII. Tobol'skii okrug*. Sverdlovsk: Izdanie orgotdela Uraloblispolkoma, Uralstatupravleniia i okruzhnykh ispolkomov.

———. 1930. *Olenevodstvo Tobol'skogo severa v tsifrakh. Po materialam pripoliarnoi perepisi 1926–27 g.* Tobol'sk: USU.

Utvik, Unni K. 1985. *Kolasamene: fra tsarens undersetter til sovjetiske borgere*. Master's thesis, Department of Russian, University of Bergen.

[V Koidentskoi] 1925. 'V Koidenskoi tundre'. *Severnoe khoziaistvo*, no. 9: 111–13.

Vaccaro, Ismael, and Karma Norman. 2008. 'Social Sciences and Landscape Analysis: Opportunities for the Improvement of Conservation Policy Design'. *Journal of Environmental Management* 88, no. 2 (July): 360–71.

Vasil'ev, Vladimir I. 1970. 'Nentsy i entsy Taimyrskogo natsional'nogo okruga (ocherk khoziaistva, byta i etnicheskikh protsessov, protekaiushchikh na Eniseiskom Severe)'. In *Preobrazovaniia v khoziaistve i kul'ture i etnicheskie protsessy u narodov Severa*. Moskva: Nauka.

———. 1975. 'Problema formirovaniia eniseiskikh nentsev (K voprosu ob etnicheskoi prirode etnograficheskikh grupp v sostave sovremennykh narodnostei Severa)'. In *Etnogenez i etnicheskaia istoriia narodov Severa*. Moskva: Nauka.

———. 1979. *Problemy formirovaniia severo-samodiiskikh narodnostei*. Moskva: Nauka.

———. 1994. 'Nentsy'. In *Narody Sibiri i Severa Rossii v XIX v. (Etnograficheskie kharakteristiki)*. Moskva: Nauka.

Vasilevich, Grafira M. 1951. 'Esseisko-Chirindinskie Evenki (Po kollektsii V.N. Vasil'eva, MAE N1004)'. *Sbornik Muzeia Antropologii i Etnografii*, no. 13: 154–86.

Vasmer, Max. 1953. *Russisches etymologisches Wörterbuch*. Heidelberg: Carl Winter Universitätsverlag.

Verbov, Grigorii D. 1936. 'Lesnye nentsy'. *Sovetskaia etnografiia*, no. 2: 57–70.

———. 1937. *Kratkii nenetsko-russkii i russko-nenetskii slovar'*. Salekhard: Iamal'skii okruzhnoi komitet novogo alphavita. Tipografiia redaktsii gazety 'Nar'iana Ngerm'.

———. 1939. 'Perezhitki rodovogo stroia u nentsev'. *Sovetskaia etnografiia*, no. 2: 43–66.

Viget, Endriu, ed. 2002a. *Ocherki istorii traditsionnogo zemlepol'zovania khantov*. Ekaterinburg: Tezis.

Viget, Endriu. 2002b. 'Ekonomika i tranditsionnoe zemlepol'zovanie vostochnykh khantov'. In *Ocherki istorii traditsionnogo zemlepol'sovania khantov*, ed. E. Viget. Ekaterinburg: Tezis.

Vitiugov, Anton A. 1923. 'Olenevodstvo'. *Severnoe khoziaistvo*, no. 3: 3–10.

Vizgalov, Georgii P. 2000. *Salymskii Krai*. Ekaterinburg: Tezis.

Von Sadovszky, Otto. 1995. *Fish, Symbol and Myth: A Historical Semantic Reconstruction*. Budapest: Akademiia Kiado.

VSNKh [Vyshii sovet narodnogo khoziaistva]. 1927. *Ekspeditsiia v Cheshskuiu gubu 1925 goda*. Arkhangel'sk: izd-vo nauchno-tekhnicheskoe upravlenie VSNKh.

Zherebtsov, Liubomir N. 1982a. 'Formirovanie etnograficheskikh grupp komi (zyrian)'. In *Finno-ugorskii sbornik*. Moskva: Nauka.

———. 1982b. *Istoriko-kul'turnye vzaimootnosheniia komi s sosednimi narodami*. Moskva: Nauka.

———. 1985. 'Problemy etnicheskoi istorii naroda komi'. *Trudy Instituta iazyka, literatury i istorii Komi filiala AN SSSR*, no. 36.

Zhilinskii, Aleksei A. 1923. 'K voprosu o sporakh olenevodov Kaninskoi tundry'. *Severnoe khoziaistvo*, no. 1: 45–48.

———. 1925. 'Pushnoi promysel v tundrakh Severa'. *Severnoe khoziaistvo*, no. 1: 74–79.

Zhitkov, Boris M. 1904. 'Otchety ekspeditsii Imperaterskogo Russkogo Geograficheskogo Obshchestva na Kanin p-ov v 1902'. *Zapiski Imperaterskogo Russkogo Geograficheskogo Obshchestva po obshchei geografii* tom 41, vyp 1: 1–170.

———. 1913. *Poluostrov Iamal*. St. Petersburg: Tipografiia M.M. Stasiulevicha.

Zhuravskii, Andrei. 1909. *Iz byta i kul'ta Arkhangel'skikh samoedov Izvestiia Arkhangel'skogo Obshchestva izucheniia Russkogo Severa*. Arkhangel'sk: Gubernskaia tipografiia.

Ziker, John P. 2002a. *Peoples of the Tundra: Northern Siberians in the Post-Communist Transition*. Prospect Heights, IL: Waveland Press.

———. 2002b. 'Raw and Cooked in Arctic Siberia: Seasonality, Gender and Diet among the Dolgan and Nganasan Hunter Gatherers'. *Nutritional Anthropology* 25, no. 2: 20–33.

———. 2007. 'Subsistence and Food Sharing in Northern Siberia: Social and Nutritional Ecology of the Dolgan and the Nganasan'. *Ecology of Food and Nutrition* 46: 445–467.

Ziker, John P., and Michael Schnegg. 2005. 'Food sharing at meals: Kinship, reciprocity and clustering in the Taimyr Autonomous Okrug, Northern Russia'. *Human Nature* 16, no. 2: 178–210.

Zuev, Vasilii F. 1947. *Materialy po etnografii Sibiri XVIII veka (1771–1772)*. Moskva-Leningrad: Nauka.

Notes on the Contributors

David G. Anderson is Professor of Anthropology, University of Tromsø. He researches the history and ethnography of the circumpolar Arctic and has conducted fieldwork in Eastern Siberia (Taimyr, Evenkiia, Zabaikal´e), the Russian North (Kola), Northern Norway and in Canada's Mackenzie Delta. His current research is on the different visions of history among settler states and aboriginal peoples and how this is linked to the growing debate on indigenous rights. His English-language monograph *Identity and Ecology in Arctic Siberia* was published by Oxford University Press and his recent publications include two co-edited books from Berghahn Press – *Ethnographies of Conservation* and *Cultivating Arctic Landscapes*.

Tatiana Argounova-Low is a teaching fellow at the Department of Anthropology, University of Aberdeen. She started working with the Polar Census materials in 2003 as a Leverhulme Research Fellow when she travelled to do her fieldwork among the Essei Iakuts. While identity, economy and social life of native communities remain her main interests, her current research focuses on movement, mobility, and interpretation of road phenomenon in Siberia.

Elena M. Glavatskaya is a professor of history at the Ural State University. She researches the history, ethnography and religious traditions of the Uralic and Siberian indigenous peoples and has conducted fieldwork in the Urals, and North-Western Siberia. Her current research interests are on the evolution of religious landscapes and how best to map them, and on use of photographs for reconstructing historical processes in the late 19th - early 20th century in the Urals and Siberia. She is the author and co-author of numerous books in Russian and English on the religious traditions and livelihoods of Siberian indigenous peoples. Her latest English-language publication is an article on photography in *Jahrbüecher für Geschichte Osteuropas*.

Evgenii M. Ineshin is a researcher and lecturer (*dotsent*) at the Irkutsk State Technical University. He is interested in the adaption of ancient man in mountainous regions at the border of the Pleistocene and Holocene epochs and conducts archaeological and ethnographic research in the Baikal-Patom plateau north of Lake Baikal. In 2006 he defended his *kandidatskaia* thesis titled 'Chelovek i prirodnaia sreda na rubezhe pleistotsena i golotsena na Baikalo-Patomskom nagor´e' and is the author of more than 40 works in Russian and foreign languages.

Peter Jordan is Reader in the Department of Archaeology, University of Aberdeen. He has wide-ranging research interests in the archaeology, ethnoarchaeology and ethnohistory of northern hunter-gatherers. Recent publications include: *Material Culture and Sacred Landscape: The Anthropology of the Siberian Khanty*, and *Ceramics before Farming: The Origins and Dispersal of Pottery among Hunter-Gatherers of Northern Eurasia from 16 000 BP* (edited with Marek Zvelebil) and an edited collection *Landscape and Culture in Northern Eurasia*.

Stanislav Kiselev is a lecturer in the Department of Ethnography and Anthropology at St Petersburg State University. He was also a post-doctoral research assistant for a project on the Polar Census in the Russian North and Western Siberia funded by the Norwegian Research Council and based at the University of Tromsø. He researches the socio-economic conditions of the indigenous peoples of the European North of Russia. His past work has been on the ethnography and identity of the borderlands between Russia, Belorussia and Poland which he published in his co-edited book *Etnicheskaia identichnost´ na pogranich´e kul´tur*. He is presently organising several field expeditions to the Kola peninsula, Evenkiia and the Bolshezemel tundra.

Konstantin B. Klokov is Professor of Regional Politics at St. Petersburg State University. He was also a research fellow for a project on the Polar Census in the Russian North and Western Siberia funded by the Norwegian Research Council and based at the University of Tromsø. He started his research career investigating the hunting and trapping economy of the Enisei River basin in the 1970s. His interests now extend to the traditional livelihoods of indigenous peoples in Western Siberia, Taimyr, Iakutiia and Chukotka. He has been the Russian co-odinator of two Arctic Council projects and an international project on the 1926/27 Polar Census funded by the Research Council of Norway. He is the author and co-author of numerous books in Russian and in English on the traditional livelihoods of indigenous people. His most recent English-language publications appear in the *International Journal of Entrepreneurship and Small Business* and *Polar Research*.

Igor Semenov is Chief Executive Officer of EthnoExpert, a company which works in the fields of environmental, historical and cultural studies and ESIA procedures. Since 2004 he has been studying the history and identity of the peoples of the European part of the Russian North in the Nenets Autonomous *okrug* and in the Arkhangel´sk and Komi regions. He worked as a lecturer and Associate Dean in the Department of Ethnography and Anthropology at Saint Petersburg State University until 2009. He was also a post-doctoral research assistant for a project on the Polar Census in the Russian North and Western Siberia funded by the Norwegian Research Council and based at the University of Tromsø. In 2006 he founded the Northern Expedition Centre at Saint Petersburg State University to support interdisciplinary field research in the Arctic. His most recent publications are in the *Vestnik Voronezhskogo Gosudarstvennogo Universiteta* and the serial publication *Polevaia Etnografiia*.

Gunnar Thorvaldsen is Professor at the Norwegian Historical Data Centre, The University of Tromsø. He is the author of the monograph *Databehandling for historikere [Information technology for historians]* among other monographs, and has published several methodological and articles on the social and population history of Scandinavia in *Historical Methods*, the *Scandinavian Journal of History*, and *Sibirica*. His most recent publication is an article about the creation of a Historical Population Register for Norway.

Elena A. Volzhanina is a senior scientific researcher at the Institute of Northern Development, Siberian Division, Russian Academy of Sciences in Tiumen´. Her scientific interests include the ethnography, ethnodemography, and ethnic history of the indigenous peoples of the North during the 20th century to the first decade of the 21st century. She is the author of a monograph entitled *Etnograficheskie protsessy v srede nentsev Iamala v XX - nachale XXI veka* and has published her archival and field research in the journals *The Archaeology, Ethnography and Anthropology of Eurasia* and *Vestnik arkheologii, antropologii i etnografii*.

John P. Ziker is Associate Professor of Anthropology, Boise State University. His interests include indigenous land tenure systems and their sustainability, demographics, human sociality, the circumpolar north, and post-socialist societies. He is the author of *Peoples of the Tundra: Northern Siberians in the Post-Communist Transition*, from Waveland Press. He has authored numerous articles on Siberia for the journals *Human Nature, Nomadic Peoples*, and *Ecology of Food and Nutrition* and with Konstanin Klokov has recently edited, in Russian, a collection on the Polar Census in the Russian North and Western Siberia.

Index